Apostates, Hybrids, or True Jews?

Apostates, Hybrids, or True Jews?

*Jewish Christians and Jewish Identity
in Eastern Europe, 1860–1914*

RAYMOND LILLEVIK

☙PICKWICK *Publications* • Eugene, Oregon

APOSTATES, HYBRIDS, OR TRUE JEWS?
Jewish Christians and Jewish Identity in Eastern Europe, 1860–1914

Copyright © 2014 Raymond Lillevik. All rights reserved. Except for brief quotations in critical publications or reviews, no part of this book may be reproduced in any manner without prior written permission from the publisher. Write: Permissions, Wipf and Stock Publishers, 199 W. 8th Ave., Suite 3, Eugene, OR 97401.

Pickwick Publications
An Imprint of Wipf and Stock Publishers
199 W. 8th Ave, Suite 3
Eugene, OR 97401

www.wipfandstock.com

ISBN 13: 978-1-62564-530-2

Cataloging-in-Publication data:

Lillevik, Raymond.

    Apostates, hybrids, or true Jews? : Jewish Christians and Jewish identity in eastern Europe, 1860–1914 / Raymond Lillevik.

    xiv + 378 p. ; 23 cm. Includes bibliographical references and index.

    ISBN 13: 978-1-62564-530-2

    1. Messianic Judaism. 2. Gurland, Rudolf Hermann (1831–1905). 3. Lucky, Christian Theophilus (1854–1916). 4. Lichtenstein, Isaac (1825–1908). 5. Jesus Christ—Jewish interpretations. 3. Judaism—Relations—Christianity. I. Title.

BR158 L444 2014

Manufactured in the U.S.A.

Maps «Hungary» (etc.) used with permission.

To Margareth, Ole Martin, Kristoffer,
—and Jakob, who was born the same year as this project.
You make each day a blessing to me.

*Vår sang skal
deg opphøye,
o Gud, som alt formår,
du ser oss med ditt øye
hvor vi i verden går.
Når vi har endt vår gang,
skal nye røster heves
og synge Sions sang!*

—Petter Dass

Contents

List of Illustrations   ix
Foreword by Oskar Skarsaune   xi
Preface   xiii
Acknowledgments   xv

1   Introduction   1
    Presentation   1
    Jewish Believers in Jesus: The Road Less Taken   2
    Previous Research   7
    Method: A Narrative and Analytical Approach   8
    Sources   10
    Constructing Identities   14
    The Problematic Term "Jewish Christian"   19
    Jewish Identification: Sergio DellaPergola   20
    Outline   26

2   Eastern European Jews between 1860 and 1914 and the Christian Missions   28
    Introduction   28
    The Term "Eastern Europe"   30
    The Jews   31
    Christian Mission Work to the Jews   37

3   The Biographies of Gurland, Lucky, and Lichtenstein   42
    Rudolf Hermann (Chaim) Gurland (1831–1905)   43
    Christian Theophilus Lucky/Chaim Jedidjah Pollak (1854–1916)   89
    Rabbi Isaac Lichtenstein (1825–1908)   142

4   Analyzing the Relationship between Jewish Identity and
    Faith in Jesus   174
    Introduction   174
    The Relation to Judaism and the Jewish Tradition   174
    The Relation to the Jewish People   238
    The Relationship to the Christian Tradition and Doctrines   273
    The Relation to the Christian Community   290
    The Relationship to Jewish-Christian Groups and Individuals   310

5   Conclusion   333
    Three Jewish-Christian Identities   333
    Further Perspectives   339

    Appendix: The False Doctrines of Talmud   345
    Introduction   345
    Text: "False doctrines of the Talmud"   346

    Bibliography   359
    Index of Subjects and Names   379

Illustrations

Maps

1. East Central Europe, 1910   29
2. Jews and Armenians in East Central Europe, ca. 1900   33
3. The Pale of Jewish Settlement   34
4. Hungary   36

Figures

5. Rudolf Hermann Gurland   43
6. Christian Theophilus Lucky   89
7. Isaac Lichtenstein   142

Foreword

RAYMOND LILLEVIK'S STUDY IS an interesting and timely contribution to the study of profiled Jewish-Christian leaders of the late nineteenth and early twentieth centuries. They played important roles in the pre-history of what later was called Messianic Judaism, although they did so in quite different ways.

Lillevik's study is pioneering in more than one respect. First, none of these three Jewish-Christian leaders have ever before been portrayed and studied in such depth and detail as in this book. It therefore brings new data and new knowledge.

It is also pioneering in another respect. Lillevik analyses the nowadays important concept of identity with regard to the three Jewish-Christian leaders. It goes without saying that this was an acute problem for persons who, according to the common perceptions of their time, were trying to straddle two incompatible identities: Jewish and Christian. More specifically, Lillevik asks how the three leaders themselves understood and practiced their problematic double identity.

I find Lillevik's choice of the three persons treated in this book to be well considered. His biographies of them are accurate and nuanced, and his analysis of their challenges with regard to identity is well grounded in a theoretical framework based on cutting-edge scholarship in the field.

Lillevik has shown great acumen in his handling of the sources, and his nuanced portrayal of the double identity of the three leaders is enlightening. It demonstrates a wide spectrum of possibilities and choices as far as identity formation for Jewish Christians is concerned, in a period marked by upheavals and changes with regard to culture, religion and politics in a turbulent Eastern Europe.

In our days, when attention to questions of identity formation has reached new heights in scholarship, Lillevik's book is a timely contribution, demonstrating that the issue is not an entirely new one, and that lessons learned from people living more than hundred years before us, are still of general relevance, and of special relevance to modern day, so-called Messianic Jews.

The book will be of great interest to church historians, missiologists, scholars in interreligious studies, sociologists of religion; but also for a wider group of interested readers, comprising present day Jewish Christians, be they inside or outside the movement of organized Messianic Judaism, and also Christians in general who have an interest in things Jewish.

Prof. dr. Oskar Skarsaune,
Author of *In the Shadow of the Temple* (2002),
Co-editor of *Jewish Believers in Jesus: The Early Centuries* (2007).

Preface

This book compares three Jewish men who believed Jesus was the Messiah, and is a revised version of my PhD dissertation from 2013 by The Norwegian School of Theology (MF) in Oslo. The project began in 2004 when I became aware of the Caspari Center's Project, Jewish Believers in Jesus from Antiquity to the Present. Quite early the professors Reidar Hvalvik and Oskar Skarsaune advised me to make some research on some central Jewish believers in Jesus in modern age, and I began digging.

The research and writing took place while I have been working full-time as a teacher in my village Nesna in Northern Norway. Added that I have tried as best as I could not to let my family, our congregation, and other people that I am responsible to feel they were neglected because of my hobby, it has taken a long time to get it finished. The main disadventage about this way of doing things is that I have prioritized *what* to write, and not *how* to do it. The careful reader may therefore find some inconsistencies when it comes to formalia in the references. I am not sure if this is an apology or a way of boasting, but it is at least honest. Personally, I am grateful to have had the oportunity to work on this topic, and would be even more thankful if the history described in the following could become a blessing.

Acknowledgments

WORKING ON THIS PROJECT, the people I have met while writing has been a key in my motivation. The old Norwegian word *dugnad* indicates the sort of unpaid work or projects people in the village or the neighborhood do to have things fixed, more or less on their own initiative, like repairing the playground, building the sport club-house, run the local church etc. I think it is an appropriate term to describe what I have been part of the last nine years. Except for the concrete result itself, a consequence of a *dugnad* can be the good feeling of being part of a team, or quite simply to have friends in a wide but fundamental sense. I have come to understand that I have been more than privileged in many ways during the work on this book. Sincere thanks therefore go to a lot of people:

Professor Reidar Hvalvik, for patient, energetic and clear guidance and help, far beyond what could be expected. I wish my own students had a supervisor like him.

Professor emeritus Oskar Skarsaune, for sharing his insight, enthusiasm and to-the-point comments at important stages during this project.

Hilary le Cornu, to whom I am particularly grateful and in debt for her translation of the *Edut leIsrael* material. Without her efforts, the project would not have been possible.

The staff at the libraries at *Nesna University College* and *MF Norwegian School of Theology*, for friendly efficiency and overbearence for almost a decade.

Caspari Center, *Den norske Israelsmisjon* and *Den Evangelisk-Lutherske Frikirke* for financial support, giving me opportunities to take some time off to look for sources or make some sort of text out of my notes. After the dissertation was completed, *Egede-instituttet* followed up, helping me in the same way in the process towards publication.

Not least, I am grateful to the administration, board and collogues at *Kristen Videregående skole i Nordland*, whose patience and flexibility with me have been impressive as well as encouraging. For years this school has allowed me to take out overtime as short-time leave in order to let me work in peace.

A number of people who have been providing and making accessible source material, often with much efforts: Dr. Tatjana Aleksejeva and Dr. Ilya Lensky at the museum *Jews in Latvia* for material on Pucher and his oponents; Nicholas J. Kersten from *Seventh Day Baptist Historical Society* for information about Lucky in the USA; Pastor Hans-Heinrich Gurland for digging up and transcribing his grandfather's handwritten manuscripts and letters; Jorge Quiñónez for providing *Edut leIsrael* and the works by Lichtenstein; Dr. Ellie R. Schainker and Dr. Mitchell Leslie Glaser for sending me their dissertations; Dr. Sípos Ete Álmos, Professor Oddvar Johan Jensen and Dr. Sandra Gintere for sending me their books or articles; Nathanael Finestone for material on the Gurlands and the Feinsteines; Ildiko Szayer and pastor Marton Zsolt for totally surprising (as well as touching) help with the translation of Hungarian material on Lichtenstein; Dr. Winfried Schultze at the *Humboldt-Universität* in Berlin for providing material on Lucky, and Torstein Bryne for checking out references in the last minute.

Cindy Osborne, Caroline Ruth Meaddow-Smith and Renee Waara for linguistic help. Osborne also did an excellent job on the proof editing. Thanks also to my colleagues, Jorunn Nilsen and Olaf Pona, for their assistance with the German texts when I have been rushing into their offices with another hundred-and-fifty-year old obscure word, sentence or paragraph. Gratefully, not many know how much these things were needed.

Dr. Stephan Bitter, Professor Torleif Elgvin, Professor Tormod Engelsviken, Dr. Anne-Marie Kool and Pastor Torkild Masvie for encouragement, practical help, advice and for connecting me to important networks and persons.

Professors and PhD students at MF Norwegian School of Theology 2010–2012; the staff at CEEAM at Karoli Gaspar University; Dr. Kovács Ábrahám, lecturers and participants at the NIME conference in Höör, Sweden, May 2011, and the CEEAM conference in Budapest June 2012, for constructive criticism, fruitful discussions and practical help. A special thanks to Gunnar Elstad and Sverre Lauvås for warm hospitality and friendship when I came to Oslo.

Nesna, 2014

1

Introduction

Presentation

Chaim Gurland, Chaim Jedidjah Pollak and Isaac Lichtenstein were all Jews born in Eastern or Central Europe in the 19th century, and they all embraced the Christian faith. Their attitudes to Judaism and Christianity were, however, very different.

Rabbi Chaim Gurland, later known as *Pastor Rudolf Hermann Gurland* (1831–1905), from Lithuania, was in his lifetime one of the most famous and prominent characters within the evangelical church and its mission to the Jews, especially in the Russian Empire.[1] Gurland apparently followed the traditional pattern for converted Jews, leaving behind all connection to his Jewish background, and none of his descendants cultivated any connection to their Jewish origins.[2] In this Gurland appears representative of the vast majority of Jews who were baptized during this period. However, a close reading of the sources concerning Gurland seems to modify this image.

Chaim Jedidjah Pollak, later known as *Christian Theophilus Lucky* (1854–1916), from modern-day Ukraine, was a gifted scholar of Jewish tradition who made a significant contribution to the Christian missions and churches that were involved in evangelizing the Jews. He was baptized and was ordained in a Protestant denomination in the USA. He accepted Christianity and published Christian periodicals for Jews both in

1. Lillevik, "Rudolf Hermann Gurland," 22–23.
2. Hans-Heinrich Gurland, in a letter to Raymond Lillevik, November 2004.

1

Hebrew and English (*Edut leIsrael* and *The Peculiar People*), yet fiercely criticized traditional mission work to the Jews. Lucky maintained that Jewish believers in Jesus should stay within the Jewish people and their traditions as much as possible.

Rabbi Isaac Lichtenstein (1825–1908) openly confessed his belief in Jesus while still in office as a relatively highly-ranking Hungarian rabbi. He never joined any Christian denomination by being officially baptized, but baptized himself in a synagogue *mikve* (ritual Jewish bath). In a number of publications and letters in response to criticism from both Christian and Jewish circles, he defended his belief in Christ and his ambivalent relationship to Judaism and the Christian church.

The aim of this dissertation is to present critical biographies of Gurland, Lucky and Lichtenstein and analyze how these three Jews viewed their Jewish identity in relation to their Christian faith. For the sake of comparison, Gurland is assumed to represent the standard or stereotypical convert missionary who assimilated into non-Jewish society, while Lucky and Lichtenstein represent different attitudes and strategies for Jewish believers in Jesus to maintain a Jewish identity. The chronology of the dissertation will therefore follow the order in which Gurland is described and discussed first, followed by Lucky and Lichtenstein.

Jewish Believers in Jesus: The Road Less Taken

The existence of Jesus-believing Jews who claim some sort of Jewish identity (today often called Messianic Jews) has traditionally been regarded as controversial or quite simply neglected by the majority of people in both Christian and Jewish tradition.

From the Jewish point of view, a Jewish believer in Christ has been regarded as an apostate, a *meshummad*, lost to the Jewish nation as well as to Judaism as a religion. Because of the traumatic experiences of the Jewish Diaspora in Christian Europe since antiquity, the antipathy towards Jewish converts to Christianity can be quite strong. Traditionally, a conversion to Christianity has therefore been regarded as social suicide as well as an attack on the Jewish community.[3] The consequences of such a conversion still vary, but even today baptized Jews are explicitly regarded as non-Jews, having "separated themselves from the national destiny of the Jews." This leads to conflicts within families as well as ju-

---

3. Harris-Shapiro, *Messianic Judaism*, 177.

dicial and political consequences.⁴ After having lost a member of the family to the Christian faith, some traditional Jewish families observe *Shiva*, the traditional week of mourning for the dead, while according to the Israeli Supreme Court, Jesus-believing Jews who immigrate to Israel cannot become Israeli citizens: "But the Jewish people has decided during 2,000 years of its history" that Messianic Jews "do not belong to the Jewish nation and have no right to force themselves on it."⁵

At the same time, the church has tended to suspect these Jewish Christians of syncretism or the "Judaizing" of Christianity. Since the beginning of the Constantinian period, the idea of being a Jew and a Christian simultaneously has been regarded as impossible, or at the very least controversial. For many Christians, Jewish believers in Jesus with a strong Jewish identity not only represented some sort of religious and cultural hybrid, but also challenged the traditional framework of Christian tradition and belief, even the understanding of what a Christian is.

This phenomenon is a paradox, as the first Christians were all Jews who also worshiped the God of Israel. However, the fact that the majority of the Jewish people followed what became rabbinic Judaism, and that the majority of the church very soon consisted of Gentiles, led to an estrangement between the two religious bodies.⁶ After Constantine, the number of converted Jews was never high, except for the enforced mass conversions in Renaissance Spain. The number of Jewish conversions to Christianity increased significantly during the 19th century; according to estimated numbers from the beginning of the 20th century approximately 200,000 Jewish persons were baptized during the 19th century.⁷

---

4. Hertzberg, "Jewish Identity," 370.

5. Justice Menachem Elon quoted in *New York Times*, December 27, 1989 in the article "Israeli Court Rules Jews for Jesus Cannot Automatically Be Citizens." See http://www.nytimes.com/1989/12/27/world/israeli-court-rules-jews-for-jesus-cannot-automatically-be-citizens.html. Although the State of Israel grants its inhabitants religious freedom, a Christian from a Jewish background will not be given status as a citizen. This practice has been confirmed several times in Israeli decisions in court cases on the Law of Return since 1950. For references to the Law of Return since 1950 and the different cases of the Israeli authorities vs. Brother Daniel (1962), Eileen Dorflinger (1978) and Beresford (1989 and 1992), see Stern, "Court Cases," 87–96; Cohn-Sherbok, *Messianic Judaism*, 199.

6. Hvalvik, "A New Sect," 19–26. See also Nerel, "Eusebius' *Ecclesiastical History*," 65–86.

7. Thompson, *A Century*, 264.

This was a result of the European emancipation and the new possibilities of advancement within European society. Baptism was frequently regarded as the sole key to upward social mobility: "they moved from nominal Judaism to nominal Christianity."[8] However, the increase in converts is also due to increased missionary efforts by many Protestant churches and mission organizations starting around 1800, especially in Great Britain and the USA.

Over the next 100 years an increasing number of converts became more aware of their Jewish heritage. Some of the converts became part of small congregations designated for Jews by both denominational and non-denominational missionaries.[9] After World War 2 (WWII) and the establishment of the State of Israel, Jewish-Christian (in English-speaking countries called Hebrew-Christian, later Messianic) congregations slowly emerged across the church landscape. In 2004, there were about 200 self-identified Messianic congregations in the USA and 80 in Israel.[10] Their ties with traditional churches vary widely, but all base their confession of faith on the New Testament. In addition, there are also an unknown number of Jewish believers in Jesus in traditional churches all over the world.

Because of the shock of modern anti-Semitism, and particularly the *Shoa* (the Holocaust), many of the major Protestant churches in Europe and North America have more or less abandoned traditional mission work to Jews, replacing it with inter-religious dialogue.[11] In addition, European mission work has lost its influence in general. Before WWII, the predominant mission activity among Jews came from British missions like the London Society for Promoting Christianity amongst the Jews and the Mildmay Mission to the Jews. After the war, American organizations took over that position.[12]

In this new religious atmosphere, mission work toward the Jewish people is often regarded as attempted spiritual destruction of a people already threatened by assimilation, and theologically superfluous. The claims of Messianic Jews are troublesome for the on-going dialogue between Christians and Jews, as they seemingly blur the traditional

---

8. Endelman, *Jewish Apostasy*, 9.
9. Glaser, "A Survey," 421.
10. Zaretsky, *Jewish Evangelism*, 23–27.
11. Rudnick, *Studium zum christlich-jüdischen Gesprach*.
12. Ariel, *Evangelizing*, 215.

boundaries between Judaism and Christianity. Although conversions in both directions continue, the traditional pattern, in which the convert assimilates into the new community, is usually followed. When some Jews insist on having a place in both communities, this disturbs many people's image of what makes a Jew.[13] However, in the last two decades there has been a certain shift in the awareness of the phenomenon among scholars. While Jewish academic articles and studies during the 1970s and 1980s either ignored the movement of Jesus-believing Jews or found it hard to take them seriously, from the mid-1990s the tendency has been to describe the converts more impartially and less stigmatically.[14]

Contemporary Messianic Jews still face many challenges, not only from traditional Jews and Christians, but also in the form of internal tensions. Although many Messianic Jews find a place within the Messianic movement, many also place themselves in traditional churches and denominations.[15] Although the question "Can Jews believe in Jesus and

13. Describing a certain Jewish identity today is a very complex task. Traditionally, Jewish identities were defined by where people were living and how they practiced Judaism. Generally there was a distinction between Sephardim and Ashkenazim, but these were usually broken down into several sub-groups depending on where the person came from. In relation to religious practice, people would either be pietists (the *Hasidim*), formalists (*mitnagdim*) or modernists (*maskilim*). For the last 200 years, parallel to growing anti-Semitism and assimilation, there has been a disintegration of Jewish identities. Today there is much debate not only on whether Jewishness should be defined in secular or religious terms, but also between different religious Jewish denominations like Orthodox, Conservative, Reform, and Reconstructionist, just to mention a few. Sergio DellaPergola states, "Judaism is a multi-faceted complex of normative, cognitive, behavioural affective and other types of expression. It can be at the same time religion, ethnicity, culture, organized community, social group, collective and personal historical memory, folklore, and more. Therefore, no single indicator or measure can adequately catch the complexity of Jewish identification. Jewish identification can and should be described and measured through a variety of different indicators" (DellaPergola, "Jewish Identity/Assimilation/Continuity").

14. Ariel, *Evangelizing*, 268–73. See also the bibliography in Schainker, "Imperial Hybrids," 317–31.

15. This includes the Roman Catholic and the Orthodox as well as the Protestant churches. It is therefore interesting to see how e.g., Russian Jewish Christians see themselves as a part of the Russian Orthodox Church, Kornblatt, *Doubly Chosen*. As the characters that will be treated in this study all became more or less associated with Protestant churches and Jewish missions, the situation within the Roman Catholic and the Orthodox churches is not a topic here. However, it should be noted that particularly since the establishment of the State of Israel, so-called Hebrew Catholics have become a factor of certain weight within the Catholic Church in Israel, and a competitive force against Palestinian Catholics. Nerel, "Nostra Aetate," 47–58.

still be Jews?" is answered with a "Yes," the practical consequences are intensely debated. Some of the discussion is related to the general internal Jewish discussion about Jewish identity that has been going on since the Enlightenment. However, theological disagreements on topics such as the doctrine of the Trinity, Christology, soteriology (teaching on salvation) and the role of the Torah also surface.[16]

From the Christian mission's point of view, the challenges facing Jesus-believing Jews are not unique. For centuries both Protestant and Roman Catholic missions increasingly have had to deal with issues related to contextualization of the Christian message, particularly related to the churches in the non-European world. Traditionally, mission activity has led to a certain adaption of the missionaries' culture among the new Christians, and in most churches in the non-Western world issues concerning local identity are discussed. In recent years there have been discussions related to so-called Muslim Background Believers and Jesus Bhaktis. As the terms indicate, these are groups of people from a Muslim or Hindu background that seek to combine Christian faith with their cultural identity while living in their traditional context.[17] This phenomenon in many ways resembles the positions of Lucky and Lichtenstein.

In this study I seek to describe the idea of sameness, coherence and continuity in regard to the combination of Christian faith and being Jewish as it was understood by three particular individuals. Why have I chosen to study Gurland, Lucky and Lichtenstein for this purpose? First of all, the embryonic period of the modern Messianic movement is usually held to be the last decades of the 19th century, when Jewish/Hebrew Christians and the mission societies first faced the discussion about Jewish-Christian congregations that followed the growing national consciousness among the Jewish people at that time. Lichtenstein, Lucky and Gurland represented different solutions to the issue of Jewish Christians' relationship to their Jewish identity. The fact that they were either rabbis or talmudic scholars makes them significant because it is interesting to see how Jews rooted in the Jewish people and with a good understanding of Judaism viewed the relationship between Judaism/Jewish tradition and Christian faith. It is no coincidence that

---

16. Karabelnik, "Competing Trends," 52; Telchin, *Some Messianic Jews Say*.

17. For some, this means that they participate in the prayer in the mosque, and during the recitation of the Muslim creed they profess faith in Jesus instead. Chandler, *Pilgrims of Christ*, and Blystad, "Muslimske Jesus-disipler," 6–7.

Kai Kjær-Hansen counts Lucky and Isaac Lichtenstein among the four "big" Jewish Christians around the year 1900, together with Joseph Rabinowitz (1837–1899) and Yechiel Lichtenstein (or Herschensohn; ca. 1830–1912).[18] Gurland appears as a character who is representative of the many Jewish Christians who associated with mainstream denominations instead.

Second, the quantity of the literary material from Gurland, Lucky and Lichtenstein lends itself to research and comparative study. Because of the confiscation and destruction of the German and Austrian Jewish mission archives as well as the *Shoa* itself, much of the material is today only available in Scandinavia, Great Britain and the USA.[19]

Third, the stories about Gurland, Lucky and Lichtenstein are in many ways part of a rather unknown chapter of Scandinavian church history. All three of them had significant contact with the mission societies in Norway and Denmark. In the 1860s and 1870s, Gurland was one of the first missionaries of the Norwegian Israel Mission, and was later employed by a Norwegian-American mission, while Lucky and Lichtenstein cooperated with missionaries and representatives from these missions.[20]

Previous Research

Much of the available information about these three has never been collected or compared. Basically, this dissertation is therefore the first academic contribution to provide new historical knowledge and understanding of Gurland, Lucky and Lichtenstein.

In his work about Jewish mission history in the 1890s, Joh. de le Roi presents Gurland, Lucky and Lichtenstein, giving his readers his evaluation of them and even advice on how one should relate to Lichtenstein and Lucky. Later Jewish mission literature and histories of Hebrew Christianity only describe one or two people in each work, with the exception of Oskar Skarsaune's work in Norwegian on the Norwegian Israel Mission, which includes all three. Few Jewish studies

---

18. Kjær-Hansen, "Lucky," 3. In comparison, Mark Kinzer operates with very much the same list, although exchanging Yechiel Lichtenstein with Paul Levertoff, Kjær-Hansen, "Mark Kinzer," 4.

19. Baumann, "The History," 26.

20. Lillevik, "Rudolf Hermann Gurland" and "Lucky—møteplager?," 22–24.

on conversion to Christianity in the modern age focus on individuals, and when they do, it is often within the context of assimilation or studies on cults and identity. One of the few individuals who have been studied by both camps is Joseph Rabinowitz, from Kishinev (today's Chisinau[21] in Moldova/Bessarabia), the founder of the first Jewish-Christian synagogue in modern times. That congregation was a result of the same cultural process that influenced Gurland, Lichtenstein and Lucky.[22]

Method: A Narrative and Analytical Approach

To be able to provide new insight about Gurland, Lucky and Lichtenstein, the first step is to make a critical reconstruction of their life-stories, depending on what is possible to know from the sources and what is believed to be relevant for the question about identity. However, this dissertation does not limit itself to presenting biographies of these three individuals, but seeks to analyze their perception of Christian faith and Jewish identity. This raises several methodological challenges. As far as the approach to sources is concerned, there is not any established use of theory that has won canonical status in historical studies.[23] This makes the choice of methods even more crucial, and basic questions need to

---

21. Due to the historical and political events of the twentieth century many places in Central and Eastern Europe have changed names one or several times the last 150 years, and/or there have been a great variety of spelling standards, depending on the languages. Cities like Stanislau (now Ivano Frankovsk), Kishinev (today Chisinau) and Mitau (now Jelgava) are good examples of this. Although not always consistent, I have used the names that were in use in the timespan of this dissertation.

22. The following list presents some of the works that refer to Gurland, Lucky, or Lichtenstein: Joh. F. A. de le Roi: *Geschichte der Evangelischen Judenmission seit Entstehung des neueren Judentums* (3 vols.; 2nd edition; Schriften des Institutum Judaicum in Berlin no. 9; Leipzig: J. C. Hinrichs'sche Buchhandlung, 1899), vol. 2 (Grossbritannien und die aussereruopäischen Länder während des 19. Jahrhunderts); Thompson, *A Century of Jewish Missions*; Hugh Schonfield, *The History of Hebrew Christianity from the First to the Twentieth Century* (London: Duckworth, 1936); Jacob Jocz, *The Jewish People and Jesus Christ: The Relationship between Church and Synagogue* (3rd edition; Grand Rapids: Baker, 1979); Oskar Skarsaune, *Israels venner— Norsk arbeid for Israelsmisjonen 1844–1930* (Oslo: Luther Forlag, 1994); Glaser, "A Survey"; David Eichorn, *Evangelizing the American Jew* (New York: Jonathan David Publishers, 1978); Steven J. Zipperstein, "Heresy, Apostasy, and the Transformation of Joseph Rabinovich," in *Jewish Apostasy in the Modern World* (ed. Todd Endelman; New York: Holmes & Meier, 1987), 206–31; Kai Kjær-Hansen, *Joseph Rabinowitz and the Messianic Movement: The Herzl of Jewish Christianity* (Edinburgh: Handsel, 1995).

23. Rüsen, *History*, 93.

be considered. Social identity is connected to self-definition and self-understanding, and in many ways it constitutes a person's values and worldview. An analysis of an individual's Jewish identity therefore demands a systematic approach, making it possible to single out certain variables and elements of Jewish identity. On the other hand, a connection of Jewish identity to one or several individuals makes it necessary to deal with historical and biographical questions as well, as the formation of identity follows the personal development of the individuals. This development is influenced by their cultural, social and ideological context. It therefore seems most relevant to use both the analytical and narrative approaches in the outline, a combination that is well known in literature and biographical studies.[24] Based on a large selection of source material by and about Gurland, Lucky and Lichtenstein, I will describe and discuss their ideas in light of relevant aspects of their historical and cultural situation as well as a functional theory on Jewish identity.

Consequently, this dissertation builds not only on church and mission history before World War 1 (WWI), but also on modern Jewish history, studies in Judaism and studies in Jewish demography. The specialization of scientific disciplines makes it difficult for many scholars to give statements about phenomena that lie under another discipline, and as a Lutheran theologian, I do not claim any professional competence in Jewish studies. However, to address the topic I believe this approach most useful, although I risk being criticized for being light-handed on certain issues.

In the following I seek to describe and explain history, and will not explicitly establish normative theological solutions for either Jewish or non-Jewish believers. Neither is it my intention to make affirmative research on behalf of sympathizers or opponents of the Messianic movement. Nevertheless, it is well known that historical comparison can easily carry some sort of political agenda in the choice of comparative situation, hidden or not.[25] In light of the controversial aspects related to Jewish believers in Jesus, many will probably find that there is an element of sympathy to the phenomenon in the choice of topic for the study itself. I am also aware that reconstructing the lives and views of Gurland, Lucky and Lichtenstein can become part of constructing contemporary Jewish-Christian identity (or identities). However, regardless

24. Longum, *Drømmen*, 15.
25. Penslar, *Israel in History*, 4.

of any controversial aspect of the choice of topic, the dissertation itself follows ordinary scientific values.

Sources

Neither Gurland, Lichtenstein, nor Lucky operated with a clear program on Jewish identity for Jewish believers in Jesus, with the partial exception of Lucky, and even he did not discuss the topic systematically. Consequently, most of the material I have found on identity and faith in Jesus is not written in a systematic form, but rather as autobiographies, mission reports, conference minutes and more or less polemical articles and letters. The material I have used for this study is primarily selected from the literature where Gurland, Lucky and Lichtenstein describe, comment, or discuss issues that are related to Jewish identity. In addition, I build upon material from people who were friends or coworkers with them, where the same issues are in focus and related to Gurland, Lucky and Lichtenstein. Both my presentation of their life stories and my analysis also rely on some secondary sources that are important for understanding the socio-political, religious and cultural contexts of the individuals.

The material was produced in certain contexts and situations, and the content is determined by demands about which we cannot be sure we know everything. In addition, most of the sources were written in the context of Christian mission, and the reader needs to consider the ideological background and purpose of the particular material. The background and context might have influenced what material was selected or omitted, and how it was edited. It is necessary to take into account that the individuals behind the source material were not only observers, but their perspectives may have influenced the material. Not least, they could also have operated as agents for their own or others' interests, a natural dimension in many sources historians deal with.

When reading Gurland's, Lucky's and Lichtenstein's ideas about issues like, e.g., Jewish-Christian congregations or the Zionist movement, one must consider the possibility that they would write what was expected of them, or that they had certain agendas when writing. This is an obvious aspect when reading much of Gurland's material, which usually was aimed at friends and supporters of the Jewish missions. This may also have been the case even for Lichtenstein's writings and Lucky's

Hebrew journal *Edut leIsrael*. At different periods Lucky cooperated on the journal with different mission societies in New York and in Berlin, and it must be considered whether this influenced his editorial work. Isaac Lichtenstein's material may have been colored by how he clearly was in opposition to the leadership of the Hungarian Reform Jewish community before WWI. In addition, from the 1890s, he and his books were dependent on financial support from a committee of mission leaders in Britain.

Similarly, one must consider the motives for writing of those who wrote about Gurland, Lucky and Lichtenstein. Both Gurland's widow, Helene Gurland, and Joh. de le Roi wrote for friends of the Jewish missions in the German societies in general, and would possibly highlight material that was of particular interest in these circles. However, Helene Gurland also appears to have in mind her contemporary Baltic German society. Moses Löwen, August Wiegand, Max Weidauer and Gisle Johnson not only had been either sympathizers or opponents of Lucky, but at the time they wrote, some of them were involved in discussions about Jewish identity for Jewish Christians in the mission societies. Theodor Zöckler's (one of Lucky's friends) article about *Edut leIsrael* in *Saat auf Hoffnung* in 1892 and 1893 is particularly interesting in this regard. This article does not only present much material from the Hebrew journal translated to German, but was published at a time when Lucky's agenda caused much debate among the Jewish missions in Germany. The same issues were highly controversial when David Baron and Ragnvald Gjessing wrote about Lichtenstein as well.

The main languages for this study are English and German. As *Edut leIsrael* was written in late 19th-century Hebrew, I have been dependent on Hilary Le Cornu's English translation of many of the Hebrew volumes.[26] In addition, in the 1890s Theodor Zöckler wrote a detailed article about this journal that includes much material translated into German, which I also refer to.[27]

Obviously this material must be read in its biographical context as much as possible. The written material by Gurland, Lucky and

26. Unpublished translations by Hilary Le Cornu of excerpts of *Edut leIsrael* 1 (1888); 2 (1890); 3 (1891); 4 (1897); and 5 (1898). The volumes from 1897 and 1898 are entitled *HaEdut*. The Hebrew material is made available by Jorge Quiñónez at http://vineofdavid.org/remnant_repository/theophilus_lucky/.

27. Zöckler, "Judentum und Christentum," *Saat auf Hoffnung* 29 (1892) 205–15; 249–65; 30 (1893) 41–54. The English translation in the notes is mine.

Lichtenstein extends over several decades, which means that the investigation must take the relevant time span into consideration. While Lichtenstein's literary production took place from 1886 to about 1900, Lucky's was between 1888 to close to the beginning of WWI. In Gurland's case his biography uses material that spans from his teenage letters in the 1840s to his death in 1905. However, the use of (auto) biographies as sources must also be done with much care. Narratives and personal stories are usually not straightforward and accurate reproductions of life as it was lived, and the reader of the material must consider several characteristic features of the genre:[28] 1) Memory is a reconstruction of past events, interpreted in light of contemporary need to create meaning. In addition, the passage of time erodes a person's narratively constructed identity, making it necessary to reconstruct it time after time.[29] 2) The biographical narrative draws out from the background those elements that compose the plot that is the focus of attention. 3) The use of culturally available plots, like the conversion narrative pattern, not only shapes the reconstruction but may lead to exclusion of material.[30]

These considerations are relevant for all of the persons who are the objects of this study. In particular they are relevant for Gurland's *In zwei Welten*. The biographical material on Lucky is special, as he seems to have avoided, and perhaps even mocked, the standard conversion narrative. On Lichtenstein, the biographical material is scarce. Still, the material is in no way worthless for any of them. The notion that historical narrative explanations are selective and interpretative does not mean that any actual occurrences referred to in the narrative are fictional and mere projections of the narrator.[31] The challenge is to balance methodological skepticism of the sources while writing history based upon them.

In addition, writing biographical sketches of Gurland, Lucky and Lichtenstein is in itself something that needs consideration. Stephen Walton describes the fundamental elements of modern biographies as a combination of a human life, described more or less chronologically,

---

28. Polkinghorne, "Narrative Psychology," 9–18, 9.

29. Ibid., 14.

30. In pietistic and evangelical circles, salvation was largely understood as the experience of conversion. This consequently formed the conversion narrative genre, describing the convert as moving from darkness to light in the given scheme of spiritual experience. Hindmarsh, *The Evangelical Conversion Narrative*, 15.

31. Polkinghorne, "Narrative Psychology," 18.

with some sort of (pseudo)intimacy, usually describing the erotic life of the individual. In addition, the individual is supposed to represent values or ideas worth paying attention to or even imitating. The disposition of the biography is usually based on anecdotes. Walton claims it is misleading and positivistic to believe that a biography can explain how a person "really" was, and he thinks scholars instead should let the sources speak for themselves as much as possible.[32] In fact, the life and the work of an individual can be totally irrelevant for each other, and consequently he wants more focus on the works of the individual, and less on the person himself.[33]

Although I find Walton's perspectives valuable, I disagree with this separation of the subject from her/his work. Generally, in fruitful research one cannot separate the subject from the work, although one needs to distinguish between them while (re)constructing a life story. I also disagree with his view of anecdotes as useless. As a biography tries to combine the characteristic and original about a person with how this person represents his own background and contemporary society at the same time, anecdotes may be adequate and relevant sources. The anecdotes found in the sources used in this dissertation usually describe exactly what was felt to be characteristic about Gurland, Lucky and Lichtenstein, and how they acted in extraordinary or unexpected ways. In fact, research on identity often relies on insights from social sciences, and I believe it is essential to keep in mind some of the criticism these disciplines have met on behalf of human free will. One of the most famous critics of the social sciences, Hannah Arendt, not only distrusted these sciences for misunderstanding the social society they tried to understand, she also claimed these sciences underestimated human freedom itself.[34] On the other hand Gurland, Lucky and Lichtenstein were children of their times, like everybody else, and it is important to survey the socially determined aspects in their attitudes to Jewish identity.

---

32. Walton, *Skaff deg eit liv!*, 32–34.
33. Ibid., 37.
34. Baehr, *Hannah Arendt*, 4.

Constructing Identities

Individual and Social Identities

Identity refers to the totality of characteristics that individuals hold to constitute their self, which is based upon pre-adult identifications with behavior and values of persons close to the child. Later these identifications are (usually) integrated in society.[35] The term "identity" is related to *idem*, and describes an idea of sameness, continuity and coherence for a thing or a person at all times and in every situation. In social sciences the term is usually used in two ways: self (or personal) identity and social (or collective) identity.[36] While the first use for many is particularly associated with Erik Erikson's theory on identity formation, the latter refers to the idea of belonging to and identifying with certain groups, like ethnicity. Social (or collective) identity, which refers to the idea of similarity with a group, includes a notion of being different and separated from others. Studies in social identity are related, among others, to Fredrik Barth's ideas of boundaries and boundary crossing, as well as to Benedict Andersson's discussion of large social groups as "imagined communities." Related to this is the term "collective identity," which is based on memory and collective practices that usually define a frame of reference for constructions of solidarity and trust.[37]

Barth has pointed out that it is not so much the culture enclosed in an ethnic group that defines the group, but the ethnic boundaries. These boundaries make it possible to identify other individuals as fellow members of the group who are "playing the same game," sharing the same criteria for evaluation and judgment. On the other hand, the dichotomization of others as strangers implies an assumed restriction of common understanding and mutual interest.[38] Within complex polyethnic systems with close inter-ethnic contact (as in pre-WWI Eastern Europe, chapter 2 below), the cultural characteristics have to be constant to maintain the established social system. It is only these systems that

---

35. Meyer, *Jewish Identity*, 6.

36. Friese, "Introduction," 1–13, 1.

37. Ibid., 6–7, and Eder et al., *Collective Identities*, 19. However, among scholars the term is not yet fixed. In some studies collective identity refers to the identity of a social group as such, while in most cases it refers to the sense of belonging and identification of the individual.

38. Barth, "Introduction," 9–38, 15.

survive a flux of members (like converts) from one community to the other.[39] As newcomers, converts could be more or less free to participate in their new society, but often they would nevertheless be "disabled" in their interactions with the majority language and culture.[40]

Complications on Identity

However, in spite of being one of the most central topics in disciplines like psychology and sociology in the 20th century, identity as an academic topic is controversial amongst scholars. While social studies like feminist and postcolonial theory for decades have paid particular attention to social identity, within social theory and philosophy some have questioned the concept altogether. One of the reasons for these frustrations is the term identity itself, as the content of the word has not been fixed. Nevertheless, the idea of belonging to social groups, or the individual feeling some sort of continuity or discontinuity, is not a new phenomenon. Admitting that the term identity is "insufficient," Peter Wagner nevertheless claims that the phenomenon it represents is well worth investigating, as "personal identity and collective identity do occur."[41] I therefore believe that fruitful research is not always dependent on a scholarly consensus about the term as such, but on whether the concept of identity or social identification helps give relevant knowledge for historical research.

In addition, one needs to consider whether the object of study can be adequately grasped by the traditional distinction between social and personal identity. Individual claims of continued Jewish identity while professing Christian faith not only seriously challenge a master narrative and blur traditional boundaries, but may evoke identity complications on a personal level as well. The aspect of solidarity in any social identity is often related to a memory of collective trauma or triumphs.[42] As central memories in the Jewish community are associated with disastrous Jewish-Christian relations, the traumatic experience is often integrated in Jewish identity. When studying identity among Jewish believers in Jesus, one therefore cannot overlook the significant antipathy to the phe-

39. Ibid., 19–21.
40. Ibid., 32.
41. Wagner, "Identity and Selfhood," 32–55, 48.
42. Alexander, "Toward a Theory," 1–30.

nomenon in the Jewish community. In the Jewish consciousness, Jewish believers in Jesus are regarded as not only lost coreligionists or some sort of national traitors, they are often an outright abnormity. Individuals from this group can even be described in pathological terms, as in the titles of the studies by Carlebach and Schainker: *Divided Souls* and "Imperial Hybrids."[43]

Jewish believers in Jesus have in some works been associated with psychiatric diseases. In his survey of American Hebrew Christians from the 1950s to the 1970s, Sobel concludes that "Hebrew Christians tend to be essentially marginal people who suffer from a long list of defeats and frustrations ranging from the psychological to the economic to the social."[44] This perception is related to the fact that some of the boundaries that are drawn by social identity can be understood as natural, objective and inaccessible, and are thus removed from the arena where things can be changed.[45] For many Jews the distinction between Jews and Christians would be such a boundary. Consequently, Jewish believers in Jesus would find that the perception that Jews who believe in Jesus are traitors is internalized in their worldview even after their conversion.[46] Personal identity may be a manifestation of social identity, which certainly is the case here, making any absolute distinction between these concepts of identity rather fruitless for this study.

While Gurland, Lichtenstein and Lucky identified themselves in different ways with the Jewish people, the general opinion in the Jewish community, then and now, would be that having embraced Christian faith, they no longer belonged to the Jewish community. Does this mean that making any references to their Jewish identity would be an anachronistic example of how the terms "Jewish" and "identity" were emptied of their contents?[47] A Jew who converts to Christianity usually represents

---

43. Carlebach, *Divided Souls*; on Schainker, "Imperial Hybrids," see footnote 14 above [x-ref].

44. Sobel, *Hebrew Christianity* as quoted by Kjær-Hansen, "Neither Fish nor Fowl," 9–18, 15. Sometimes the tragedy of Hans Herzl, son of Theodor Herzl (the main Zionist ideologist), is used by Jewish anti-missionary circles to illustrate this point. Herzl converted to Christianity in the 1930s, and suffering from depression, he later committed suicide; Glaser, "A Survey," 239. Kjær-Hansen rejects this idea, referring to Siegel, *Depression*, 85–87.

45. Friese, "Introduction," 4.

46. Ariel, *Evangelizing*, 47.

47. Hruby, "Zur Problematik," 76–87.

a radical break with his former orientations in life. To describe converts to Christianity as Jews would be to stretch the concept of continuity and coherence too far for many Jews, although it was the same person who made the religious reorientation from Judaism to Christianity. This raises the question of who represents an authentic version of Jewish culture and identity, as it implies that Jewish believers in Jesus cannot be regarded as legitimate carriers of such an identity.[48]

Philosophers associated with deconstruction theories made the concept of the subject and personal identity their main target in the 1960s. Foucault denied any correspondence between the terms of identity and any essential self. Consequently we need to deconstruct our historical selves. However, although Foucault has influenced cultural studies as well as psychiatry, etc., cultural studies generally has returned to a modified version of the traditional Western understanding of the human subject and identity, leading Strozier to note that there is usually a weak connection between many studies and the theory in this respect.[49] In general, though, the understanding of identity and history as being fluid has made a great impact on Western thinking. This process has also made some Jewish scholars more nuanced and inclusive in their view of the place of Jesus-believing Jews in the Jewish community. Dan Cohn-Sherbok suggests that Messianic Judaism should be placed within the Jewish people in the same way as traditionally Jewish denominations like the Orthodox, Reform and Conservative Jews.[50] Others, like Shoshanah Feher and Carol Harris-Shapiro, describe the Messianic movement as bridge-builders between Judaism and Christianity.[51] Daniel Boyarin says:

> I suggest that the affiliation between what we call Judaism and what we call Christianity is much more complex than most scholars, let alone most lay folk, imagine and that that complexity has work to do in the world, that we can learn something from it about identities and affiliations.[52]

---

48. Max Weber calls such agents that claim to represent a collective memory "carrier groups." Alexander, "Toward a Theory," 11.

49. Strozier, *Foucault*, 267. See also Paul Veyne's criticism of the antipathy toward Foucault among historians, recorded by Clark, *History, Theory, Text*, 71–73.

50. Cohn-Sherbok, *Messianic Judaism*, 203–9.

51. Harris-Shapiro, *Messianic Judaism*; Shoshanah Feher, *Passing over Easter*.

52. Boyarin, *Border Lines*, xii.

Jewish Identity between 1860 and 1914

These new approaches to Messianic Jews are apparently related to the general attitude about cultural and religious pluralism in the Western world today, at least in major academic circles.[53] Still, I do not believe one need to make Gurland, Lichtenstein and Lucky into deconstructionists to label them "Jewish." First of all, Gurland, Lichtenstein and Lucky publicly claimed they belonged to the Jewish people, and Lichtenstein and Lucky even insisted they were within the Jewish tradition. Second, around 1900, Eastern European Jewry could very well operate with several types of Jewish identity. When discussing the role of Zionism for the Jewish identity of Norwegian Jews, Vibeke Banik claims that Jewish communities even prior to the establishment of the State of Israel contained several different and parallel Jewish identities, so-called double identities.[54] At least in certain political contexts this phenomenon appears to have been used for later Jewish-Christian identities. In her studies on how Soviet Jews in the 1960s and 1980s rediscovered their Jewish identity after becoming members of the Russian Orthodox Church, Judith Kornblatt explains how Russian Jewry distinguishes between being ethnically Jewish (*evrei*) or belonging to the religious community (*iudai*).[55] Thus it was, within a certain cultural context, possible to create a space where Jews in the Diaspora could be (Orthodox) Christians and still be looked upon as Jewish.[56] Although what Kornblatt is describing is strongly connected to the particular cultural situation within the Soviet Union, it nevertheless indicates how, in the modern age, one could find ways to identify oneself as Christian and Jewish at the same time. According to Ellie Schainker, the phenomenon described by Kornblatt may even be traced back to the beginning of the 19th century. In the Russian Jewish community, conversion to Christianity did not have to be the end of being Jewish in every aspect.[57] Such double identities,

---

53. E.g., within queer theory, which may describe Jewish believers in Jesus as a showcase for its own understanding about identity as result of construction; Roden, "Introduction," 1–18, 10.

54. Banik points to how the Bund (the Jewish Socialist party) in Poland, which wanted to combine a Jewish and a Polish identity, cultivated a context and ideology where a double identity was possible. See Banik, *Solidaritet*, 43 and 75.

55. Kornblatt's spelling.

56. Kornblatt, *Doubly Chosen*, 49; and Gershenson, "Ambivalence," 175–94, 176.

57. Schainker, "Imperial Hybrids," 294.

where individuals or groups were combining Christian and Jewish identification markers, could also be observed around 1900, according to Banik. The Jewish acculturation in Europe during the 19th century did not necessarily lead to a weakened Jewish identity as such. For example, Banik refers to how Jewish women in German countered the German culture by combining German/Christian traditions with a certain Jewish twist.[58]

For other Jews, this modern self-definition as Jews was, and is, highly problematic. Double identities, even attachment to Zionism, could be seen as an expression of weak identification with the Jewish people. Today, religiously oriented Jewish scholars claim that a secular Jewish identity becomes increasingly meaningless, at least when it comes to maintaining collective identity and a sense of mutual belonging. Jonathan Sacks is representative of these claims when insisting that Jewish unity is a religious concept: "Jewish unity is in the end an irreducibly religious concept. There is no coherent secular equivalent."[59] As Gurland, Lichtenstein and Lucky also were religiously motivated, it is of interest to see whether they were content with a secular Jewish identification, or if religious and Jewish identity had meaning for them.

The Problematic Term "Jewish Christian"

James Carleton Paget points out how the term "Jewish Christian" and the German *Judenchrist* have been used in different ways among scholars as well as in pious literature, and suggests that one should consider new terms for describing these individuals.[60] However, while these considerations are particularly relevant within the field of early church history, for Jewish believers in Jesus in the last decades before WWI the situation was different. Although not very precise, the terms "Judenchrist," "Hebrew Christian," and "Jewish Christian" were nevertheless used by sympathizers as well as opponents of the phenomenon. The problem was not the term itself, but what it tried to describe, namely how individuals with a Jewish background could embrace Christianity with some sort of

---

58. Banik, *Solidaritet*, 78.
59. Sacks, *One People?*, xii.
60. Paget, "The Definition," 22–52.

legitimacy. In spite of the obscurity of its meaning, "Jewish Christian" appears to have been used relatively often.[61]

However, the discussion about technical terms is probably not as controversial as the theme itself. If we understand social identity according to Anderson's "imagined communities," where the collective identity is founded and shaped by identification with certain boundary markers, it is understandable that the concept of "Jewish Christian" would not make sense for representatives of either Christianity or Judaism.[62] According to Peter Wagner, the idea of personal and collective identity is associated with some sort of fundamental continuity and coherence.[63] For Jews in general, and particularly within traditional Judaism, Jewish individuals expressing faith in Jesus represent neither continuity nor coherence within a Jewish framework. Within these frames the term Jewish Christian therefore becomes meaningless, at least when speaking about a continued Jewish identity, because of the phenomenon itself and not necessarily semantics.

Nevertheless, as Wagner points out, in spite of the confusion often related to identity discourse, "there is 'something' that is being investigated."[64] For him the problem does not lie so much in the research findings as such, but in the inadequacy of the term "identity." For the same reason I use the terms Jewish/Hebrew Christian and Jewish believer in Jesus interchangingly in this dissertation. Both terms are adequate for my purpose, namely to describe the discourse about the phenomenon itself: ethnic Jews who show adherence to Christ and the Christian faith while maintaining some sort of continued Jewish identity.

Jewish Identification: Sergio DellaPergola

As Vibeke Banik points out, an essentialist framework stresses social identity (like ethnicity) as a fixed category, while a constructionist framework focuses on how the content of identities is fluid and changes throughout history. While the essentialist approach will have a rather

---

61. Some of Lucky's followers claimed that "Jewish Christian" was the best term, while Gurland and Lichtenstein do not seem to have used it very often. Anonymous "What's In a Name?," 110.

62. Friese, "Introduction," 4.

63. Wagner, "Identity," 48–49.

64. Ibid.

exclusive attitude against elements that do not fit into the collective memory, constructionist ideas will be able to see significant differences within one social group.⁶⁵ Such a cultural approach to the formation of identity opens up for the individual choices related to forming an identity, something that makes it relevant to see cultural concepts (e.g., Zionism) as central Jewish identification markers. As I see it, a cultural and constructionist approach also appears useful for studying Jewish identity among Jesus-believing Jews in the decades before World War 1. Theoretical perspectives are necessary not least to distinguish between important and unimportant source findings, and I have therefore chosen Sergio DellaPergola's categories as my key reference for Jewish identification.⁶⁶ The use of DellaPergola's categories and variables not only serves the aim of effectively extracting facts from the sources, but also constitutes a paradigm of Jewish identity to which Gurland, Lichtenstein and Lucky can be compared. Likewise, by the use of relevant theoretical knowledge, here represented by DellaPergola, missing empirical information can be located. Lastly, this system makes it possible to suggest a generalization of how Gurland, Lichtenstein and Lucky were building an identity.

Although DellaPergola describes Christian Jews in his own works as people with a distanced relationship to the Jewish community, he still claims that any survey on social identity first of all has to relate to the individual's self-identification. DellaPergola operates with a number of variables of Jewish identification which he holds to be manifestations of Jewish identity, based on the assumption that identity is created by a series of identifications during childhood and later. These variables are organized in three categories representing differing attitudes to Jewish identity: A) Particularistic; B) National-community; and C) Universalistic. DellaPergola thereby makes a distinction between religious and non-religious identities, which is usually done within contemporary Jewish demographic studies to include people of Jewish origin who would not be included in traditional halakic terminology. Category A is regarded as the strongest identification to Jewish religious and cultural tradition, while C identifies those with the most distanced relation to this part of the Jewish heritage.⁶⁷

65. Banik, *Solidaritet*, 32–34.
66. DellaPergola, "Jewish Identity," 25; and Rüsen, *History*, 103.
67. *Particularistic* (the Jewish tradition): 1) Form a family and honor parents; 2)

In this project I use DellaPergola's categories of Jewish identification for identifying and structuring Gurland's, Lucky's and Lichtenstein's sense of identification with Jewish tradition and the Jewish people. In other words, I use categories A and B, but not C, as I want to focus on identification concepts that are commonly held to be explicitly Jewish. To describe and discuss the attitudes to Jewish tradition and the Jewish people, I focus on some core concepts/variables given for Jewish identification with the particularistic or national-community categories that are expressed in the sources. I do not intend to apply all of DellaPergola's variables in the two categories, but will use the lists of variables as a help to extract elements that are connected to Jewish identity from their writing or their life-stories, and to find if there are elements missing that one should expect to be there. The core concepts of Jewish identity that will be discussed in depth will, to some extent, vary with each individual, as the issues which are commented on or described in the material sometimes differ.[68]

However, applying contemporary concepts of Jewish identity to pre-WWI individuals may appear to be a questionable approach for several reasons. First of all, when reconstructing the past one needs to avoid what John Henry named "Whiggism," i.e., the tendency to judge

---

Study Tanak; 3) Believe in God and be a religious person; 4) Give Tzedaka; 5) Celebrate Jewish holidays; 6) Study Talmud; 7) Participate in the Seder of Pesach; 8) Fast on Yom Kippur; 9) Observe the Sabbath; 10) Observe kashrut at home; 11) Circumcise male children; 12) Have Bar-Mitzvah and Bat-Mitzvah; 13) Not marry non-Jews; 14) Have a religious burial; 15) Study Torah; 16) Belong to an Edah (Jewish origin group); 17) Feel part of the Jewish people; 18) Be a Jew.

National-community (the Jewish people): 1) Help the needy; 2) Live in Israel; 3) Support Zionism or other Jewish nationalist ideas; 4) Peace among Edoth of the Jewish people; 5) Peace among religious/secular Jewish people; 6) Love your neighbor; 7) Speak Hebrew or Yiddish; 8) Strengthen Hebrew or Yiddish; 9) Be a Zionist or other Jewish nationalist.

Universalistic: 1) Be at peace with one's self; 2) Pay income tax as due; 3) Be a decent person; 4) Take care of your environment; 5) Succeed in studies; 6) Succeed economically; 7) Peace between Israel and its neighbors; 8) Peace among Jews and Arabs. See DellaPergola, "Jewish Identity," 25; and Ahituv, ed., *Historical Atlas*, 466–67.

Concerning the use of languages in category B, there is not always necessarily a connection between language and identity, as pointed out by the social anthropologist Øyvind Eggen. In the cases of Gurland, Lucky, and Lichtenstein, however, there seems to be a relationship between these concepts that will be discussed in each case. See Eggen, "Troens bekjennere," 55.

68. One example is Zionism, which was regarded as important by Lucky as well as Gurland, but which Lichtenstein does not even mention in his writings.

and interpret the past in terms of the present.⁶⁹ In particular, I will argue that one cannot understand the ideas or positions of pre-WWI Jewish believers in Jesus to be direct anticipations of the situation of the current Messianic movement. There is also a risk that the source material from the decades before WWI will be presented and analyzed in light of contemporary variables without considering that they are constructions and products of history, and possibly of only limited durability.⁷⁰ With the radical historical experience and development of the Jewish people over the past 150 years, it would be anachronistic to simply apply contemporary variables of identification directly to Jews living before WWI. One obvious example is the relationship to the State of Israel, one of the strongest elements of Jewish identity after 1948.⁷¹ Referring to the current situation for Jewish identity, Jonathan Sacks claims that until the last decades of the 19th century, for Jews to "define themselves as Jews without reference to religious belief or halakic practice would have seemed . . . a contradiction in terms."⁷²

Nevertheless, in the late 19th and early 20th century most of the thoughts and processes that shaped modern Jewry had been visible and discussed for decades, and with some adjustments I believe DellaPergola's variables and categories are still valuable for a historical project.⁷³ After all, in the wake of the Enlightenment, anti-Semitism and Zionism in the last decades of the 19th century, Jewish identity and identification was highly debated within and outside Jewish circles. Elements of the debate were a combination of the stereotypes of what was Jewish claimed by non-Jewish societies, as well as the Jewish religious, cultural, political and linguistic experiences in the Diaspora, the exclusion by European

69. Henry, *Scientific Revolution*, 3–4.

70. Wagner, "Identity," 51–52.

71. Indeed, Robert Paine claims that within a Zionist framework, Jewish Israelis would identify more strongly with Jewish history before the revolts in 70 and 132 than to Eastern European Jewry before 1948. Paine, "Israel," 126–36.

72. Sacks, *One People?*, 214.

73. The absence of the State of Israel can, to some extent, be compensated for by references to Jewish nationalism such as Zionism. As described by Banik, several decades before the State of Israel Zionism became a key marker for Jewish identification in many Jewish communities. However, it can be argued that Zionism has a different function before and after 1948, in the sense that before the creation of the State of Israel, the state was regarded as a means to avoid assimilation, while today Zionism is a means in itself to identify as Jewish. Banik, *Solidaritet*, 81, and Kahn-Paycha, *Popular Jewish Literature*, 126.

nationalism, and the religious aspects of divine selection.⁷⁴ The outcome of the process is a striking continuity in the way of thinking within the Jewish communities in the last 200 years. In spite of the time span and of the crucial experiences of *Shoah* and the creation of the State of Israel, Sacks states that:

> ... to a degree that is quite striking, Jews remain heirs of the nineteenth century. The disintegration that took place then still haunts Jewish existence today. The ideological battle-lines are the same. The same questions are asked and receive the same conflicting answers. Much has changed in the Jewish world, but our habits of thinking have not.⁷⁵

Another question is whether a phenomenon as complex as Jewish Christians may be grasped sufficiently by sociological categories at all. The fact that social identity builds on social relations might have made Gurland, Lucky and Lichtenstein express themselves differently from one situation or context to another, in a way that may obscure the findings. This does not necessarily mean that they would contradict themselves, but rather focus on different aspects depending on whether they were involved in, e.g., a polemical dispute or dealing with family relations. Such questions must be considered during the dissertation.

For a project like this it is essential that the text material be expressed through the methods, and not the opposite. When applying DellaPergola's scheme like this, there is a risk that Gurland, Lucky and Lichtenstein are described as more Jewish than they actually were, particularly since I have omitted DellaPergola's third category, "universalistic." In addition to DellaPergola's two categories, I have therefore added a number of concepts that I have arranged into three categories, representing (from a Jewish perspective) traditional transgressions or taboos, namely Christian doctrine, the Christian community, and the contemporary (premature) Hebrew Christian movement or individuals associated with this movement. Traditionally, a friendly relationship to these phenomena is seen as a clear expression of boundary-crossing from the Jewish majority's point of view.⁷⁶ A combination of DellaPergola's iden-

---

74. For Jewish nationalists, the implication of the last was that marriage to non-Jews was unwanted. See variable 13 in DellaPergola's category *A*, and Banik, *Solidaritet*, 81.

75. Sacks, *One People?*, xiii.

76. DellaPergola excludes "those of Jewish descent who have formally adopted another religion" from what he calls the "core Jewish population," and locates this group

tification markers with such examples of boundary-crossing visualizes the complex situation for many Jewish believers in Jesus since the 19th century.

This way of structuring the material as well as the different phenomena is not something I have copied from others, but is based on some core concepts found in the sources. These concepts are believed to be representative examples of what was found characteristic of their identification with the non-Jewish community. These examples, which I see as core concepts or markers for such social identification, are therefore not always symmetric. When dealing with Gurland's, Lucky's and Lichtenstein's attitudes to Christian tradition and doctrine, baptism and ideas on supersessionism in regard to Christianity vs. Judaism are central topics. However, these attitudes would be expressed within the framework of certain traditions or denominational preferences, and also in contrast to others, directly or indirectly. Similarly, the discussion on their relationship to the Christian community will focus on official church membership, but also needs to consider the potential tension between the status of being baptized or unbaptized and their real social or ideological position among Christians at the same time. Much of this material is expressed in the discussions on mission strategy and phenomena that took place within Christian Europe and the USA, particularly the assimilation process and anti-Semitism.

While these two categories (relationship to Christian tradition and to the Christian community) reflect the categories for identification to Christianity, I also use a third, which reflect Gurland's, Lucky's and Lichtenstein's identification with other Jewish believers in Jesus. This category constituted a social group or a more or less loose community of contemporary fellow Jewish believers in Jesus. In this community, one can either assume some degree of mutual acceptance for Jews who wanted to combine their national identity with a Christian faith, or that the topic was an arena for controversy. The fame and influence of the persons I have found in the sources varies, and sometimes the most influential were not very well known in all circles. Except for the social

---

in the "enlarged Jewish population." On the other hand, he claims that the concept of a "core Jewish population" is meant for those who identify themselves as Jewish, and ultimately rests largely on self-identification and "people's subjective, individual awareness of belonging and willingness to belong (directly or indirectly) to the Jewish collective." DellaPergola, *World Jewry*, 9–11.

dimension, the issue of Jewish identity and faith in Jesus in this loose network was highlighted in discussions about independent Jewish-Christian congregations and Torah observance for Jewish Christians.

In addition to DellaPergola's two first categories, I have therefore used the following list to structure the dissertation:

The relationship to Christian tradition and doctrine: 1) Baptism; 2) Ideas of supersessionism/replacement theology; 3) Theological and denominational preferences (like pietism, dispensationalism, millenarianism and liberal theology).

The relationship to the Christian community: 1) Church membership; 2) Mission societies and mission-strategic preferences; 3) Anti-Semitism.

The relationship to contemporary Jewish (Hebrew) Christian groups and individuals: 1) Gurland's, Lucky's and Lichtenstein's relationships with famous and/or influential contemporary Jewish believers in Jesus (like Joseph Rabinowitz, David Baron and Yechiel Herschensohn-Lichtenstein, as well as the relations between Gurland, Lucky and Lichtenstein themselves); 2) Gurland's, Lucky's and Lichtenstein's relationships to fellowships of Jewish believers in Jesus (e.g., the Hebrew Christian Alliance); 3) Gurland's, Lucky's and Lichtenstein's position in the debates about Torah observance for Jewish believers in Jesus and Jewish-Christian congregations.

Outline

Based on the above-mentioned considerations the book follows this outline:

1. Introduction
2. Eastern European Jews between 1860 and 1914 and Christian missions
3. The biographies of Gurland, Lucky, and Lichtenstein
4. A comparative analysis:
    a. The relationship to Jewish tradition
    b. The relationship to the Jewish people
    c. The relationship to Christian tradition and doctrine

d. The relationship to the Christian community
   e. The relationship to Hebrew Christian groups and individuals
6. Conclusion

2

Eastern European Jews between 1860 and 1914 and the Christian missions

Introduction

> The world in which Marc Chagall grew up is no more now than shards of memory. The log cabins of his Vitbsk served to stoke the ovens in Treblinka. His fiddlers on the roof have flown to Paradise . . . via Hell.[1]

With these words, Sidney Alexander summarizes a basic dimension for anyone trying to reconstruct the lives of Jewish individuals from Eastern Europe before 1914. The extraordinary disaster of the two world wars and the Holocaust has created a gap that surpasses the ordinary historical distance every historian has to deal with. The world Gurland, Lucky and Lichtenstein lived in has not only changed, but has disappeared, not to say been murdered. Aside from the emotional or existential element of this situation, it also raises certain challenges when the worlds of these three individuals are to be reconstructed. One of these challenges is that access to relevant source material is difficult, particularly Jewish sources. Another aspect is that contemporary studies on the Jewish communities in this part of Europe either tend to follow previous or current state borders—obscuring the contact across these borders—or the opposite, giving overviews that become so general that the content may lose its connection to the concrete communities. In this study I will try to combine both the general and the concrete perspectives. The following section presents a general and brief overview

---

1. Alexander, *Marc Chagall*, 17.

of Eastern Europe and its Jewish population in the last century before WWI. Thereafter I present the biographies of each individual, which I follow up with analysis. Descriptions and in-depth discussions of relevant issues that are significant to understanding each individual will be given when this is most natural, be it either the local political context or ideological and cultural ideologies and phenomena. While this approach will give the best grasp of the context, the downside is that the survey may include some overlap.

FIGURE 1: East Central Europe, 1910

Map from Magocsi, *Historical Atlas of Central Europe*, 119.

The Term "Eastern Europe"

The term "Eastern Europe" is disputed, and neither politicians nor geographers agree fully on the content.[2] Some scholars and politicians tend to use the term "East Central Europe" when focusing on the countries and regions where Gurland, Lichtenstein and Lucky mainly operated, but this use is not fixed. For Piotr S. Wandycz the term denotes Poland, Hungary, Slovakia and the Czech Republic (Bohemia), while others (like Paul Robert Magocsi) include territories like Ukraine, Belarus and the Baltics, regions that are central for this dissertation. In addition to the discussion of its geographical unity, the demographic situation in central Eastern Europe was, and still is, very complex, characterized by a diversity of nationalities, languages, religions, cultures and customs. Not least, until WWII the region was also home to the largest Jewish population in the world.[3]

A significant characteristic of East Central Europe is that while Western Europe after the Middle Ages experienced development towards capitalism and industrialization, the agrarian character of Eastern Europe proved much more enduring.[4] Until 1870 only the Czech lands were influenced by industrialization, and compared to the West, the national and ethnic problems were more complex and acute.[5] In the West the state formed the nation; in the East nationalism often included a protest against an alien state or regime.[6] For example, between 1794 and 1905 the Poles were engaged in no less than six uprisings and one revolution against Russian rule.[7] Nevertheless, until the 19th century the Judaeophobia that was common elsewhere in Europe was less pronounced in the East.[8] In the wake of modernization and new ideologies this was about to change. From being ideological companions before 1850, liberalism and nationalism became counterparts in the decades before WWI. The radical socialists as well as the nationalists were in-

---

2. Wandycz, *The Price of Freedom*, 1, 7–8.
3. Eberhardt, *Ethnic Groups*, 3.
4. Wandycz, *The Price of Freedom*, 6.
5. Ibid., 7, 135.
6. Ibid., 138.
7. Ibid., 10. However, most nationalist organizations in Russia and Austria-Hungary did not seek outright independence, but social reforms as well as cultural and political autonomy; Roshwald, *Ethnic Nationalism*, 33.
8. Wandycz, *The Price of Freedom*, 10.

creasingly influenced by Social Darwinism, which regarded the liberals and middle class as being traitors to either class or nation/race. Two ethnic groups that were associated with both liberals and the new middle class, and which often played a significant economic function in this part of the continent, were the Germans and the Jews.[9] For Gurland, Lucky and Lichtenstein the connections between these two groups became significant, as the German-speaking context would frame much of their lives.

Around 1900, 1.7 million Germans lived in the Russian Empire, in settlements surrounded or intermixed with settlements containing other groups. These Germans were often referred to by regional names, like Baltic, Bessarabian and Black Sea Germans. Germans living in Austrian Galicia were likewise called Galician Germans. Their presence was due to the slow migration of Germans eastward from the Elbe River between the year 700 and the 18th century, in a combination of military conquest, peaceful colonization, natural or forcible assimilation of surrounding ethnic groups, and invitations from local rulers who found their technical skills attractive. Their political and economic power in the 19th century differed, from wealthy landowners and barons in the Baltic Russian provinces to Galician Germans who hardly could manage on their own. As these minorities often had little contact with each other, the German population in Eastern Europe was characterized by its cultural, confessional and linguistic complexity.[10] Nevertheless, the German language and culture had great influence in these regions, and due to their privileged political and economic status they were often very loyal to their regimes, e.g., in the Russian Empire.[11]

The Jews

A characteristic feature of the Jews in this part of the continent were that although they often had been there as long as (or even longer than) some of the "native" populations, they had no territory of their own. In addition, most of them resided in towns and cities where they were

9. Ibid., 167.
10. Kühl, *Tyskere i Øst*, 24–25, 87.
11. Magocsi, *Historical Atlas*, 104. As late as WWI more than a hundred thousand Russian Germans fought on the Tzar's side against Germany and Austria, in spite of several decades of nationalistic politicies against the Russian German population before the war. Kühl, *Tyskere i Øst*, 88.

associated with urban professions, and therefore they often played a significant role in the economic, cultural and, to some degree, political life of the countries where they lived. It is estimated that in 1900, of the 10.6 million Jews in the world, 70 percent lived in East Central Europe. Seventy percent of these (7,468,000) lived in the Austrian province Galicia and in the Russian territory where Jews were allowed to live, the Pale of Settlement. The remaining areas with significant Jewish settlements were 1) Russian Bessarabia, Austrian Bukovina and Romanian Moldavia; 2) Northeastern Hungary; and 3) Budapest and Vienna.

All of these three regions or cities were, during the 19th century, exposed to significant immigration by poverty-stricken Jews from Galicia and persecuted Jews from the Pale, the latter group mainly after the outbreak of severe pogroms in Russia from 1881 onwards. In addition, between 1880 and 1914, 350,000 Jews immigrated from East Central Europe to Western Europe, while 2.4 million moved to the United States.[12] This mass migration was due to the rise of modern anti-Semitism as well as the worsening of economic conditions for the Jewish population in the region. In addition to the demographic changes, the Jewish community was also increasingly transformed from within as a result of growing religious indifference and diversity between traditionalists and reformers, as well as increased cultural assimilation into non-Jewish communities. As a reaction to growing anti-Semitism and European nationalist movements, several expressions of Jewish nationalism and political activism became widespread, like Zionism and Bundism (the Jewish Socialist movement in Russia and Poland). The traditional language in the Jewish communities was Yiddish, a combination of medieval German dialects, Hebrew, Aramaic and Slavonic languages. Most of the Yiddish-speaking Jews in this part of Europe were called *Ostjuden*, a term that indicated their adherence to traditional Judaism or Hasidism as well as their lower social status, poverty and lack of higher education.[13] During the 19th century an increasing number of Jews also learned to use their neighboring languages, as well as Hebrew. Hebrew was traditionally used among rabbis for religious purposes, but Jewish Enlightenment pioneers (*maskilim*) and later Zionists incorporated the classical language in their own ideology.

---

12. Magocsi, *Historical Atlas*, 107–9.
13. Stokke, "Auswanderer," 9.

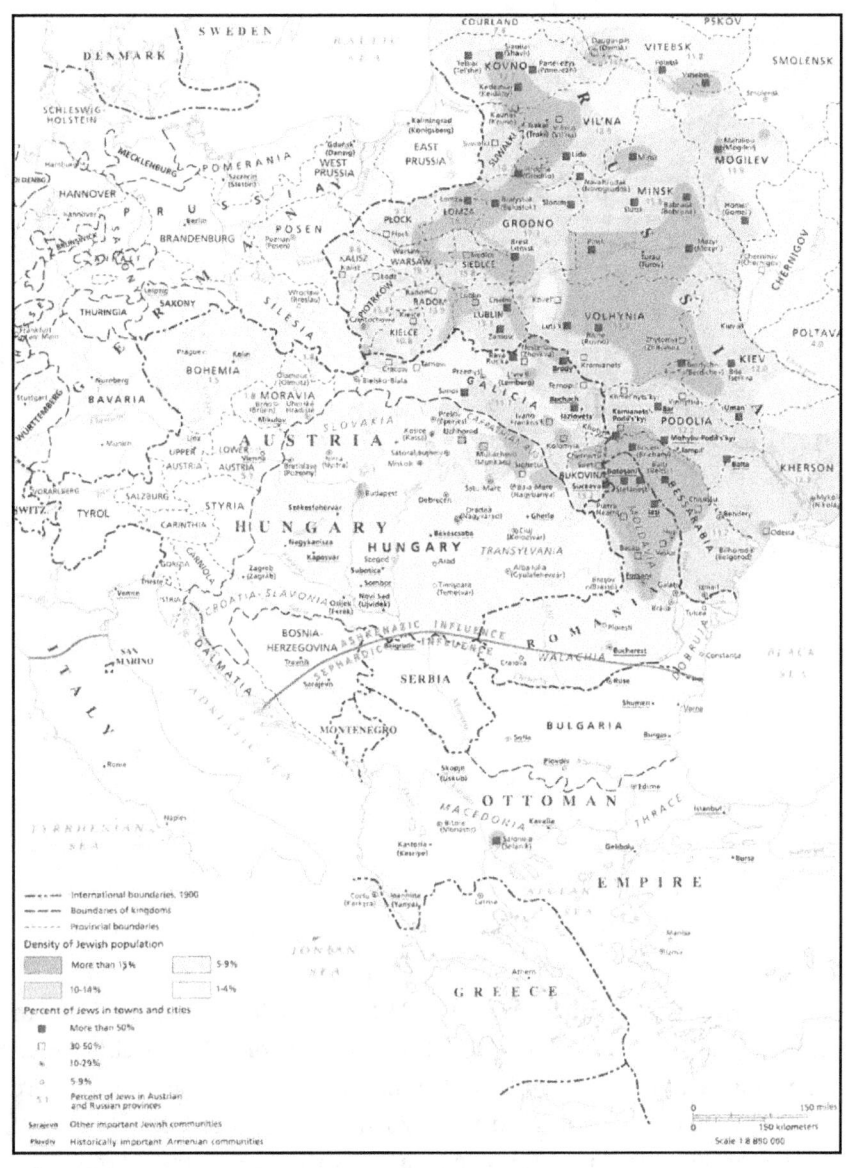

FIGURE 2: Jews and Armenians in East Central Europe, ca. 1900
Map from Magocsi, *Historical Atlas of Central Europe*, 109.

FIGURE 3: The Pale of Jewish Settlement. Map found at http://jgsla.org/articles/tag/pale-of-jewish-settlement. No permission.

During the century before WWI the majority of the Jews in Eastern Europe lived in the territories of the old Polish-Lithuanian Commonwealth, which after partitions in 1772, 1793, and 1795 were divided between Prussia and the two major multi-ethnic empires of Austria and Russia. In the Russian Empire, Russians dominated the highest strata in the government, while Germans and Poles filled important functions in the regional and central administration of the empire. The German elite that had ruled the Baltic since the conquest by Teutonic Knights in the Middle Ages retained its hegemony over the Latvian and Estonian peasants, a situation similar to the position of Polish landowners in Ukraine and Belarus. Before the Russification in the last decades of the 19th century, these groups were free to pursue their own politics of cultural assimilation of the native populations (i.e., making the native peasants into Germans or Poles).[14] For the Russian Jews the situation was different. Most of the Jewish population was forced to continue living in the territories of the previous Polish-Lithuanian Commonwealth, now called the Pale of Settlement (Russian *chertá osédlosti*). Since the partition of Poland in the last decades of the 18th century, Lithuania was a province in the Russian Empire, and the Jewish communities were autonomous entities in most of their internal affairs.[15] However, the Russian Jews gradually found themselves more and more restricted, and in 1844 the traditional body of Jewish self-government, *kahal*, was abolished.[16] Until the Pale of Settlement was abolished by the provisional government in 1917, on the average the area of the Pale covered one million square kilometers, extending from the Baltic Sea to the Black Sea. Here Jews were permitted rights of domicile, employment and trade, and the territory contained 94 percent of the Russian Jews—according to the official census in 1897, 4,899,300 people.[17] Eighty-two percent of the Jews lived in towns and villages, forming 37 percent of the urban population. In other parts of Russia, such as Kurland and St. Petersburg, Jews had to be born there in order to live there.

After the partitions of Poland, Austria got Galicia, and consequently the Habsburg regime had to deal with masses of Hasidic Jews who were quite different from its traditional Jewish population. In spite of the Hungarian revolt against Habsburgian rule in 1848–1849, Hungary was established as an autonomous nation in a double monarchy with Austria in 1867, the so-called *Ausgleich*. This privileged position in the Austrian Empire was due to the crisis after the Austrian defeat in the war with Prussia in 1866. Although the other ethnic minorities were also offered more liberty, they ended up being dominated by the Hungarian (Magyar) majority.[18] The empire of Austria was now divided into a dualist state, where the states of Austria and Hungary shared the king, army and foreign policy. The Hungarian majority was reluctant to promote

14. Roshwald, *Ethnic Nationalism*, 21.
15. Mendes-Flohr and Reinharz, *The Jew*, 378–79.
16. Klier, *Imperial Russia's*, 1, 6.
17. Bobe, "Four Hundred Years," 34.
18. Berend, *History Derailed*, 264.

social reform to the other nationalities, although the Jews at times were regarded as political partners.[19] The Hungarians understood themselves as a fragile nation surrounded by enemies, and expected to be culturally subsumed under the Germans or the Slavs if they were not careful about development. The Hungarian governments therefore enforced a strong Magyarization of the country, something a majority of the Hungarian Jews identified with.[20]

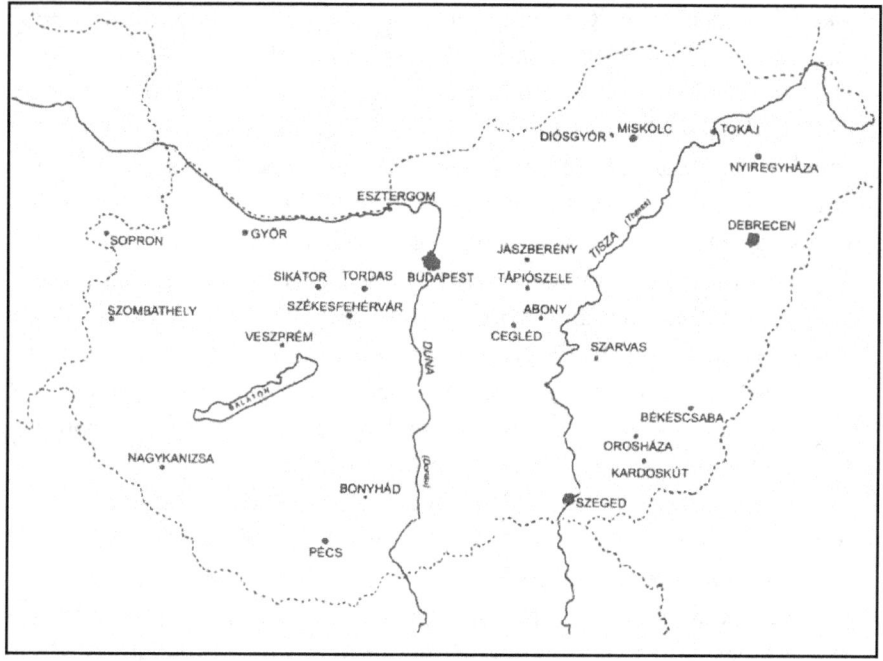

FIGURE 4: Hungary. From Terray, *Et liv i grenseland*, 231.

For both Germans and Jews, it was characteristic that as groups of non-indigenous origin they were dramatically over-represented in the new business and middle-class elite during the 19th century, due to their urbanization and strong orientation to business and education.[21] However, while the Germans often were assimilated into their sur-

19. Wandycz, *The Price of Freedom*, 180.
20. Ibid., 9, 143.
21. In Romania the Greeks were another group that filled this new strata in the modern society. Berend, *History Derailed*, 199.

rounding societies, the Jews often remained in many aspects outsiders and aliens.[22] As the Jews were associated with the emerging capitalist society and new ideologies like liberalism and socialism, the traditional Judaeophobia in the Christian communities was revitalized by the new anti-Semitism in the last decades before WWI. However, while traditional Jew hatred was based on religious rivalry, anti-Semitism was associated with Social Darwinism and the new ideas about race.

Christian Mission Work to the Jews

Parallel to this development, during the 19th century there were established a number of Protestant mission societies with the purpose of converting Jews, and much of their effort was focused on the Jews in Eastern Europe. These societies were based in Western and Central Europe, as well as in Scandinavia, and until WWII the Anglican and British free-church societies were regarded as the leading force in this movement. This activity, together with the changes within Eastern European Jewry, constitutes the background for the approximately 200,000 Jews baptized during the 19th century.[23] For the vast majority of them, conversion was connected to a wish for assimilation and disengagement from the Jewish community, and in many cases the conversions were not, or were only partly, the result of missionary efforts. In mission circles before WWI, Gurland, Lucky and Lichtenstein awoke much interest, and several of these societies had much contact with one or several of them. It is therefore natural to present those societies which are most relevant for this study.

The Jewish missions were organized in the same pattern as other Protestant mission enterprises: Church missions (usually associated to free churches) and mission societies (independent societies with a democratic structure and a certain denominational tendency). Their strategies were first of all preaching and later also establishing Christian schools to create a population with Christian values.

---

22. Ibid., 200–201.
23. Le Roi, *Judentaufen*, 49; Thompson, *A Century*, 264.

The London Society for Promoting Christianity amongst the Jews and Die Berliner Gesellschaft zur Beförderung des Christentums unter den Juden (The Berlin Society for Promoting Christianity among the Jews)

The London Society for Promoting Christianity amongst the Jews (founded in 1808) is usually regarded as the first mission society aimed at Jews to be established in modern times, and was to become the largest mission society focusing on Jews before 1900. By then the society operated with missionaries in Eastern Europe as well as in most of the relevant British colonies and countries under British influence. The *Berliner Gesellschaft* began in 1822, supported by the Prussian king, and was inspired by the London Society. From its foundation to 1900 the society is said to have had 25 missionaries in Posen, Hungary and Czernowitz. The Berlin Society's journal was *Nathanael: Zeitschrift für der evangelischen Kirche an Israel*. The society was closed by the Gestapo on January 23, 1941. The German Society kept a much lower profile than the British did, but nevertheless the Berlin Society involved itself with Gurland as well as Lucky. While Gurland was associated with the Berlin Society during his studies in Berlin, the society secured the financial platform for the establishing of Lucky's *Edut leIsrael* between 1889 and 1893.[24]

The Mildmay Mission to the Jews

After 22 years in service with the London Society, Anglican vicar John Wilkinson (1824–1907) founded a new Jewish mission under the Mildmay Foundations in June 1876, due to disagreement on the return of the Jewish people to Palestine. Wilkinson's society also became an outlet for individuals and Protestant church bodies who did not feel free to deal with the London Society, which primarily was a Church of England affiliate. From the beginning, the new Jewish mission was linked to the Mildmay Institutions in London, particularly the Mildmay Conference Hall, which was used for public meetings. The Mildmay Mission was nondenominational, and in 1905 it employed 53 missionary workers in its ten institutions on all continents. One of these institutions was a workshop for Jews in Odessa, run by Gurland's assistant and successor Rosenberg. The society published the monthly *Trusting and Toiling*, as

---

24. Le Roi, *Geschichte*, 1:142 and 153; Glaser, "A Survey," 232.

well as the Yiddish journal *Dibre Hayomim* every second month. The society was, from the 1880s, associated with Rabinowitz in Kishinev, who to a large extent was supported by the society. At the same time, the Mildmay Mission was supporting the publication of Salkinsons's Hebrew translation of the New Testament in 1885, the so-called "New Testament Movement." Because of this work, Gurland was associated with the Mildmay Mission already in 1887, and in 1900 he became the superintendent for all the society's workers in the western part of the Russian Empire. Lichtenstein and Lucky were never associated with this society as such, but Wilkinson was central in the committee that was established for Lichtenstein's financial support in 1893.[25]

Der Evangelisch-Lutherische Zentralverein für Mission unter Israel

The *Zentralverein* (central union) was founded in Leipzig in 1871 with professor of theology Franz Delitzsch (1813–1890) as chairman. Since 1863, Delitzsch had published the Jewish mission periodical *Saat auf Hoffnung*, which followed Gurland with much interest starting in 1864. The society coordinated the work of many German and Scandinavian Mission to Israel societies, of which the most important were the Norwegian, Bavarian and Saxonian societies. *Zentralverein* had a strong Lutheran and pietistic profile, and many of its members and leaders had, like Delitzsch himself, experienced a spiritual breakthrough during revivals in their youth. From 1861 to 1891 the Norwegian society had a particularly close relationship to the *Zentralverein*, mainly due to the personal friendship between Carl Paul Caspari and Franz Delitzsch. *Zentralverein* was behind the *Institutum Judaicum Delitzschianum* seminary in Leipzig, which was founded in 1880 (but did not get started until 1886).[26]

The Hebrew Christian Testimony

This non-denominational society was founded in 1891 by the two Jewish converts David Baron (1857–1926) and Charles Andrew Schönberger. Baron had been working for several years with John Wilkinson for

---

25. Le Roi, *Geschichte*, 2:296 and 300; Pruter, *Jewish Christians*, 29; Wilkinson, *The Life of John Wilkinson*. See also Le Roi, "John Wilkinson," 50–58.

26. Burgmester, "Franz Delitzsch," 13–29; Skarsaune, "'En Lærd af Guds Naade'"; Glaser, "A Survey," 233; Rengstorf, "85 Jahre Institutum Judaicum," 30–68.

the Mildmay Mission before the founding of the Hebrew Christian Testimony, and Schönberger had been working for, among other societies, the Scottish Free Church in Budapest, and from 1884 he was in Vienna. While he was closely associated to Lichtenstein, Baron became an ardent opponent to Lucky.[27]

The Scandinavian Societies

The Norwegian Israel Mission (*Den Norske Israelsmisjon*) is the oldest of the Scandinavian Israel mission societies. It was founded in 1844, and sponsored Gurland from 1867 to 1876. From the 1880s the Norwegians did mission work in Romania and later in Budapest, where their missionaries came in touch with Lucky and Lichtenstein. The Danish society (*Den Danske Israelsmission*), founded in 1885, got in touch with Lucky already in 1890 and maintained contact with him and his Jewish followers until the 1930s in Lvov/Lemberg. The Swedish society (*Svenska Isralesmissionen*), founded 1875, had some work in Odessa at the time Gurland was there, and its chairman, Theodor Lindhagen, appears to have become one of Lucky's sympathizers. Although these organizations were independent, theologically and personally they were closely associated with the denominational and revivalist factions of the Lutheran state churches in their countries. Still, disagreement about mission strategy related to Jewish-Christian congregations caused much strife within them.[28]

American societies: The Sabbath Tract Society and The Zion Society of Minneapolis

The Sabbath Tract Society was the branch of the Seventh Day Baptist denomination (SDB) that was responsible for publications for internal as well as external use. Consequently, the society was closely connected to SDB theology and denominational interests. From 1886 Lucky was associated with this society, and even after his return to Galicia he occasionally received financial support from its board. The Zion Society (Norwegian: *Sionsforeningen*), founded by Norwegian immigrants in the 1870s, was associated with the Lutheran tradition in accordance with the

---

27. Thompson, *A Century*, 111; Le Roi, *Geschichte*, 2:176–79; Glaser, "A Survey," 283; and http://www.messianictestimony.com/aboutus.html.

28. Skarsaune, *Israels venner*, 28–209; Torm, *50 Aars arbejde for Israel*; and Edvardsson, *Kyrka och judendom*.

different immigrant synods. Although not said explicitly, the inspiration behind their mission activity was probably from the Norwegian Israel Mission. At minimum, the immigrants must have been well informed about the Norwegian mission activity, which seems to be confirmed by the fact that the society "took over" Gurland from the Norwegian society in the 1890s.[29]

29. Waldeland, *Jøderne og Jødemisjonen*, and *Seventh Day Baptists in Europe and America*.

3

The Biographies of Gurland, Lucky, and Lichtenstein

To analyze their views on Jewish identity, I believe it is necessary to read texts by Gurland, Lucky and Lichtenstein in light of the lives they were living, and vice versa. Hence, this section does not intend to give a complete biography of each individual, but seeks to establish information about their lives that is relevant and adequate for the analysis. I therefore dwell on material that relates to the five categories of identification that were presented in the introduction, which will be discussed more systematically in the analysis in chapter four. Still, some issues or processes need more thorough discussion than others in the following three biographical sketches in order to get a broader or more nuanced picture of the events.

Rudolf Hermann (Chaim) Gurland (1831–1905)

FIGURE 5: Le Roi, *Rudolf Hermann Gurland*, second front page.

Introduction

The primary source for the following sketch of Rudolf Hermann (Chaim) Gurland is the biography *In Zwei Welten: Rudolf Hermann Gurland: Ein Lebensbild* (*IzW*), which was published by his wife, Helene Gurland, in 1907.[1] Except for some printed material, her main sources were hand-

---

1. Gurland, *In zwei Welten*, 1911. The English translations of quotations in the notes are mainly taken from an unpublished translation of unknown date in the possession of Hans-Heinrich Gurland. As my copy is not complete regarding Gurland's life before his conversion, the quotations from this period are translated by me. (Translations from both sources have been edited for clarity.) *IzW* was published several times after 1907, and some of the editions differ slightly from each other. E.g., the Norwegian translation, *I tvende verdener*, 1912, which I assume is based upon the 1907 original, contains some details that are lacking in the 1911 version that I have used as the main source. In addition, the part that describes Gurland's discussion with synagogue members in Kishinev had been published several times in different editions since 1864. See note 165 below [x-ref]. In her work on the Jewish society in Kurland and Rige until WWI, Svetlana Bogojavlenska refers to Gurland and discusses his role in the polemic between the Jewish and Baltic German leadership in the 1870s (see pages 72–73). Her main source on Gurland's biography is the 1907 version of *In zwei Welten*. See Bogojavlenska,

written diary notes and letters by Gurland that were in her possession. Another biographical source is a little book by the German historian of Christian missions to the Jews, Joh. F. A. de Le Roi, *Rudolf Hermann Gurland*. This volume was published in 1906.[2] Although le Roi generally must be considered well-informed, I nevertheless regard the publication by Gurland's widow as a better source when the narratives differ.[3]

In many ways the narratives about Rudolf Hermann Gurland follow the standard literary pattern of Jewish converts from the 19th and early 20th century, which can be found in contemporary Protestant Jewish mission periodicals and biographies in Europe and North America. Basically, the form of these (auto)biographies is structured according to interpretative patterns provided by Christian theological concepts like providence, God's law, and the order of salvation (*ordo salutis*).[4] This standard narrative focuses on conversion and baptism as the crucial events that transform the life of the individual, often described metaphorically as leaving the dark world of paganism or Judaism to enter a new world of light. In Gurland's case, the biography's title signals the same pattern.[5] Like most evangelical autobiographies and conversion narratives, *IzW* and le Roi's book have many parallels to the modern novel. This means that these narratives must be regarded as something more than sources for historical reconstruction, as the genre itself determines what material is considered significant and how different phenomena should be interpreted. In addition, one needs to consider what audience the books were aimed at. Both Helene Gurland and le Roi wrote for friends of the Jewish missions in the German societies in general. However, Helene Gurland also appears to address her contemporary Baltic German society.

Die jüdische Gesellschaft, 115–19.

2. Le Roi, *Rudolf Hermann Gurland*.

3. A substantial summary of Gurland's life in German is published by Gurland's grandson, Hans-Heinrich Gurland and Stephan Bitter; see Bitter and Gurland, "Gurland, (Chaim) Rudolf Hermann," cols. 551–72.

4. Hindmarsh, *The Evangelical Conversion Narrative*, 6–8.

5. Ibid., 1–3.

Family Background

Chaim Gurland was born in Vilnius in 1831 to Raphael (Feidel or Faytel) Gurland (died 1862) and Ida, born Rabinowitz (died after 1882).[6] Nicknamed *Litvaks*, Lithuanian Jews spoke a distinct form of Yiddish, also used in today's Latvia and Belarus.[7] According to *IzW*, Chaim's grandfather was not born Jewish, but was a Spanish philo-Semite in Portugal who converted to Judaism when he migrated to Holland.[8] The sources say nothing about whether it was at his conversion to Judaism that he took the surname Gurland, but alternatively this might have taken place when his son Raphael settled in Lithuania after facing a family crisis in Holland, where Raphael's wife converted with their daughter to Christianity.[9] In Lithuania he married Ida Rabinowitz, daughter of a

---

6. In Anonymous, "Belarus and Lithuania: Census & Family Lists from Various Districts, 1795–1900," there appears one Chaim Gurland, born about 1830 in Stakliskes in Trakai, some kilometers southwest of Vilnius, and whose father is Faytel Gurland. As the list reports that he converted in 1864, this could well be the same persons as in *IzW*. This raises certain questions concerning the descriptions of his family life in the biography, as the wife Gena (Gisa?) is also described as a convert by the census. According to *IzW*, Gurland and Gisa divorced in August 1863, and it was his new wife Marie who converted with him the following year. Either the list has confused Gurland's second wife with his third, or the biography for unknown reasons has changed the facts here.

7. Levin, *The Litvaks*, 10. As the Jewish communities in the Russian empire were characterized by huge cultural differences, I relate Gurland to regional (Lithuanian, Ukrainian and Latvian) Jewish contexts more than to the general Russian Jewish history when natural. Zipperstein, *Imagining Russian Jewry*, 10.

8. The Portuguese Inquisition functioned between the 1530s and 1791 to round up, among others, Marranos who were backsliding in secret to Judaism. Holland became the new home for thousands of Marrano refugees who returned to Judaism. Considering the background of Chaim Gurland's grandfather, it is possible that he had a Marrano background. Le Roi describes the family background slightly differently. Gurland's grandfather was a Christian who converted to Judaism in Holland, due to the strong philo-Semitism of the country. After his conversion he fled to Poland. Le Roi, *Rudolf Hermann Gurland*, 3; Yovel, *The Other Within*, 222; and Phillip, "Spätbarock," 2: 23–86, 27.

9. The name Gurland appears with slightly different spellings in sources from tsarist Lithuania, and according to *IzW*, 9, the name means "stranger in the land," which probably refers to the Hebrew *g-r* ("alien").

Up to about 1800, Jews in Eastern and Central Europe had no hereditary surnames in the current fashion. Between 1797 and 1845, the Jewish population in this area was gradually compelled to accept or choose hereditary surnames. Jewish surnames could be derived from Hebrew or Yiddish first names, the person's occupation (mainly religious occupation), nicknames, abbreviations, or local/habitation names, which was common in the German-Yiddish contexts, but there are several examples of Slavonic

rabbi in Vilnius, and Raphael became a devoted rabbi himself. Chaim Gurland was the first son of this marriage.

Without saying so explicitly, *IzW* seems to suggest that Raphael's dramatic background explains much of his behavior in his relationship with Chaim. Helene Gurland describes Raphael Gurland as a depressive character: ". . . One rarely one saw him laughing, as if the life in itself was a sin, the birth an event of bad luck."[10] Gurland's memories of his early family life are rather gloomy, and the autobiography claims that his father's fear of the law and its impossible demands also became his own.

When Chaim was five, his father began giving him religious training at home, hoping to see him as his successor. This was possible since the Russian government left the education of children to their parents.[11] Gurland gives a claustrophobic description of this situation. Fellowship with other children was rare, as the teaching took all his time. His father instructed him in the Hebrew Bible, and later he was introduced to Talmud and Kabbalah, following an extended curriculum compared to the traditional Jewish religious elementary school, the *heder*. Knowledge in other subjects was not encouraged, but Chaim familiarized himself with history and drawing by asking other children for help in secret. In addition to Hebrew, he also learned Russian, which his father held to be unnecessary.[12]

Consequently, Chaim developed much opposition to his father, and he felt they not only were living in different worlds but that life under his father was a life in some sort of prison. This description of Chaim's childhood and relationship to his father may resemble a common phenomenon pointed out in several studies of religious conversion, where the father has been absent, weak or abusive. Although stressing that these studies are later, in his work on Jewish mission to the Jews in the

---

local names as well. From this it is possible that the name Gurland somehow also refers to Kurland, north of Lithuania. Unbegaun, *Russian Surnames*, 347, 337.

10. Gurland, *IzW* (1911), 10–11: " kaum je hat man ihn lachen sehen, als ware das Leben an sich schon Sünde, das Geborenwerden ein Unglück."

11. An additional motive for this was probably to find a way to avoid his son being enlisted in the Russian army, as rabbis or rabbinic students were exempted from military service according to the law of 1827. As Jewish recruits could be conscripted from the age of twelve and taken to military schools, these "cantonists" or "Nicholas' soldiers" usually lost their bonds to the Jewish community by the time they were dismissed after twenty-five years of service. Levin, *The Litvaks*, 67.

12. Gurland, *IzW* (1911), 34.

USA from 1880 to 2000 Yaakov Ariel nevertheless suggests that there is a similar pattern among Jewish converts in the USA around 1900:

> In all the different autobiographical accounts and the many testimonies in missionary magazines of that period, I have not found one that described a person who converted while living with a warm and supportive two-parent family.[13]

However, although the observation by Ariel appears to fit with Gurland's experience, other sources contradict or modify this pattern in regard to Jewish converts to Christianity. Ellie Schainker indicates that strained family relations were not always the case for converts, not even in Russia. Converts could have strong bonds to their families, something that explains how Gurland could maintain contact with his mother and parts of his family for years after his conversion.[14]

Gurland studied at a *heder* in Vilnius between 1842 and 1847, and between 1848 and 1851 he attended the famous *yeshiva* (theological seminary for Talmud studies) in Volozhin hin, in today's Belarus.[15] This *yeshiva*, founded in 1802 by Rabbi Chaim Ben Isaac Volozhiner (1749–1821), became the model for all the *yeshivot* founded in Lithuania in the 19th century, and the institution was a stronghold in the opposition to the Hasidic movement. However, when *Haskalah*, the Jewish Enlightenment movement, was established in Vilna and Kovno starting in the 1840s, the conflict between the *Hasidim* and *mitnagdim* (the traditionalists) to some extent ceased, and was replaced by the battle against the *maskilim*, the followers of *Haskalah*. *Haskalah* ideology was of course banished from the *yeshiva* in Volozhin as well as the other

---

13. Ariel, *Evangelizing*, 41. See also Rambo, *Understanding*, 53, 11, 157.

14. Schainker, "Imperial Hybrids."

15. Due to the *heder* system, almost every Jewish boy was able to read and write. However, the Talmud instruction that took place there was something the government as well as Jewish supporters of reform wanted to change. The system for education within the Jewish society in Vilnius of the period was that most boys from the age of 4 or 5 went to a *heder*. The traditional *heder* education lasted until age 13. The syllabus began with learning the Hebrew alphabet, and then went on to the Pentateuch with Rashi's basic commentary. After this the pupils read selected portions of the Talmud with the traditional commentaries. After Bar-Mitzvah, they could continue studies of the Talmud in smaller groups, trained by a teacher who was a regular scholar; this was called a small *yeshiva*. For those with the opportunities and right abilities could then go to one of the bigger *yeshivot*, like Volozhin. From the beginning of the century, *maskilim* tried to reform the education system, also in Vilinus. Levin, *The Litvaks*, 95–99; and Klier, *Imperial Russia's*, 6.

yeshivot, but it nevertheless leaked in among some of the students.[16] Although Gurland's biography does not mention *Haskalah* sources explicitly, the biography dwells heavily on his religious doubts and unrest during his years at the different schools. In some of his letters to his cousin and pen pal Samuel, Gurland shows little respect for many parts of Judaism, particularly regarding the obscurity of Talmud and other parts of the Jewish oral tradition.

> Even the speculative ideas from even the greatest, best and brightest rabbi, Moses Maimonides, in this regard seem to me to be an unsuccessful attempt. His theosophical theories are in reality a dangerous play with words, as he admits that they are not grounded on revelation but on pagan philosophy, especially Plato and Aristotle.[17]

> You know what I think about the doctrines of Talmud and Kabbalah. For every day I am convinced that not only is a big part of Talmud and Kabbalah inauthentic, but also that they cannot be recognized as the Word of God, as they contradict themselves.[18]

However, Chaim evaluated the Hebrew Bible differently from the oral tradition, and regarded the *Tanak* (the Hebrew Bible) as divine in contrast to the words of Talmud and Kabbalah. Still, even parts of the word of God were unclear, particularly texts referring to the promised Messiah:

> I have to make it clear to you that I do not disparage the Holy Scripture as I do Talmud. No, since I began to study it from the start again, the Holy Scripture day by day has become more holy and dear to me, while Talmud looks more like a gallery of characters without life.... Oh, that the loving God would have mercy

16. A process described in autobiographies and novels like Solomon, *In the Thicket*; and Gordon, *Between Two Worlds*.

17. Gurland, *IzW* (1911), 29. "Selbst die spekulativen Ideen des grössten, gelehrtessten und tiefsinnigsten unserer Rabbiner, des Moses Maimonedes, scheinen mir in dieser Beziehung ein misslungener Versuch zu sein. Seine theosophischen Theorien sind im Grunde ein gefährliches Begriffsspiel; den wie er selbst gesteht, hat er sie nicht aus dem Boden der Offenbarung, sondern aus der heidnischen Philosophie, hauptsächlich aus Plato und Aristoteles genommen!"

18. Ibid., 35. "Du weisst, wie ich zur talmudischen und kabbalistischen Lehre stehe. Ich bin täglich überzeugter, dass nicht nur ein grosser teil des Talmuds und der Kabbala unecht [ist?], sondern auch, dass dieselben nicht als Wort Gottes anzuerkennen sind, da sie sich gegen daselbe richten."

on me and by his Spirit give light on the several places in the Holy Scripture that are obscure to me!"[19]

Synagogue Ministry and Retirement

After graduating from Volozhin in 1851, Gurland spent some years in different vocations. In 1852–1853 he was a teacher for his uncle's family, the chief rabbi in Lemberg (today's L'vov/L'viv in Ukraine).[20] According to Stanislawski, Lemberg was one of the most important places for the *Haskalah* and non-traditional synagogues in Eastern Europe (others

---

19. Ibid., 44–45. "Ich wollte Dich nur aufmerksam darauf machen, dass ich mit dem Talmud zugleich nicht auch die Heilige Schrift verachte. O nein, den seit ich beide von neuem studiere, wird mir die Heilige Schrift täglich heiliger und lieber, während mir der Talmud wie ein leblose Bildergalerie erscheint. . . . Ach, dass der liebe Gott mir gnädig sein und die vielen Stellen der Heiligen Schrift, die mir noch dunkel sind, durch seinen Geist erleuchten wollte!"
Helene Gurland explains that the letters were translated from Yiddish to German by her husband as part of his preparations for the biography. However, the utterances above fit neatly with a traditional conversion narrative, describing how the future convert responds positively to the Bible while he experiences the Jewish tradition as dark or obscure. Today, readers of *IzW* have no choice but to trust Helene Gurland that the letters to Samuel are authentic. In any case, the reflections on Talmud and Kabbalah also match contemporary *Haskalah* ideas, see the analysis of Gurland's relation to Jewish tradition in 4.1.

20. Around 1850, the city contained the largest Jewish community in Austria. Gurland's uncle probably belonged to the Orthodox camp, but his identity is not clear. From 1846 more than 700 Jewish children attended the modern Jewish school in the city, indicating the influence of modern Judaism in the region. The school reforms in Lemberg can perhaps explain Gurland's reform efforts when he later became rabbi in Wilkomir, particularly regarding the education system. Four years before Gurland came to the city, in September 1848, the Lemberg state-appointed rabbi and leader of the progressive Jewish community, Abraham Kohn, was murdered. Between 1849 and 1854 the city was under martial law and ruled directly by the Austrian government, due to the city's role in the 1848 revolution. As the Orthodox population had been loyal to the Habsburg regime during the revolution, in contrast to Kohn and the modern Jews, they were in favor with the authorities during Gurland's stay in Lemberg. Kohn's successor as rabbi for the progressive Jews was therefore picked by the Austrian authorities in 1849 from among the Orthodox. I have not been able to confirm *IzW*'s information about Gurland's uncle's position as chief rabbi, but with his background at Volozhin I reckon he must have lived with some relatives in the Orthodox community of the city. If he associated himself publically with the progressive Jews in Lemberg, I do not think he would have been given a post as rabbi in Wilkomir. Stanislawski, *A Murder in Lemberg*, 5, 29, 49.

were Tarnopol and Brody).[21] Here Gurland must have had access to most of the *Haskalah* literature and influence.

However, in 1854, he succumbed to the expectations that were directed at him by the family, and accepted a post as rabbi and director in a synagogue in Wilkomir (today's Ukmerge) in Lithuania, north-west of Vilnius. Obeying his father's wish, he married the local chief rabbi's daughter.[22] Wilkomir was regarded as an important rabbinical seat in Lithuania, and was famous for its many distinguished talmudic scholars. Before WWI, 150 of Wilkomir's residents were certified as rabbis. Wilkomir was a stronghold for traditional Jews and had a reputation for its religious conflicts, first between the mitnagdim and *Hasidim*, and later with the *maskilim*. Many progressive Jewish leaders experienced difficulties in Wilkomir, and due to his untraditional views on the Torah and his religious doubts, Gurland's career in Wilkomir was neither long nor peaceful.[23]

In Wilkomir he openly worked for reforms in the local Jewish schools (a characteristic feature for him also as a Christian minister and missionary), and to begin with he was able to gain some support. One of the inspirations for his reform efforts may be Isaac Baer Levinsohn's *Teduah beYisrael,* published in Vilnius in 1828. This work had become a major reference for Lithuanian *maskilim*, who also became a significant audience for *Haskalah* newspapers and periodicals. Levinsohn argued strongly for a systematic education in Hebrew and the Torah, as well as the learning of foreign languages. In addition, he stressed the need for Jewish youth to learn practical skills and crafts. Gurland's initiative on school reforms was therefore only one of several in Lithuania and Wilkomir at the time. The *maskil* Max Lillienthal (1815–1882) worked hard during the 1840s and 1850s to reform the Jewish education system and establish new schools.[24] The first Hebrew newspaper ever, *Hamaggid*, which was published in Prussia from June 1856, had 60 subscribers in

---

21. Ibid., 17.

22. Her name remains unknown in the sources. The reason why she is not identified is not explained by Helene Gurland, who does not refrain from giving detailed information about Gurland's two other Jewish wives, Gisa and Marie.

23. One of the leading Russian *maskilim*, Moshe/Moses Leib Lilienblum, was forced to leave the city, Ellenson, "The Orthodox Rabbinate," 165–88, 175.

24. Feiner, *Haskalah*, 161.

Wilkomir alone.[25] After the establishment of the first two Reform Jewish elementary schools in Vilnius in 1841, a number of similar schools were started. The curriculum at these schools included secular subjects as well as the Hebrew Bible and Talmud.[26]

Nevertheless, most of the Jewish children continued to be in traditional Jewish schools, and generally the period is characterized by opposition to the reforms. Several rabbis and leading figures of the Jewish community were strong and sometimes violent opponents of the *Haskalah*, especially in Kovno and Wilkomir.[27] Generally, while the traditional Jewish communities in the last decades of the 19th century were increasingly less condemning of the reformers, this was not the case in Russia in the 1850s. As early as January 1855, the hostility towards Gurland's progressive profile reached a climax when one of the members of the congregation stole his passport and tried to get him trialed and conscripted as a recruit for the Russian army.[28] He was rescued by a Baltic German judge who discovered the plot by luck.[29]

From the beginning, Gurland felt the years in Wilkomir were a mistake. He felt the day of his ordination in Wilkomir, March 8, 1854, was the worst day in his life: "When I heard the words from the chief rabbi—'Do you promise to teach and live according to God's written and oral commands, that is the Torah and the Talmud, which was given us through Moses?'—for me, it was like standing on the edge of the Abyss."[30] Two and a half years later, in January 1857, at the age of 25 he publically declared his position towards the Talmud and the Kabbalah. His mar-

25. However, as Feiner points out, the number of subscribers does not necessarily mean that all of them were members of the *Haskalah* movement. Many would be Jewish merchants, etc., who were inclined to support its ideas. See ibid.

26. Levin, *The Litvaks*, 96–97.

27. Ellenson, "The Orthodox Rabbinate," 175.

28. According to the Russian law of 1835, Jews without passport could be conscripted to the army. A year later, this rule was relaxed. Klier, *Imperial Russia's*, 13.

29. The judge in this narrative is the Baltic German Alexander de Roberti. As Roberti is contrasted with the fanatic and corrupt Jewish accuser as a sensible and righteous man, the story in many ways foreshadows Gurland's later experiences when he finds the solution to his existential crisis within German culture and virtues. Gurland, *IzW* (1911), 60.

30. Ibid., 34. "Als ich die Worte des Ober-Rabbiners vernahm: 'Verplichtest du dich, das Gesetz Gottes schriftlich und mündlich, d. h. die Thora und den Talmud, welche uns durch Mose übergeben worden, zu üben und zu lehren?' da war es mir, als stände ich am Rande des Abgrundes . . . ."

riage was annulled by the family, and his one-year-old daughter stayed with her mother. Several years later, Gurland tried to reconcile with his daughter, but the effort led to nothing. Gurland had by then become a Christian, and the sixteen-year-old daughter refused to have a *goy* as her father.[31]

For the following six years Gurland moved from place to place in the Pale. He cannot have been totally rejected by his family, as he was employed as a tutor for three years at his uncle's home in Dünaburg (today's Daugavpils in Latvia).[32] This was probably a less difficult place for Gurland than Lithuania. Although the Jewish community contained most of the religious factions within Baltic Jewry, the tensions between them were not as high as in many other places.[33] Later he made a living as an instructor in calligraphy.[34] Convinced that Judaism needed reform, he began writing a work titled *"Das Judentum und die Reformversuche des 17. und 18. Jahrhunderts."* The work was never published, as he converted to Christianity before he was finished.[35]

In 1862 Gurland married the young Jewish woman Gisa Bogatirowa, who he met in Orsha (in today's Belarus). This marriage also suffered from Gurland's tense relation to traditional Judaism. The turmoil became intense when Gurland began giving public lectures about the need for reform, and he was accused of being a Christian.[36] Less than a year after the wedding, Gurland's mother-in-law annulled the marriage, and when their daughter Sophie was born on August 7, 1863, in Uman in today's Ukraine, Gurland did not even know where they were.[37] Around

---

31. Ibid., 66.

32. Of these events Le Roi gives a slightly different version: After Volozin he became assistant rabbi in Lemberg for his uncle, the chief rabbi. Between 1857 and 1860 he was rabbi and director of the rabbinic seminary at Berditshew, where he first encountered Reform Judaism. At first he fought against this influence, but later he joined the *Haskalah* camp. Le Roi also describes only one divorce. Le Roi, *Rudolf Hermann Gurland*, 4.

33. Amir, "Dvinsk," 262–68.

34. Gurland's handwriting in letters and reports is impressive. Some of these texts are still available at the Norwegian Israel Mission's archive in Oslo.

35. Gurland, *IzW* (1911), 66: "Judaism and the reform attempts in the 17th and 18th centuries."

36. Ibid., 70.

37. Accrding to Feiner, Uman was regarded as a Hasidic stronghold in the Russian empire—in spite of a small circle of reformers in the Jewish community there. However, we do not know if Gisa's family had any connection to Hasidism. Feiner, *Haskalah and History*, 162.

1870 he found them in Odessa, and thanks to financial help he managed to pay his former mother-in-law to bring his daughter to him.[38]

The Conversion

According to *IzW*, Gurland had never considered conversion to Christianity as an option, although he on several occasions showed some sympathy to Christianity in his letters to Samuel. However, in the summer of 1863 he came into contact with the German Army minister Ernst Karl Rudolf Faltin (1829–1918) in Kishinev, capitol of the Russian province Bessarabia.[39] Since 1859 Faltin had been the minister of a small Protestant church for the German Diaspora in the town. His congregation consisted of approximately 300 immigrants from Würtemberg, and in the beginning he had no plans for doing missionary work among the Jews, which in any case was illegal for anyone other than the Russian Orthodox Church.[40] Nevertheless, a number of Jews began consulting the German minister, and many even applied for baptism. In such cases Russian law did not prevent a Protestant minister from baptizing Jews. Eventually Gurland heard about Faltin and decided to contact him.

In about 1860, he got a Hebrew New Testament from a Jewish merchant. Here Gurland read the Sermon on the Mount and the rest of the Gospel of Matthew for the first time, but he was troubled by Paul's doctrine about the atoning death of Jesus.[41] He claims in the biography that he never intended to become a Christian. Rather his thought was to confirm his theory that Judaism contained the core of Christianity, as Jesus said he did not want to annul the Law and the Prophets. Gurland's opinion was that if Judaism was released from the Talmud, this reformed Judaism would perhaps correspond to a Christianity that likewise liberated itself from dogmatic theology and went back to the ethical doctrine of the Sermon on the Mount.[42]

---

38. In 1885, Sophie Gurland married a pastor from Kurland: Emil Bielenstein (1858–1953), the son of the Baltic German minister and scholar of Latvian linguistics and folklore August Bielenstein; Bitter and Gurland, "Gurland, (Chaim) Rudolf Hermann."

39. Hennings, "Aus dem Tagebuch," 74–76.

40. Skarsaune, *Israels venner*, 138.

41. Gurland, *IzW* (1911), 71.

42. Ibid., 70.

However, the friendship with Faltin proved to be crucial for Gurland's future, and several years later he would call Faltin his "own Philip" (referring to Acts 8:26–39). Eventually Gurland told Faltin that he struggled with the meaning of Isaiah chapter 53, giving Faltin an opportunity to explain the Christian interpretation of this and several other parts of the Hebrew Bible. Faltin's interpretation made a great impression on Gurland, and soon followed several weeks of spiritual agony:

> I then went home. It had become late, and my wife was asleep. In me and about me there was night. Deeply frustrated I said to myself: "You are standing at the crossroad, and have to either go deeper into the darkness or closer to the light." In my spiritual agony I fell on my knees and cried: "O God of Israel, Abraham and Jacob, you have no pleasure in the death of a sinner. You want him to repent and live! O God of my salvation, who so often has helped me in my life, reveal your power, rescue me from these doubts out of the night that surrounds me, and place me on the way of light!"[43]

In most conversion narratives of the 19th century, descriptions of spiritual struggles are common, and they sometimes overshadow the persecution that could come from the convert's surroundings. According to Ariel, however, for Jewish converts the content of their agony very often circled around the same topic, namely their Jewish identity:

> The most difficult thing for converted Jews was not the reserved, suspicious, or outright resentful attitudes in the Jewish or Christian communities but their own uneasiness. . . . The major dilemma that faced converted Jews was how to have peace of mind with a choice and an action that they had been brought up to regard as a betrayal of their people and heritage.[44]

---

43. Ibid., 76. "Dann ging ich nach Hause; es war spät geworden und meine Frau schlief. In mir und um mich war es Nacht; erregt sagte ich mir: "Du stehst nun am Scheidewege, der dich entweder tiefer in die Finsternis hinein oder näher zum Lichte bringen wird." In der Seelenangst, die mich erfasste, wandte ich mich an Gott, ich warf mich auf die Knie und schrie: "O Gott Israels, Abrahams und Jakobs, Du hast keinen Gefallen am Tode des Sünders, Du willst, das er sich bekehre und lebe! O, Du Eretter, der Du so oft in meinem Leben mir geholfen hast, offenbare Deine Macht, reisse mich aus diesen Zweifeln, aus der Nacht, die mich umgibt, und führe mich auf den Weg des Lichtes!""

44. Ariel, *Evangelizing*, 47. Although Ariel focuses on Jewish immigrants to the USA, his observations are probably relevant for this study, as most of the immigrants between 1880 and 1914 in Ariel's work came from Eastern Europe, in particular Russia.

Similar agony is expressed in this narrative about the later Jewish missionary Leopold Cohn (1862–1937):

> For several days my heart ached with sorrow and depression. . . . How could I love the hated One? How could I take his name upon my lips since He is the Crucified One and since His followers in every generation and in every country have hated my people, robbed my brothers of all that was good and fair, killed, tortured and degraded them? How could I, a true Jew, join myself to such a band of the enemies of my own flesh and blood?[45]

Gurland's conversion narrative appears somewhat atypical to this pattern. When comparing Leopold Cohn (as recorded by Sevener) and Ariel with Gurland's narrative, it seems that although Gurland was in agony about whether to become a Christian or not, his relationship to the Jewish people was not an element in this struggle. The question is whether the absence of concern for his Jewish identity is representative of his attitude to his people, meaning that his identification with Judaism and the Jewish people was weak, or whether it has been omitted on purpose. In fact, in spite of the emotional description of his struggle, it is not very clear what the agony actually was about, except for changing religion as such. In 1854 he had written to Samuel that conversion to another religion could not be so bad after all, in fact it could be said to be a patriarchal deed.[46] However, it seems that when the question of conversion became acute, Gurland nevertheless met doubt and psychological obstacles.

In the traditional Lutheran pietistic pattern of *ordo salutis* (the emotional and psychological chronology and pattern which conversions were expected to follow), it was expected that the potential convert would feel crushed under the word of the law, which would make room for the redemptive experience of the gospel. This experience is probably reflected by his reference to how God "hast keinen Gefallen am Tode des Sünders" and to Isaiah 53. Still, compared to the stories of prominent Lutheran and pietistic revivalists, Gurland's conversion narrative is not very substantial at this point. His depressions are referred to as a natural

---

45. Sevener, *A Rabbi's Vision*, 13.

46. Gurland, *IzW* (1911), 36. According to Jewish tradition, Abraham was a convert to Judaism.

part of becoming a Christian, and explained in Pauline terms: "He did not understand that it was the labors of the new man."[47]

Finally, Gurland was convinced that he needed to become a Christian, and soon began preparations for his baptism. The close contact between the rabbi and the German pastor did not pass by unnoticed, leading to a clash in one of the local synagogues in Kishinev.[48] He decided to become a missionary to the Jews, and it is possible that Faltin encouraged him in this, but it is not reported in the sources.

In this period, i.e. in 1863, Gurland married for the third time. His new wife was his hostess in Kishinev, the Ukrainian Jewish widow (Maria) Krupitz (1836–1876).[49] She was later baptized together with Gurland and changed her name to Marie Emma Whilhelmine Krupitz. According to Pastor Nicolai Baron von Stackelberg, Marie was first married at the age of 12. When she was 18 her husband passed away, leaving her alone with two children. When she married Gurland her children were taken from her by her family, as her new husband was considered an apostate due to his outspoken views on traditional Judaism.

Gurland's New World

On April 26, 1864, Gurland and his wife were baptized by Pastor Faltin. In accordance with church tradition and Russian law, their names were changed. That Gurland chose "Rudolf Hermann" indicates that the minister was his godfather. Marie was named after Faltin's wife, Emma. The law in 1850 did not allow Russian Jewish converts to take new surnames.[50]

---

47. Ibid., 71. "Es waren die Geburtswehen des neuen Menschen, die er aber nicht verstand." However, Gurland's conversion narrative was not the only one that did not quite fit into the traditional Protestant conversion narrative and the scheme of ordo salutis. This was also the case with Carl Paul Caspari in Germany, the contemporary Jewish Christian who became a professor of theology at the university in Christiania (today's Oslo). Skarsaune, "En Lærd af Guds Naade," 56.

48. Gurland, *IzW* (1911), 79–92. This debate is discussed in the analysis of his relationship to Jewish tradition.

49. Ibid., 71. She was born August 6, 1836, in Belaja Cerkov'. Here her name is said to be Marie Krupitz, but the sources do not say anything about her Jewish first name. See Bitter and Gurland, "Gurland, (Chaim) Rudolf Hermann."

50. Schainker, "Imperial Hybrids," 149; and Stanislawski, "Jewish Apostasy in Russia," 189–205, 193. The name Hermann may be after the famous German Jewish convert Hermann of Cologne (Judah ben David ha-Levi, born about 1109), who was baptized in 1129 and later became abbot of the monastery at Scheda. Cohen, "The Mentality," 20–47, 29.

Russian law dictated that Jewish converts moved away from their former communities to avoid relapse, and consequently between 1864 and 1867 Gurland and Marie lived in Berlin.[51] Here he attended *Berliner Heidenmissionshause*, supported by the Jewish mission society *Berliner Geshellschaft der Förderung des Christentums unter den Juden*.[52] This home for proselytes had been established the same spring, and was run by some of the teachers at the seminary, Freudenberg and Mitte.[53] Other than being a place for Jewish converts to find accommodation, a central goal for the home was to help the converts to adapt to a Christian lifestyle, which probably also meant assimilation into German culture. The home therefore tried to have converts come in contact with Christian German families. The friendship between Gurland and the Wunder family, as well as with Max Besser, was therefore no coincidence. For Gurland this acculturation and the new friendships were refreshing. Some years later Gurland even entrusted his daughter Sophie to the Wunders' care.

The Berlin society (*Berliner Geshellschaft der Förderung des Christentums unter den Juden*) was established in 1822, and was the first Jewish mission society on the European continent that was created in the image of the London Society for Promoting Christianity amongst the Jews. Although Gurland never was employed by the Berlin society, the society nevertheless had him listed as one of its own missionaries.[54] In Berlin, Gurland found his theological platform, located within the system of traditional Lutheran doctrine. He was also exposed to the writings of Friedrich Schleiermacher (1768–1834), August Neander (1789–1850) and the idealistic philosophy. However, the seminary did

51. Schainker, "Imperial Hybrids," 216.

52. Harling, "Zum Gedachtnis," 85–87, 86. Of course not all converted Jews became missionaries, but it is clear that many of the missionaries working among Jews in Eastern Europe were Jews themselves. According to Ariel, the same phenomenon was apparent in the Jewish mission societies in the USA around 1900. This strategy of making Jews into missionaries was one of the things Lucky was later to criticize, as it only made the impression that people converted because of prospects for future income. Ariel, *Evangelizing*, 27–33.

53. Ziethe, *Funzig Jahre*, 47.

54. The Society's main strategy was to give public lectures for Jews, and at the 100 year anniversary in 1922, the Berlin Society claimed to have baptized 3,000 Jews during its ministry. At that time the society was eager to prove that Jewish candidates for baptism needed proper instruction first, probably reflecting the increasing antipathy towards Jewish mission work in German society. E. Schaeffer, ""Bilder des Rückblicks," 34–53, here 35 and 39–45.

not give him a complete theological qualification compared to standard Lutheran ministers, although according to le Roi he also went to the university.[55] This situation did not prevent him from later being ordained as a minister.

For Gurland the three years in the Prussian capital were a two-fold experience. He suffered much from bad health (lung problems), but was highly stimulated both intellectually and spiritually by his studies. He was not the only Russian Jew who felt the German culture was refreshing. From the 1860s, in the wake of German state-building, Jewish intellectuals in Russia were increasingly attracted to German culture and the new German state.[56] After leaving Berlin, he continued to keep in touch with several good friends, like the Wunders, as well as his pen pal Max Besser, who became assisting lecturer in Halle for Fr. Aug. G. Tholuck (1799–1877).[57] The correspondence between Gurland and Besser plays a similar role in *IzW* as the letters to his cousin Samuel during his years at Volozin, as it supplies the biography with Gurland's own reflections.

On October 15, 1867, Gurland became *pastor adjunctus* (curate) in Kishinev, and became Faltin's assisting minister.[58] However, the little German church in Kishinev needed financial support to do this. By now the story of Gurland's conversion had been spread widely by the press, pamphlets and rumors, and several sponsors volunteered to support the ministry of the converted rabbi.[59] The money soon came, often channeled via Professor Franz Delitzsch in Leipzig, the later leader of the *Evangelisch-Lutherische Zentralverein für Mission unter Israel*.[60]

Mission to the Jews in Russia

The legal context of Jewish conversion to Christianity in tsarist Russia can be summarized thus: The Imperial Code of Laws guaranteed free-

---

55. Le Roi, *Rudolf Hermann Gurland*, 13.
56. Klier, *Imperial Russia's*, 156.
57. Bitter and Gurland, "Gurland, (Chaim) Rudolf Hermann."
58. Ibid., 5.
59. The story of Gurland's conversion was published several times, the first in 1864 as three articles entitled "Aus dem Tagebuche eiens bekehrten russischen Rabbiners," *Der Friedensbote für Israel* (Berlin: 1864) 77, 83–85, 90–94. For a complete list of publications about Gurland's conversion, see Bitter and Gurland, "Gurland, (Chaim) Rudolf Hermann" and Hennings, "Aus dem Tagebuch," 82–83.
60. Bitter and Gurland, "Gurland, (Chaim) Rudolf Hermann."

dom of religion to all religions. Only the official religion of the Russian Empire, the Russian Orthodox Church, had the right to seek converts. Other Christian churches as well as Judaism and Islam were strictly forbidden to be involved in any missionary activities under threat of severe punishment. If someone wanted to become Russian Orthodox, nobody was allowed to interfere in that decision. Jews were permitted to convert to any tolerated version of Christianity, while Christian citizens could only in extraordinary circumstances be allowed to become members of a non-Orthodox church.[61]

The numerical extent of Russian Jewish converts in the decades before WWI cannot be precisely set, but a conservative estimate by Stanislawski states that 41 percent (84,500) of all Jewish converts in Europe during the 19th century came from Russia.[62] Of these, 69,400 were baptized into the Russian Orthodox Church, 12,000 into the Roman Catholic Church, and 3,100 into different Protestant denominations, mostly the Lutheran church.

How the Russian authorities viewed mission work towards the Jews is a subject of some dispute among scholars. According to Stanislawski, the Russian government supported and encouraged Jewish conversions, but was ambivalent towards non-Orthodox mission work due to the danger that Orthodox believers would be influenced by Protestants. This is the background for the restrictions that were put on mission societies like the London Society for Promoting of Christianity amongst the Jews, which was never allowed to work in the Pale of Settlement in Russia itself, but only in Congress Poland (where "the worst that could happen" was the conversion of some Catholics). However, there was also some ambivalence towards converted Jews in the Orthodox Church, as described by John Klier and Ellie Schainker. They oppose the traditional description of the tsarist regime as aiming for the conversion of Jews to Christianity, and believe the government as well as church authorities were reluctant about this sort of work, especially its practical implications. Particularly from the 1880s, they feared the "Judaizing" of the Orthodox Church, which made the authorities not only refrain from supporting endeavors like Rabinowitz's work in Kishinev, but actively

---

61. Stanislawski, "Jewish Apostasy in Russia," 192.
62. Ibid., 190.

thwart them, describing them as an artificial obstacle to the expected disintegration of Russian Jewry.[63]

In his studies on Russian Jewish apostates, Stanislawski analyzes a group of Jewish converts to the Russian Orthodox Church in Lithuania. Using this material and analysis on Gurland, or other Lithuanian Jews who converted to a Protestant church, must of course be done with caution. It was probably differences in the conversion process that influenced whether one went to the national majority church (with strong bonds to the tsarist regime) or to minority churches related to Central Europe, like the Lutheran church. Still, Stanislawski's analysis is useful for giving a general picture about the background and context of the conversions. In his attempt to analyze material about 244 Jewish converts in the period between 1819 and 1911, Stanislawski distinguishes between voluntary and involuntary converts (like the 70,000 conscripted Jewish soldiers under Nicholas I). When it comes to the majority of the converts who voluntarily sought baptism in the Orthodox Church, Stanislawski divides his material into the following five categories: 1) Those seeking educational or professional advancement; 2) The economically successful; 3) The criminals; 4) The believers; and 5) The destitute and desperate.

The two first groups had much in common, but generally the first category consisted of people who wanted an opportunity to advance socially and economically, while the second group were mainly successful people who wanted to stabilize their place among the wealthy circles of Russian society. Although these two groups consisted of many famous Jews, they were not numerous. Gurland reported about his encounter with some representatives from these groups.[64]

With regard to the criminals, it should be noted that until 1862, Russian Jewish citizens facing the threat of a court sentence could in many cases be released if they accepted baptism.

Although all the applicants in the documents naturally emphasized their sincere conviction of the supremacy of the Christian (Russian Orthodox) faith, Stanislawski believes that most of them were motivated primarily by social or economic reasons. Still, he finds that at least a handful of them seemed to be driven by mainly religious motives, and all of these were women. However, he mentions two men who became

63. Schainker, "Imperial Hybrids," 115–17.
64. Le Roi, *Rudolf Hermann Gurland*, 18.

missionaries or workers for the Jewish mission. It seems that since their conversion was soon followed by mission jobs, Stanislawski is inclined to place them under one of the first two categories.[65]

The vast majority of the converts in Stanislawski's material belong to the last category, the destitute and desperate. Most of these were young (between 15 and 30), and Stanislawski concludes that this group is a symptom of the major changes and challenges Russian Jewry went through during that century, and which led masses of Jews into great poverty and increased neglect of their Jewish origins.

However, Schainker points out that most of the 84,500 conversions of Jews in southern Russia to the Orthodox Church were not a consequence of any systematic church ministry, but rather part of a social process. In her thesis, she explains what elements of the social framework of the Pale of Settlement made widespread conversion to Christianity possible, and in particular she relates the phenomenon to social mobility as well as the informal contacts and networking between Jewish converts and the Jewish community. According to her thesis, the image of the Pale and the *shtetl* (Jewish village) as places of compact and insulated Jewish communities is mistaken. Instead she describes Russian Jewish communities as places inhabited by Jews as well as Christians of all categories, who interacted on a daily basis. Here converted Jews would be able to maintain some sort of collective identification with their Jewish background, and in many cases family and community continued to play key roles in a convert's life.[66]

In fact, the policy of the empire was partly to sustain Jewish institutions, not to undermine them. For the sake of political stability it was part of Russian policy of the 19th century to give institutional support to the different religious confessions of the empire, whether Islam, Judaism, or the Lutheran church in the Baltics.[67] Nevertheless,

---

65. Alexandr Shkafel, born in 1848 in Vilnius, graduated from the Lithuanian Church Seminary in 1871. In 1877 he had a job in Brest-Litovsk where he was "assigned to induct Jewish children to Christianity." Yosef/Pavel Dreyzin graduated from the governmental-sponsored rabbinical seminary in Zhitomir, then worked as a rabbi in several places in the Pale of Settlement before he was baptized in 1891 at the age of 48 together with his three children. His wife did not convert. Dreyzin completed a translation of the New Testament and various saints' lives into Yiddish. Stanislawski, "Jewish Apostasy in Russia," 196.

66. Schainker, "Imperial Hybrids," 14, 16 and 21.

67. Ibid., 120.

the modern profile of the new schools and state-appointed rabbis were not very welcome in the Jewish community. In addition, the reluctance of the Orthodox Church to carry out mission activity towards the Jews was regarded as a problem by several of the converts. There was a widespread belief that Jewish converts needed material and social assistance, for example in the form of one-time monetary and clothing stipends. Because of this system, conversions from Judaism were often regarded as mercenary and insincere.[68] Nevertheless, before 1850 the Russian regime had no problem welcoming conversions based on socio-economic motives, as well as those based on religious motives that were preferred by the church.[69]

In a situation where parts of the Jewish community were open to contact with Christians and converts, while the official church refrained from supporting mission activity, the existence of Protestant churches or mission activity would probably be regarded with some interest by many Jews. If that were the case, it would partly explain Faltin's unexpectedly successful career as a missionary among Russian Jewry in the 19th century. In fact, as Schainker points out, urban Russian Jews preferred conversion to Protestant churches.[70] Generally however, it was groups four and five in Stanislawski's list that became the targets for Protestant mission work, and already in the 1850s Faltin was facing the dilemma of what to do with applicants for baptism whom he suspected were motivated mainly by economic and social reasons. On the one hand this group was the most receptive to the church, at least outwardly, but on the other there was no doubt that he and later Gurland preferred authentic believers.[71]

---

68. Ibid., 116 and 125. Until 1837 this was the custom for converts from all religions in the empire, but it later applied only to Jews. An adult Jewish convert would be granted 30 rubles. Men were generally regarded with more suspicion than female Jews, as Jewish women were regarded as more pious and as their status in Talmud gave them even more to gain by conversion. As a result, male conversions were often suspected to be motivated by instrumental purposes, while female conversions could be perceived as a moral act. Ibid., 110–11.

69. Ibid., 59.

70. Ibid., 58 n. 87, and 70–71.

71. Le Roi, *Rudolf Hermann Gurland*, 14.

Gurland's Mission Work

Back in Kishinev, Gurland immediately took up his ministry, as several Jews already were waiting for Christian teaching. In his reports he describes the problems this work faced.[72] Some of the local Jews could be quite hostile, especially towards those Jews who went to church for preparation for baptism. In his reports and letters he writes about how some Jews would travel from Odessa, Bessarabia, and even from Lithuania for Christian teaching. Some of the proselytes later became missionaries themselves.[73] However, in spite of this he reveals in his letters a feeling of loneliness. He missed his German friends and the intellectual atmosphere of Berlin:

> I feel so lonely, so abandoned and low, and I seek consolation in God, and relief in my official work. Some people think my homesickness and longing for Germany is merely imagination and reverie, but all the same, this sentiment fills my heart [sic; "seele" means "soul," but the English translation has changed this for some reason] entirely. I should like an air-bath in Germany, I long to breathe German air and German warmth in order to revive and make progress. Perhaps the Lord will help. That would be grand![74]

In 1868 Gurland was offered a small post as a professor of Hebrew at a local Greek Catholic University. For the sake of intellectual challenge he accepted the post, although he for unknown reasons never began the job.[75] However, in the biography Gurland also describes his missionary

---

72. During a period of four months in Kishinev, Gurland had 29 applicants for baptism. However, when it was revealed that hope of financial support from the church was a central motivation for most of them, only 5 young men were allowed to begin instruction for baptism. During the two and an half years he worked in the town, 320 Jews contacted him for baptismal instruction, but only 20 completed it. Le Roi, *Geschichte*, 1:342; and Le Roi, *Rudolf Hermann Gurland*, 14.

73. Ibid., 37; Gurland, *IzW* (1911), 135.

74. Gurland, *IzW* (1911), 130. "Ich fühle mich so einsam, so verlassen und suche Trost in Gott, Linderung in meinem Amte. Viele halten mein Heimweh nach Deutschland für Einbildung und Schwärmerei, aber dies Gefühl erfüllt meine Seele ganz und gar. Ich möchte ein Luftbad in Deutschland nehmen, deutsche Luft und Warme einatmen, um aufzuleben und mich fortzuentwickeln; vielleicht hilft Gottes Gnade mir dazu. Herrlich ware es!"

75. Ibid., 128. It is possible he was meant to replace the Jewish Christian Iakov Brafman (b. 1824), who between 1860 and 1866 taught Hebrew at Minsk Theological Seminary. However, since taking this post would imply conversion to the Russian

work with much enthusiasm and warmth, mixed with several humorous anecdotes. Although he complains about the long mission journeys in Ukraine and Belarus, many of the stories are from these travels.[76]

The happiest experience in his years in Kishinev was when finally he got in touch with his former wife Gisa and their daughter. This time his former mother-in-law agreed to hand her granddaughter, Sophie, over to Gurland for a certain amount of money. He had to promise that the girl would not be baptized before the age of 14, and that Sophie's mother could visit her whenever she wanted. After the agreement was officially settled, he took the daughter with him. By then Sophie was about 6 years old. Still, Sophie did not stay long in Bessarabia. In 1870 she was sent to Berlin to stay with the Wunders.[77] Gurland claimed he was worried for her security, as he had received some threats.[78] He was also concerned that she should have an upbringing and education in Germany.[79] Sophie stayed in Berlin until she moved with her father and Marie to Kurland the following year.

Orthodox Church as well as moving to Minsk, I do not find this very likely. Schainker, "Imperial Hybrids," 178–82.

76. Gurland, *IzW* (1911), 139.

77. In particular it was Miss Sophie Wunder who took care of Gurland's daughter. Some months after Sophie Gurland's departure to Berlin, Gisa came to Kishinev to see her. At this occasion Gurland made her agree that their daughter could be baptized sooner than first agreed; ibid., 135.

78. It is possible that he was afraid she was going to be kidnapped. Reports of use of force against Jewish apostates and converts in the form of harassment and violent insults were not uncommon in Russia. The Russian press several times ran stories of Jewish violence towards converts. Still it can be questioned if this is overestimated in the conversion narratives for propaganda purposes. Nevertheless, there were cases taken to court to have the conversions annulled. Most cases were about the Jewish family who wanted the court to annul the conversion of a relative; the reasons were related to claims of insanity or the age of the convert. Sometimes the Jewish families were accused for using violent force in attempts to get their family member back. Schainker, "Imperial Hybrids," 28, 46, and 288. In addition to Gurland, the sources claim that Lichtenstein and Lucky also experienced physical insults. However, serious injuries to Jewish converts appear to have been extremely rare, and homicide is not heard of. According to Stanislawski, most religiously sanctioned murders within the Jewish community before the late modern age concerned "informers." However, there were never sanctioned killings of heretics or apostates in this period; these people were instead excommunicated. Nevertheless, Stanislawski claims that the murder of Rabbi Abraham Kohn in 1848 in Lemberg was a turning point in Jewish history, as it inaugurated an era when assassinations for religious or political reasons among Jews could happen. Stanislawski, *A Murder in Lemberg*, 114.

79. Gurland, *IzW* (1911), 141.

The Ministry in the Baltic 1871–1894

During a stay in Germany with the missionary von Carl Axenfeld in Rheinland in 1870, Gurland came in touch Pastor Gustav Seesemann (1839–1913) from Mitau, in the Baltic province Kurland. Seesemann encouraged Gurland to work as a part-time missionary for the Lutheran church in Kurland and Livonia.[80] That Gurland would follow Seesemann's advice was not obvious; it perhaps seemed more likely that he would go to Germany, where he had several friends. Here many friends of the Jewish mission also wanted to have him in their ranks, and as late as the 1880s he was asked to take a post in the mission work in Rhineland. When Gurland accepted the post, it may have been because it brought him closer to his Jewish family. The story of Gurland's attempt to get in touch with his first daughter indicates this. This contact must have taken place shortly after he came to Kurland, based on the information that she was about sixteen by then. From his mission reports it also appears that he spent some periods in Lithuania, particularly Vilnius, which may suggest the same thing.

Between 1561 and 1795 Kurland was a Polish duchy or tributary state managed by German nobility, and while Livland and Estonia became parts of the Russian Empire during the 16th century, the territory was not changed into a Russian province until 1795.[81] The capitol Mitau, today's Jelgava, was the seat for the semi-autonomous German government and parliament of Kurland. Aside from being the political capital of the province and home of the local parliament, Mitau was also an important communication hub and school society.[82] In 1832, the new Russian church laws organized the evangelical churches of the Baltic provinces as a division of the Russian Orthodox Church, with the Tsar as the churches' principal. However, in real life the churches ran themselves, and the ministers were appointed by the councils of the German nobility, although formally by the Russian government. The

---

80. Bitter and Gurland, "Gurland, (Chaim) Rudolf Hermann."

81. Kurland is today one of three Baltic Russian provinces that in 1918 became the Republic of Latvia; the two others are Livonia (with its capital Riga) and Latgale in the east. In Latvian, Livonia is equal to the regions Vidzeme in the north and Latgale in the east, while Kurland is synonymous to the regions Kurzeme and Zemgale. Latgale belonged to the Pale of Settlement. Šteinmanis and Anders, *History*, xvi, 48; and Eberhardt, *Ethnic Groups*, 22.

82. Hirschhausen, *Die Grenzen*, 38, 125.

Lutheran church was organized in independent consistories for Kurland and Livland, a system which lasted until 1920.[83] The organization of the churches had the character of the German *Landeskirchen*, with the assemblies of all the ministers, the synods, as a key element.[84] Although there were separate congregations for Baltic Germans in some places, most congregations were a mix of Germans and Latvians, with the leading strata filled with Germans.

According to Wilhelm Neander, the interest in mission work became widespread among the congregations in Kurland in the 1850s. One of the leading organizers for this was Eduard Neander, the *pastor primarius* (official or head minister) in Mitau, whose position Gurland would later take. In 1865, the synods of the Lutheran churches in Kurland had the mission to the Jews on their agenda.[85] In a speech (and later an article) arguing for this work, Pastor W. Müller praised the Pietists and the Moravians for their concern on these matters, and describes mission work towards Jews as a matter of love. However, for him the mission activity was also meant to replace political emancipation and prevent the influence of the Jews on Baltic society. Müller held the emancipation of Jews as an attack on the superiority of Christianity that only fit the interests of Reform Judaism, with its plea for a *HumanitetsStaat* that eventually would lead to the superiority of Judaism.[86] To prevent this, Müller agitated for the establishment of a regional mission society. In a later article in the *Baltische Monatsschrift*, Müller goes on to explain his views regarding mission work vs. emancipation. Referring to what he holds to be deconstructive elements in Judaism, he claims that the emancipation process will not lead the Jews to the sort of contact with Christianity they need. As the emancipation of the Jews in Russia would only lead to damaging effects on society, the synod should go on with mission activity towards the Jews.[87]

---

83. Duzmans, *Lettland*, 54.

84. Neander, *Die deutschen*, 6, 10, 61. See also Bogojavlenska, *Die jüdische Gesellschaft*, 112.

85. Le Roi, *Geschichte*, 1:332, and Müller, "Ueber Judenmission," 22, 89–116; 99 and 107.

86. The term is not very clear, but probably indicates a state where religion and confessions are irrelevant for the lawmakers; see Bogojavlenska, *Die jüdische Gesellschaft*, 107.

87. Müller, "Zur Characteristik," 483–99.

It is difficult to know to what extent Müller was representative of Baltic clergy in these matters, but he met resistance in the Baltic German press at the time. In editorial notes to Müller's articles, the editor of the *Baltische Monatsschrift* several times objected against the idea of mission work toward the Jewish population, as it would only attract opportunists. In the 1880s however, the Baltic German press had become more supportive to this.[88] Still, *IzW* and writings by Gurland mainly dwell on the first motive mentioned by Müller, i.e., Christian love for the Jewish people. According to Seesemann, the new mission work was a result of visits by the London Society in the 1860s, but Faltin's work in Kishinev might have been an important inspiration as well.[89] As indicated by Müller, inspiration may also have come from Baltic Moravians, the pietistic movement established by Duke Zinzendorf (1700–1760) in Herrnhut during the 18th century. The influence of this movement was significant and widespread among the native population in the Baltics since the 18th century.

The church's first calling of a missionary was directed to a local Jewish convert named Adler, a choice that proved to be unfortunate for the mission.[90] Stationed in Bausk, south of Mitau, he soon provoked controversies with the local Jewish population. In addition, he was regarded as unsuitable for the work for personal reasons. Still, the circle behind this fiasco wanted to make a new effort, and managed to convince Gurland that he should move his mission work to the Baltics. Gurland moved to Mitau in 1871, where he took the post of curate for the surrounding congregations combined with mission work to the Jews. In 1881 there were more than 48,000 Jews in Kurland, and in 1897 they composed 9 percent of the total population; however, in several professions Jews were overrepresented, e.g., in medicine.[91] Scholars on Baltic Jewry describe the Jewish population in the provinces as Germanized and carriers of German culture, and the first Jewish immigrants in the 16th century were already affiliated with German culture.[92] Most tradi-

---

88. Bogojavlenska, *Die jüdische Gesellschaft*, 110 and 120.

89. Gurland and Seesemann, "Fra de russiske Østersjøprovinser," 59.

90. Adler was described by the Baltic mission secretary Seesemann as a "disaster," Gurland and Seesemann, "Fra de russiske Østersjøprovinser," 59; Gurland, *IzW* (1911), 141; and Seesemann's letter to Gurland in the Norwegian version of *IzW* (1913), 248–50.

91. Dribin, "Kurzeme's and Zemgale's Jews."

92. Bogojavlenska, *Die jüdische Gesellschaft*, 97.

tional communities in Kurland and Livonia were heavily influenced by the Jewish communities in Lithuania, whence many of the immigrants came. The only Jewish educational institution to be found in all three provinces was the *maskilim* system or the Talmud Torah, giving rich and poor children the same religious education. For adults there was *Bet Hamidrash*, social clubs where one could study Torah or Talmud.[93] However, the *Haskalah* and the desire for contemporary education in Germany also influenced the Jews in Kurland, who were rather receptive to Western culture compared to Jews in Lithuania.[94] During the Russification in the last decades before WWI, the Jews became an increasingly Russifying element. This was valuable for the tsarist regime vs. the local (Baltic German) authorities.[95]

In spite of being in Russian territory, the German population continued to be the ruling class in the provinces. The German landowners managed to maintain their traditional privileged position as the ruling class, but from the 1860s the new political situation nevertheless led to an increase of Russian and Jewish immigration, particularly to Riga. While the Germans in 1867 composed 43 percent of the total population of Riga, in 1913 they composed only 16 percent. In the last decades before WWI the modern urbanization, industrialization and growing national consciousness of the four ethnic groups in these provinces led to a strong cultural and political mobilization that became a main issue of political life, particularly in Riga. The non-German populations demanded opportunities for political participation, economic emancipation and cultural independence. Expressions related to ethnicity became sensitive carriers of associations of loyalty, hostility and dependency, like the terms "Baltic" and "Latvija," which both were new terms around 1850.[96] Imitating Baltic Germans, in the 1860s Latvians, Jews and Russians established associations and societies that became part of the public life of the city and the provinces, and were the backbone of the contemporary multicultural conflict lines.[97]

In addition to the demographic changes, the assassination of Tsar Alexander II in 1881 led to major political and cultural challenges for

93. Godin, "Jewish Traditional," 217–21.
94. Lipschitz, "Jewish Communities," 276–84, 276.
95. Bobe, "Four Hundred Years," 34–36.
96. Hirschhausen, *Die Grenzen*, 342–52.
97. Ibid., 374.

the Baltic German population. Tsar Alexander III deeply distrusted Baltic Germans as well as the native population of the provinces, and adapted a policy that sought to transform the Baltic provinces into an integrated part of Russia. In practice the administrative system of the Baltic provinces became a mixture of old and new, as some institutions were Russified, others not. In spite of the challenges, the Baltic German elite retained most of the control, despite being on the defensive.[98] In the end they could not avoid the introduction of Russian as the administrative language, and in 1888 Russian replaced German as the language of instruction in schools.[99] Many Baltic Germans in Kurland and Livland emigrated, and from 1881 to the 1930s the German population dropped significantly. Most of those who remained in the provinces (and the later republic of Latvia) moved to the cities, particularly Riga, due to the loss of privileges.[100] Moving to Germany was not considered an option for many, as Baltic Germans were alienated culturally from Germany and the ongoing industrialization there.[101]

While the German nobility still had most of the cultural and political power in the Baltic provinces, in the 1850s Latvian nationalism was manifested for the first time. The Latvian population was religiously divided among Lutherans, Roman Catholics and Orthodox.[102] Paradoxically, the new national Latvian consciousness was partly a consequence of the work of many of the German ministers, who in their pastoral and scholarly efforts had given much attention to the Latvian language.[103] One of the most famous of these ministers and scholars was Sophie Gurland's later father-in-law, pastor August Bielenstein (1826–1907).[104] Later the policy of Russification only strengthened anti-Russian sentiments among the Latvians as well as the Germans.[105]

---

98. Bilmanis, *A History*, 250.
99. Hirschhausen, *Die Grenzen*, 152, 162; Raun, *Estonia*, 62.
100. Balodis, *Lettlands*, 228.
101. Wittram, *Baltische Geschichte*, 196.
102. Balodis, *Lettlands*, 226.
103. Spekke, *History of Latvia*, 280.
104. Gintere, "August Bielenstein"; Gurland, *IzW* (1911), 170.
105. Zake, *Nineteenth-Century*, 8.

Mission Work, Controversy, and Promotion

For 25 years Gurland was part of these demographic and political changes in the Baltic. On June 27, 1871, he was appointed as a minister, based in Mitau, with the particular purpose to teach Christianity to Jewish proselytes.[106] From 1871 to 1873, Gurland worked full-time as a missionary minister, which included much traveling in all the Baltic provinces. Still supported by foreign mission societies (like the Norwegians and Swedes), he worked in various arenas. Besides direct contact with Jewish society, he also tried to educate the German clergy in the Baltics about Judaism and the Jewish people and to inspire them to support the mission work.

Gurland's mission work did not seem to have many results in the form of Jewish converts, something he openly discusses in his reports. On the other hand, he gives vivid descriptions of personal meetings he had with Jewish as well as non-Jewish people on his many journeys. These detailed reports of discussions on his travels usually deal with conversations with Jews. In addition, Gurland devotes much space in his reports to reflections on and descriptions of the Jewish school system.[107]

Gurland's interest in Jewish education would, in the end, cause the most significant controversy between him and the Jewish religious leadership in the Baltics. In an article in 1875 explaining the Jewish character, Gurland describes his visits to some Jewish schools in Vilnius.[108] Partly described as a flashback to his own Litvak childhood in the same area, Gurland gives a detailed description of some of the lessons. Without any attempt to appear neutral, he has difficulty deciding whether to categorize the pedagogy as well as the physical environment as tragic or as comic, and argues that establishing schools, particularly for Jewish girls, should be a natural part of the mission activity.[109] His main rea-

---

106. Bitter and Gurland, "Gurland, (Chaim) Rudolf Hermann."

107. Gurland wrote several reports which include some stories from the *heders* he had been visiting. How he managed to get permission from the *melameds* (teachers) to do so, he does not say; perhaps it was due to his connections with the German nobility. Gurland's narratives seem to support Schainker's thesis that the doors between Jewish society and a convert like Gurland were not always as closed as one would think. One should also have in mind Pucher's accusation below, that Gurland made up at least one of these stories. However, the Baltic German population does not seem to have believed Pucher about this.

108. Gurland, *Bericht*, 32–36.

109. During the early 1870s, the Baltic German churches had established several

son for involving the churches in Jewish education is what he regards as the general spiritual decline in the Jewish population, as talmudic Judaism had outlived itself and become an object of disgust, irony and blasphemy. Consequently, Jewish children would grow up as pagans, spiritually speaking, if they were not rescued by Christianity.[110] Other than the evangelistic purpose, the main goal of such schools for Jewish girls would be to let them learn the Old Testament redeemed from the Talmud and traditional commentaries, which he believed would strengthen their moral upbringing and future family life.

In September 1875, Gurland's stories in *Bericht* led to a public clash between the Baltic German and Jewish populations in Mitau. Mitau was a multicultural community, known for its high percentage of Jews (21% in 1860). From 1859 to 1893, the most famous rabbi in Mitau was crown rabbi Shlomo Pucher, who had great impact on local Jewish society as well as good relations with the Russian authorities.[111] Pucher met Tsar Alexander II twice, in 1861 and 1867, a contact that influenced the relatively friendly Russian attitude towards the Jews in the Baltic.[112] Rabbi Pucher became Gurland's most prominent Jewish opponent in Mitau and Kurland.[113] Although controversial for his reform efforts, Pucher seems to have been one of the few "official rabbis" (i.e., state-appointed rabbis) who gained respect in a Jewish community in Russia.

Even before Gurland turned up, Pucher had made himself known with several public attacks on the Lutheran church's new initiative in mission activity towards Baltic Jews. In the 1860s, in response to the new Protestant mission activity towards the Jews in the Baltic, Pucher defended in sermons and in the German press the advantages of Judaism.[114]

---

elementary schools for Jewish girls. However, we do not know if these schools were result of Gurland's efforts. ibid.

110. Ibid., 26–31.

111. Levin, "Mitau." Here Pucher is named Focher. In most Russian Jewish communities a dual rabbinate evolved after the introduction of so-called crown (or state) rabbis. Usually these state-elected rabbis had very little support in the Jewish community, and were rather isolated within the community they were supposed to lead. Rabbi Pucher appears to have been an exception to the rule, probably due to the more positive attitude to Reform Judaism found in Kurland. Klier, *Imperial Russia's*, 8.

112. Dribin, "Kurzeme's."

113. This information was given in an email to the author from Dr. Tatjana Aleksejeva, research specialist at the "Jews in Latvia" museum, and Ilya Lensky, director of the same museum; April 2, 2009.

114. Šteinmanis and Anders, *History of Latvian Jews*, 159.

In an open letter to the Lutheran clergy in 1867, Pucher claims that there is no Jew who converts to Christianity because of religious convictions, and he describes Jewish mission as an attack on human liberty and dignity.[115] He also expresses dismay over the synod's decision to place Adler in Bausk, based on the assumption that the progressive Jewish population in Mitau apparently are "less" Jewish than those in Bausk, where the Jewish population is said to be more nationalistic.[116] Pucher finds this assumption offensive to the Mitau Jews, and demands a public apology. In an article later that year, Pastor Müller rejects Pucher's address and demands, and defends Adler from Pucher's accusations of being an opportunist.[117]

After Gurland's arrival in 1871, Pucher addressed him and the Baltic German clergy on at least one occasion, attacking Gurland and the mission activity. In this letter of September 1875, Pucher accuses Gurland of being a fraud who not only has made up fantastic stories about individuals and schools in Vilnius, but also has given an impression of his former co-religionists as uncivilized.[118] In addition, Pucher claimed that Gurland had never been a rabbi, referring to anonymous sources in Kishinev.[119]

We probably do not have the full picture of the reactions from either Gurland or the German population to Pucher's accusations, as *IzW* mentions the controversy only briefly, and we hear nothing about if and how Gurland responded to the accusations. Instead, *IzW* focuses on the indignation the Baltic German population felt on Gurland's behalf. According to Helene Gurland, the article was seen as an attempt to slan-

---

115. Russian Jews were familiar with converted compatriots, and a conversion did not necessarily cut all ties with the family or the Jewish community. In fact, converts like the St. Petersburg professor Khvolson, who admitted that his baptism was part of his strategy for professional mobility, could even be admired in the Jewish community. However, conversions based on religious convictions were more difficult to handle. See Schainker, "Imperial Hybrids," 179.

116. Pucher, "Offenes Sendschreiben," 217–41.

117. Müller, "Ein offenes Wort," 374–85.

118. Pucher, *Offener Brief*. Pucher claims that he had investigated Gurland's information, and states that the tragic and hilarious heder he describes in the *Bericht* does not exist. To prove this he gives a list of 6 heders close to the synagogue in Vilnius with between 6 and 20 students, not the 130 described by Gurland. In addition, he denies the use of the pedagogic methods described in Gurland, *Bericht*. Pucher, *Offener Brief*, 8–9.

119. Le Roi also says that Gurland had been a rabbi in Kishinev, Le Roi, *Rudolf Hermann Gurland*, 5.

der Gurland, and therefore students from the local high school arranged a torchlight procession in support of him, during which the crowd hooted and howled outside the state-appointed rabbi's house in Mitau.[120] This event did not lead to any open hostilities against the Jewish community, but considering the peaceful relationships that usually existed with the Jews in the Baltic, an event like Baltic German students rallying and shouting outside the state rabbi's home was practically unheard of. Both Jewish and Baltic German leaders would be careful not to worry the regime in St. Petersburg, whose main concern was political stability between the ethnic groups. It is difficult to know from the sources what impression this march made on the Jews in Kurland, but after this the sources are quiet about any controversy whatsoever between Germans and Jews in Kurland. Considering that Pucher and Gurland were stationed in the same city for more than 20 years before they both moved to Riga in the early 1890s, this silence is striking.[121] Still, although *IzW* does not comment on the relationship between the two religious leaders after 1875, Helene Gurland obviously feels a need to remark that relatively few Jews mourned Pucher's move from Mitau to Riga compared to the reaction to her husband's move.[122]

The reaction from the Baltic German population suggests that Pucher's open letter was considered to be more serious than a questioning of religion or Pastor Gurland's integrity, although a feeling of solidarity with the pastor may have been part of the reaction. Pucher's good relationship with the tsar probably gave the controversy a political dimension as well, although this is never explicitly said in the sources. When, in the 1860s and 1870s, Pucher openly challenged the Lutheran church and later Gurland, his defense of the Jewish Baltic minority was probably also seen as an attempt to undermine the position of the Baltic

120. Gurland, *IzW* (1911), 158. Considering Helene Gurland's age, the crowd of students that visited Pucher's home probably included of some of her friends, or at least people she knew.

121. However, an anonymous pamphlet claimed to be written by a rabbi in Mitau, stirred a heated debate in the Baltic German press in 1883. The pamphlet described a revolting story about a Jewish convert who had taken his one-year-old son with force and with assistance from the police and had him baptized in Mitau. The reactions in the press were clearly against the author, who was accused for fraud and having put the relationship between the Germans and the Jews at stake. See Bogojavlenska, *Die jüdische Gesellschaft*, 119–20.

122. Gurland, *IzW* (1911), 193. See also Bogojavlenska, *Die jüdische Gesellschaft*, 120.

Germans. When Pucher explicitly reminded his readers about the mission's failure with Adler, this would probably have been felt like a provocation to the Baltic German society. This does not necessarily mean that the content of Pucher's accusations was irrelevant, considering the failure with Adler. Precisely because of Adler it would probably have been even more humiliating for the church (and the Baltic community) if Gurland lost public trust. However, Gurland's negative view of Jewish schools in Russia was not new or something he was alone in. Already in Wilkomir he had been involved in reforms of the Jewish school system, and similar conditions were reported by other converts, missionaries and Jewish historians as well.[123]

The controversy did not lead to any public conclusion, at least not directly. Instead, Gurland was promoted the following year. In 1873, Gurland had been asked to combine his mission work with serving as curate for Pastor Neander at the Trinitatis Kirche in Mitau.[124] Although Gurland's ties to the church in Mitau thereby grew stronger, in 1876 he had, according to *IzW*, almost decided to accept a post as missionary for the *Rheinisch-Westfälischen Judenmission* in Cologne. However, when Neander was about to retire in spring 1876, Gurland was asked by the church authorities in Kurland to replace him as *pastor primarius*.[125] This plea shocked him, apparently making him concerned for the mission work as well as how he, as an outsider, would be viewed within the clergy. He nevertheless accepted the post, which he held for the next 17 years. One of the reasons for this was the discussion he had with one of the province ministers, Carl Baron von der Recke-Paulsgnade, who declared to him that he had to see this as a sign from God.[126] He was formally appointed to the post of *pastor primarius* at the Triniatiskirche

---

123. Meyersohn, "Das Unterrichtswesen," 196–202. Reports of grave conditions and methods in the heder schools were also widespread among progressive Jewish intellectuals and official Russian bureaucrats, particularly in the 1870s and 1880s. Zipperstein, *Imagining*, 42–45; and Haumann, *A History*, 144.

124. The German population in Mitau belonged to three separate congregations, of which two used the large *Trinitatiskirche* from 1615. Most of the pastor's children's services, lectures for confirmation candidates, Bible lectures, etc. took place in the sacristy in the church's choir; Neander, *Die deutschen*, 44.

125. The church patrons of Mitau decided on May 3 to call Gurland as Neander's successor, Gurland, *IzW* (1911), 162.

126. Baron Carl von der Recke-Paulsgnade (1817–1902) was "Landesbevollmächtigter" (state secretary) of Kurland, central in enforcing the agrarian reforms under Alexander II; Wittram, *Baltische Geschichte*, 165, 307.

in Mitau on October 10, 1876 (one month before his wife died at the hospital in Tallinn). This meant that one of the most important posts among the clergy in Kurland was now held by a former rabbi. The question is whether Gurland's promotion was part of a strategic game in light of the discourse with Pucher. While on the one hand it secured prestige for Gurland, it could have also reduced the tension between the Baltic German and Jewish communities. Dworkowich, Gurland's successor as a missionary, was soon moved to Riga.[127]

For many in the leading strata in Kurland it was not obvious that Gurland should have this post, and about 15 years later this led to tensions between him and other clergymen in Kurland. By then his ethnic as well as his educational background were regarded as problematic by an increasing number of the clergy, who found it difficult to understand the choice of Gurland as a leading minister in light of his lack of university education.[128] Still, Gurland was popular among many in the local congregations, as he had a special concern for children and young people in his ministry.

That Gurland, intentionally or not, was cut off from his work as a missionary seems to have troubled him. During his ministry years, Gurland seriously considered going back to mission work several times. On some occasions, mission societies in Germany offered him a job as a missionary, but Franz Delitzsch advised him to stay where he was.[129] However, at this point the sources differ. While Helene Gurland claims that Franz Delitzsch encouraged him to stay at his post in Kurland, le Roi says he did the opposite. On one of Gurland's visits with Delitzsch, the professor is supposed to have begged him to return to mission work.[130]

---

127. Le Roi, *Rudolf Hermann Gurland*, 35. Paulus Dworkowicz replaced Gurland in 1877, and settled in Riga in 1878. In 1883 he was replaced by P. Eisenschmidt, but due to new restrictions on the Baltic German community by Russian authorities it was difficult to maintain this work. See Le Roi, *Geschichte*, 1:334–35.

128. In addition there are indications that Gurland was regarded as alien by some, in the sense that his personality had certain Jewish characteristics. "Odessa," 3; and Fauerholdt, "National-Jüdiches Christentum," 13–24, 23.

129. Gurland, *IzW* (1911), 166.

130. Le Roi, *Rudolf Hermann Gurland*, 35–36. This disagreement, which is based on different quotations from Delitzsch, may possibly be explained as different opinions held by Delitzsch at different times or in different situations. I assume that Le Roi's quote is from the same source Gurland refers to in his letter to the Zion Union in 1892, which Gurland dates not very long before Delitzsch's death in 1891; Waldeland, *Jøderne og Jødemisjonen*, 7. By then, in his relations with the local church authorities,

Already in 1878, Gurland applied to the Norwegian Israel Mission to become the society's full-time missionary (the application was turned down, apparently for financial reasons).[131] That Gurland sent this application the same year that he married Baronesse von Drachenfels strongly suggests that he was sincere about his interest in mission work, but perhaps also that he found himself in an uncomfortable position as *pastor primarius*. However, the mission periodicals still presented material from Gurland, who continued to be involved in mission to Jews when this was natural, especially on his journeys. Some of these reports could be rather long, as he quotes almost complete dialogues and discussions. According to le Roi, Gurland also baptized several Jews during his years as *pastor primarius*.[132]

On his journeys in the Baltics and St. Petersburg, Gurland established relations with Protestant revivalists in the western part of the Russian Empire. On his visits to St. Petersburg, Gurland stayed with Countess Lieven of Mesothen (a town south of Riga), Countess Gagarin and the wife of Peter Schuwaloff of Ruhenthal (Rundāle Palace in today's Pilsrundāle).[133] These were sympathizers of the retired Imperial Guard colonel, Wassilij Alexandrowitsch Paschkow (1831–1902), one of the richest landowners in Russia. Under the influence of the evangelists Lord Radstock (1838–1913) and Baedeckers (1823–1906), Paschkow had become sympathetic to evangelical Christianity. Aside from supporting Radstock's and Baedecker's evangelistic work in Russia financially, during the 1880s Paschkow arranged public evangelistic meetings in his own palace in Newa-Quai in St. Petersburg.[134] At some of these meetings there were up to 700 participants present, and his sympathizers were sometimes nicknamed "Paschkowites." The movement was particularly popular in aristocratic circles, and does not seem to have reached the

---

Gurland was in quite a different situation than in 1879 (see below). However, as neither Helene Gurland nor Le Roi explains the context of their sources, it is also possible that their use of Delitzsch quite simply reflects their different personal opinions about where Gurland belonged—in the mission or in Kurland.

131. Skarsaune, *Israels venner*, 117.

132. Le Roi, *Rudolf Hermann Gurland*, 37.

133. According to Gurland's son, Schuwaloff once visited their home in Mitau. Bitter and Gurland, *Unsichtbare Kirche*, 29.

134. Coad, *A History*, 193.

lower classes.¹³⁵ According to *IzW*, Gurland also met Paschkow on one of his journeys to Germany or Britain, where Paschkow was exiled.¹³⁶

The same year Gurland was appointed to the post in Mitau, 1876, Marie Gurland died. When Gurland's daughter was placed in Berlin for the sake of her upbringing, one of the reasons mentioned was that Marie was not very good at this, and I assume her health was the main reason. In 1874 Marie's mental and physical health had been gradually declining for several years, until she could no longer take care of herself.¹³⁷ According to Helene Gurland, the loss of her two children was something she never found a way to handle in spite of the initial comfort of having Sophie with them. The fact that she and Gurland never had children was also a blow to her. In her final two years she suffered from a brain disease. In 1875, Gurland followed the doctor's advice and sent her to a hospital run by the Lutheran church in Reval in Livland (today Tallinn in Estonia). Gurland visited her on his mission travels in Estonia and to St. Petersburg. During her last two months at the hospital she suffered several strokes, and she died November 7, 1876.¹³⁸

Familiy Reconciliation

In 1878, at the age of 47, Rudolf H. Gurland was married again, for the fourth time, to 25-year-old Helene Baronesse von Drachenfels (1853–1916). She came from one of the oldest and most respected families of the German nobility in Kurland, and the couple had six sons.¹³⁹ In spite of the central role Rudolf Hermann Gurland had among his descendants, their Jewish heritage played a minor part for the family after his death, and the children had no significant contact with Jews or the Jewish community. While Gurland was alive, however, he was able to keep in touch with several relatives. According to Ariel and Schainker,

---

135. Gurland, *IzW* (1911), 180, 207; Holthaus, "Weitblick." According to Hebly, *Protestants*, 64, Sophie Lieven is the author of *Eine Saat die Reiche Frucht brachte* ("A Seed That Bore Rich Fruit") (Basel, 1952).

136. Gurland, *IzW* (1911), 181.

137. Perhaps this is the reason Gurland felt he lacked family life in Kishinev; see Gurland, *IzW* (1911), 128.

138. Le Roi, *Rudolf Hermann Gurland*, 34.

139. Ernst Gurland (1880–1946), Max Gurland (1882–1925), Paul Gurland (1884–1963), Rudolf Gurland (1886–1947), Wilhelm Gurland (1887–1932), and Hellmut Gurland (1891–1946), Bitter and Gurland, "Gurland, (Chaim) Rudolf Hermann."

Jewish converts in Russia as well as Northern America managed to retain ties with their families and the Jewish community if they wanted to, in spite of resentment from the families.[140] This appears to have been the case with Gurland, who managed to have some contact with his own family as well as the families of his first two wives. Although these relations were quite strained, Gurland had supported his mother financially since his father died in 1862.[141] In October 1879, the mother surprisingly left Vilnius in secret to visit her son and his family in the rectory in Mitau for several weeks. Gurland was able to find a Jewish housewife to maintain a kosher kitchen during her stay. In these weeks he and his mother had some sort of reconciliation, including on the matter of the *Kaddish*.[142] However, though Gurland often explained the gospel and Christianity to her, she never left Judaism. She spent most of the days in her room, praying. Even though she went to the local synagogue, the increasing influence of Reform Judaism in Mitau made her not feel at home. In spite of Gurland's attempts to persuade her to move in with them, she returned to Vilnius after some weeks. Gurland continued to stay in touch with her by correspondence and visits, and was able to disuade her from moving to Jerusalem. When the family neglected to inform him about her death before her funeral, he became very upset.[143]

Gurland's Last Years in Kurland

Gurland's last years in Mitau were difficult, and eventually led to his withdrawal in 1894. In the 1880s the Russian Empire increased its efforts to take control of its domains. This had radical consequences for the German population in the Baltic provinces, whose political autonomy came under increasing pressure. The official language was now Russian, and for the Baltic Germans it was especially provoking

---

140. Schainker, "Imperial Hybrids," 1–2.

141. Gurland *IzW* (1911), 113.

142. "Hazkarath Neshamot": The son's prayer for the deceased parents. Gurland promised her that he always mentioned her in his prayers. ibid., 170.

143. Gurland *IzW* (1911), 171. According to Helene Gurland, Ida Gurland was very proud of her son and his position in Kurland. Considering the tensions with his father and his break with Judaism, this may sound strange. Nevertheless, it is possible that she, at her visit to the rectory in Mitau, expressed some of the affection many in the Jewish community felt for successful converts; see Schainker about Khvolson, in Schainker, "Imperial Hybrids," 297.

that German schoolchildren had to have all their lessons in Russian. The German aristocracy and clergy became more and more frustrated with the Russian policy, and parts of the Baltic German population now encouraged resisting the reforms. Although Gurland did not approve of the new regime, he could not follow the calls for resistance and felt rather uncomfortable about the Baltic German uproar. This lack of patriotism by Gurland was seen by some as provocative, but he does not seem to have encountered any form of anti-Semitism as such. Generally anti-Semitism was not widespread at this time among either Germans or Latvians. M. Laserson points out that as late as in the revolutionary chaos of 1918 and 1919, "the Germans did not reveal any sign whatsoever of anti-Semitism at the time."[144]

Gurland's background as a foreigner was nevertheless now used against him by some of the German clergy, who felt that his post should be held by a man of more patriotic background and mentality. According to his son, Rudolf Gurland, the father left Mitau due to illness and difficult conflicts related to frustration about the fact that a stranger had had the most prominent ministry in the country.[145] In his article in *Saat auf Hoffnung* in 1912, Fauerholdt refers to Gurland's awkward social situation in Kurland. Although Fauerholdt formulates the details rather vaguely, he seems to believe that some of Gurland's difficulties came from the fact that he converted when he was an adult, and thereby struggled with being acculturated like other converts.[146] In addition, it could be that Gurland's limited academic theological education was regarded as a problem. Usually pastors with only theological seminary education ended up as curates, which was the case for some Latvian ministers. These could be described rather patronizingly as "*halb-pastoren.*"[147] This appears to have been a factor in Gurland's case as well.[148]

---

144. Laserson, "The Jews," 94–186, 98; Šteinmanis and Anders, *History*, 33. Nevertheless, Bogojavlenska reports about a few attacks on Jewish shop owners by Latvian gangs in the early 1880s. While some Latvian nationalists described Jews as parasites, others claimed they set a standard for how a suppressed people could build up a nation. Bogojavlenska, *Die jüdische Gesellschaft*, 80–85.

145. Bitter and Gurland, *Unsichtbare kirche*, 23.

146. Fauerholdt, "National-Jüdiches Christentum," 23.

147. German slang for "incomplete pastor."

148. Gurland's lack of university education was regarded as a problem by some, at least in the beginning. See "Odessa," 3; Le Roi, *Rudolf Hermann Gurland*, 35; and Neander, *Die deutschen*, 11.

Retirement and Health Problems

In 1894, Gurland moved to Riga to take up mission work among Jews again, after working part-time as a missionary since 1893. The son Rudolf Gurland remembers the family's grief when they left.[149] Going to Riga, Gurland could not take over from his own successor there, Dworkowitz. Instead he had agreed to work for the American mission society Zion's Society for Israel (*Sionsforeningen*).[150] The church periodical *Lutheraneren* had published Gurland's reports and essays about the mission to the Jews for years, and shared the same Lutheran profile as the Norwegian Israel Mission.[151]

Before May 1892 the *Sionsforeningen* had received two letters from Gurland, in which he explained his wish to return to the Jewish mission:

> I'm well prepared to join the ministry of the Jewish mission again, and would prefer to stand in your honorable Zion Union instead of serving with a Jewish mission in England or Germany, wherefrom I already have received requests. Through Pastor Meyersohn I know what spirit rules among you. . . . If the Zion Union should wish to have me in its service, I would be pleased with an annual salary of 2,000 rubles ($1,000) instead of my current salary as a minister of 6,000 rubles, and for the future will abandon any retirement pension and widow's pension, as my wife has some money from her home and I under no circumstances would burden the mission's finances. Only as long as I'm able to work and actually do what I'm supposed to do, I expect humble support for living from the relevant mission society.[152]

From January, Gurland worked in Riga until September 1896, when he moved to Odessa with his wife and their youngest sons. However, already from 1887 Gurland had cooperated with the Mildmay Mission's project of handing out New Testaments in Hebrew and Yiddish to Jews in Eastern Europe, by managing a Bible depot for the society.[153] This

---

149. Bitter and Gurland, *Unsichtbare Kirche*, 23.

150. Meyer, "Protestant Missions to Jews," 112. At Gurland's death the society ran three missionary centers in Minsk, Chicago, and Odessa.

151. One of the society's first missionaries, employed from 1880, was the Jewish-Christian pastor Theodor Karl Meyersohn. Meyersohn had been baptized by Gurland in Mitau in 1874. See Le Roi, *Rudolf Hermann Gurland*, 37.

152. Waldeland, *Jøderne og Jødemisjonen*, 121; my translation.

153. Le Roi, *Geschichte*, 2:261. Between 1886 and 1906, 1,195,483 Hebrew, Yiddish and Ladino Hebrew New Testaments were distributed by the Mildmay Mission; Meyer,

work was the result of a new political situation at this time. The Russian government now allowed the work of colporteurs, which made it possible to establish Bible depots in several cities within Russia. Gurland now used his influence among the Baltic clergy to encourage them to participate in the campaign.

To establish a mission work in Riga was natural. Most of the Jews in Livonia lived in Riga, and in the last decades before WWI the city experienced immense growth related to industry and trade.[154] However, Gurland's efforts in his last years were stymied by an increasing decline of his health. Since he left Berlin in 1867 he had been to rehabilitation for lung problems at German baths several times. The health conditions were not improved after leaving Mitau, as the new work included much traveling. He was advised to move to a climate more suitable for him. In 1896, the 65-year-old Gurland and his wife therefore moved to Odessa with their youngest sons, working for both the American and the British societies.[155]

Gurland's Odessa

Although there are no explicit complaints in *IzW*, Helene Gurland shows little enthusiasm about this move to the cosmopolitan port on the Black Sea.[156] The encouraging events that are mentioned are often related to their life and social network in the Baltics, like visits from the Russian and Baltic German nobility from Kurland and St. Petersburg. In his memoirs, the son Rudolf Gurland is more positive about the city where he grew up as a teenager, although not much is said about the time in Odessa except for mentions of his school and vacations in Kurland.[157]

During the 19th century, Odessa had become a key commercial and industrial city in southern Russia, and the Jewish community had an important role in industry, banking, export and trade. Over one third belonged to the working class. In 1867 the population of Odessa was

---

"Protestant Missions to Jews", 97. See also Nerel, "The 'Flagship'" 49–56.

154. Kirby, *Baltic World*, 201; Bobe, "Four Hundred Years," 23.

155. Le Roi, *Rudolf Hermann Gurland*, 35.

156. Gurland, *I tvende verdener*, 316. While the German version of *IzW* from 1911 does not mention Lieven's name, the information from the Norwegian translation seems to be partly confirmed by Gurland's son's memoirs in *Unsichtbare Kirche*; see below.

157. Bitter and Gurland, *Unsichtbare Kirche*, 29.

about 128,000, and in 1910 it had increased to 620,000. With 49 percent Russians, 31 percent Jews, 9 percent Ukrainians and 11 percent other ethnic groups, it was the biggest multicultural city in Russia. While the political discussions in Russia's second cosmopolitan city, Riga, were closely associated with ethnicity, politics in Odessa was more focused on local problems and conflicts between the classes.[158] According to Zipperstein, as early as the 1870s the Jewish community in the city was characterized by ritual laxity and acculturation, due to the general materialism and unusual opportunities for Jewish traders.[159]

In the 1890s the city had become central for progressive Jewish political and cultural life, particularly Zionism and the revival of the Hebrew language.[160] The proto-Zionist movement *Hibbat Zion* had Odessa as their headquarters, and the city was home to a number of central Zionists like L. Pinsker, M. L. Lilienblum, Achad Ha'am, J. Klausner, and V. Jabotinsky.[161] Many of these were former *maskilim* who abandoned the path to Jewish assimilation because of the Russian pogroms in the 1870s and 1880s.[162] Odessa's position as the center for Russian Zionism was not due only to the size of the city, but also to the fact that Odessa was Russia's main outlet to the Black Sea and the Mediterranean Sea, and therefore the main channel for Jewish emigration from Russia to *Eretz Israel*/Palestine. Most of these emigrants represented a practical Zionism that wanted to colonize Palestine step by step.[163] The Jewish nationalists wrote and discussed in both Yiddish and Hebrew, but particularly the latter, which also made Odessa a center for Hebrew literature and culture. In his encounter with the Jewish society in Odessa, Gurland met this ideology constantly. The last part of *IzW* therefore contains

---

158. Hirschhausen, *Die Grenzen*, 371.

159. About 90 percent of the local Jewish-owned shops were open on the Sabbath, Zipperstein, *Imagining*, 66.

160. For the Jewish community in the city itself, Jewish intellectuals played a marginal role; in the early 1890s this group consisted of about twenty persons. Zipperstein, *Imagining*, 77 and 81.

161. Pinsker was a famous proto-Zionist and author of the Zionist manifest *Auto-emancipation* (1882); Lilienbum was author of *The Revival of Israel on the Land of Its Ancestors*; and Ha'am was founder of the Benei Moshe Society, with its headquarters in Odessa. http://www.jewishvirtuallibrary.org/jsource/judaica/ejud_0002_0015_0_15016.html.

162. Anti-Jewish outbreaks occurred in Odessa on four occasions during the century (1821, 1859, 1871, and 1881), in addition to a number of attempted attacks; ibid.

163. Anonymous, "Odessa," *Enclycopedia Judaica*; Vital, *A People Apart*, 605.

extracts from his reflections on contemporary Jewish nationalism.[164] Considering the heated discussions in the missions about the nature of Zionism, Gurland's attitude appears rather ambivalent:

> I follow the Zionist movement with warm interest, and listen carefully to the judgment of the Jewish press. However, from them you will hear much that is unclear, confused and fantastic.[165]

The nationalism that was growing among Russian Jewry was reflected among Jewish believers in Jesus as well. In 1896, the topic of Jewish-Christian congregations had been on the agenda in Jewish mission circles for more than a decade, provoked by persons like Joseph Rabinowitz.[166] Rabinowitz lived in Kishinev, not very far from Odessa. Here he had, since the mid-1880s, founded an independent church/synagogue, and received permission from the Russian Ministry of Interior in 1884 to run a prayer house for his "New Israelites" society in Kishinev. The Russian government nevertheless did not grant him a license to act as a minister, but Rabinowitz's work raised much interest among the mission societies as well as the Russian public.

"New Israelites" was one of at least three parallel Jesus-believing movements in southern Russia in the 1880s. The two other groups were "New Israel" and "Spiritual Biblical Brotherhood." "New Israel" was established by Jacob Priluker in 1882 in Odessa. Priluker abandoned

---

164. The original context or intended audience for this material in *IzW* is not explained. My suggestion is that it is written with supporters of the Mildmay Mission in mind; see my discussion about Gurland's attitude to Zionism in chapter 4.2.

165. Gurland, *IzW* (1911), 204. " Ich verfolge die Zionistische Bewegung mit warmen Interesse und horche aufmerksam auf die Urteile der Jüdischen Presse, aber man bekommt viel Unklares, Verworrenes und Phantastisches zu hören."

166. Joseph Rabinowitz was a Ukrainian Jew who in the 1870s left Hasidism for *Haskalah*, although he maintained a deep concern about the Jewish people and Judaism. Long before his conversion to Christianity in the early 1880s he had come to the conclusion that traditional and contemporary Judaism confused ends and means concerning the Talmud's function. As he saw it, the goal of the halakic literature was, to begin with, to strengthen Israel's national spirit, but instead it had a significant position of its own, independent of national concerns and the Jewish people's real needs. The Talmud should serve a provisional role in Jewish life, and its primary role was to bring Jewry intact to the future. Zipperstein, "Heresy," 211. However, Zipperstein believes Rabinowitz's outspoken tendency to deemphasize Talmud before his conversion was influenced by his brother-in-law, Yechiel Herschensohn-Lichtenstein, and not his Hasidic background as such. He was permitted to establish a synagogue called Betlehem in Kishinev in December 1884, but never had any formal right to function as a minister or rabbi. ibid., 216.

Talmud, kosher observance and circumcision, and introduced Russian and Sunday observance for his group in an attempt to forge a rapprochement between Judaism and Christianity. He thus expected the Russian state to grant them civil liberties equal with Christians. He later immigrated to Britain. "Spiritual Biblical Brotherhood" was founded by Jacob Gordin in Elizavegrad in 1880. The society began prior to the pogroms as a group of about 30 members who rejected talmudic Judaism and encouraged Jews to do agricultural labor. Due to lack of followers and increased Russian repression, Gordin and about 60 followers immigrated to the USA in 1891. In October of the same year, the Russian police closed the Brotherhood for fear of revolutionary activities and ordered the arrest of Gordin.[167] Like Gordin, Rabinowitz also had trouble with the Russian authorities and was accused by local Russian leaders of being a Western agent doing sectarian Christian work in Jewish disguise. In 1886, the Russian Orthodox Synod ordered the police to stop his activities, but the police did not find anything incriminating against him.[168]

From the outset, all these groups appeared to be rather obscure attempts to be integrated into the Russian community. However, this perspective would probably be a misunderstanding of Rabinowitz's position, which was much closer to Protestant missions than the others. While Gordin and Priluker promoted intermarriage and rejected all displays of Jewish particularism, this was not the case with Rabinowitz, who cannot be categorized as an assimilationist though he favored conversion. Generally Russian authorities believed that Jewish conversions were insincere, with mercenary motives. According to Schainker, this was an important reason for the skepticism toward groups like Rabinowitz's. One suspected that their main motivation for their "hybrid" identity, wanting to be officially Christian while maintaining a Jewish way of life, was to escape the restrictions laid on Russian Jews.[169]

According to Schainker the three groups challenged the Russian state and church in two ways: 1) They introduced religious choice within Judaism, and thus became a destabilizing element for one of the confessions of the empire; and 2) Priluker, Gordin, and in particular Rabinowitz were regarded as carriers of evangelical ideas that could

---

167. Schainker, "Imperial Hybrids," 196.

168. Schainker in particular refers to the retired general Shumlianskii's letter to the over-procurator of the Synod, ibid., 197, 200, 250.

169. Ibid., 129.

undermine the hegemony of the Russian church and culture, as well as introducing unwanted political ideas in the Russian countryside. In this they were regarded in the same way as Russian Protestant groups like Stundists and Baptists, and lay groups and sects within the Russian Orthodox Church.

Rabinowitz's congregation consisted of Jews who confessed a creed of Christian doctrines, but who also claimed that they and their faith were Jewish. In spite of being supported by several foreign mission societies, it never joined any denomination or traditional church.[170] During the 1890s, Rabinowitz's work was one of the most controversial issues in British and German mission societies, but Gurland does not seem to have taken part in the debate. Gurland's old friend and colleague, Rudolf Faltin, had, however, become one of the strongest opponents of Rabinowitz's work. The content of Faltin's criticism is obscure. Skarsaune believes that traditional chauvinism is the main explanation, while Kjær-Hansen suggests that it all came down to Faltin's feeling of being overshadowed by Rabinowitz.[171]

Both Gurland and Rabinowitz were closely connected to both the Mildmay Mission and Franz Delitzsch. On this background, it is striking that *IzW* never says anything about Gurland's position concerning the discussion and situation in Kishinev, but only gives a brief note about Gurland's relationship with Rabinowitz in general:

> When they [the Jewish converts] were supposed to be baptized, Gurland usually sent them to his highly respected spiritual father in Kishinev, superintendent Faltin, who still worked under a great blessing for Israel until he also became ill and had to lay down his ministry. After this the proselytes living there and Jews who were seeking salvation streamed to Odessa. This increased when the Jewish-Christian congregation in Kishinev disintegrated after the death of its founder, Joseph Rabinowitz. Gurland had more and more often come in friendly contact with him.[172]

170. Delitzsch, "Ein südrussiches," 106–10.
171. Skarsaune, *Israels venner*, 168; Kjær-Hansen, *Joseph Rabinowitz*, 127–42.
172. Gurland, *IzW* (1911), 197. "Zur Taufe sandte Gurland sie dann meist nach Kischinew zu seinem hochverehrten gesitigen Vater Probst Faltin, der nach wie vor in grossem Segen unter Israel wirkte, bis auch er kränklickeitshalber sein Amt niederlegen musste. Da strömten dann auch die dortigen Proselyten und heilsbegierigen nach Odessa, und das steigerte sich, als die judenchristliche Gemeinde in Kischinew durch den Tod ihres Gründers Josef Rabbinowitsch, mit dem Gurland auch öfters in freundschaftliche Berührung gekommen, sich ganz auflösste."

Another of Gurland's Jewish-Christian friends while living in Odessa was the Ukrainian Julius (Yiddle) Feinstein (1859–1899). He was Gurland's employee, working as a colporteur at the Bible shop of the Mildmay Mission in Odessa. Feinstein and his wife Ester both had a Hasidic background, but Julius had been a believer already in the 1880s, apparently associated with the local Baptist church. After his conversion he tried to make *aliyah* (immigration to Palestine), but was stopped in Constantinople by the Ottoman immigration rules. Ester, then his non-Christian fiancée, later became a believer herself. When they moved back to Odessa, Julius was employed by the Baptist community in Odessa as hall keeper in combination with his trade. In 1897 he was engaged by the Mildmay Mission to assist Gurland with the distribution of New Testaments and was supposed to take care of the Bible depot. The sources indicate a warm relationship:

> Especially J. Feinstein (Julius/Yiddle) had become dear to him. As colporteur he had become a faithful friend and assistant. Deeply shaken at his death he exclaimed: "I am heartily sad because of you, my brother Jonathan."[173]
>
> I thank my dear Saviour from the bottom of my heart for fulfilling my warmest wish and deigning to use me as his humblest worker in His vineyard. I also thank dear Pastor Wilkinson, for the confidence shown me, and the salary granted in the past year, and would thank dear Oberpastor Gurland especially heartily, for having treated me always with brotherly love, in spite of my defective education and my ignorance, and for guiding and encouraging me with the greatest kindness, when my courage was often low. It was a good and blessed work in one spirit, joyful in hope, patient in tribulation, instant in prayer.[174]

In 1900 the Mildmay Mission promoted Gurland, appointing him as superintendent for all their missionaries in western Russia. Now he had the responsibility of supervising Mildmay's stations in the empire, like those in Warsaw and Minsk. This again included much traveling, which

---

173. Gurland, *IzW* (1911), 198. "Ganz besonders lieb war ihm Joseph Feinstein, der ihm als Kolporteur ein treuer Gehilfe und freund wurde und bei dessen plötzlichem Tode er tieferschüttert klagte: 'Es ist mir leid um dich, mein Bruder Jonathan.'" I do not know why the English manuscript here gives only the first letter in the first name and indicates Julius/Yiddle. If the translation is based upon the 1907 version of *IzW*, it is possible that the 1911 version aimed to be more precise.

174. Wilkinson, "Colporteur."

Gurland combined with regular journeys to Kurland and rehabilitation in Germany.[175]

Mission Activity and the Kishinev Pogrom

Russian authorities had an ambivalent attitude to foreign mission activity within its borders, and although there were new opportunities for some of the mission societies during the 1880s, missionaries faced many obstacles. Generally the western part of the empire was open for Jewish missions, and consequently there were less restrictive rules in Poland. This was possible as the society's workers aligned themselves with the Russian Bible Society.[176] The material was mostly in Yiddish. At the turn of the century, a home and workshop were founded in Odessa for the care of new believers and to provide them with vocational training. This work was connected to Gurland and Rosenberg.[177] The history books of the Zion Union provide readers with an overview of Gurland's efforts in Odessa. While the first overview describes the number of converts and other Jewish contacts, the second describes the literature work.[178]

In 1903 the mission felt the outbreak of the pogrom in Kishinev. This has become one of the most infamous pre-Holocaust pogroms in Russia, and quite early there were strong indications that it was initiated by the government itself. The pogrom was the climax of the tensions that began after the assassination of Tsar Alexander II in 1882. That year the May Laws were enacted on the more than 5 million Jewish inhabitants, strictly limiting their lives and opportunities to make a living and forcing great numbers to emigrate.[179]

The pogrom in Kishinev started on Sunday, April 6, and initiated other pogroms that did not cease until 1905. During the Kishinev pogroms, 45 Jews were killed and 400 wounded, and 1,300 houses and shops were destroyed.[180] This tragedy had a great impact on the rest of Europe. According to Håkon Harket, the shocking impact of the pogrom was partly because of the relatively peaceful period after the 1880s, and

---

175. Gurland, *IzW* (1911), 198.
176. Glaser, "A Survey," 109.
177. Ibid., 79.
178. Blegen, *Zionsforeningens*, 240.
179. Glaser, "A Survey," 71; Wilkinson, *In the Land of the North*, 24.
180. Harket, *Historien*, 224.

partly because this time there was no doubt where the source of the violence could be found: the leading ideologist of the empire, Konstantin Pobedonostsev, and minister for domestic affairs Vjacheslav K. Phleve. The pogrom was therefore regarded as a well-planned mass murder.[181] Thousands of Jews escaped to Odessa, where Gurland found himself in a horrible situation. Although he and the other missionaries put all their efforts into relief work for the refugees, he had difficulty handling the situation emotionally:

> And when the years of famine came, and in the year 1903 so-called Jewish pogroms (persecution of Jews) broke out at Kishinev, all the oppressed and persecuted Jews came in crowds to Gurland, so that this sudden pressure of work nearly overtaxed his strength and he was not able to listen to every individual Jew and still less able to provide help for all, and had to call upon [Christian] friends again and again for help. Gurland's sensitive mind and heart suffered terribly when he heard of the cruelties committed against Jews [without consideration of age and sex]. It made him ill to see those emaciated faces, pale with terror, and to hear the dreadful reports of the refugees; he could hardly stand it altogether but for the love and sympathy shown by [Christian] friends of the Jewish mission who, again and again, filled his hands to enable him to at least alleviate some temporal needs and wants.[182]

In the wake of the pogroms Gurland's health declined significantly. Before Easter 1905 his health became increasingly worse, and he died in Odessa on May 21, 1905. At the request of his previous congregation in Kurland, he was buried in Mitau. The sermon at the burial was given by his son-in-law, Pastor Emil Bielenstein.[183]

181. Ibid.
182. Gurland, *IzW* (1911), 197. "und als dann die Jahre der Hungersnot kamen und 1903 die grosse Judeverfolgung über Kischinew hereinbrach; da kamen die Bedrängten und Verfolgten in so grosser Menge zu Gurland, dass es fast seine Kräfte übersieg, auch nur alle anzuhören, wieviel mehr für alle zu sorgen, und er immer wieder die Hilfe seiner Freunde anrufen musste. Gurlands weiches Gemüt litt furchtbar unter all dem Grauenhasten und Schrecklichen, das die Judenverfolgung brachte. Er wurde ganz krank, wenn die armen Geflüchteten, mit schreckensbleichen Gesichtern sich um ihn drängend, von all den Graumsamkeiten und Scheusslichkeiten erzählten, die sie miterlebt; er konnte es nicht anhören, und er wurde erst wohl, wenn die Liebe und Teilnahme der Missionsfreunde ihm immer wieder die Hände füllte, dass er wenigstens äusserer Not abhelfen konnte mission."
183. Gurland, *IzW* (1911), 205–18. Gurland's last days and his funeral took place

Gurland's efforts on behalf of the Jewish refugees were appreciated among the Jewish community, and were recognized in his obituary in *Allgemeine Zeitung des Judentums* (June 30, 1905), as well as among some mission circles.[184]

Christian Theophilus Lucky/Chaim Jedidjah Pollak (1854–1916)

FIGURE 6: Seventh Day Baptists in Europe and America, 387

Introduction

Three of the five major sources about Lucky's life—the obituaries by William C. Daland in *Sabbath Recorder*, Max Weidauer in *Saat auf Hoffnung* and Gisle Johnson in *Missions-Blad for Israel*—do not say much about his life before conversion, nor about his conversion itself.[185]

---

under the dramatic political circumstances caused by the revolutionary turmoil in 1905. During the weeks before and after his death, Odessa experienced a number of strikes and riots. On the 13th of June a regular rising took place in the city. The following day the town was shelled by the battleship Potemkin, and thousands of people were killed during the following bloodshed. Bascomb, *Rødt mytteri*, 84.

184. Harling, "Zum Gedachtnis," 86; Terray, *Et liv i grenseland*, 50.

185. William C. Daland was one of Lucky's friends in the Seventh Day Baptists (SDB) in New York. He had a Baptist background, but became a member of the SDB when he studied at Union Theological Seminary together with Lucky in the early 1880s.

The two other sources, the obituaries in *Nathanael* in 1917 (issues 1 and 2) by August Wiegand and Moses Löwen, provide readers with more detail.[186] However, these versions differ, particularly on the events around his conversion and baptism. In addition, Löwen's and Wiegand's conversion narratives also relate very differently to the expected pattern of the genre of conversion stories.[187]

As Lucky's biography is obscured by markedly different conversion stories, it is difficult to know which of the narratives is authentic. Löwen's version is not only very substantial, but also less shaped by the conversion genre, and I therefore hold this text to be the best of the competing stories. I believe that the different narratives are due to Lucky himself. Several of those who knew Lucky personally mention that he was reluctant to divulge private information.[188] Löwen tells how, in 1890, Lucky persuaded him not to reveal how he had become a believer: "But please don't tell people about it, right? They don't need to know everything!"[189] According to Wiegand, in matters related to his

---

Between 1889 and 1898 he edited the journal *The Peculiar People*. He worked as a pastor in New York, Rhode Island and London, and later became president of the Seventh Day Baptists.

Max Weidauer, a German Lutheran minister in different German congregations in Galicia from the late 1890s to WWI, published the article "Erinnerungen an Ch.Th. Lucky" in *Saat auf Hoffnung* (1923) 166–68, 171–80, 209–14.

Gisle Johnson was a Norwegian pastor and missionary for the Norwegian Israel Mission. Between 1904 and 1919 he was stationed in Galatz, and between 1921 and 1946 in Budapest. In 1923 he published "Fra vor missions fortid: vor berøring med Lucky," *Missions-Blad for Israel* 97 (in two different issues in the autumn of 1923) 225–27, 248–51, as a response to Weidauer's article the same year.

186. Löwen, "Christian Theophilus Lucky," 1–25; Wiegand, "Chajim Jedidjah Lucky," 41–63. Löwen and Wiegand met Lucky in 1889. Löwen was a Jewish Christian who edited *Edut leIsrael* together with Lucky between 1890 and 1892, but later became one of his opponents. Wiegand was a German Lutheran pastor, and supported Lucky for the rest of his life. Wiegand was also the pastor who took care of Lucky's funeral. Their different views on Lucky's agenda probably color the obituaries.

187. Hindmarsh, *The Evangelical Conversion Narrative*, 1–3, 6–8. Wiegand is closer to this genre than Löwen, as he describes Lucky as someone moving from unbelief to belief and with a specific moment of conversion, while Löwen refrains from such references.

188. The Norwegian missionary Gisle Johnson described him as a "strange man that it was extremely difficult to get a clear picture of, even for those who knew him" (Johnson, "Fra vor missions fortid," 225).

189. "Aber nicht war, du sagst es den Leuten jetzt nicht? Sie brauchen nicht alles zu wissen!" (Löwen, "Christian Theophilus Lucky," 6).

personal life Lucky was practicing the Jewish proverb "Megalleh téphach u-mekasseh tiphchajim."[190] One example of what this could mean can probably be found in Lucky's behavior when describing his own baptism to his German friend Pastor Weidauer. In that particular situation, Lucky apparently wanted to confuse the local Jews. Probably this was because he wanted to avoid being regarded as a traditional apostate, but in any case the episode shows that he was willing to use or obscure his own narrative for his own purposes.[191]

The periodical *Peculiar People*, which usually expressed Lucky's views in most matters, shows a clear antipathy towards the traditional symmetric conversion narratives, which it found to be an integrated part of much of the humbug related to Jewish mission activity.[192] In addition, Wiegand describes how, in his editorial work, Lucky used pseudonyms and fabricated correspondents and readers.[193] These factors make a plausible explanation for the incoherence in parts of his biography. It probably also means that biographical information that one assumes came from Lucky should be used with some caution. In addition, the reader must take into account the agenda of the writers of the source material, who by no means were neutral to Lucky. Theodor Zöckler's article about *Edut leIsrael* in *Saat auf Hoffnung* in 1892 and 1893 is particularly important in this regard, as parts of it are important for the later analysis of Lucky's identification with Jewish tradition. Here Zöckler not only described and discussed the journal, but the article must be assumed to be influenced by his own role as one of Lucky's moderate sympathizers in the controversy around his agenda at the time.[194]

---

190. "Show one palm, when hiding two palms" (Wiegand, "Chajim Jedidjah Lucky," 46).

191. Weidauer, "Erindringer," 209. I have used this Norwegian translation of the original German article: Max Weidauer, "Erinnerungen an Ch.Th. Lucky," *Saat auf Hoffnung* (1923) 22.

192. "Editorial Notes," in *The Peculiar People* 1 (1888–89) 110–112; 112. also Hindmarsh, *The Evangelical Conversion Narrative*, 8.

193. Wiegand, "Chajim Jedidjah Lucky," 54.

194. Zöckler, "Judentum und Christentum" (1892) 205–15, 249–65, and (1893) 44–54.

Childhood and Growing Up in Galicia

Chaim (Wolf/Been) Jedidjah Pollak was born on September 11, 1854, in the small town of Tysmienica (Polish)/Tysmenitsa (Yiddish), close to Stanislau in Austrian Galicia, today part of western Ukraine.[195] Most writers understand Galicia to be the territory obtained by Austria at the partition of Poland in 1772.[196] The territory consisted of a number of ethnic groups: Ukrainians/Ruthenians, Poles, Jews, Armenians, Germans and Karaites.[197] After being ruled tightly from Vienna, as part of the *Ausgleich* in 1867 Galicia became a semiautonomous province run by the Polish majority until 1914.[198] Ethnically and politically, the Jews were caught between the Ukrainians and the Poles, who competed for political and economic power in the wake of the *Ausgleich*. Polish boycotts and violence towards Jews increased before 1914, with outbreaks of violence in 1898, 1902 (Lemberg) and 1903.[199]

The majority of Galician Jews lived in close-knit communities and maintained a traditional economic and religious way of life until WWI.[200] Their cultural, religious and linguistic heritage made them a distinct group, which dominated in petty trade, inn keeping, artisanship and free professions in the towns and shtetls.[201] They were mainly Yiddish-speaking, unassimilated and remained relatively uninvolved politically.[202] In spite of different opinions about national rights, internal autonomy

---

195. Wiegand, "Chajim Jedidjah Lucky," 41. The town was, until 1945, named Stanislau in German, but like Tysmenitsa and many other places in the region, the spelling differed according to the different ethnic groups: Stanislav (Yid.) or Stanislawow (Pol.). It is today named Ivano Frankovsk. Lucky's family name was Wolf, relating to Jacob's blessing in Genesis 49 where Benjamin was likened to the wolf, Unbegaun, *Russian Surnames*, 341; and the claim that Lucky belonged to the tribe of Benjamin, Randolph, "Christian Theophilus Lucky," 206–8.

196. Magocsi, *Galicia*, xiv.

197. Wandycz, *The Price of Freedom*, 177; and Magocsi, *Galicia*, 28. E.g., the Jewish population of Tysmienica composed about one third of the town's population; Anonymous, "Tysmenitsa," 15:1492.

198. *Ausgleich* is the term for the political reorganization that made the Austrian empire into a dual state (Austria and Hungary) and which granted some privileged ethnic minorities more political influence.

199. Prusin, *Nationalizing*, 7.

200. Ibid., 5.

201. Ibid., 1.

202. Markovits and Sysyn, *Nationbuilding*, 154.

and Zionist ideas, the majority of the politically involved Jews were loyal to the Habsburg Empire, and the Jewish-Galician intelligentsia preferred German culture and education.[203]

Economically, the Jews were middle-class in a traditional agrarian community, and Jews were over-represented in professions like law, medicine, the arts and journalism, but the majority lived in crushing poverty that forced many into prostitution or emigration.[204] The depressive economic and social situation had serious consequences for the Galician Jews: In 1890, 85 percent of the Jewish Galician population was below the official minimum standard of living, and death rates in the Jewish community were disastrous.[205] The building of the railways, the new industrialized Polish farmers and the Austrian electoral reforms created an important push factor for Jewish emigration, and this became even stronger due to the flood of Jewish refugees from Russian pogroms as well as increased anti-Semitism among the Ukrainian and Polish populations. Of the 281,150 Austrian Jewish emigrants to the USA between 1881 and 1910, 85 percent were from Galicia, one tenth of the approximately 2 million Eastern European Jews that came in the same period.[206] Lucky was therefore among the first Galician Jews who migrated to the USA when he came to New York at the beginning of the 1880s.

According to Löwen, the source that provides essential information about Lucky's closest family and his childhood, Lucky's parents were the shopkeepers Aaron and Esther Pollak.[207] Aaron was an old widower when he married the young Esther, and Chaim (later Lucky) was their only son. Lucky never knew his father, as Aaron died when he was very young.[208] Due to the little shop, his mother was able to take care of the

---

203. Prusin, *Nationalizing*, 4.

204. Ibid., 3.

205. Hödl, *Als Bettler*, 16, referring to Mahler, "The Economic Background," 255–67. Lucky was primarily interested in the cultural and religious consequences of this situation and not the economic aspects of it; see the profile in the Hebrew journal and the analysis of his identification with the Jewish people.

206. Mahler, "The Economic Background"; Hödl, *Als Bettler*, 18; also Markovits and Sysyn, *Nationbuilding*, 154 and 155 n. 16.

207. Löwen, "Christian Theophilus," 3. According to the SDB *Yearbook* of 1917, Lucky was left an orphan, and was thereafter in care of a relative; SDB *Yearbook* (1917), 22.

208. Ariel's comments on the significance of the father for converts (Ariel, *Evangelizing*, 41).

boy and pay for some education for him. People became aware of the boy's intellectual capabilities early on, and he also received some education in German and Polish. As he became a skilled user of Hebrew, he probably attended a *heder* and later a Talmud school in his hometown or nearby.

Esther died when Lucky was a teenager, and to make a living he worked as a tutor while he continued his own education in the evenings.[209] He was restless and changed residence and studies frequently until he came to Berlin in the beginning of the 1870s. According to the American sources, his father had wanted him to become a rabbi, something which is never mentioned in the German or Scandinavian sources.[210] Nevertheless, almost all sources describe the boy as pious and concerned about his biblical studies and religious affairs. He was not only interested in Judaism, but everything religious. In this regard some of the sources include several anecdotes about the little boy's curiosity,

---

209. Did Lucky have wealthy relatives? According to the obituary in the SDB's *Yearbook* in 1917, Lucky seems to have inherited about 750,000 dollars, which he could not get so long as he refused to accept a demand from the aunt in charge of the money that he embrace the Roman Catholic faith. Obviously, that Lucky was heir of so much money is hard to believe. The fact that Galicia was regarded as one of the poorest regions of Europe at the time makes it even less plausible, particularly as his family background seems so obscure in the sources. If members of his family had been that wealthy, it is reasonable that their names would have been mentioned in some of the sources. In addition, considering the audience of the obituaries, one can also find motives for constructing or exaggerating such a story, as it tends to 1) emphasize Lucky's noble Jewish patriotism; 2) describe him as someone who did not convert for opportunistic reasons; and 3) fit very neatly into the generally strong antipathy towards the Roman Catholic Church among Seventh Day Baptists (and most Protestants in general). On the other hand, precisely because of the implausibility of the story, for the author of the article in the *Yearbook* there was a certain risk of being looked upon as a fraud by inventing a story like this. Also, if Lucky had wealthy relatives or some access to money in his family, it could give some explanation of another mystery that puzzled Lucky's missionary friends, namely how he, who due to his poverty often had his meals with friends, was able to finance his many travels. In addition, Lucky attended several educational institutions in Breslau and Berlin, which usually was possible only for students from wealthy families. There were, however, exceptions to the rule, e.g., when the teachers in Breslau agreed to sponsor Lucky. It was usually the distinguished families who sent their sons to yeshiva; these institutions did not usually offer equal opportunities to all. Still, there are known exceptions to this rule as well. It is therefore difficult to decide on the veracity of this story. *SDB Yearbook* 1917, 22; and Shapiro, *Between the Yeshiva World*, 4.

210. Velthuysen, "Christian Theophilus Lucky," 196–98.

for instance that he tried to observe how representatives from the different local religions behaved and practiced their rituals.[211]

Lucky did not only meet different religions on his doorstep, but was also confronted with the different factions and movements in the Galician Jewish community. Although the local rabbis in his hometown favored traditional Judaism, the young Lucky was fascinated by different Hasidic dynasties and local rabbis, and according to Wiegand he was particularly fond of the rabbi in Wiznitz/Wischnitz (Ukrainian: Wyschnyzja).[212] The group surrounding this rabbi was a typical Hasidic dynasty, associated with non-ascetic mysticism, dancing and song, and its leader was the *zaddik* or the *rebbe* (Hasidic leaders were called "rebbe," not rabbi).[213] Although there appears to have been opposition to this movement (e.g., from the local rabbis in Tysmenitsa), by 1830 Hasidism

---

211. Widauer, "Erindringer," 168.

212. Wiegand, "Chajim Jedidjah Lucky," 42. Until 1918, the town was part of Austria-Hungary, and lies today in the western part of Ukraine, close to the border with Romania. The "Wunderrabbi" mentioned by Wiegand is probably Rabbi Menachem Mendel (d. 1885), author of *Zemach Tzadik* and founder of the Haggar dynasty in Wiznitz. His dynasty had strong links to the first *Hasidim*, and his court won great reputation. The dynasty is today present in the State of Israel. http://www.jewishgen.org/yizkor/Bukovinabook/buk1_089.html.

213. Schwarzfuchs, *A Consise*, 133. The Hasidic dynasties are the result of a mass movement under the leadership of the famous Israel Ben Israel, called Ba'al Shem Tov (1700–1760). In spite of the different dynasties, the Hasidic movement had (and has) some common doctrines: 1) God is present in everything, including evil. 2) Evil was at one time divine and fell from its divine status, but can be restored and sanctified again. 3) The relationship between the adherent and God was characterized by strong emotions, although expressed traditionally through prayer and Torah observance. 4) Contemplative reading of each word and letter in the Torah. 5) The perfect relationship to God was only reached by the rebbe, but he could mediate some of this to his adherents. 6) Hasidic ethical thinking was individual and non-ascetic. 7) Traditional messianic expectations. Illmann and Harviainen, *Judisk historia*, 130.

The rebbe was regarded as the mediator between God and the adherents, and often able to perform miracles. The rebbe could sometimes be enormously popular and rich, living in a castle with a large crowd of adherents living together with him. These rabbis, like, e.g., the zaddik in Czortkow, lived in castles among extreme Jewish poverty. They were regarded with enormous respect even among the poor of the local non-Jewish population, which according to Hödl to a great extent explains the authority they had in the Jewish population. The whole Jewish community could feel the charm of the rabbis' prestige even among non-Jews, which could be one of the few reasons for respect the Galician Jews were able to experience. A strong national sense in combination with a conservative religious ideology made the *Hasidim* oppose any pressures towards assimilation from the Austrian government, and often emigration as well. Mahler, *Hasidism*, xiv; and Hödl, *Als Bettler*, 25.

had become the most characteristic form of Jewish life in Galicia.[214] Later, the *Haskalah* movement won much influence in some strata of the Jewish population. Zionism and Socialism also became dominant factors in Jewish life in Galicia.[215]

Although Hasidism was characteristic for Galicia, some scholars claim that generally rural areas were influenced by Hasidism, while some of the cities were influenced by *Haskalah*.[216] In any case, Hasidic doctrine does not seem to have had lasting influence upon Lucky. During his studies he changed his religious and political profile several times, and associated himself with Socialism, Pantheism and Anarchism, Reform Judaism, and finally with Jewish nationalism and Zionism (not to mention the Christian faith). Jews who did not follow the *Hasidim* often had to choose between assimilation and Zionism. However, for the assimilationists it was not obvious to which ethnic group one should belong. In the first decades they fought among themselves about whether one should acculturate to the German or Polish community, and when the Zionist movement grew stronger, the main struggle was between assimilationists and Zionists.[217] Lucky went from being a German Liberal to a Pole of Jewish confession. Later he was fascinated by Karl Marx, and particularly anarchism as described by Max Stirner, author of *Eine und Sein Eigentum* (1844).[218] Possibly this interest in secular ideologies was inspired by the *Haskalah* movement in his hometown, which around 1850 was a center for this movement in eastern Galicia.[219]

Löwen describes Lucky's shifting attitude to different ideologies as an expression of his characteristic restlessness.[220] This description is perhaps somewhat unfair. A young Jewish intellectual in the last part of the century in Galicia probably had quite a lot to deal with when work-

---

214. Markovits and Sysyn, *Nationbuilding*, 229; Anonymous, "Horowitz," 8:986.

215. For a contemporary description of the Hasidic environment in Galicia, see Guttry, *Galizien*, 87–104.

216. Sharot, *Messianism*, 186.

217. Skrypek, *The Problem*, 2.

218. Löwen, "Christian Theophilus Lucky," 4. Max Stirner is pseudonym for Johann Kaspar Schmidt (1806–1856), a German philosopher associated with left-wing Hegelianism and anarchism, who by his ethical solipsism held that all religions and ideologies rest on empty concepts. The same is true for the state and other social institutions that claim authority over the individual. Anonymous, "Stirner, Max," 2006.

219. Anonymous, "Stanislav," 15:338.

220. Löwen, "Christian Theophilus Lucky," 5.

ing on politics as well as religion, and trying out different worldviews could be a method for sorting out what he found credible. Considering Löwen's difficult partnership with Lucky in the early 1890s, this may be the reason for his statement.

Studies in Breslau and Berlin

At the beginning of the 1870s, Pollak studied at different rabbinic seminaries in the new German state. In the last part of the 19th century there were three major rabbinic seminaries in Germany, and all of them were central in the process that intensified the fragmentation of the Jewish community in the region. The neo-Orthodox *Der Jüdisch-Theologische Seminar* in Breslau was founded in 1854, and was the oldest.[221] In 1872, the Reform-inspired *Die Hochschule für die Wissenschaft des Judentums* was established in Berlin, and in 1873 the competing *Rabbiner Seminar für das Orthodoxe Judentum*, which wanted to combine Torah observance and modern science.[222] Both the Breslau seminary and the institutions in Berlin provided not only traditional scholarship but also modern education for rabbis and teachers. The curriculum of the seven-year program at the seminary in Breslau included both Jewish tradition and other subjects like classical languages (Greek and Latin), and was more or less copied by the *Hochschule* and the *Rabbiner Seminar* in Berlin.[223]

Pollak began at the school in Breslau about 1871 or 1872. According to Wiegand, he first went to the *yeshiva* in Pressburg (today's Bratislava) before going to Breslau, but this does not seem to have been for a long time.[224] At the school in Breslau the teachers thought his Jewish educa-

---

221. Run by Zacharias Frankel (1891–1875), who tried to balance the religious and historical aspects of Judaism. He also claimed some liturgic reforms, but maintained use of Hebrew. See Roemer, *Jewish Scholarship*, 50–52; and Illmann and Harviainen, *Judisk historia*, 150.

222. Rürup, *Jüdische Geschichte*, 201.

223. The studies included Bible exegesis, including the targums, Hebrew and Aramaic, Palestinian geography, historical and methodological introduction to the Mishna and the Talmud, Babylonian and Palestinian Talmud, classical languages and realia, the history of Judaism in relation to the history of Jewish literature, Midrash, religious philosophy and ethics, ritual practice, and Mosaic criminal and civil law, particularly talmudic family law. In addition, pedagogy, catechesis and homiletics were taught. Schwarzfuchs, *A Concise History*, 101.

224. Löwen, "Christian Theophilus Lucky," 5; and Wiegand, "Chajim Jedidjah Lucky," 42.

tion was satisfactory for enrollment, but wanted him to finish his high school education before he did his final work at the seminary itself. As he apparently had no money, the school sponsored him, only to discover that the restless student was more interested in other subjects than in Latin and Greek. After some months he left and went to Berlin.[225]

From autumn 1872 to January 1877, i.e. from age 17 to 22, Chaim lived and studied in Berlin at different religious and secular institutions. If the information from the sources is combined, we see that Lucky became a student at both of the Jewish institutions in the German capital in addition to attending the university. The first winter, he was admitted as a student at the *Hochschule* under its headmaster Abraham Geiger (1810–1874), during the first year the institution existed. The aim of the *Hochschule* was to study Judaism in the light of modern methods and a modern worldview, and from the very beginning the school was associated with the Reform movement.[226] We do not know what motivated Lucky to begin at the *Hochschule*, but its profile was clearly different from the moderate modern school in Breslau and the traditional *yeshiva* in Pressburg. Lucky therefore seems to have been influenced by Reform ideas at the time, or at least he was curious about them. The *Hochshule* also wanted Lucky to finish studying high school subjects, which he now did.

Having finishing the *gymnasium*, it seems that Lucky in 1873 also attended the *Rabbiner Seminar*.[227] This seminary was founded by the

---

225. Wiegand, "Chajim Jedidjah Lucky," 42. In Breslau, Lucky met one of the people who would become one of his strongest opponents after his conversion: Joh. F. A. de Le Roi, the later historian of Jewish missions, who had been working in Breslau as a missionary to the Jews since 1866. From a missionary's point of view, the outcome was poor. Apparently, Le Roi's way of speaking about "the Jews," combined with Lucky's experience of a couple of Jewish baptisms at about the same time, seems to have convinced him that the mission was just another expression of anti-Semitism.

226. Other teachers were David Zvi Hoffmann, Abraham Berliner, and Jacob Barth. Roemer, *Jewish Scholarship*, 52.

227. The information about Pollak/Lucky at the *Hochschule* as well as the *Rabbiner Seminar* is solely based on the obituaries; I have not succeeded in getting in touch with the archives of either the *Hochschule* or the *Rabbiner Seminar*. However, in an editorial note in Wiegand's obituary, Hermann Strack refers to a list of students at the *Hochschule* from 1872–1873, which he claims was given him by one of the lecturers at the institution, Dr. Ismar Elbogen. Here the young Pollak is included (Wiegand, "Chajim Jedidjah Lucky," 43). There appears to be no reference to Lucky's stay at the *Rabbiner Seminar* in any other source I have found. It is therefore possible that Löwen and the other sources have confused these two institutions. Still, as the first year of the *Rabbiner Seminar* fills the gap between his year at the *Hochschule* and his studies at the university, it is

Orthodox rabbi Israel Hildesheimer (1820–1899) in 1873, as a reaction to the establishment of the liberal *Hochschule* the previous year. The seminary was neo-Orthodox in outlook, but Hildesheimer insisted that the students be familiar with the scientific method. The *Rabbiner Seminar* in Berlin became the center for German Jewish orthodoxy, and tried to combine loyalty to the Torah with scientific methods.[228]

If Lucky attended the *Rabbiner Seminar* in Berlin, this would either be during the winter after his year at the *Hochschule* (in that case, the first year of this school as well) or while he was at the university. Wiegand tells about Lucky's studies at this school without mentioning the seminary, but instead describes how he, during his time in Berlin, struggled with the claims of Reform and Orthodox Judaism, particularly their views on divine revelation.[229] Lucky would have ended up on the Orthodox side, following the Orthodox view of divine revelation in the Torah. This information may explain why Lucky left the *Hochschule* after only one year. Hildesheimer regarded the *Hochschule* as a destructive institution for Judaism and the Jewish community, and to make this change of schools, Lucky may have sympathized with that view.

Between November 1874 and January 1877, Lucky attended the university. Both at the *Hochschule* and at the *Rabbiner Seminar* it was common that students followed lectures at the university at the same time. The archives of the university do not give any information about what subjects Lucky was studying, except that he was at the faculty of philosophy. Neither did he obtain any degree, and he seems to have been locked out because he was lazy or did not do good enough work ("wegen unfleiss").[230] Wiegand describes Lucky as not very successful when

---

likely that the sources are right about this. Considering Lucky's Palestinian Zionism, he would also feel more at home at Hildesheimer than with Geiger. Hildesheimer's interest in Zionist ideas was religiously motivated, and in 1888 he founded a society in Berlin to support Jewish colonization of Palestine/Eretz Israel. Rürup, *Jüdische Geschichte*, 150; Roemer, *Jewish Scholarship*, 128.

228. Hildesheimer ran the seminary for the next 26 years, so in other words he was Lucky's headmaster. Until it was closed down by the Nazis in 1938 and the library moved to Tel Aviv, the seminary educated a great number of rabbis and lay leaders for Jewish communities in Central and Western Europe. More than 100 students received rabbinic certification there between 1873 and 1938. Hilker-Siebenhaar, *Wegweiser*, 154.

229. Wiegand, "Chajim Jedidjah Lucky," 44.

230. In the archives of the former *Königlichen Friedrich-Wilhelms-Universität zu Berlin* from the middle of the 1870s there is only one person enrolled with the name Chaym Wolf Pollak, registered from November 25, 1874 to January 23, 1877. He was

it came to classical logic and the art of rhetoric, as he felt more at home in talmudic discourse and with old languages than the former subjects.[231]

The information about Lucky's stay and studies in Berlin is poor, although it gives certain background for his reputation as a gifted Jewish scholar. His choice of schools also describes him as an intellectual who sought to be loyal to the Jewish tradition, although not in the mainstream of the Eastern European Jewish communities, and certainly not within Hasidism.[232] For Löwen, ambivalence was something characteristic of Lucky, and he explains many of Lucky's moves before and after his conversion by referring to his restlessness. However, there is also a possibility that Lucky was struggling with the tension between traditional Judaism and the Reform movement, which was a crucial debate for most Eastern European Jews who had migrated to Germany, and it is likely that Lucky did not know where to place himself. According to Wiegand, the issue of divine revelation in particular seems to have been important

---

registered as number 540 at the Faculty of Philosophy, but there is not given any information about which lectures or subjects he attended. As the name in the university archive was a relatively common Jewish name, there is a theoretical uncertainty whether I have found the right person. However, no other Pollak has been found, and as long as the given dates seem to fit with the other information we can assume that this is the Pollak I am trying to trace. See the email from June 28, 2007, from the head of the university archive:

> Sehr geehrter Herr Lillevik, Chaym Wolf Pollak war vom 25.November 1874 bis zum 23.Januar 1877 Student an der Königlichen Friedrich-Wilhelms-Universität zu Berlin. Er hat sich unter der Nummer 540 des 65.Rektoratsjahres (seit 1810-W.Sch.) in die Matrikel der Universität eingetragen und an der Philosophischen Fakultät studiert. Er wohnte im Wintersemester 1874/75 in der Koblanckstr. 14 b und danach in der Choriner Str. 72. Pollak wurde wegen 'Unfleiss' aus der Matrikel gelöscht und erhielt k e i n Zeugnis mit einer Nennung der von ihm besuchten Lehrveranstaltungen. Wir haben deshalb hier keine Möglichkeit mehr festzustellen, bei welchem Professor er die Vorlesungen besucht hat. Mit freundlichen Grüßen Dr. Winfried Schultze, Leiter des Universitätsarchivs.

231. Wiegand, "Chajim Jedidjah Lucky," 43.

232. Although the relationship between Jewish traditionalists in Eastern Europe and the neo-Orthodox in Germany seemed good on the surface, this was according to Marc Shapiro due to a general lack of understanding of what German Jewish Orthodoxy stood for. Those traditional rabbis who were able to read the German writings were much more skeptical. By attending the seminary in Berlin, Pollak therefore demonstrated a certain distance from traditional Eastern European Jewish attitudes to Torah studies. Shapiro, *Between the Yeshiva World*, 41.

to him, and subsequently this issue was crucial for his movement in a Christian direction.[233]

Lucky's Conversion: The Typical Story

During his time in Berlin or shortly thereafter Lucky embraced the Christian faith, but the sources do not agree on either chronology or on many of the details. Particularly when it comes to the question of his baptism, the information is both fragmented and partly contradictory. Lucky explained several times that he wanted to keep much of this to himself to avoid alienation from his Jewish surroundings,[234] and the result is a rather unclear picture of what really happened. In other words, there is no conversion narrative in a traditional sense in any of the sources about or from Lucky. Instead, the sources give four different versions of his conversion, of which the three following stories follow the typical conversion genre, while Löwen's narrative that is more asymmetric is discussed in the next chapter.

Lillie Zöckler and the SDB sources give the following short and not very specific narrative about Lucky's conversion:[235] At some point he began to study the New Testament in Delitzsch's Hebrew translation with a friend to prove the superiority of Hillel compared to the life and teachings of Jesus. In this contact with the New Testament he was particularly attracted to the mysticism in the Gospel of John and the Jewish character of Matthew.[236] The result was that during these studies he was convinced that Jesus had to be the Messiah. He was then baptized by a friend without becoming a member of any official church or denomination.

In the second version, Weidauer recalls that Lucky stated several times that he came to faith in "Jeschua" during the night, and that he felt a deeper understanding of the grace of God. Lucky described his new attitude to the message of Christ as feeling the joy of someone who knew there was an expensive pearl in a box, but now had seen it for himself.[237] Before this new attitude to Jesus and the New Testament he had been a faithful and pious Jew for long time, and this experience was consistent with his previous worldview.

233. Wiegand, "Chajim Jedidjah Lucky," 44.
234. Löwen, "Christian Theophilus Lucky," 6; and Wiegand, "Chajim Jedidjah Lucky," 46.
235. Zöckler, *Gott Hört Gebet*, 13.
236. Velthuysen, "Christian Theophilus Lucky," 196–98.
237. Weidauer, "Erindringer," 174.

Löwen and Wiegand have more substantial, but also slightly different stories. First we will have a look at Wiegand's story:

Wiegand tells how, in Berlin, Lucky came across a Greek New Testament that he read to practice the language. Although the Jewish character of the book struck him, particularly in the writings of Paul, at first he was not very concerned about the person of Jesus. This, however, changed as a result of his struggles with Orthodox and Reform views on revelation. At this point he had come to the conclusion that if the Torah was genuine divine revelation, the New Testament had to be the same. He came to this conclusion the night before his exam sermon in a Prussian synagogue, apparently as a part of his studies at the *Hochschule*. This led him to regard Jesus and the New Testament as a genuine and legitimate part of the divine revelation together with the Torah. The following morning he told his teacher Israel Lewy about his decision:

> "This night I have become a Christian."
> "What's that supposed to mean? Have you fallen into the hands of the missionaries?"
> "No, you are the first one I have spoken with. My faith comes solely from the New Testament, which I consider equal with the Old."
> "And now you are going to turn your back on our people and its holy religion?"
> "Oh no, since Jesus is the promised Messiah, faith in him is not apostasy from the religion of Israel."
> "But everyone from our people who goes to this Jesus becomes a Meshummad."
> "I will never become a Meshummad."
> "And the Torah of Moses—you are going to keep that?"
> "Yes, as the New Testament says that the first congregation in Jerusalem was faithful to the law, I will also do that."
> "That is not possible. As a Christian you cannot continue to be a Jew!"
> "Yes, I will!"
> "Then you will become an unlucky man your whole life: You will not be counted among the Christians because you are a Jew, and likewise among the Jews, because you are a Christian."
> "That is something I have to bear!"[238]

---

238. Wiegand, "Chajim Jedidjah Lucky," 44–45. "Diese Nacht bin ich ein Christ geworden!"
"Was heist das? Sie sind doch nicht den Missionaren in die Hände gefallen?"
"Nein, Sie sind der erste, dem ich mich ausspreche. Meinen Glauben habe ich allein

This story is the closest we get to a traditional conversion narrative when it comes to Lucky, and there is some similarity between this story and Gurland's report from the debate in the synagogue in Kishinev. First of all we read about how the convert had been struggling spiritually before the decision, and the next thing is a discussion between the convert and a Jewish representative. However, the differences are also obvious. While Gurland defends his choice by attacking Jewish tradition and encouraging his opponents to embrace Christianity, the discussion between Lucky and Lewy is all about whether Lucky can still be a Jew.

Wiegand's narrative seems very stringent, probably because he had to trust his own memories of talks with Lucky—if it is not fabricated altogether. After the discussion with Lewy, Lucky began traveling quite a lot. Wiegand says that he was eventually baptized in Belgrade by unregistered Baptists, as he wanted the *tevila*, i.e., full immersion in water. Later he would not answer properly on questions regarding his baptism.[239]

Lucky's Conversion According to Löwen

Both Wiegand and Löwen report that after Berlin, Lucky moved to Galicia for a short period of time. However, Wiegand mentions this very briefly; due to much suspicion there from the Jewish community, Lucky

---

aus dem Neuen Testament, das ich mit dem Alten verglichen habe."
"Und nun wollen Sie unseren Volke und seiner heiligen Religion den Rücken kehren?"
"O nein, wenn Jesus der verheißende Messias ist, dann ist auch der Glaube an ihn kein Abfall von der Religion Israels."
"Aber alle, die aus unserm Volke zu diesem Jesus gingen, wurden Meschummadim (Abtrünnige)."
"Ich werde nie ein Meschummad sein."
"Und die Thora Mosis, die warden Sie ja doch nicht halten!"
"Doch, im Neuen Testament steht ja, dass die älteste Gemeinde in Jerusalem dem Gesetze treue gewesen ist. Das werde ich auch tun."
"Das ist ein Unmöglichkeit. Als Christ können Sie nicht Jude bleiben!"
"Doch, das will ich!"
"So werden Sie zeitlebens ein unglücklicher Mensch sein: Bei den Christen werden Sie nichts gelten, weil Sie Jude sind, und bei den Juden nichts, weil Sie Christ sind."
"Das muss ich dann tragen!"

According to Wiegand, Lewy was a teacher in Breslau from 1883. It is not clear how this information fits the fact that Lucky then was in New York; see the chapter below.

239. Wiegand, "Chajim Jedidjah Lucky," 46.

was forced to emigrate. At this point Löwen's version of Lucky's conversion is more substantial as well as complex:

Lucky's first encounter with the New Testament was during his studies in Berlin, where he found a Greek-German version in the belongings of a friend. Somehow the brief excerpts he read fascinated him, and led him to visit a Sunday service at *Sophienkirche*.[240] After Berlin, Lucky (not yet converted to faith in Jesus) went back to Galicia and Bukowina to work as a tutor. In his spare time he gathered other students around him and introduced them to Max Stirner and theoretical anarchism. During his studies and the following years, he experienced getting sympathizers for his own ideas among pupils and friends. According to Löwen, Lucky had a heart for mysticism and he even started a study group for his pupils where he taught them esoteric subjects. He had a tendency to separate the pupils into different groups, something that annoyed many of them, and after a while most of them became tired of Lucky's regime.[241]

In Chernowitc some of his sympathizers vandalized and profaned one of the local synagogues and its Torah scrolls, causing great turmoil in the Jewish community. Although he was not involved, Lucky and one of his friends, Russbaum, were put under supervision, while the police arrested those who had committed the crime. Russbaum's grandfather belonged to the inner circle of the miracle-working rabbi in Sadagora, and his family was therefore able to help him immigrate to America. Lucky, however, found shelter in a small village before getting a new passport under the name Elik. In the period between the episode in Chernowitc and his emigration to the USA, Lucky frequently moved around from place to place. At the same time he stopped using his birth name and changed his name from time to time, using a number of aliases: Elik, Elk, Lucki (read "luzki"), and Lucky (read "lucky"). This mix of names was not always necessary, but Lucky always liked to play with his name, almost like a toy. He also liked to play with the names of his friends, particularly in Hebrew. According to Löwen it was during this period that Chaim Wolf Pollak changed his name to Lucky, but not yet "Christian Theophilus."[242]

---

240. Löwen, "Christian Theophilus Lucky," 6.

241. Ibid., 5.

242. According to Unbegaun, the Slavonic surname Lúckij, which derives from a local name, is in Ukrainian pronounced "Lúc'kyj." Unbegaun, *Russian Surnames*, 282.

The difficulties in Galicia and Bukowina led Lucky into much rethinking, spurring him to leave anarchistic, socialistic and pantheistic ideas, and again return to faith in God. He also wanted to migrate to America, but would have to travel through Germany, which could be difficult for a foreign Jew like him with his political history. In a letter from Russbaum he was also encouraged to emigrate. This gave Lucky the courage to try, and he went to Berlin again for the first time since his studies. Here he got shattering news: First, his previous girlfriend now had her own family. Second, he was informed that Russbaum had been baptized, which made Lucky uneasy on his own behalf. He visited the *Sophienkirche* in Berlin at least twice. Although the liturgy felt alien, the sermons about Jesus were comforting to him.

Löwen does not cite any event that is said to be the crucial moment in Lucky's conversion process, but from now on he appears to have felt spiritually connected to (at least some) Christian leaders. After some time in Berlin, Lucky traveled to Leipzig to see Delitzsch. Delitzsch had already in the 1870s become one of the most prominent leaders and scholars of the German Jewish missions, and he would probably soon be informed about the conversion of a former student at Hildesheimer's institution. According to Weidauer, Lucky had strong affection for Delitzsch and his Hebrew New Testament his whole life, something that is confirmed several times in *Edut leIsrael*.[243] The professor and Jewish mission leader very soon put Lucky in touch with Yechiel Lichtenstein, the Jewish-Christian teacher who was later to become a teacher at Delitzsch's *Institutum Judaicum* for Lutheran ministers.[244] Together

---

243. Weidauer, "Erindringer," 175; "Book review," *Edut leIsrael* 1, issue 3 (1888) 54–63; 63, and "The History of the Life of Franz Delitzsch," 95–97. *Sabbath Recorder* even claims that Lucky had been Delitzsch's student. Randolph, "Christian Theophilus Lucky," 207.

244. Jechiel (or Yechiel) Zevi Lichtenstein (1829–1912), born Herschensohn in Bessarabia. He was a rabbi in Jassy, where, in 1855, he baptized himself and some of the members of the Jewish congregation in a local river. He thereafter tried to establish a Jewish-Christian congregation in Skolian in Bessarbia. He married the sister of Joseph Rabinowitz, who became a believer in Jesus several years later. After his conversion, Herschensohn-Lichtenstein became interested in Hasidic theology and spirituality, and for a period he went to the Hasidic yeshiva in Liadi (Lithuania) in the 1860s. Consequently he developed a theology combining Jewish mysticism with Protestant Christianity. In 1868 he settled in Leipzig, where he soon became friends with Delitzsch and was employed by different mission societies. In 1886 he was employed as teacher at *Institutum Judaicum* in Leipzig. Here he wrote a commentary in Hebrew on several of the books of the New Testament. "Jechiel Zevi Lichtenstein," 122–27; and Kjær-Hansen, *Joseph Rabinowitz*, 35, 46.

with the time in Berlin, this visit seems to have been a decisive moment for Lucky's attitude to Christianity. Lucky was particularly inspired by Lichtenstein's views on Jewish Christianity. After a period of time, Delitzsch helped Lucky get to London and contact the Jewish missions there.

The outcome of the encounter between Lucky and some of the representatives of the Jewish missions in Britain would be typical of the future. The practices of the British mission provoked Lucky, and his attacks against these societies' methods and attitude to the Jewish tradition would follow him the rest of his life. Löwen claims that he was particularly involved in heated discussion with Jewish Christians like Moses Margoliuth (1818–1881), whom he accused of alienating himself from the Jewish nation.[245] Soon after, Lucky embarked on the three week long sea journey to New York.

In all of his writings, Lucky never seems to comment on the topic of baptism, except when he criticizes mission societies for being too liberal when it came to baptizing Jews, and he does not refer to his own baptism.[246] As described above, Wiegand claims he was baptized in Belgrade by local Baptists.[247] Löwen has no hard facts about when and where Lucky was baptized, but he assumes that it took place after Lucky arrived in the USA and became a member of the SDB.[248] Weidauer claims that Lucky was baptized, although he admitted he did not know the details, except that the event was not connected to any church. He assumed it had taken place in America, in living water, performed by a Christian with Jewish-Christian witnesses, and certainly not registered in any church protocol. The lack of information was not because Weidauer had not tried to find out. He recalls how, at one of Lucky's visits in Wygoda in 1900, some of

245. Margoliuth was a Jewish convert from Suwalki in Polish Galicia. He had lived in Britain since the 1830s and became an Anglican minister and scholar, as well as one of the founders of the Hebrew Christian Alliance. Between 1877 and 1881 he was the vicar of Buchinghamshire. He was author of *The Fundamental Principles of Modern Judaism Investigated* and several other books, and in the 1840s began publishing *The Star of Jacob*, a Hebrew Christian monthly magazine. Jacobs, "Moses Margoliuth"; Berg, "Keren," 39–41; and Pruter, *Jewish Christians*, 33.

246. As I cannot be sure if I have come across all the issues of *Edut*, it is difficult to know for certain whether this topic was ever commented upon in the Hebrew journal; but that this is never picked up by any of his German or American readers I find implausible.

247. Wiegand, "Chajim Jedidjah Lucky," 46.

248. Löwen, "Christian Theophilus Lucky," 14.

the local Jews observed Weidauer with Lucky. Since Lucky's appearance gave no doubt about his ethnic and religious background, Weidauer assumed that the local Jews would later ask him if his guest was baptized, and asked Lucky what he should tell them. Lucky's answer was: "As they understand it, no."[249] All in all Lucky tried hard to keep his friends in the dark when it came to this event. Gisle Johnson indicates a certain spiritualism in Lucky's attitude to baptism, describing the spiritual understanding of baptism by one of Lucky's followers.[250]

Although the lack of information about Lucky's baptism is striking, there is every reason to believe it took place. Lucky's later partners—orthodox Lutherans (like Delitzsch and later Landsmann and Pohlmann in New York) and Seventh Day Baptists—would argue fiercely against each other on many topics, but neither would normally give anyone the position Lucky had without some sort of proof of a theologically valid baptism. Even an opponent of Lucky's, Le Roi, does not question Lucky's baptism. These arguments I find relevant also to the question of whether Lucky went through baptism several times, as most Baptists as well as Lutherans would not accept repeated baptism.[251] However, if being baptized several times was not regarded very positively by his partners, that could also be a reason for holding back this information.

Although none of the sources gives a definite date or place for the baptism, it probably cannot have taken place until after he left the university. This is due to the situation the baptism would put him into in the Jewish community in Berlin, although Jewish conversion to more or less nominal Christianity was a common phenomenon in Berlin of the 1870s.[252] I also find it probable that Lucky was baptized before he left Europe, as he would have met even less understanding in both Britain and the USA if he could not relate to a personal baptism. In this context it is interesting that Lucky became friends with Yechiel Lichtenstein in Leipzig, who had baptized himself in his youth. When he first came to

249. Weidauer, "Erindringer," 209.

250. Terray, *Et liv i grenseland*, 121, 170.

251. Naturally, most Baptists would claim that infant baptisms are not valid. Still, if a person is baptized as an adult believer like Lucky, the baptism is usually not supposed to be repeated. However, for the Seventh Day Baptists this may have been different. It appears that Friedländer, the first editor of *The Peculiar People*, was expected to be baptized again in spite of being baptized as a believer in 1863. *Seventh Day Baptists in Europe and America*, 1338.

252. Endelmann, "The Social and Political Context," 83–107, 83–85.

faith in Christ in the 1850s, he and some friends had baptized themselves in a river in Romania. Later, under the influence of Delitzsch, he was convinced that this baptism was not biblical and decided to be publically and formally baptized in a church.[253]

Lucky must certainly have heard about this and been challenged on the topic himself by Delitzsch and Lichtenstein if he was not yet baptized. Further, he must have been baptized before Delitzsch would send him with his recommendation to Britain and the USA. It is therefore possible that Wiegand's information that Lucky was baptized in Belgrade is true, but from the sources it is impossible to tell if it took place before or after his visit in Leipzig. I assume, however, that he was baptized in Belgrade or somewhere in Germany before he met Delitzsch, as he had been on the move in secret for a long time before he set out for Germany again, and he would probably not go to Belgrade before he went to Britain.

Due to this obscurity it is also not completely clear when Pollak took his new names, and although he continued to use his Jewish name as an editor, among non-Jewish friends and contacts he became known as Christian Theophilus Lucky. However, Theophilus ("the one who loves God") is in Hebrew *Jedidiah*, so in this respect he probably wanted to deliberately stress the continuity between his Jewish background and his new Christian faith.

Wiegand's version is that after his conversion and discussion with Lewy, Lucky went back to Galicia and Bukowina, working as a tutor for some Jewish families. In contrast to Löwen, who says that Lucky still had not had a Christian breakthrough at this point, Wiegand says that Lucky used his spare time to share his Christian beliefs and inspire friends and colleagues to study Judaism and stay with their people. In particular he used the Jewish festivals to explain how the Hebrew Bible is completed and fulfilled in the New Testament. According to Wiegand, the story "Eine Pesach-ereignisse" was created during this period.[254] In this story the tutor, Eliakim (who he claims is identical with Lucky), not only convinces his Jewish host family that Jesus is the Messiah, but also strengthens their Jewish identity. *The Peculiar People* printed an English version of this narrative.[255]

253. Skarsaune, *Israels venner*, 176–77.

254. Wiegand, "Chajim Jedidjah Lucky," 50. See also idem, "Passah-Ereignisse," 165–86; and idem, [K.I.M.], "The Story of Passover," 126–40.

255. The narrative describes "Mr. E.," a tutor for a secular Jewish family, who pos-

Lucky in New York and at Union Theological Seminary

In the 1880s, Lucky spent most of his time in the USA, where he not only got his education in Christian theology but also established an important personal network. This was particularly the case with his relationship to the Seventh Day Baptists in New York, as this church helped him to establish and run the two periodicals *Edut leIsrael* and *The Peculiar People*. The sources differ on whether Lucky arrived in New York in 1882 or 1880.[256] If Löwen's information about Lucky's stay in Britain before he went to America is correct, Lucky had at least one meeting with Moses Margoliuth there. His departure from Britain must have taken place before Margoliuth's death on February 25, 1881, probably in 1879 or 1880.[257] Arriving in New York in the early 1880s, Lucky was part of the wave of Jewish immigrants from Eastern Europe to America. As a young male Jewish immigrant in New York (in 1880 Lucky was 25–26 years old), he fit perfectly with the rest of the Jewish newcomers, as the vast majority of them were young men. Before he began at Union Theological Seminary (UTS), Lucky made his living working in a cigarette factory and as a day laborer.[258]

Soon after his arrival in New York, Lucky came in touch with people who would become important friends and contacts for him later. Following Delitzsch's advice, he moved in with the Jewish-Christian missionary Daniel Landsmann (d. May 13, 1896), who was working for the Lutheran Church—Missouri Synod.[259] Landsmann was born in Belarus and had written a couple of articles for *Saat auf Hoffnung*. He and his German wife were happy to meet Lucky, but the relationship

---

sibly resembles Lucky himself. Through his lessons he is able to make the household more conscious of being Jewish and of Jewish traditions, and at the Passover meal he reveals himself and his faith in Jesus. Ten years later he meets the family in Vienna, and discovers that the wife and her Jewish husband have become Christians. The narrative stresses that Israel is the olive branch which the Gentiles have been grafted into. Without saying it explicitly, the narrative thus is also an attack on traditional Christian supersessionism. Daland claims that the story is true, and that most of the characters were still alive; Anonymous, "A Translated Extract," 30–53.

256. *Seventh Day Baptists in Europe and America*, 1382; Wiegand, "Chajim Jedidjah Lucky," 49; and Kjær-Hansen, "Petra Volf's Reminiscences," 100.

257. Andersen, *Israelsmissionen*, 70; and Kjær-Hansen, "On Lucky's Where-abouts," 17–21, 18.

258. Wiegand, "Chajim Jedidjah Lucky," 50.

259. Randolph, "Christian Theophilus Lucky," 206–8.

between Landsmann and Lucky was never easy. In fact, their discussions about the national identity of Jewish Christians as well as about Luther could become so heated that Landsmann's wife had to get between Lucky and her husband several times. Still, they continued to be friends, and Lucky would later recommend Landsmann's books in *Edut leIsrael*.[260] According to Löwen, Lucky always visited or stayed with him and his wife when he later visited New York.[261]

After some time in New York, Lucky also became friends with Pastor H. Pohlmann of the Lutheran Independent Church, who in 1882 began having services for German emigrants and Jews, and Pohlmann let him preach in his church.[262]

In the fall of 1882, Lucky began a three-year course in Christian theology at UTS, which at the time was one of the two most important Presbyterian institutions in the country, together with Princeton. However, both before and after the formalization of the denominational relations between UTS and the Presbyterian Church, the institution operated quite independently and was open to students of other denominations. The relaxed practice of accepting students had, however, one limit: until 1906, every student had to be a member of a Christian church.[263] As Lucky did not become a member of the SDB until 1885, he must have belonged to another denomination when he began his studies in 1882, probably Pohlmann's congregation. According to *Sabbath Recorder*, the UTS at first was reluctant to admit Lucky to the seminary, due to recent thefts by some Jewish students. He was therefore accepted on probation.[264]

---

260. Löwen, "Christian Theophilus Lucky," 12; "Book reviews," *Edut leIsrael* 1, issue 2 (1888) 42, and "Book review," in *Edut leIsrael* 1 (issue 3, 1888) 62; Le Roi, "Daniel Landsmann," 52–56.

261. For example in the autumn of 1909, to renew his American citizenship. See Philips, "Ch. Theophilus Lucky," 690.

262. Pohlmann's congregation did not belong to any of the Lutheran synods, and was located in the church building at 87 Attorney Street, which belonged to the Methodists under the name Wesley Chapel. As Pohlmann was allowed to use it for Lutheran services when possible, it was also called "Evangelische-Lutherische Bethanien Kirche." He lived as a widower next door to the church, without any regular salary. Löwen, "Christian Theophilus Lucky," 12. also Andersen, *Israelsmissionen*, 70–75.

263. Handy, *A History*, 112.

264. Randolph, "Christian Theophilus Lucky," 208.

The curriculum for the three years at UTS was largely a prescribed one, and included studies in Greek and Hebrew. Once a week voluntary classes were held in different oriental languages like Arabic, Assyrian, biblical Aramaic, Chaldean, and Syrian, and later Lucky's friends would describe him as exceptionally skilled in several of these languages.[265] Most students maintained their work for their churches and missions. Participation in prayer was mandatory and monitored. Although the majority of the students were Presbyterians and Congregationalists, Lucky probably met representatives from most Protestant denominations there.

During Lucky's years at UTS, the institution was troubled by increased theological tensions, resulting in a heresy trial against Professor C. A. Briggs in 1891–1893 for his use of historical critical methods. At the time Lucky was at UTS, Briggs represented the seminary in the joint periodical with Princeton. As Princeton at that time represented a much more traditional view of the methods used for biblical and theological research than did Briggs, much attention was given to the question of biblical interpretation. On the latter topic, the issues revealed marked differences between the two Presbyterian institutions, as Briggs rejected the dogma of verbal inspiration and the theory of original biblical autographs. In 1888, the periodical came to an end due to problems in cooperation.[266]

The controversy around Briggs was, of course, noticed among the students, but as far as I know it was never mentioned explicitly by either Lucky himself or his friends from the seminary. However, *The Peculiar People* as well as *Edut* would later express skepticism toward modern ideas concerning Old Testament theology, and never seem to have identified with modern theology in that sense.[267] In fact, during the 1870s Lucky had already been deeply involved in the modern debate about the possibility of divine revelation and its consequences for the Torah.[268]

---

265. Philips, "Ch. Theophilus Lucky," 690; Velthuysen, "Christian Theophilus Lucky," 196–97, 208.

266. Handy, *A History*, 58.

267. "The Feast of Tabernacles," 66–67; and "The Sabbath Day," 1–15. (Note the new name of the periodical in 1897–1898, the chapter about the periodical below.) In the last article Lucky clearly reads the Bible literally, e.g., dating the creation to 2500 years before Moses.

268. Wiegand, "Chajim Jedidjah Lucky," 44.

Lucky—A Missionary and a Seventh Day Baptist?

Lucky's relationship to the SDB relates to two of the most obscure parts in his biography, namely his baptism and church membership. Did he belong to a Lutheran church or an SDB church, and did he ever work as a missionary?

On May 1, 1885, Lucky had his final exam and obtained a graduate diploma, which was the standard qualification from UTS. A couple of months later, on August 16, he was ordained by Pohlmann in the Independent Evangelical Lutheran Church in New York City. He was then thirty years old.[269] However, Lucky did not work as a pastor. According to Löwen and Wiegand, Lucky only wanted this title to get American citizenship, which was very important to him.[270] Löwen claims that Lucky had no intention at all of working for either the church or the mission societies.[271] However, this contradicts others, like Le Roi, R. Andersen, and SDB sources. According to Le Roi, Lucky became a member of the SDB and worked as a missionary for them to the Jews in Strychance, Austria, from 1885 to 1886, and to the Jews in New York City from 1886 to 1889. Le Roi claims he went to Galicia after being ordained by Pohlmann.[272] Kai Kjær-Hansen also describes Lucky as a missionary between 1885 and 1886.[273] *Edut* also refers to a visit in Romania, which possibly is the same event.[274] However, it is puzzling that according to the SDB articles as well as Le Roi, Lucky had become a member of the

---

269. Randolph, "Christian Theophilus Lucky," 206–8; and Le Roi, *Geschichte*, 2:388.

270. Löwen, "Christian Theophilus Lucky," 15; Wiegand, "Chajim Jedidjah Lucky," 53.

271. Löwen, "Christian Theophilus Lucky," 15.

272. Le Roi, *Geschichte*, 2:388.

273. *Seventh Day Baptists in Europe and America*, 381.

274. "Letters from Romania," 146–52. During this stay in Romania, Pohlmann claims that Lucky, despite severe difficulties, was able to convert several Jews, of which two are named: Dr. Russbaum and Dr. Joseph Paulus Becker Taubes. While Taubes, described as twenty-seven and a former rabbi in Chernowitz, is reported as having immigrated to New York and later being associated to the Methodist church, Pohlmann says nothing more about Russbaum. His name, as well as his connection to Romania and Chernowitz, is striking when compared to Löwen's story about Lucky's friend of the same name in Romania. Nevertheless, although Löwen's and Pohlmann's narratives indicate that a person named Russbaum was involved in Lucky's life this period, content and chronology seems to be confused. Andersen, *Israelsmissionen*, 70–75.

SDB shortly before he was ordained in the Lutheran congregation, and none of the sources seem to be bothered by it!

Lucky's relationship with the SDB was established during his studies at UTS. At the seminary, Lucky became acquainted with some Seventh Day Baptist students who would later become significant leaders of their church, such as Rev. Ira Lee Cottrell, Rev. Earl Saunders, and later professor and church president William C. Daland. Daland was a Baptist who joined the SDB during his studies at UTS, and would later be Lucky's editorial partner for years to come. On October 1, 1886, after returning to New York from Europe, Lucky began his work in New York under the Seventh Day Baptist Missionary Society, a ministry that lasted until 1889.[275] Lucky's fascination with this little church is not difficult to understand. He was used to Jewish Christians who celebrated Sundays, and he probably felt relieved to come across Gentiles who celebrated the Sabbath. He attended SDB services in New York, and having sought membership for some time was admitted to the church on February 14, 1885.[276]

According to Löwen, Lucky must have been baptized in front of witnesses from the SDB before he could be ordained in their church.[277] Löwen seems to think that the SDB congregations would regard Lucky's previous baptism, whether it was in a Lutheran context or not, as alien and invalid. This, however, does not have to be the case. Within the traditional Baptist decentralized church structure, these decisions would usually be a matter for the local congregations, and it is therefore difficult to verify or falsify Löwen's statement.

However, the picture of Lucky's relation to the SDB and the Lutheran church raises some problems. According to the 1917 *SDB Yearbook*, Lucky was both admitted as an SDB member in February and then ordained as a Lutheran minister in August 1885. Apparently the *Yearbook* editor did not see any difficulties in this paradox. In fact, Lucky's respect in some Lutheran and German Jewish mission circles (Delitzsch, Landsmann and Pohlmann) helped him to be accepted

---

275. "Christian Theophilus Lucky," *Seventh Day Baptist Yearbook* (1917), 22–23.
276. Ibid.
277. Löwen, "Christian Theophilus Lucky," 14–15. He claims that Lucky also was ordained by the SDB church, and is probably thinking about his position in the SDB Missionary Society.

within the SDB.²⁷⁸ Lucky read and spoke several Slavic languages, as well as French, German, English, and later Dutch (in addition to Latin and the biblical and oriental languages studied at UTS), which must have been a tempting opportunity for the missions.²⁷⁹ It is also possible that the church found Lucky's network among the Lutherans useful for its contacts with other Protestant churches. For the leadership of the SDB, Lucky must have been a very interesting character in very interesting times, due to the massive Jewish immigration that was then taking place. At the beginning of the 1880s the Baptists regarded the Jewish mass immigration as an event led by God, and they expected large numbers of Jews to convert when they finally escaped the spiritual and political prisons of Europe.²⁸⁰ When meeting someone like Lucky, it would probably be very tempting to interpret this as part of the same divine providence, as mission to the Jews was a rather new and interesting phenomenon among Baptists as well as many other Protestant communities.

Protestant mission was a new experience for most of the Jewish immigrants as well. Most of them were from Eastern Europe, and were used to Christian churches being more or less hostile to the Jews, and many of them were raised to say *Shaketz teshaktzeno* ("You shall despise it!") when passing by a church. Some of the means the newly founded missions used to reach the Jewish community, basically poor working-class immigrants from the 1880s to WWI, was to offer them medical, educational and relief services. Most of this activity was sponsored directly or indirectly by Protestant church bodies, although some of the missions severed their connection with the denominations when they were well established on their own, as was the case with Arno Gaebelein's New York–based *Hope of Israel*'s relationship with the Methodist church.²⁸¹ In 1902, Luis Meyer of the Chicago Mission estimated that 4,033 Jews had joined a Protestant church. In addition, some thousands had joined non-Protestants churches like the Roman Catholic and Unitarian churches. In spite of the small number of converts, considering that there were less

---

278. Ibid., 11; and Randolph, "Christian Theophilus Lucky," 206–7.

279. According to Lillie Zöckler, Lucky spoke thirteen languages (Zöckler, *Gott Hört Gebet*, 13). also Kjær-Hansen, "Petra Volf's Reminiscences about Lucky," 37, note 36.

280. Davis, *Immigrants*, 43.

281. Ariel, *Evangelizing*, 23–27.

than 2 million Jews in the country, the results were substantial compared to the percentage of converts from other Protestant mission fields.[282]

Many of the missions used Jewish converts as missionaries. Between 1900 and 1910 about 120 converts served as ministers, and around WWI about 200 served as evangelists to the Jews.[283] Generally these Jewish missionaries were regarded as traitors twice over in the Jewish community. The resentment was just as strong in America as in Europe, even from secular Jews, who usually did not regard conversion to Christianity from a religious but from a social perspective.[284] However, prejudice and suspicion towards Jewish converts were widespread among Christians as well, and some Jewish missionaries were involved in scandals related to fraud and financial manipulation. *The Peculiar People* often attacked the work of one of them, Hermann Warsawiak.[285]

Lucky appears to have experienced the same distrust against baptized Jews in many circles. There are certain hints that parts of the SDB had problems trusting Lucky in the beginning, reportedly due to bad experiences with former Jewish baptism candidates/Jewish believers.[286] The need to confirm Lucky's integrity seems sometimes to have been an issue, as *Sabbath Recorder* underlines both his reputation among the German Lutherans as well as the church's own process before he was accepted as an SDB member in 1885.[287] However, his membership did not remove all doubt about his sincerity. According to Courtiss I. Randolph in his obituary in *Sabbath Recorder* in August 1917, the SDB leadership suspected Lucky of trying to make "business" when arguing for a free position as a missionary while still receiving financial support.[288] The

282. Ibid., 22, 39.

283. Ibid., 33.

284. Ibid., 60, 67.

285. "Editorial Notes," 112, and "At Least be Corteous," 94–96 (incomplete pagination in my copy), 95.

286. Randolph, "Christian Theophilus Lucky," 208.

287. See, e.g., "Brother Lucky's Work," 409. Here the journal presents excerpts of letters about Lucky from several German mission leaders.

288. The obituary quotes an observation by one Dr. Main: "Almost, if not quite, the saddest chapter relates to the fact that our people could not understand him. Most of our leaders and people misunderstood him in two particular ways: 1. Jews are full of prejudice against a Christian Jew who receives a salary from Gentiles. Naturally our board wished to pay him a definite salary and receive from him the regular, formal, detailed reports. *He* wished us to give him a modest honorarium, quarterly or annually, and allow him to make, not 'official,' but informal and general reports concerning his

reason for this is probably to be found in the average attitude towards Jews in general and particularly baptized Jews. The fact that many Jews who were baptized seemed not to fulfill general expectations about their resulting of life was probably a painful disappointment in many mission circles, and some seem to have been eager to present Lucky as an exception to the rule.[289]

Lucky apparently did not only belong to two different denominations, but was ordained in at least one of them as well. One does not have to be a traditionalist with an interest in details of church doctrine to find this confusing. First of all, theological topics like baptism and observance of the Sabbath or Sunday would most probably make any combination like Lucky's case impossible, especially in light of the generally polemic atmosphere against most traditional churches one finds in the SDB's publications from the period.[290] What makes it even stranger is that nowhere can there be found any discussion of Lucky's peculiar denominational position. Naturally, SDB and Lutheran sources tend to emphasize their own connection with Lucky, but usually his connection to the other community is also referred to. In the SDB sources, Lucky's and *Edut leIsrael*'s connection to Delitzsch seems in fact to have been highly valued. Even for Le Roi, one of Lucky's strongest critics when discussing mission strategy, his position in SDB is not regarded as a problem, at least not explicitly.[291]

In other words, Lucky's status in regard to his church membership—whether in the Lutheran church, where he gained his ordination

---

fields and labors. *Of course* that was not 'business'! In my judgment his efficiency and joy would have been quadrupled could the board have had some of his idealism. 2. He greatly desired to follow the method of St. Paul, not the methods of a modern board working among the Jews. The modern method is to take converts into the church whose missionaries have been the means of the conversion, Baptist, Episcopalian, Methodist, Presbyterian, etc. Paul's method was simply to urge Jews to accept Jesus as the Savior and Lord, and then allow them to observe honored customs, if they so desired, and would not observe them as essential for salvation, or press them upon others. Here, too, our board and people failed to rise to his level, which was both scriptural and rational" (Randolph, "Christian Theophilus Lucky," 207–8).

289. Ariel, *Evangelizing*, 27.

290. The same denominational attitude can be found in some orthodox Lutheran writings as well, for instance in the Missouri Synod or among Norwegian immigrants in the USA.

291. According to Le Roi, H. Friedländer (= Friedlander) and Lucky had done much harm to Christian mission work among the Jews (Le Roi, *Geschichte*, 2:190–93, 389).

and thereby an American passport, or in the SDB, which seems to have supported him the rest of his life—remains obscure. One must wonder whether this obscurity is what Lucky wanted.

Edut leIsrael *and The Peculiar People*

Already before he finished his studies at UTS, Lucky and Daland established a society for a future journal in Hebrew, the Hebrew Publishing Society.[292] In 1887, Lucky had convinced the leadership of the Tract Society of the Seventh Day Baptist Church to establish *two* periodicals: one in English aimed at Christian readers who needed to become aware of the mistakes of Christian mission work among the Jewish people, and one in Hebrew aimed at Jewish readers to establish a stronghold for Jewish Christianity. Both papers were established in the little town of Alfred Centre, NY, and the first issues of *Edut leIsrael* were published starting in September 1888.[293] The English paper was started in April 1888, under the name *The Peculiar People*.[294] While Lucky was editor of *Edut leIsrael*, *The Peculiar People* was edited by the Jewish Christian Zevi Hermann Friedlander in cooperation with Joseph Landow.[295] However,

---

292. Andersen, *Israelsmissionen*, 71.

293. *Seventh Day Baptists in Europe and America*, 1338. Alfred is today a village located in the town of Alfred in Allegany County in the state of New York. At that time it was called Alfred Centre (http://en.wikipedia.org/wiki/Alfred_(village),_New_York). It seems that the congregation in the village was one of significance for a long time, with several educational institutions belonging to the church. In its last years *The Peculiar People* was seated in Plainfield, New Jersey, e.g., *The Peculiar People* 9/1 (1896) 1 (front page).

294. Ibid.

295. H. Friedlander (1830–1888) was born to a Jewish family in Schneidemuehl, and was baptized in 1852. In 1863, he became a missionary for the London Jews Society. He worked for several years in Jerusalem, and founded the Artuf Colony between Jerusalem and Jaffa. On July 6, 1886, he was compelled to resign from the London Jews Society, and thereafter he had problems supporting himself and his family. Friedlander had commenced keeping the Sabbath and was looking forward to baptism (Le Roi, *Geschichte*, 2:190–93; Anonymous, "A Great Need," 67–69; 68; and *Seventh Day Baptists in Europe and America*, 386, 1338). Joseph Landow was born in 1859 in Galicia, a descendent of Rabbi Ezekiel Landow in Prague, and grew up within strictly orthodox Hasidism. In 1886, he met a Jewish Christian in Czernowitz, Bukovina, who preached the gospel to him. He went to the USA to assist with *Edut leIsrael*, and was ordained to ministry in SDB in April 1888. Landow was *Edut*'s typesetter in Alfred, where he appears to have suffered from some kind of illness. He was still weak after being ill when he went to Galicia, "To the dear readers in the camp of the Hebrews, the Edut says," in

it is clear from the beginning that *The Peculiar People* strongly identified itself with *Edut leIsrael* and its editor.

From the beginning of 1888 to November, Friedlander edited *The Peculiar People* weekly.[296] *The Peculiar People* was accused by Christian readers of not supporting the Christian mission, and not even having its own mission work. To this Friedlander's answer was that he did not want to talk about their own mission work, as they did not meet those "model foes who succumb to the power of our persuasion. Our stories have all no symmetrical endings—they break off at the wrong point." *The Peculiar People* instead wanted the Christian press to report on the mission's failures as well as its victories.[297] How exactly *The Peculiar People* was financed is not very clear. From its own columns, it is clear that due to the lack of subscribers the periodical suffered from a lack of money.[298] This was apparently the case for *Edut leIsrael* as well.[299]

Edut leIsrael represented a very foreign system of thought even in mission circles, which did not give it much financial support. The language and attitude in the journal were much more concerned with living in the midst of the Jewish people than traditional missionary tracts in Hebrew. However, it was clear from the beginning that the journal would not be greeted with enthusiasm by the Jewish public. Due to the resentment, *Edut* compares the journal's situation with being lovesick.[300] *Edut leIsrael* was supposed to strengthen Jewish values in light of Jesus, and

---

Edut leIsrael 1/7 (1888) 120. About Landow's work in Europe, it is mentioned that he gave 20 addresses, no baptisms, but had several adherents ("A Brief Notice of a Brief Life," 61–63, 61; and *Seventh Day Baptists in Europe and America*, 384).

296. From July 13 to November 16, sixteen issues were published. See Anonymous, "A Great Need," 67–69; 67.

297. "Editorial Notes," 110–12; 112. The "success language" *The Peculiar People* refered to, is also commented on by Kovács in his study of the Scottish Mission. Kovács, *The History*, 365.

298. "Editorial Notes," 71.

299. Ibid. In the mid-eighties, Lucky and the Tract Society had been promised an inheritance from the Seventh Day Baptists Mr. Delos C. Burdick and Mrs. Hanna Burdick. This, however, never happened, as it was prevented by a court decision; Randolph, "Christian Theophilus Lucky," 207. As late as 1911, Lucky still thought it would be possible to get this money. He then was trying to establish another periodical in cooperation with Philip Cohen in Johannesburg: *The Messianic Jew*. See Anonymous, "The Work of Brother Ch. Th. Lucky," 267. In 1888 *Edut leIsrael* published a brief obituary about Burdick, see "Memorial Stone in the Book," 85.

300. "To the Dear Readers in the Camp of the Hebrews, the Edut Says," 65–67, 65–66; and "Word to the Reader," 1–8, 7.

to work for peace among Jews—understood as between Jesus-believing Jews and non-believing Jews. In spite of its focus on the New Testament and Jesus, when Lucky in the first issue states the editorial purpose of the journal, it is the spiritual and nationalistic goals that are mentioned. Here there is no mention of Christianity, the New Testament or Christology at all. Still, it was characteristic for *Edut* and Lucky to combine Jewish and Christian writings.[301] According to Wiegand, Lucky always insisted on rewriting all New Testament names and words in Hebrew using what he assumed were the original words, like Paul being changed into "Sha'ul ha-kodesh," and likewise Peter into "Schimon Kefa."[302] Culturally, the journal had a conservative profile, not focusing much on socio-economic issues.[303] When commenting on the major challenges for contemporary Jews in the USA or Galicia, the journal mainly focused on what it found to be national, spiritual and cultural disintegration, not poverty in itself. Lack of assistance to impoverished Jewish newcomers is primarily regarded as a national problem and a national betrayal. In particular, the journal criticizes Marxism, which is said to be a destructive force for the collective consciousness of the Jewish people.[304]

---

301. "This Is the Task Set Before 'The Witness,'" 6; and "Thoughts from HaEdut," in *Edut leIsrael* 2/1 (the volume is not given but from the year I assume it is the second, Sivan 1890), 5.

302. Wiegand, "Chajim Jedidjah Lucky," 54. Usually the term would be transcribed "ha-kadosh."

303. Lucky wanted the journal to be associated with other contemporary Hebrew journals like *Hamaggid, Hamelitz, Hazephira* and *Chabatzeleth*, see *The Peculiar People* 9 (1897) 237–40, 239.

304. "Thoughts from the 'Edut,'" in *Edut leIsrael* 1/2 (1888) 25–29; 27, 28–29. By 1920, about 23 percent of the Jews in the world lived in America, transforming the image of Jews in the USA. By 1910, 90 percent of American synagogues called themselves Orthodox. The American Jews from Germany were not very enthusiastic about this massive immigration, as the newcomers were much less willing to be culturally integrated into American society. While the new immigrants were poor, Yiddish-speaking and observers of traditional Judaism (after a while many turned to Conservative Judaism), the German Jews were Reform and middle-class citizens and now feared for their social status because of the massive immigration of traditional Jews. The affiliation to traditional Judaism does not necessarily mean that the new immigrants were more observant than the established Jews were, but is probably partly due to the need for regional ties and social familiarity. In addition, the Orthodox did not constitute a homogenous group but were separated into different organizations. Although some temporary relief programs were initiated from the beginning, they were not able to provide the immigrants with sufficient help. Rom, "The American," 3, 31–32, 44–46, 79.

At the beginning of 1889, the journals met serious problems: Both Friedlander and Landow had died. These events led to an abrupt halt in the publication of both journals. On June 29, 1889, Lucky returned to Eastern Europe and Galicia.[305] After Lucky's return to Europe, he managed to re-establish *Edut leIsrael* in Lemberg/Lvov. In New York, the Tract Society assumed the publication of *The Peculiar People* as a monthly journal from April 1889, with Daland as editor. He served in that position until 1898, when lack of funds caused the journal's closure. In 1894, Rev. S. S. Powell and Prof. W. C. Withford were added to the editorial staff.[306]

Why did Lucky leave everything that had been built in Alfred, only to do it all over again in Europe? As with his arrival in America, the reasons for Lucky's return to Europe are complex. According to *The Peculiar People*, Lucky stopped his work due to bad health, while *Sabbath Recorder* claims Lucky was eager to discuss mission strategy with certain mission societies, which he apparently was able to do in Leipzig.[307] However, Wiegand claims his return was due to Lucky's enthusiasm, caused by the work and writings of Joseph Rabinowitz and Isaac Lichtenstein, and in particular an invitation from Wilhelm Faber in Leipzig.[308] The return may also have been an attempt to save *Edut* after the death of Landow, whose function was apparently not to do traditional missionary work, but first of all to make *Edut leIsrael* known in the Jewish communities in Eastern Europe.

Another possible explanation for Lucky's return to Europe can be found in the narrative by Löwen, who says that at the time *Edut leIsrael* was established, a small group of young Jesus-believing Jewish men settled in Alfred Centre. Löwen does not say what they were supposed to

---

305. William C. Daland, "Brother Lucky's Travels," 652. The same year Lucky's pamphlet *Passover Events* was published by the Seventh Day Baptists, *Seventh Day Baptists in Europe and America*, 1339.

306. *Seventh Day Baptists in Europe and America*, 1338. Daland worked as pastor in New York, Rhode Island and London. Prof. W. C. Withford was professor of biblical languages and literature at Alfred Theological Seminary from 1893. See ibid., 1338, 1373, 1398.

307. "Book Review," *The Peculiar People*, 3 (1891) 156–60; 157, and excerpts from letters from Franz Delitzsch, William [= Wilhelm] Faber, and Johannes Müller in "Brother Lucky's Work," 409. Nevertheless, according to Skarsaune, it appears that the mission leaders in Leipzig had begun their reorientation already in 1888 (Skarsaune, *Israels venner*, 184–86).

308. Wiegand, "Chajim Jedidjah Lucky," 53.

do, but probably they were sympathizers who wanted to stay with Lucky. Lucky was registered as a missionary at the time, and gathering a group like this could be counted as part of his work.[309] The plans for them apparently changed after a while, as the whole group left Alfred, and three of them, named Reuter, Karmen, and Japhe, returned to Galicia.[310] According to Löwen, Lucky actually sent them back so "Sie sollen nichts ganz vergojischen"—in other words, to avoid their being assimilated into their non-Jewish surroundings.[311] Reuter, who was from Lucky's hometown Tysmenica, later met Löwen in Berlin. Reuter was complaining that Lucky forced him and the others to stay in the synagogue and the Jewish community, which, according to Löwen, Reuter feared would lead him away from the Christian faith.[312] Lucky seems to have feared the cultural effect of the assimilation process on Jewish Christians in America, a fear that he probably shared with Joseph Rabinowitz, who after his visit to the USA around the same time strongly warned Jews against immigration to America.[313] Philip Roth's comment on the American experience of assimilation expresses what some feared and other hailed: "Immigrants flowed into America, and America flowed into them."[314] About 1900, the concern about Jewish acculturation to Anglo-Saxon American society and the loss of Jewish identification was intense in some immigrant communities in New York, which only deepened the distance to the majority of Jewish immigrants who valued this

309. Most Jewish converts were male immigrants; according to Ariel this was due to the different social positions of men and women. There was a widespread feeling of freedom among the male Jewish immigrants, while Jewish women generally held on to Jewish practices (Ariel, *Evangelizing*, 45, 298–99).

310. Löwen only mentions these three names, without identifying them in any more detail.

311. Löwen, "Christian Theophilus Lucky," 16: "They were not to be totally gentilized." This fear was probably related to intermarriage. According to Ariel, many of the Jewish male immigrants married non-Jewish women and settled in non-Jewish areas. See Ariel, *Evangelizing*, 45.

312. "Reuter weinte in Berlin vor mir wie ein Kind" ("In Berlin, Reuter was crying like a child in front of me"). So Löwen, "Christian Theophilus Lucky," 16. Löwen obviously felt this story was a parallel to the personal relationship between himself and Lucky, where Löwen felt Lucky overruled his (Jewish Christian) sympathizers and their views.

313. Kjær-Hansen, *Joseph Rabinowitz*, 176.

314. Eyerman, "Formation," 110.

process.³¹⁵ It is therefore possible that Lucky believed that if *Edut leIsrael* were to be able to go on and reach Jews in Eastern Europe, he and the journal would need a traditional Jewish context to achieve its purpose, and therefore sought to place it in Eastern Europe.

Due to many complications, e.g., Friedlander's and Landow's deaths, Lucky's return to Europe and the tense fellowship with Löwen later on, the publications became irregular. In Stanislau, M. Löwen, who worked for the *Berliner Missiongeschellscaft*, became Lucky's co-editor. From 1892 *Edut leIsrael* was published in Berlin until it was halted at the end of the year.³¹⁶

Both Wiegand and Zöckler inform us that many of the names of the writers of articles were fabricated, such as Eljakim, Ha-mazliach, Ben-Israel, Isach Jehudi, etc. All of them were Lucky's pseudonyms.³¹⁷ According to Wiegand, Lucky seems to have thought of these names as prototypes of a future congregation of Jewish-Christian believers. From Löwen we know that Lucky used to play with names in general, be it his own or others', and his use of pseudonyms may reflect this behavior.

In addition, it should be considered whether Lucky's use of pseudonyms and anonymity were somehow part of his agenda or way of working in general. There have always been different motives and reasons for anonymity and the use of pseudonymous publications. However, the phenomenon became much less common in the 20th century; the decline of the use of anonymity began in the late 19th century, although anonymous publication was still widespread at that time.³¹⁸ Anonymity has often attached to playfulness or even mischief, like the use of fake

---

315. Gurock, "Jewish Communal," 260. Both Yiddish and English-speaking Jewish papers in New York promoted Americanization and encouraged the newcomers to adopt the customs and language of their new homeland. Rom, *The American*, 42–43.

316. Zöckler, "Judentum und Christentum," (1892) 205. Lucky did not accept this situation, and tried several times later to restart the journal. The restart in 1897 was the fourth attempt. Anonymous, "Zwei neue jüdische Zeitschriften," 163–68.

317. This does not mean that all of the material in the journal came from Lucky. Löwen himself says that he wrote articles for *Edut* while it was still headquartered in New York, and even more so in Lemberg. However, as Lucky was the heart of the project, the deal was that he had to produce most of the texts himself.

318. Griffin, *The Faces*, 8, 14. Traditional reasons for anonymity are shame, fear of consequences and diffidence, or authors could chose anonymity if they felt their authorial persona conflicted with their daily one. These reasons do not seem very relevant in Lucky's case.

personae.[319] This was also used by famous authors like Mark Twain and the earlier Jonathan Swift, who, according to Mullan, "liked to make trouble, and anonymity helped him to do so."[320]

Although some of Lucky's opponents in the Jewish mission would feel that the comment about Swift was accurate about him as well, it is more likely that his use of literary anonymity and pseudonyms was related to his habit of playing with names in general, rather than creating mischief or misleading his readers. Lucky's German friends were familiar with this practice. According to Wiegand, the uniform style of the journal would make this obvious to anyone who was able to read Hebrew, and therefore his intention could not have been to mislead. Wiegand's own explanation, that Lucky's fabricated personae were meant to represent the future Jewish-Christian church, therefore seems to be relevant.

The Return to Europe and Galicia

On July 22, 1889, Lucky arrived in Leipzig and met Delitzsch and his coworkers Wilhelm Faber and Johannes Muller, the secretary of the *Zentralverein*. The friendly relationship between the leaders of the *Zentralverein* and Lucky would prove to be significant for both parties in the following years. Among the leaders as well as the students at the *Institutum Judaicum*, Lucky made friends who would become some of his closest sympathizers as well as coworkers in Galicia. For the *Zentralverein* the contact with Lucky influenced work on its new mission strategy. At this point Delitzsch's health was declining, and Gustav Dalman, Faber and Muller were more and more taking over responsibility for the *Zentralverein* and the institute. Lucky and the German ministers used the opportunity to discuss the work they wanted him to do: Establish Jewish-Christian congregations in Eastern Europe. According to Löwen, Faber and Müller were enthusiastic about Lucky and his ideas.[321] For Gustav Dalman, the attitude to Lucky would soon become more tense.[322]

319. Mullan, *Anonymity*, 6 and 294.

320. Ibid., 14. Today disguise, according to John Mullan, has rather become mock disguise, used to advertise the adaptability of the author rather than conceal his identity.

321. Löwen, "Christian Theophilus Lucky," 17.

322. At the start of *Edut* and *The Peculiar People* in 1888 and 1889, Dalmann expressed sympathy with Lucky and Friedmann's journals. However, after Lucky's return to Eastern Europe, Dalman raised strong protests against the new Leipzig program,

The next summer the general conference of the *Zentralverein* decided on its new strategy: Its workers should stay away from working as traveling evangelists and establishing homes for proselytes. Instead, they should seek to create Jewish-Christian fellowships that were part of the Jewish environment around them, and not let new Jewish believers in Christ be alienated from the Jewish nation. The missionaries should therefore concentrate on building attractive Christian evangelical congregations for the Germans living in the Eastern European heartland of Orthodox Christianity and Greek Catholicism. Then Jewish individuals would come by themselves to observe these fellowships, and eventually establish their own congregations for fellow Jews with help from the evangelical pastors. This was how Rudolf Faltin had been doing his work in Kishinev since the late 1850s, but now the missionaries should encourage new believers to stay within the Jewish community as much as possible.

According to, e.g., Le Roi and the *Sabbath Recorder*, all of this was due to Lucky's influence.[323] However, as Skarsaune points out, in 1889 the Leipzig institute had been working with these ideas for some time already. In fact, a Leipzig candidate had been stationed in Chernowitz since 1888 to try out this concept.[324] Although the leaders of the *Zentralverein* since 1888 were likely well informed about *Edut leIsrael*'s and *The Peculiar People*'s existence and views, the influence from Lucky and his American friends was probably limited in the beginning. Nevertheless, the impression that Lucky's views were significant for the strategic reorientation in Leipzig is probably not unfounded. Lucky's reappearance on the European scene would at the very least be felt as a confirmation of being on the right track, and Lucky's friendship with several of the most outspoken followers of this new strategy would also strengthen the impression that Lucky's and the *Zentralverein*'s views were merged together.

There are some indications that the Lucky-Leipzig relationship was not flawless, however. Wiegand, who was student at the Leipzig institute

and left the society in autumn 1890 for this reason. Although not mentioning Lucky by name, he nevertheless states that the mission methods of the Seventh Day Baptist have "taken over" ("die Herrschaft gewonnen hatten") within the *Zentralverein*. See Dalman, "Missionsrundschau," 59; and Dalman, "Mein Verhaltnis zur Leipziger Judenmission," 92–93.

323. Anonymous, "Brother Lucky's Work," 409.

324. Skarsaune, *Israels venner*, 185.

by then, says that Faber was totally unprepared for Lucky's appearance in the summer of 1889, and did not quite know what to do with him in the beginning. Wiegand gives the impression that the journey with Müller and the candidates to Rabinowitz in Kishinev was more like an act of improvisation. In addition, while Lucky during this summer established a cordial friendship with several of the German ministers, the friendship he had established with Yechiel Lichtenstein before he went to America, cooled down. Löwen describes how the returned Lucky used every opportunity to try to convince the institute lecturer that he should start observing Jewish customs. To begin with, Lichtenstein apparently found the idea entertaining, but finally he had had enough, and yelled at Lucky that he should leave him alone. Lucky apparently never forgot this event. In a letter to Löwen much later, he complained about Lichtenstein's lack of loyalty to his Jewish background. Lichtenstein's outburst in Leipzig was added to two other sins by him: His third marriage was to a Gentile woman, and he had shaved his beard.[325]

But Lucky's concern was not only about Jewish-Christian congregations; he wanted to re-establish *Edut*, this time in Europe. The sources do not say anything about whether this was a topic in Lucky's discussions with the *Zentralverein* leadership, but it is a striking fact that in spite of an apparent overlap in views and the mutual warm feelings between Lucky and some of members of the Leipzig society, the *Zentralverein* never took any responsibility for *Edut leIsrael*. Instead, the main support behind the journal came from *Berliner Geshellschaft der Förderung des Christentums unter den Juden*, the oldest of the German mission societies.

During his stay in Leipzig in the summer of 1889, Lucky was planning a long journey in Eastern Europe with some of the representatives from the Leipzig institute and *Zentralverein*. But before this journey took place, Lucky first visited the Jewish Christian Moses Löwen in Berlin, whom he asked to help with *Edut* and to approach the Berlin society for financial support. Löwen was from Sambour in Galicia, had been baptized only two years before Lucky turned up, and had been serving the London Society for Promoting Christianity amongst the Jews since 1888. Löwen was perplexed and not very optimistic about asking a mis-

---

325. In light of the enthusiasm towards Herschensohn-Lichtenstein in several issues of *Edut*, where he is called Even-Tzehar, this conflict is surprising.

sion society to support a journal with *Edut*'s profile, but to his surprise, the Berlin society accepted the project the same autumn.[326]

After visiting Löwen in Berlin, Lucky returned to Leipzig. The following fall he was traveling with Muller and the candidates Wiegand and Meissner in Austria, Hungary, Serbia and Bulgaria. In August he was in Constantinople, heading for Palestine, but did not get the *tezkhra* of the Turkish government.[327] Early in 1890 he appears to have settled in Stanislau, although he retained his American citizenship. At the end of August and beginning of September Lucky stayed with Joseph Rabinowitz, who had led the "Sons of Israel of the New Covenant" congregation since 1884.[328] This visit seems to be the only time Lucky met Rabinowitz. As neither Lucky nor *The Peculiar People* later comments much on Rabinowitz's work, it seems probable that some disagreement took place.[329]

Edut leIsrael *and the Berlin Society*

The same autumn, the mission society in Berlin decided to support *Edut leIsrael* financially. According to the deal between Lucky and the Berlin society, Lucky was supposed to produce material for the journal, and was free to live in Stanislau, while Löwen was stationed by the Berlin society in Lemberg, about three hours away via rail.[330] Lucky did not get any salary; the support from the Berlin Society financed the publication and distribution of *Edut*, as well as the employment of Löwen.

The purpose of the agreement was two-fold: the Berlin society did not have any responsibility for the Seventh Day Baptist and Jewish nationalist Lucky, and Lucky on his side was not formally connected to the mission. The Danish Israel Mission was contacted, and it was agreed that this society would establish their own station in Stanislau with the

326. Löwen, "Christian Theophilus Lucky," 18.

327. The Ottomanian license to enter Palestine.

328. Anonymous, "Brother Lucky's Work," 409. According to Lillie Zöckler, this was where Lucky first met August Wiegand and Max Meissner (Zöckler, *Gott hört Gebet*, 14).

329. As Rabinowitz did not care about observing Sabbath regulations, it is very likely that Lucky was critical of what he saw in Kishinev, particularly in light of his encounter with Yechiel Lichtenstein the same summer; Kjær-Hansen, *Joseph Rabinowitz*, 149; and Kjær-Hansen, "Controversy about Lucky," 46–64; 46 n. 2.

330. Blom, "Reiseerindringer," 123.

German minister August Wiegand.[331] In May 1890, Löwen settled in the Galician capital Lemberg (today Lviv, Ukraine), and the first edition of the reborn *Edut leIsrael* was published the following month.[332] The reasons why the Berlin Society accepted this agreement are not clear, and the society's official historian is silent about this partnership.[333] However, at the beginning of the 1890s, the leadership of the Berlin Society also had sympathy for some of Lucky's and the *Zentralverein*'s agenda. At least they observed the flaws of traditional mission work. In a report to the Norwegian Israel Mission in 1890, the Berlin Society's chief theologian, Hermann Strack, admitted that placing converts in homes for proselytes and making them into paid missionaries had bad effects, both because it attracted candidates with the wrong motives, and because it destroyed the missions' and the converts' reputation among Jews as well as in the churches.[334] It is possible that this consideration was the background for the agreement. Nevertheless, after a couple of years Löwen and the Berlin Society would abandon the publication of the journal.

The Second Edut leIsrael *1890–1892*

From the beginning of 1890, Stanislau was Lucky's base until 1914, when the town was on the frontlines during WWI.[335] In May 1890, Löwen also settled in Lemberg to establish *Edut leIsrael*. Until 1892 Lucky edited *Edut leIsrael* together with Löwen, but later he published some issues of the journal alone.

With about 20,000 inhabitants, Stanislau was smaller than Lemberg, but was regarded as an influential town for the Jewish population in eastern Galicia. After WWII it was renamed Ivanov Frankovsk and became part of Western Ukraine (then Ukrainian S.S.R.). In 1880 the Jewish population of the town was 10,023 (53% of the population).[336] Lucky was not the only Jewish writer who settled down in Stanislau to reach the Jewish community, although he appears to have been the first

---

331. Torm, *50 Aars arbejde for Israel*, 33.
332. Anonymous, "A Great Need," 67–69.
333. Schaeffer, "Bilder des Rückblicks aus hundert Jahren Missionsgeschichte."
334. Skarsaune, *Israels venner*, 185.
335. Löwen, "Christian Theophilus Lucky," 19. According to Wiegand, Lucky settled there during Easter (Wiegand, "Chajim Jedidjah Lucky," 56).
336. Anonymous, "Stanislav," 15:338.

to establish a Jewish journal. Between 1900 and 1914 the town hosted several Jewish magazines; all were short-lived. In addition to one Hebrew monthly, *Ha-Yarden* (1906–1909), there were several Yiddish weeklies: *Stanislaver Nakhrikhten* (1902–1912), *Der Yiddisher Veker* (1905–1907) and *Stanislaver Gloke* (1909–1914). Observing the short lives of the Hebrew and Yiddish papers in Stanislau before WWI, it seems likely that publishing Jewish papers in Galicia was not easy economically, and the religious profile of *Edut* would probably not help in attracting subscribers.

Löwen reports that in spite of having few subscribers, many Jews were interested in the journal, and he and Lucky received numerous visitors and letters.[337] However, lack of subscribers was not the journal's biggest difficulty. Löwen openly talks about the different problems they met, but according to him, the main challenge was related to Lucky's working habits and personality. In particular, Lucky felt the anguish of being supported by the Berlin Society and still claiming independence from the mission; he wanted to cut any bond to a mission society, and he wanted Löwen to follow him. He could make small things into existential questions. Not least, he demanded eagerness for the rabbinical law not only from his own person, but from Löwen as well, who was not willing to do this on principle. Some of the German ministers supported Lucky in these disputes, and one of them, Johannes Müller, claimed that Löwen's non-Jewish wife should let herself be Judaized.[338] Löwen says it took several years before Wiegand and Zöckler could see the situation from Löwen's point of view.[339] This conflict between the German ministers is reflected in the debates in *Saat auf Hoffnung* and *Nathanael* between 1891 and 1894.[340] Still, the problems were not always about

337. Löwen, "Christian Theophilus Lucky," 20.

338. Ibid., 21.

339. Löwen claims that Lucky would have approved of what he reported in the obituary, as he insists that they were cordial friends their whole lives in spite of their disagreements. On other controversial issues, they often shared the same perspectives. In any case, Löwen's obituary seems to be colored by the conflict between them in Stanislau. It is possible that he also had in mind the relationship to, e.g., Wiegand, who at the same time was writing a parallel obituary for Lucky in the same journal, *Nathanael*.

340. the debate between Müller and Wiegand vs. Dalman, Strack, and Löwen. See the articles "Falsche Wege," 161–81 (according to Kjær-Hansen the author was Dalman, referring to Reinar Dobert [ed.], *Zeugnis für Zion*, 44 n. 96); Löwen, "Zur Abwehr wieder eine neue Verunglimpfung der Judenmission," 33–50; Wiegand, "Eine kritische

Löwen and Lucky; the "ordinary" difficulties missionaries expected to meet often made things worse. At the end of 1891, Löwen had fallen into depression, and in January 1892 the Berlin Society had had enough. Löwen went back to Berlin and published a final double edition (issue 8-9) without Lucky's assistance.

HaEdut *and Other Journals*

After the closure of *Edut leIsrael*, Lucky waited until 1907 before he was able to establish a new Hebrew journal, called *HaEdut* (or *haEduth*).[341] The content and ideology were the same as in *Edut leIsrael*, but according to Löwen, Lucky only managed to publish seven or eight issues. However, the collection of Lucky's Hebrew writings published on the Internet by Jorge Quiñónez contains at least 9 issues of *HaEdut* from 1897 and 1898. Except for some sporadic support from the SDB, it is not clear who Lucky cooperated with in this, or from where he got financial support. According to Löwen, Lucky continued to have the same ambivalent attitude to financial support from mission societies, and he assumes that this was the reason for the new journal's few publications.[342]

In 1898 the American journal closed down as well. In 1910 Lucky established another journal in English, *The Messianic Jew*, together with the Jewish-Christian missionary Philip Cohen from Johannesburg. In 1903 Cohen, supported by the Dutch Reformed Church of Transvaal, opened the Jewish Missions of the Dutch Reformed Church of Transvaal in Johannesburg. The financial support for the journal probably came from this work.[343] However, Lucky also was in touch with the SDB about this project. *Sabbath Recorder* reports on Lucky's enthusiasm and new hope in relation to this new journal, and on his plans to visit the General Conference together with Cohen to be associated with the Seventh Day Missionary and Tract boards.[344] However, this journal did not survive for long. Possibly only one issue was published, as the partnership be-

---

Stimme über die Judenmission," 150–56; Wiegand, "Zumitten Israels," 150. Kjær-Hansen, "Lucky and the Leipzig Program," 22–27; 22; and Zöckler, "Die Missionsarbeit in Galizien," 216–20.

341. Löwen, "Christian Theophilus Lucky," 22–23.

342. Ibid.

343. Strack, *Yearbook* (1906), 112. *The Messianic Jew* was published by The Messianic Jew, 134 3rd Avenue, Melville, Johannesburg.

344. Anonymous, "The Work of Brother Ch. Th. Lucky," 267.

tween Lucky and Cohen soon came to an end. According to Wiegand, Lucky quit the cooperation with Cohen because of disagreements on small things, and the fact that Lucky did not find it easy to cooperate with partners who held on to their independence.[345]

Although this journal did not last for long, Cohen and Lucky managed to have their voices heard at a strategic time, as the World Mission conference was held in Edinburgh in 1910. Here the establishing of national churches was one of the topics, and Cohen and Lucky probably found it strategic to use this event to express their views. The publication of *The Messianic Jew* induced David Baron to write an article against Lucky and his sympathizers in *The Scattered Nation* in 1911.[346] From April 1911, Lucky also wrote some articles in *De Boodschapper* under the name Jedidjah, but from then on, his health began to decline.[347]

Lucky's Friends among the Missionaries

Soon after settling down in Stanislau, Lucky became a voice that missionaries to the Jewish people had to pay some attention to, although often with some frustration. Otto von Harling was somewhat representative of the ambivalent attitude to Lucky among several missionaries. Once he witnessed how Lucky criticized the Jewish Christians at a meeting for their lack of Torah observance, while other Jews were present. After an outburst from von Harling in private during a break, Lucky began emphatically to explain during the meeting how the Hebrew Bible points to Christ.[348]

For some of the Danish missionaries to the Jews in Galicia, Lucky even became something like a supervisor.[349] Johannes Volf and his wife Petra were the first Danish missionaries the Danish Israel Mission sent to Przmysel (in today's Poland) in Galicia, in 1905. Lucky was his advisor for contact with the Jews. The Volf family and Lucky got along very

---

345. Wiegand, "Chajim Jedidjah Lucky," 61; *The Messianic Jew: Organ of the Jewish Messianic Movement* 1.

346. Baron, *Messianic Judaism*, 423–32.

347. Velthuysen, "Christian Theophilus Lucky," 198; Löwen, "Christian Theophilus Lucky," 24.

348. Harling, *Pionerarbeide i Galati*, 14, 25; Anacker, "Meine Reise nach Galizien," 86.

349. Volf, "Mindeblade om Pastor Johannes Volf," 92–118, 98.

well, and Lucky became the godfather of two of their sons. Several times he also preached in the evangelical church in Przmysel.[350]

In addition to the friendship with the Volf family, Lucky's more lasting friendships from 1889 onward seem to have been with the pastors of small German Lutheran Diaspora congregations in Stanislau: August Wiegand, Theodor Zöckler and Max Weidauer. Wiegand, as well as his successors Zöckler and Weidauer, were primarily congregational ministers, but nevertheless combined their traditional ministry with mission work among the Jews in the area. Wiegand and Zöckler were trained by the *Institutum Delitscianum* in Leipzig, and influenced by Leipzig's strategic thinking. Most of their work was related to the Germans living in the German colony in Stanislau and the districts nearby. Not only were most of these Germans impoverished, but the children were heavily influenced by Polish society.[351] Shortly before 1900, when Zöckler's church managed to employ a second minister, Max Weidauer, the German population in the area had grown to about 1,300.[352]

From 1889 to 1890 Wiegand lived in Lucky's house, where he came in touch with several of Lucky's friends and adherents. Due to his second exam in theology, he left Stanislau in January 1891 and became a minister in Mecklenburg, Germany.[353] In addition the sponsor, the Danish Israel Mission, seems to have had second thoughts about him, as Wiegand became very critical of traditional missions to Jews. According to the general secretary of the Danish mission society, Axel Torm, Wiegand's ministry was characterized by much love for Jews, but he became one-sided in his views on mission strategies and methods. Theologically he

---

350. Another missionary who praised Lucky's friendship was Gisle Johnson from the Norwegian Israel Mission. Johnson met Lucky a few times in 1903 and 1904, during Johnson's first years as a missionary in Galicia, and during the next ten years, they corresponded. Johnson, however, never supported Lucky's agenda in the same way as Volf. See Johnson, "Fra vor missions fortid," 248.

351. Wiegand, "Chajim Jedidjah Lucky," 56. According to Lillie Zöckler her husband was inspired by the institutions and school run by the little Catholic society in his own hometown, which was the key for the little minority's survival in a Protestant environment (Zöckler, *Gott hört Gebet*, 19).

352. Ibid., 25.

353. According to Lillie Zöckler, Wiegand had planned to return to Stanislau, but found that he had to stay in Germany to take care of his widowed mother (Zöckler, *Gott hört Gebet*, 15–18).

even became dangerous, as it seemed he was limiting Jesus to being a Jew within ordinary Judaism and nothing else.[354]

Wiegand's successor, Theodor Zöckler (1867–1949), became another companion of Lucky's, although he was not as outspoken as Wiegand. He would become the most famous Lutheran pastor in Stanislau and eastern Galicia. He was stationed in Stanislau immediately after Wiegand's departure in 1891, and stayed there until the Germans fled the Red Army in 1944. Like Wiegand he was, in the beginning, dependent on financial support from the Danish Israel Mission, but after some years, in 1893, he was employed by the German Evangelical Church to minister in Stanislau. Until he married Lili Bredenkamp in January 1893, Zöckler also lived in Lucky's home, and even used his home every week for lessons in Christianity for the German children.[355] For Zöckler, the mission work and the German Diaspora ministry needed each other, as the mission needed a living church community to make Christianity attractive for the Jewish population.

The German ministers and the Jewish editor appear to have found themselves on the same quest: to help their countrymen find Christ and be strengthened in their own national identity. Between 1895 and 1898 Zöckler established several institutions in the area, which after WWI numbered about 600 residents, including an orphanage, a German school that also hosted many Jewish children, an old people's home, and a home for disabled and psychiatric patients from all ethnic groups in the area.[356] The institutions were based on a revival in the local congregation in the summer of 1895. Some of the Jewish children were baptized, but to Torm's frustration, Zöckler was very strict about accepting Jewish applicants for baptism.[357]

Zöckler was positive toward Lucky but not uncritical of him. As Zöckler saw it, Christian liberty included the right to observe the law, a paradoxical parallel to the liberty to not observe the Torah in the Letter to the Galatians.[358] However, he did not follow Lucky's views on every matter about Jewish Christianity. For Zöckler it was alright for Jewish Christians to "live as Jews," but theologically one had to focus first of all

354. Torm, *50 Aars arbejde for Israel*, 35.
355. Zöckler, *Gott hört Gebet*, 18.
356. Volf, "Mindeblade," 105.
357. Torm, *50 Aars arbejde for Israel*, 83.
358. Dalman, *Die Allgemeine Konferenz*, 20.

upon conversion and be born again. Although Jewish believers in Jesus have the right to form their own fellowships, Zöckler emphasizes that the focus on national Christianity in any form must not contradict the universal idea of Christianity.[359]

Zöckler also took care of Lucky's well-being in general, and in the last years before WWI more or less employed him as a teacher of Hebrew, Old Testament and Judaism for the candidates at the *Paulinum*, a home for theological candidates in Stanislau founded by Zöckler in 1908. The institution was founded to train theologians for ministry in the Diaspora congregations as well as to inspire them for the mission to the Jews.[360] However, considering Lucky's age and economic situation it was just as important that Lucky at the same time had a place to live.

Many of the sources comment on Lucky's poverty in Stanislau. According to Weidauer, Lucky lived in several places during his years in Stanislau; one of these was under the Bistritzbridge in a wood shack, filled up by his bed, Talmud and lots of books.[361] He got clothes from friends, and for Weidauer it was a mystery how Lucky managed to make a living, not to mention how he was able to travel so much. First of all he seems to have traveled a lot in Galicia, visiting neighboring towns and talking with Jews.[362] However, he was also reported to have been in Russia, Romania, Serbia, Germany, England, Holland, South Africa, and the USA.[363] According to SDB sources, he must have been in the USA at least twice after his return to Europe in 1889, in 1893 and 1909.[364] He came to dinner at Zöckler's home twice a week, and later he went to a family by the name of Opdenhoffs, before settling at the *Paulinum*.[365] Although Weidauer assumes that Lucky ate with Jewish friends as well, he believes he was often hungry, but never begged or borrowed money from anyone. Nevertheless, eating with his non-Jewish friends was not without problems, as Lucky expected his meals to be kosher, much to the

---

359. Zöckler, "Judentum und Christentum," (1893) 45.

360. Zöckler, "Aus Galizien," 138. also Torm, *50 Aars arbejde for Israel*, 83. In Torm's opinion Zöckler sometimes waited too long with the baptism of Jews because he wanted to know their motives. Sometimes Jewish children at the orphanage also were baptized.

361. Weidauer, "Erindringer," 167.

362. Reinen, "Missions: Correspondence," 518.

363. Velthuysen, "Christian Theophilus Lucky," 196–98.

364. Philips, "Ch. Theophilus Lucky," 690–91.

365. Anonymous, "Missionen i Stanislau," 159.

distress of non-Jewish wives. The Norwegian missionary Gisle Johnson unabashedly described Lucky as "a nightmare for any housewife."[366]

The sources include a detail that perhaps explains why Lucky, in spite of being a rather difficult friend or guest, was not only tolerated, but even warmly welcomed in some places: His ability to remember most people he had met combined with a deep loyalty to those he regarded as friends. When Lucky became friends with several of the candidates from Leipzig and other missionaries, he remembered even the birthdays of their children with visits or postcards. Thereby, Wiegand says, the difficult guest won the hearts of the parents.[367] When possible, Lucky shared social and spiritual fellowship with the German ministers, and he participated more or less regularly in Zöckler's and Weidauer's little staff in Stanislau.[368] Still, Weidauer says that Lucky could become intensely affected during discussions, which made it difficult to talk with him. One of the things Weidauer and Lucky disagreed on was anti-Semitism, an ideology of which Weidauer seems to have been more understanding.[369]

Lucky's Jewish-Christian Fellowship

During their ten years of correspondence, Johnson had only one argument "that seemed to bite on" Lucky, namely that Lucky did not seem to have an alternative when he criticized the Jewish mission.[370] It is true that Lucky never managed to establish a Jewish-Christian congregation, but that does not mean that he never tried. In Galicia and Bukowina he had a circle of Jewish individuals who viewed him as their leader. It is probably this circle which is referred to in his death notice: "On behalf of the believing Jews who are faithful to the Law."[371] Weidauer thought that

---

366. Johnson, "Fra vor missions fortid." The relationship between Lucky and Johnson's mother was an exception to the rule: "After a brief moment of the one observing the other, the ice was broken, and the old father Lucky, in spite of how strange he could appear, also knew how to behave like a gentleman—when he wanted to" (Terray, *Et liv i grenseland*, 50).

367. Wiegand, "Chajim Jedidjah Lucky," 56.

368. Weidauer, "Erindringer," 171.

369. Ibid., 177.

370. Ibid.

371. English translation from Velthuysen's obituary in *De Boodschopper* (Nov. 1916); Velthuysen, "Christian Theophilus Lucky," 196–98. I have not succeeded in finding more information about Fliegelmann. Another character who is rather obscure in the sources is Alexander Waldmann, Lucky's co-writer of the declaration at the mis-

the circle of Jews who sometimes assembled around Lucky related to him as a person and teacher, rather than being a religious community.[372] Some of these followers of Lucky were probably members of a group in Braila led by a Jewish Christian named L. W. Horowitz, who under supervision by von Harling worked for the Norwegian Israel Mission. However, after some years Horowitz's enthusiasm for the mission as well as Protestant Christianity seemed to have left him. According to von Harling this was partly Lucky's fault, as he believes Horowitz gave up his Christian ministry due to broken hopes about a Jewish-Christian colony in Palestine that Lucky had encouraged him to work for.[373]

From the end of the 1890s to 1904, Lucky cooperated with Professor Ernst F. Ströter in an unsuccessful attempt to establish a Jewish-Christian colony in Haifa.[374] In connection with this, Lucky gradually took over Horowitz's group in Galicia. A group like this was exactly what Lucky had been looking for, and he connected Horowitz's

---

sion conference in Stockholm in 1911. However, around 1910–1911 he seems to have been counted among Lucky's friends. Lindhagen, "Is there Ebionitism," 78–84, 78; and Baron, *Messianic Judaism*, 4.

372. Weidauer refers to a meeting about this issue, in Stanislau between Professor Ströter, Lucky, a Jewish Christian from Warsaw, a missionary from the Jewish mission in Braila (Horowitch?), Zöckler, Wiegand, pastor Opdenhoff and Weidauer. The result was poor. Weidauer, "Erindringer," 178.

373. Ibid., 3, 19. See also Skarsaune, *Israels venner*, 200–201.

374. Professor Ernst Ferdinand Ströter (1846–1922) founded "The Hope of Israel Mission" in 1892, together with Rev. A. C. Gaebelein in New York. After a conflict about the doctrines to be preached, they split; Strack, *Yearbook* (1906), 115; and Löwen, "Christian Theophilus Lucky," 20. Ströter was a dispensationalist in the late 1800s, and was very active in the "prophecy conference movement" in America and Germany. Between 1865 and 1869 he studied evangelical theology in Bonn, Tübingen, and Berlin. Later he joined the Methodist Church and immigrated to the USA in 1869. He was offered a position as a professor of historical and practical theology at Central Wesleyan College in Warrenton, Missouri. After six years he got another position in theology at the University of Denver, Colorado. In 1894, he quit his academic career and began working for the Jewish mission in the USA. In 1899, he returned to Germany and Eastern Europe to work for the mission there. He traveled much in Russia (13 visits), and he went to Palestine at least 3 times. In 1911–1912 he was in South Africa. In 1907, he began publishing the periodical *Das Prophetische Wort*; after his death it was continued by Heinrich Schaedel until 1937. Ströter was an independent theologian and sparked much debate. When he in 1915 publicly supported the doctrine of universal salvation, he lost much support from old sympathizers. However, according to Karl Barth, Ströter's exegesis in *Die Judenfrage und ihre göttliche Lösung* (1903) was "in spite of significant mistakes useful to read" ("trotz ihrer kräftigen Irrtümer nützlich zu lesen sei"; quotation from Hirschfeld, «Ernst Ferdinand Ströter,» 1.

group in Braila to a Palestine union in Dusseldorf headed by Professor Ströter. This Christian Zionist society held that Israel's political restoration would precede a national spiritual awakening, inspired by Romans 11 and Ezekiel 37. By 1903 the group came in contact with the Jewish Christian Simon Bauer, a baker who by then was planning to build a biscuit factory in Safed. Already in February 1904 they held a conference in Düsseldorf about the project. A month later, on March 10, the group *Amiel* was constituted. Bauer, Lucky and Ströter's plan was to employ workers and thereby establish some sort of Jewish-Christian colony, unpolluted by influence from the missions. Baptism was not a precondition to being employed, and the group in Braila was now supposed to be the core of this colony.[375]

According to Johnson, the group was excited about these plans for a long time, although it seemed that for group members the main thing was not the spiritual aspect but the prospect of making a living in Palestine. Only a couple of them were baptized and took part in Communion.[376] Lucky managed to convince the Norwegian mission to pay for an excursion to Palestine for Horowitz and Ströter, as well as a Russian Jew, to examine the opportunities more properly.[377] However, after several months in Palestine, in the summer of 1904, they returned to

---

375. Except for the theological perspectives behind this strategy, the link to the Zionist enterprise could also be a way to relate to the generally positive attitude to Jesus found among many Zionists before 1948. Sadan, "Jesus of Nazareth," 59–64; 59. Ströter explains his theology in his book *Die Judenfrage und ihre göttlicher Lösung nach Römer Kapitel 11*. However, the year after its publication it was criticized by P. L. Anacker in *Saat auf Hoffnung* for confusing Israel's future mission to the world with the mission to the Jews (Anacker, "Zu Prof. Ströter's Judenfrage," 33–39).

376. Horowitz was eager to maintain his leadership of this group, and Johnson believed he was the only outsider to sometimes be invited (Johnson, "Fra vor missions fortid," 249).

377. It must be mentioned that when Gisle Johnson wrote his article about Lucky in 1923, he was himself involved in a conflict about mission strategies and mission settlements in Palestine within the Norwegian Israel Mission. The missionary Arne Jonson (not a relative of Gisle Johnson) was, for some time during the 1920s, successful in persuading the Norwegian mission board to support the establishing of such a Jewish-Christian colony in Motza in Jerusalem. According to Skarsaune, there is reason to believe Arne Jonsen was inspired by Lucky. Gisle Johnson's anecdote is probably colored by the ongoing discussion among the Norwegian friends of Israel. Gisle Johnson opposed and ridiculed Arne Jonson's ideas fiercely, and regarded Lucky's Jewish Christianity as an illusion. Nevertheless, Johnson was impressed by Lucky, and cherished his sermons from the Old Testament. See Johnson, "Fra vor missions fortid," 250; and Skarsaune, *Israels venner*, 221, 226–33.

Europe with broken dreams, as the project seemed impossible to implement. In the fall of 1904 Horowitz was fired by the Norwegian mission society, after openly regretting that he had been baptized. Although still claiming to believe in Jesus, he wanted to be buried in a Jewish cemetery.[378] In spite of his antipathy toward the traditional Jewish mission, Lucky was not happy when Horowitz left the Norwegian mission, as the group in Braila seems to have dissolved.[379]

Lucky's network of Jewish believers in Jesus in Galicia and Romania was never very substantial, and from the outset it was never regarded as a congregation. In spite of this, for decades later missionaries and mission journals could find individuals who had been part of Lucky's network. Kurt Hruby refers to a "Luckyianer" from Galicia in the 1930s, who until his death claimed that Jesus was Messiah and that Jewish believers should be baptized, but neither leave their people nor abandon the Jewish traditions.[380] In late 1911 or early 1912 Lucky met the young Henry Einspruch (born 1892), a Galician Jew and *halutz* (a Zionist pioneer) who was on his way home from Palestine after contracting malaria. Lucky convinced him to embrace Christ, and he went to America. In 1941 Einspruch published the first modern New Testament in Yiddish, which was revised in 1959.[381]

The Struggle for a New Mission Strategy

In the decades before WWI, the ideas of contextualization of the Christian message and national churches gained influence among Protestant churches and mission societies in general, and it is only to be expected that similar discussions took place in the Jewish missions. When they did, it seems that it often was Rabinowitz's work or Lucky's

---

378. Together with a number of Jesus-believing Jews, Johnson in 1922 founded *Agudath Ma'aminim*, a union for Jewish believers in Budapest. Already during his work in Romania before WWI he had tried to establish groups like this, but in vain. In addition, the group in Braila disintegrated soon after he came to Romania. Johnson was eager not to call it a congregation, as this would make it mandatory that all members were baptized. See Terray, *Et liv i grenseland*, 118–22.

379. According to Johnson, Bauer became one of Lucky's closest friends in his little circle of Jewish Christians. Löwen describes an unamed "Bäckergeselle" in this circle, and I assume this is the baker Bauer. Löwen, "Christian Theophilus Lucky," 20; and Johnson, "Fra vor missions fortid," 248, 250.

380. Hruby, "Zur Problematik," 78.

381. Ariel, *Evangelizing*, 88.

ideas and criticism that came into focus; these also set the agenda for discussions at several international conferences on Jewish mission between 1890 and 1911.[382] During the 1880s there had been a serious debate about the work of Joseph Rabinowitz and his congregation in Kishinev, and at the conference in Barmen in 1890, Rev. Bernstein from Frankfurt and London agitated for the view that mission societies should work to establish Jewish-Christian congregations.[383]

Generally, the participants in these discussions were more inclined to accept, or at least listen to, criticism against missionary methods than to consider Jewish-Christian congregations.[384] What caused more tension were Lucky's ideas about Jewish-Christian congregations and Torah observance for Jewish Christians. Lucky's opponents feared that this was a new version of the old Ebionitism, or at least some sort of religious syncretism. Lucky's ideas were particularly debated at the conference in Leipzig in 1895 and in 1911 in Stockholm.[385] Here Wiegand and others claimed that not only should one seek to establish Jewish-Christian congregations, but also that Jewish Christians have the right to voluntarily observe the law or not observe it. While this idea was received with some sympathy among a minority of missionaries, most of the Jewish Christians present disagreed with almost all of it. Still, it was the main missions' unwillingness to change strategy that Wiegand and Lucky's other supporters found most provoking.[386] Löwen claims that Lucky modified his views in the last years of his life, at least when it came to

---

382. The international conferences for Jewish mission societies between 1871 to 1911 were as follows: the 1st conference was in Berlin in 1871; the 2nd was in 1883 in the same place; the 3rd was in Barmen in 1890; the 4th was in Leipzig, June 6–8, 1895; the 5th was in Cologne, October 6–9, 1900; the 6th was in London, October 21–22, 1903; and the 7th was in Amsterdam, April 24–25, 1906. See Strack, *Yearbook* (1906), 5. The 8th conference was held in Stockholm, June 7–9, 1911; see Strack, *Yearbook*, (1913), 6.

383. Strack, *Yearbook* (1906), 6. As far as I know, Lucky never participated on any of the international conferences himself. Instead, his non-Jewish sympathizers were willing to represent his ideas, particularly Wiegand.

384. Wilkinson, "The Moral Defensibility," 60.

385. Two of the approximately 100 participants at the Stockholm conference were Paul Levertoff from the London Jews Society and Rev. Wiegand; Strack, *Yearbook* (1913), 7.

386. Lindhagen, "Is there Ebionitism," 84.

working for the missions. During their last meeting in 1913, Lucky acknowledged Löwen's position, while regretting his own stubbornness.[387]

The War Years in Holland 1914–1916

During Lucky's last years he became increasingly depressed. This was apparently due to lack of results in his work, as well as the devastation of the war in Galicia. At the outbreak of the war, Lucky was on a journey to the USA to participate in the Seventh Day Baptist General Conference in Alfred, and in August he was in Holland with Rev. Gerard Velthysen in the SDB church in Rotterdam.[388] For the next two years, Lucky worked as a preacher in Velthysen's congregation in Rotterdam and in other congregations in Holland.

In 1916 he spent some months in England, but as Lucky's sympathy in the war lay with Germany and Austria, the antipathy towards German Christians in Britain was very disappointing for him. According to him Russia, which he held to be the Jewish people's worst enemy, was to blame for the war.[389] According to Wiegand, Lucky's hope for a German victory was connected to his belief that this would open the doors for a massive Jewish immigration to Palestine.[390] His opinion about Russia must have been strengthened by reports of the war's enormous destructive impact on society in Galicia, not least for the Jewish population. Between 1914 and 1915, Galicia was occupied by the Russian army, which started an intense Russification campaign with persecution and deportation of Jews from the war zone (Kurland, the kingdom of Poland and Galicia), as the Jews were regarded as hostile by the Russian army.[391] In 1915 the Russians were forced to flee Galicia, but in June 1916 the Russians

---

387. Löwen, "Christian Theophilus Lucky," 2. Löwen considered this event so significant that it is described already in the prologue of the obituary. Still, the narrative may also serve as a defense for Löwen vs. Wiegand and others of Lucky's sympathizers in Germany.

388. Velthuysen (born 1834) had been brought up in the Dutch Reformed Church, and became a Baptist before he became a Seventh Day Baptist in 1877, when he founded the congregation in Haarlem. In the 1870s he began publishing the Dutch journal *De Boodschapper*, which since 1876 was the Seventh Day Baptist magazine in Holland, still with Velthuysen as editor. From 1882 the journal was published as a monthly. *Seventh Day Baptists in Europe and America*, 380, 387, 1339, 1396.

389. Randolph, "Christian Theophilus Lucky," 208.

390. Wiegand, "Chajim Jedidjah Lucky," 61.

391. Prusin, *Nationalizing*, iv, 34, 53.

again occupied Stanislau. Pogroms followed immediately, and the next summer 90,000 houses were burned down and Galicia's economy was destroyed.[392] Zöckler's orphanage and other Protestant institutions were evacuated.[393]

Lucky was very worried about his Galician friends. Due to bad health and a general decline due to his age, he had to end his work for the SDB in the summer of 1916, and tried to return to Galicia via Germany.[394] In Leipzig he became ill and was sent to a sanatorium in Chemnitz, southwest of Dresden. Around October 1st he was hospitalized at *Paulsenstrasser Krankenhaus Ebenezer* in Stegliz, Berlin, where he stayed his remaining two months. On Saturday, November 25, 1916, Lucky died, and he was buried Wednesday, November 29 at 9:30 AM at the Jewish cemetery in Plau, Mecklenburg, 75 miles northwest of Berlin.[395] The funeral was arranged and conducted by his friend Wiegand, who had been pastor of the local Lutheran church since he left Stanislau 25 years earlier.[396]

It is fair to ask whether Wiegand could have been quite frank with the local rabbi, as it is not very plausible that a rabbi (or the Jewish community as such) would allow a baptized Jew to be buried in their cemetery. If the rabbi knew Lucky's religious status, it would be an exceptional case. However, as Lucky's faith was clearly announced in the German newspapers shortly after the funeral and in Wiegand's obituary only a few months later, it does not seem like Wiegand tried to hide anything about Lucky in this respect:

> Peace over Israel! Our dear pastor and friend, the Hebrew writer, Rabbi Chajim Jedidjah (Christian Theophilus) Pollak, surnamed Lucky, died Nov. 25th, 1916, just at the close of the earthly

---

392. Ibid., 51–59.
393. Glaser, "A Survey," 33.
394. Velthuysen, [name of article not given] *Sabbath Recorder* 82/2 (1917), 44; and Anonymous, "Deaths," 159.
395. Velthuysen, "Christian Theophilus Lucky," 196–98.
396. Petra Volf mentions that the funeral was also attended by one pastor Pauls from the Mennonite congregations, who gave special greetings from the Jewish-Christian congregation in Lemberg (Volf, "Mindeblade," 116). Weidauer says that when Lucky had been seriously ill some years earlier, the German friends had discussed where he eventually should be buried, at a Jewish or Christian cemetery. According to Weidauer, Lucky several times considered whether he should live his last years in America, or be buried in Palestine (Weidauer, "Erindringer," 213).

Sabbath. His name was filled with care. He was a member of the original, apostolic church of Jerusalem, zealous for the law of the fathers and witness of Jeschua in Israel. "There remaineth therefore a rest to the people of God." On behalf of the believing Jews who are faithful to the Law. B. Fliegelman, Lemberg, Galicia, Kleparu 267. On behalf of friends from the Christian Nations. A. Wiegand, Pastor, Plau in Mecklenburg, Germany.[397]

What can explain the local rabbi accepting this funeral we do not know, but Wiegand claims that Lucky's faith was not hidden from the director of the cemetery.[398] It is possible that the strain of the war generally legitimated many exceptions from many rules, including the funeral of a convert. It is also possible that Wiegand used his position as the minister in Mecklenburg in his contact with the local Jewish authorities. From their point of view, it could also have been important not to disrupt a friendly relationship with such an outspoken philo-Semite as the minister in Mecklenburg. Although it is impossible to be certain what the rabbi or the director of the cemetery knew about Lucky, it seems unnecessary to assume that the local Jewish community was intentionally left in the dark.

---

397. Translation from Velthuysen's obituary in *De Boodschopper* (Dec., 1916) in Velthuysen, "Christian Theophilus Lucky," 196. Velthuysen says that he got this text from somewhere else, and as the obituary was published in December, I assume that he relied on a notice from a German paper.

398. Wiegand, "Chajim Jedidjah Lucky," 63.

Rabbi Isaac Lichtenstein (1825–1908)

FIGURE 7: Lichtenstein, Isaac. *Judenthum und Christenthum.* Hamburg: A. Scheibenhuber, 1891 or 1892, second front page.

Introduction

Much material on Jewish life in Hungary is generally inaccessible for readers without knowledge of Yiddish or Magyar.[399] The attempt to write a biographical overview about Lichtenstein therefore inevitably suffers from the limited material that is available on Lichtenstein as well as on Jewish life in Hungary in the last decades before WWI. The most important sources about Isaac Lichtenstein's life are the obituaries from 1908 by David Baron and Ragnvald Gjessing.[400] Most of the informa-

---

399. Handler, *Blood Libel*, ix.
400. Baron, "Rabbi Ignatz Lichtenstein," 251–66. Baron knew Lichtenstein from 1888, when he worked for the Mildmay Mission, and later he became the leader of Hebrew Christian Testimony. He was central in organizing the committee to support Lichtenstein that was established in 1892. Gjessing, "Rabbi Isak (Ignaz) Lichtenstein," 171–76. Gjessing later translated the text into German: "Rabbi Isaak (Ignatz) Lichtenstein," *Saat auf Hoffnung* 46 (1909), 3–10. From 1891 he worked for the Norwegian Israel Mission in Budapest. Here he worked together with the local evangelical German congregation, and most of the contact with Jews was informal. In 1899 he returned to Norway, probably due to lack of results. In other words, he lived in Budapest during Lichtenstein's most active period. Gjessing sympathized with

tion about Lichtenstein's childhood and his life before his conversions is supplied by Gjessing, who in the 1890s worked in Budapest as a missionary for the Norwegian Israel Mission. Gjessing's information about Lichtenstein's childhood, education and self-baptism is confirmed by Marton Zsolt, who refers to Draskóczy Lázsló, "Krizstus a Tápiózselei Zsinagógában," in *Külmissziói Évkönyv* (Budapest, 1932), 67–68 and 71. However, since Marton's Hungarian source is newer than Gjessing's text I believe that it is based on Gjessing's obituary, probably the German version of it in *Saat auf Hoffnung*.[401] This is because an anonymous text very similar to Gjessing's obituary was published in Magyar in 1921: "Lichtenstein Izsák (Ignác) rabbi," in *Hajnal*, December 1921 (Volume and issue missing), 50–52.

On some occasions, Lichtenstein refers to events in his life in his writings, and we also get some glimpses of information from the Jewish press in Budapest as well as from Harold Sevener's work on Chosen People's Ministries.[402] Nevertheless, in contrast to the biographical material about Lucky, what we have about Lichtenstein for the most part appears to be consistent and without major contradictions. In some sources Lichtenstein's first name is said to be Ignatz, and according to Marton Zsolt, Lichtenstein used both Isaac (Hungarian: Izsák) and Ignatz concurrently, even when filling out official documents as a rabbi in Tápiózsele.[403] For the sake of simplicity, I have chosen to use the name Isaac.

Childhood and Education

Isaac Lichtenstein was born on Nisan 23 (April 11), in 1825, to a Jewish family in the town of Nikolsburg in Austrian Schlesien (from 1945

Lichtenstein, and later became a supporter of Arne Johnson's project to build a Jewish-Christian colony in Palestine, which caused much controversy in the Norwegian Israel Mission. Aasen, *Ragnvald Gjessing*, 20–24, 36.

401. Marton, "Zsidók útja a világ Messiásához," 34, 50. The same day he defended his Master thesis at the Baptist Theological Seminary in Budapest, June 13, 2012, Marton Zsolt met me to share the information that was relevant for my dissertation. Together with another Master student, he translated the relevant sections and pointed out the pages in his thesis.

In Hungarian the family name is placed first. When I refer to Marton and other Hungarian authors, I try to follow this rule, though not when I refer to Lichtenstein.

402. Sevener, *A Rabbi's Vision*.

403. Marton, "Zsidók útja a világ Messiásához," 33–34.

Mikulov in today's Czech Republic).[404] We do not know the names of his parents, and only know of one brother.[405] His father was a *melamed*, a teacher in a Jewish *heder*, and Lichtenstein's little living room served as a classroom as well as kitchen and bedroom. Gjessing claims the family was poor, but the parents were nevertheless able to raise at least two sons as rabbis (Isaac and his brother Abraham Jakab Lichtenstein, died 1890). From the age of nine, when he had finished the basic religious curriculum (the Pentateuch and parts of Mishnah and Gemara), his parents sent him to study the Talmud as a *Talmud-bokur* (student of the Talmud) with different Jewish scholars.

During his childhood in Moravia, Lichtenstein sometimes experienced the hatred against the Jews from their Gentile neighbors, although it is difficult to say if this happened regularly. Once he witnessed his father being struck down by a nobleman, and as a student he experienced some Gentile boys stealing his and his fellow students' clothing while they were having a bath.[406] At the age of 18, Isaac Lichtenstein finished his rabbinic education and returned home.

Lichtenstein as Rabbi in Tápiószele and His Family Life

After the end of his rabbinic studies, Lichtenstein had several posts in different Jewish communities in Northern Hungary over several years.[407] As many of the Jews who immigrated during the 19th century came from Moravia, it is possible that the young rabbi served among some of these.[408] He probably was appointed district rabbi (German: *kreissrabbiner*, Hungarian: *kerületi rabbi*) in Tápiószele around 1854, when

---

404. The name Lichtenstein is not found in the list of surnames at the local Jewish cemetery. However, the name Lichtenstein can be related to the local castle of the town, which between 1218 and the 1560s belonged to an aristocratic family named Lichtenstein; see http://www.czechatlas.com/southern-moravian-region/mikulov-chateau/ and http://www.shtetlinks.jewishgen.org/Nikolsburg/homeniko.htm. The town was the center of the Moravian Jewish community, and had even been home to the rabbi of the Golem, Rabbi Judah Loew, in the 16th century. At the time of Lichtenstein's birth, the rabbi of Nikolsburg was the influential Rabbi Banet; Kramer, *From Emancipation*, 126, and http://www.dartmore.cz/content/JewishStudies/trips.html.

405. Gjessing, "Rabbi Isak (Ignaz) Lichtenstein," 174.

406. Lichtenstein, *A Jewish Mirror*, 4.

407. Baron, "Rabbi Ignatz Lichtenstein," 251.

408. McCagg Jr., "Jewish Conversion," 142–64, 144.

he married his wife (see below).[409] The position meant that he became the official chief rabbi of the local Jewish community. One of his main responsibilities was to supervise the metrical books, the records of births and deaths for taxation.[410] The village Tápiószele (then often spelled Tapio-Tzele) is located about 70 km southeast of Budapest, in the district of Pest-Pilis-Solt-Kiskun, Hungary. As Jews had settled in the village during the 18th century, the Jewish community here was relatively young, but was in 1810 able to found a synagogue, and in 1840 a school. The same year the Jewish community numbered 396 individuals (14% of the total population).[411] One of Rabbi Lichtenstein's duties was likely to take care of these institutions. The community does not seem to have been dominated by traditionalists; as early as 1867 the school educated its pupils in Magyar.[412]

On April 26, 1854, Lichtenstein married Hoffer Fáni. His brother, Abraham, who was rabbi in Nagykata, conducted the wedding. (Judging from old photographs of the synagogues in Nagykata and Tápiószele, the Jewish community in the former village seems to have been more prosperous than the latter.[413]) The fact that many members of her family lived there in the 1880s indicates that Fáni was from Tápiószele. The obituary in an Orthodox Jewish newspaper explains the extraordinary situation in Tápiószele with its "Christian" rabbi:

> Not until the scandal had lasted a long time did the Reformed Rabbinate of Budapest succeed in inducing the representatives of the community of Tapio Tzele, composed for the most part of relatives or friends of Lichtenstein, to demand his dismissal, in order that he should withdraw from the Rabbinate.[414]

---

409. Marton, "Zsidók útja a világ Messiásához," 51. However, in 1886 Lichtenstein claims that he had been rabbi for 34 years, which indicates 1852. Lichtenstein, *Die Liebe*, 19.

410. Stanislawski, *A Murder in Lemberg*, 60.

411. Anonymous, "Tapio-Tzele," 1287–88.

412. The local Jewish primary school had teachers in Hungarian already in 1867. In 1924 the school was closed due to lack of funding from the government. Anonymous, "Tápiószele," 881.

413. Marton, "Zsidók útja a világ Messiásához," 39, 82, 84.

414. Baron, "Rabbi Ignatz Lichtenstein," 264–65. Hoffer, Lichtenstein's wife's surname before she married as well as the surname of her brother who lived in the village in the 1880s, appears to have been associated with Tápiószele already in the first decade of the 19th century; Gjessing, "Rabbi Isak (Ignaz) Lichtenstein," 174, and http://www.porges.net/FamilyTreesBiographies/Porjes.html.

Fáni and Isaac had six children, but both their sons and two of their daughters died before the parents: Wolf (August 11, 1856–August 18, 1857), Emanuel (June 29, 1859–March 11, 1887), Kathi (born March 24, 1864), Ilka (born in 1865, married to Zsigmond Neuberger in 1882), Julanka (February 22, 1867–January 19, 1869) and Aranyka (died March 5, 1874).[415]

Between 1861 and 1866, Lichtenstein was a rabbi in Szarvason; he then returned to Tápiószele.[416] However, he seems to have been doing ministry in Tápiószele during his stay in Szarvason as well, as their children were born in these two towns both before and during this period.

According to Harold Sevener, Fáni and Isaac had one grandson, named Emmanuel Lichtenstein (1892?–1979), claimed to be about 45 years old in 1936.[417] It is said that the orphaned grandson lived with his grandparents before he attended a boarding school and the gymnasium. Baron also says that Lichtenstein had some relatives who took care of him in Budapest, primarily another unnamed grandson who also was a doctor.

---

415. Marton, "Zsidók útja a világ Messiásához," 35–37.

416. Ibid., 40–41.

417. Sevener bases the story about the grandson on Emmanuel Lichtenstein's own claims in the 1920s and 1930s about this relationship. The narrative cannot be verified from Marton's master's thesis, which has surveyed Hungarian archives on Isaac Lichtenstein. However, considering that there probably would have been relatives or people who had known Isaac at the time, it is difficult to see how he could have got away with this claim if it was a fake. In addition, he seems to have showed personal integrity during the events of WWII, at least as portrayed by Sevener. Emmanuel worked under the supervision of Pastor Friedrich Forell, the director of the Swedish mission in Vienna. Until he was employed by him and Joseph Cohn from the American Board of Mission to the Jews (ABMJ, later Chosen People Ministries) he had been a journalist, but due to Nazi persecution, he had to flee and found shelter with the Swedes. According to Sevener he had earlier been baptized due to influence from his grandfather. His wife was Justina Lichtenstein (died September 4, 1966). Between 1938 and 1941 Emmanuel built up a staff of volunteers who worked to assist as many persecuted and poor Jews as possible to survive and escape from Vienna. The Swedish mission helped about 3,000 Jews immigrate, mainly to South America. When the situation became too dangerous, he was sent to Buenos Aires via Stockholm. Here, from 1942, he continued to work for ABMJ under the supervision and support of the Lutheran Church in Argentina. In addition to the work at the mission station, Emmanuel and Justina had responsibility for the Jewish-Christian congregation *Congregation El Mesias*. Together they had a son, Alexander George Lichtenstein. Sevener, *A Rabbi's Vision*, 184; and Edvardsson, *Kyrka och judendom*, 92.

The Jewish Community in Hungary:
A Seedbed for Jewish Christians?

Most scholars estimate that the first Jews settled in Hungary as far back as the 11th century. However, during the 19th century large numbers of Jews immigrated to Hungary, most of them from Galicia after the partition of Poland, and partly related to the emancipation of the Jews in the 1840s and 1867. Many Jewish immigrants also came from Moravia, and probably Lichtenstein belonged to this group.[418]

Perhaps the most striking thing about Isaac Lichtenstein was that he continued to work as a rabbi for several years after he publically announced his faith in Jesus as the Messiah. It is natural to ask if this event was related to particular conditions in the Hungarian Jewish community in the last decades before WWI. Was, for example, the Hungarian Jewish community more relaxed towards Jewish converts to Christianity?

Kramer describes the period between 1868 and 1918 as the "Golden Age" for Hungarian Jews, due to the positive political, social and economic conditions of the period. The background for this progress was that after losing the war against Prussia in 1866, the Habsburg monarchy concluded that the empire had to be reorganized. In 1867, Hungary became an independent part of the empire, and emancipation of the Jews was regarded as part of the necessary modernization of the new Hungary. Almost 50 percent of Hungary's population belonged to the Roman Catholic Church, and more than 40 percent belonged to the Reformed and Lutheran churches.[419] In December 1867 nearly all anti-Jewish laws and regulations were annulled by the Hungarian parliament. Although Judaism was not acknowledged as an officially accepted religion until 1895, the emancipation laws immediately had significant consequences for Jewish community, which soon was split into three distinct judicial entities.[420]

Traditionally, the Hungarian Jewish communities were in many ways autonomous, but in 1868–1869 progressive Hungarian Jewish leaders together with the Hungarian authorities tried to establish an overall organization for the Jewish communities. Instead, one of the consequences of this attempt was that in the following years Hungarian

---

418. McCagg Jr., *A History*, 123.
419. Sípos, "Bittet den Herrn der Ernte," 22.
420. Kramer, *From Emancipation*, 7.

Jewry was divided into three national communities or denominations: the Neologs (the progressive Jews), the Orthodox Jews, and the so-called Status-Quo. Politically this led to the founding of two national Jewish organizations in Hungary: the *Israelitischer Landessekretariat* for the Orthodox and the *Israelitische Landskanzlei* for the Neologs.[421] The Neologs wanted to modernize the Jewish educational system and centralize the communal organization, while the Orthodox fiercely opposed these attempts. The Status Quo comprised a substantial group of local communities that, for several reasons, did not want to choose between the two others, but preferred the old system.[422]

Within Neolog congregations the liturgy underwent the changes of the Reform movement, and observance of religious precepts was held to a minimum. The Orthodox, on the other hand, isolated themselves not only from the Neologs, but from Jews from other countries as well. The Status-Quo went for a middle-of-the road stance in religious matters.[423] Around 1900 the Orthodox and Status Quo represented the majority, geographically speaking, but the Neologs were dominant in Budapest and other cities. At the same time, many progressive Jews who lived in traditional communities did not establish their own alternatives.[424]

During this period, more and more Hungarian Jews identified themselves with Magyar nationalism.[425] The Jews therefore (together with the German population) became the main bulk of the new Hungarian middle class.[426] This process took place to such an extent that the Jews were looked upon as representatives of the Magyar rulers by other ethnic minorities.[427] Particularly from 1875, these groups' rights, which they were promised by the laws in 1868, were neglected in favor of the increased Magyarization of the country. In 1910 the Magyars numbered 49 percent of the Hungarian population, while the 910,000 Jews numbered 4 percent. The Magyar leadership therefore wanted to cooperate with the Jews to maintain political controll. However, they

421. Schwarzfuchs, *A Concise History*, 106.
422. Kramer, *From Emancipation*, 7.
423. Bitton, "A Decade," 113.
424. McCagg Jr., *A History*, 139.
425. Kramer, *From Emancipation*, 21; Ranki, *The Politics*, 1, 34.
426. Wandycz, *The Price of Freedom*, 175.
427. The Austro-Hungarian Empire consisted of eleven nationalities. Sípos, "*Bittet den Herrn der Ernte*," 14.

were also needed for the establishment of a Hungarian middle class. Economically, the emancipation led many Jews into successful business endeavors, and they were clearly overrepresented in media and academics. In 1900, the strongest economic group in Budapest consisted of about 1,000 families, most of them Jewish.[428]

Not least, this Jewish-Magyar symbiosis was necessary to preserve a political majority as well. Consequently, for many Jews before WWI Magyar replaced Yiddish, German and other languages as the Jewish mother tongue, from nearly 60 percent in 1880 to 77 percent in 1910. However, according to Laszló G. Terray, as late as the early 1920s the higher social strata of Budapest spoke German, as this had been the official language of the twin monarchy.[429] Although the acculturation in Orthodox circles was limited and Yiddish continued to be the language of the *yeshiva* and synagogue, more and more Orthodox Jews learned Magyar as well.[430] In 1895, when Judaism was recognized as one of the legal religions of Hungary, approximately 1.5 million Jews lived within the Austro-Hungarian Empire. From the end of the century to 1910, the Jewish population of Budapest alone grew from 50,000 to more than 200,000, composing 23 percent of the population.[431]

How did this development affect Jewish conversions, the attitude to them, and the understanding of the relationship between Judaism and Christianity? Scholars have focused particularly on the social and cultural uprooting that characterized Hungarian Jewry following the strong immigration and urbanization. In the Neolog community in particular, modernization and decline in religious observance were parallel and connected phenomena in the social development after 1867.[432] In relation to this process, attention has been paid to the apparently extraordinary numbers of Jewish converts to different Christian denominations from the end of the 19th century to WWII. In surveys of Jewish converts to Christianity in Hungary, interpretations of the phenomenon differ.[433] While Mitchell Glaser indicates a connection between political pressure/persecution and conversions to Christianity, McCagg emphasizes

---

428. Ibid., 17.
429. Terray, *Et liv i grenseland*, 103.
430. Katz, "The Identity," 13–32, 22.
431. Terray, *Et liv i grenseland*, 109.
432. Kovács, *The History*, 175.
433. Glaser, "A Survey," 115.

the cultural and social changes in the Jewish community.[434] McCagg claims that Hungarian Jews during the 19th century actually had developed some sort of tradition for conversions. For many converts the reasons were more or less opportunism, caused by discriminatory laws and customs regarding significant posts, but many famous converted Jews also argued for this choice for idealistic reasons: It was necessary to join the Magyars in their struggle for liberty and national recovery. Other scholars regard Jewish conversions to Christianity as a marginal phenomenon: Kovacs claims that the overall conversion rate in Hungary was never high, pointing out that, e.g., in 1900, 476 Jews converted to a Christian church, representing 0.05 percent of the Jewish population.[435] Similarly, Kramer believes that when compared to the size of the Jewish population, the conversion rate of Hungarian Jews was not significantly higher than that in Germany and Austria.[436] Still, while the attitude to Jewish conversions to Christianity changed from being a public and shameful denouncement of Jewish identity, it later became an embarrassing but nevertheless well-known part of the assimilation process to the Magyar community. In fact, Katz points out, the Austrian-Hungarian society as a whole still regarded baptized converts as Jews.[437]

In 1868, while most of Austria had made it legal to leave a religion without joining another, this was not the case in Hungary. In other words, if one wanted to get away from the Hungarian synagogue communities, there was no other choice than to convert to Christianity. In 1895 Hungary approved the Jewish (and Protestant) religions as officially recognized by the state, but still one could not be regarded as judicially free from a religious community nor its religious instruction until the age of 18. These laws, combined with increasing religious indifference, were, according to McCagg, significant reasons behind the increased conversions: Between 1867 and 1918 about 20,000 Hungarian Jews converted to Christianity, the majority living in towns, particularly Budapest.[438]

Lichtenstein's position in this religious landscape before his conversion in the mid-1880s is not quite clear. The Jewish community in

434. Ibid., 144, 156–59.
435. Kovács, *The History*, 243.
436. Kramer, *From Emancipation*, 27.
437. Katz, "The Identity," 15.
438. McCagg Jr., *A History*, 138.

Tápiószele belonged to the Neolog camp, which is indicated by the reactions in Budapest voiced by the Neolog leadership, and by the fact that Lichtenstein was buried in the Reform cemetery in Budapest. Gjessing also describes how the drafting of Jewish men into the military in the wake of emancipation made Lichtenstein less loyal to the dietary laws.[439] Sympathy for modern ideas was probably deeply rooted in the Tápiószele Jewish community. Even before the official separation between Neologs and traditionalists in 1868, the elementary school in Lichtenstein's community introduced Magyar in 1867.[440]

If Lichtenstein became less concerned about observance of the food regulations, he was not alone. After 1848, the Jewish communities in the Habsburg Empire faced many challenges and questions as a consequence of modernization and the new opportunities for free settlement. At the religious level, community leaders all over the country experienced greater indifference to Jewish religion and customs. The laws of 1868 intensified the process, and an increasingly greater number of Hungarian Jews ceased observing religious prescriptions, the Sabbath and dietary laws, and the Jewish communal leadership was not able—and in many places not willing—to prevent the phenomenon. For contemporary observers it seemed only a question of time until the assimilation of the Hungarian Jews would be completed. Katz believes that at the beginning of the 20th century about one third of Hungarian Jews were "fairly observant," at least to the extent that they were clearly identifiable as Jews in their outward behavior.[441]

Nevertheless, Lichtenstein does not seem to have been always associated with the Neolog agenda, neither by some of his Christian friends nor by himself. When the *Allgemeine Jüdische Zeitung* in its obituary claims that Lichtenstein belonged to the Neologs, Baron rejects this in a note: "The actual term used by this organ of 'Orthodoxy' of the 'Reformed Party' is 'Neologian.' To use it of Rabbi Lichtenstein is doubly

---

439. The emancipation of the Austrian Jews in 1867 gave traditional rabbis new problems to solve for their congregations, as the new laws demanded that Jewish men be enlisted for military service in the army. Until then rabbis and Jewish men with diplomas from the yeshiva in Pressburg had been allowed to go free, but now rabbis like Lichtenstein had to deal with his male community members as well as his sons having to abandon kosher laws. Gjessing, "Rabbi Isak (Ignaz) Lichtenstein," 174.

440. Anonymous, "Tápiószele," 881.

441. Katz, "The Identity," 17, 20.

false, for he was an 'Orthodox' Rabbi."[442] In addition, Lichtenstein's own writings from 1885 and onwards do not give the impression that he had much sympathy to the Neolog position with regard to Torah observance and the Jewish tradition.[443] Lichtenstein's attitude to Jewish Torah observance therefore seems not to be adapted to his formal position as a rabbi in a Neolog community. This also makes it more difficult to interpret his new faith in Jesus as that of a progressive Jewish individual who lapsed into Christianity more or less as a logical consequence of tendencies within the Neolog community. Still, it is not unlikely that the general cultural and social atmosphere influenced his local congregation, making it easier for him to be accepted as its rabbi even after his religious reorientation. On the other hand, I describe below how the same conditions did not make it easier for him to relate to the national Neolog leadership.

The Blood Libel of Tisza Eszlar and Lichtenstein's New Faith

Isaac Lichtenstein was almost 60 when he publically declared his newfound faith in Jesus, around 1885–1886. From then to 1892, the Jewish congregation in the Hungarian village Tápiószele became an object of heated controversy in the national Jewish communities. As late as 1929, a Magyar lexicon on Hungarian Jewry, *Zsidó Lexicon*, mentions the turmoil and the congregation's infamous rabbi:

> In the 1890s the Jewish community in the town became famous because of the Lichtenstein-affair. The motto of the pamphlet Judentum und Christentum was "Kinek a zsidó vallás nehéz, keresse üdvét Jézus kebelén (for whom the Jewish religion is too difficult, should seek salvation in the bosom of Jesus)." Resigned because of disapproval of the public. The rabbinate in the town was vacant until 1923, when it was merged with the Nagykáta rabbinate.[444]

A couple of years before Lichtenstein made his views known, Hungary had been shaken by a wave of anti-Semitism that shocked the Jewish community: the so-called Tisza Eszlar affair that took place between 1882 and 1883, and which awoke general resentment against Jews in

---

442. Baron, "Rabbi Ignatz Lichtenstein," 265, see also footnotes on the same page.
443. Ibid., 265; Lichtenstein, *Die Liebe*, 30.
444. Anonymous, "Tápiószele," 881.

the Hungarian population outside Budapest.[445] On April 1, 1882, the 14-year-old Hungarian housemaid Eszter Solymosi disappeared; it was three days before Pesach. Hungarian anti-Semites, led by parliament member Gyozo Istoczy, spread the charge that the Jews had killed the girl in order to use her blood at the Passover. Her mother accused the Jews before the local judge of having murdered her daughter, and urged him to investigate. Later a local court decided that a corpse found in the river was the girl, and that her neck showed signs of a ritual murder. Thirteen members of the local Jewish community were arrested and kept in custody for over a year. Between June and August 1883 a new trial was held, where the main witness, the 6-year-old son of one of the suspects, was put in doubt by the court, particularly after an inspection of the scene of the alleged murder. The process was intensely debated in the Hungarian public, and has been called the Hungarian parallel to the Dreyfus affair in France. After the acquittal of the accused Jews, large anti-Semitic riots followed on August 7–12, 1883, in Budapest as well as other cities and rural areas.[446]

Paradoxically, this renewed experience of hatred toward the Jews came in the middle of the so-called golden age of Hungarian Jewry. Although mainstream Hungarian Jews continued to identify themselves with the Magyar cause, Tisza Eszlar was a shock for the Jewish community. For Rabbi Lichtenstein it became a landmark.[447] In most of his writings, Lichtenstein comes back to this episode and the wave of anti-Semitism that surfaced in the wake of it. This experience not only scared him but also led him into depression, and at first his antipathy towards Christians was confirmed. However, over some time this attitude began to change as he read several articles defending the Jews written by Christian scholars who sometimes referred to the New Testament. Gjessing and Baron report that articles by Delitzsch especially made an impression on him. In response to a plea from leaders of the Hungarian Jewish committee, Delitzsch wrote an article in which he rejected the medieval idea of Jews using Christian blood in the Pesach.

445. Handler, *Blood Libel*, 12–13. For unknown reasons Gjessing dates the event to 1876.

446. According to Kramer, the affair is still central in post-war Hungarian anti-Semitism, as the accused were regarded as guilty by many as late as the 1970s, apparently unaware of the verdict of the court. Kramer, *From Emancipation*, 16, 39.

447. According to Baron, Tisza Eszlar was in Lichtenstein's region. Anonymous, "Rabbi Lichtenstein og hans Omvendelse," 65–73; 68–69.

For Lichtenstein, whose attitude towards representatives of the church was skeptical, a Christian scholar publically defending the Jews made a great impact.[448]

This led him to look up a German New Testament he had gotten several years before, when a member of his synagogue showed it to him and asked what it was about. At that time Lichtenstein had placed it on his shelf without looking more closely at it. Now he picked it out to read and while reading, he began to believe that Jesus was the Messiah:

> I looked for thorns and found roses, instead of uncovering stones—pearls, treasures above this world, instead of hate, love, instead of revenge, forgivness, instead of slavery, redemption, instead of pride, humbleness, instead of hostility, reconciliation, instead of death, life, salvation, resurrection.[449]

However, for a long time Lichtenstein did not tell anyone about this. He kept his new faith secret for two or three years while he continued to work as a rabbi, and even began to include his new views on Christ in his sermons.[450] Then, when preaching on a Sabbath about Jesus' parable of the whited sepulcher (Matt 23:27), he confessed his newfound faith for the first time.[451] In contrast to the later uproar from the national Jewish community, the local synagogue does not seem to have reacted negatively. While the obituary in *Judische Alllgemeine Zeitung* explains this with reference to Lichtenstein's relatives and friends in the community, it is also possible that his views found some sympathy among some members. According to Gjessing, the local Jewish community even accepted a Christian teacher being employed at the Jewish school. This event can

---

448. Gjessing, "Rabbi Isak (Ignaz) Lichtenstein," 173; and Anonymous, "Rabbi Lichtenstein og hans Omvendelse," 70. Still, Lichtenstein does not seem to have recovered completely after the shock of the blood libel. He comes back to this "plague" in his letter to his son in 1887. Lichtenstein, *Two Letters*, 29–30.

449. Lichtenstein, *Judenthum und Christenthum*, 8. "Denn ich forschte nach Dornen und plückte Rosen, entdeckte anstatt Kiesel—Perlen, überirdische Scätze, anstatt Hass Liebe, anstatt Rache Vergebung, anstatt Knechthaft Erlösung, anstatt Stoltz Demuth, anstatt Feindschaft Versöhnung, anstatt Tod Leben—Heil—Auferstehung." Lichtenstein writes that he had confiscated the New Testament for 33 years before reading it. Baron claims the member Lichtenstein refers to was the local Jewish teacher. Anonymous, "Rabbi Lichtenstein og hans Omvendelse," 68.

450. According to Gjessing this took place for seven or eight years, which approximately covers the gap between about 1884–1885 and the year of the Tisza affair.

451. Baron, "Rabbi Ignatz Lichtenstein," 255.

also be explained by the general attitude in the Jewish community toward learning Magyar, but nevertheless it is difficult to see how the rabbi could continue in the town for years, until the early 1890s, without some local sympathy.

The First Writings between 1886 and 1892

At about the same time he openly confessed his belief in Jesus as the Messiah, Lichtenstein met Dr. Andrew Moody, who worked for the Scotch Mission in Budapest. The meeting probably took place during the last six months of 1884.[452] Moody had come to Hungary in 1864 to work for the Free Church of Scotland's Mission to the Jews, and had significant influence on the Reformed and Lutheran churches in Hungary for the next forty years.[453]

To begin with, Lichtenstein did not identify himself, but later he revealed to Moody how he had decided to make an effort to lead his congregation to Christ, as he had been with them for a long time: "He was determined, if possible, not to separate himself from the Jews. Did not Christ belong to the Jews? was his contention."[454] Several times Moody encouraged him to publish his thoughts, an idea Lichtenstein was at first reluctant about. This nevertheless resulted in three small books: *Der Talmud auf der Anklagebank durch einen begeisterten Verehrer des Judenthums* ("The Talmud in the Dock by an Enthusiastic Worshipper of Judaism"), *Mein Zeugnis* ("My Testimony"), and *Die Liebe und die*

---

452. Moody, "Report of the Rev. Andrew Moody" (1887), 12 and idem, "Report of the Rev. Andrew Moody" (1891), 6. See also Moody, "Budapest. Report of Rev. Andrew Moody" (1892), 4–6 and idem, "Budapest. Report of Rev. Andrew Moody, B.A." (1894), 7–8. See also Kjær-Hansen, "Isaac Lichtenstein," 1–5.

453. Kool, *God Moves*, 106. During the modernization and industrialization of Hungarian society during most of the 19th century, the Protestant churches were rooted in the traditional feudal system. In spite of the political alliance between the different Protestant churches in Hungary (the Lutheran, the Reformed and the Baptists), on a religious level there were strong barriers between the communities, and due to strong rationalist influences very little mission work was initiated by these churches before WWI. Until 1910, the Reformed Church in Hungary did not involve itself systematically into mission work to Jews or other peoples, although an increasing number of its members became involved in the work of the Free Church of Scotland's Mission to the Jews in Budapest. Kovács, *The History*, 389, 394; and Sípos, *'Bittet den Herrn der Ernte,'* 210.

454. Kjær-Hansen, "Isaac Lichtenstein," 2; Moody, "Report of the Rev. Andrew Moody," (1887) 9.

Bekehrung ("The Love and the Conversion").[455] All were published in Budapest in 1886, but before Lichtenstein met Moody, he had already been in touch with the Jewish-Christian missionary Schönberger in Vienna since 1884.[456] Together with David Baron (see below), Schönberger appears to have been Lichtenstein's closest friend for the next decades.

Lichtenstein's writings naturally were met with much interest in mission circles. He had insisted on publishing *Der Talmud* first, according to Moody, "to introduce himself to the public in his real character as a true Jew, who held in high honor the commentaries and traditions of the fathers."[457] Consequently, it was not until the publication of *Mein Zeugnis*, with Lichtenstein's outspoken sympathy for Jesus, that the Jewish community in Hungary and Austria reacted. For Moody and others in the mission societies, Lichtenstein's views on Judaism and Christianity became more interesting in light of Rabinowitz's movement in Bessarabia at the same time. However, in spite of his relations to Moody, Schönberger and other missionaries, Lichtenstein refused to be associated with a mission society, not to mention being baptized. Both Baron and Gjessing inform that Lichtenstein's position also awoke the interest of the Roman Catholic Church. According to Baron, a special emissary from the pope visited Lichtenstein in Tápiószele to find out if Lichtenstein would associate himself with the Catholic Church. In Baron's version, Lichtenstein gave an answer that probably is representative of his general attitude to official conversion to any Christian church:

> I will remain among my own nation. I love Christ, I believe in the New Testament, but I am not drawn to Christendom. Just as the prophet Jeremiah, after the destruction of Jerusalem, in spite of generous offers of Nebuchadnezzar and the captain of his host, chose rather to remain and lament among the ruins of

---

455. Lichtenstein, *Der Talmud*. Using among other texts Mark 12:28 and Matt 5:17–18, the pamphlet stresses the continuity between Talmud and the New Testament, while most of the work is a defense against McCaul's accusation against the Jewish tradition. Lichtenstein, *Mein Zeugnis*. Referring to Deuteronomy and John 1:17–18, as well as paragraphs from the Talmud, Lichtenstein claims not only Jesus' messiahship but also describes him as Moses' true successor as well as the Truth sent to Earth. Lichtenstein, *Die Liebe*. While complaining about Israel's spiritual decline, he points to Jesus as the national spiritual medical doctor (referring to Matt 5:29–30; 9:12; and Acts 15:10–11).

456. Le Roi, *Geschichte*, 2:279.

457. Kjær-Hansen, "Isaac Lichtenstein," 2; Moody, "Report of the Rev. Andrew Moody" (1887), 9–12.

the holy city, and with the despised remnant of his brethren, so I will remain among my own people, as a watchman from within, to warn them and to plead with them to behold in Jesus the true glory of Israel.[458]

Gjessing mentions a similar story, but does not mention anything about the visitor being sent from the pope. Instead he claims that his name was Zettler of Maissen, and that the purpose of the visit was to ask Lichtenstein to take care of the church's Hebrew library. This is probably the same emissary Baron reports about. Lichtenstein rejected the offer, according to Gjessing, saying that "I am no Daniel that dares to go to a lion's cave."[459]

In the Jewish community Lichtenstein did not attract many followers. According to *The Peculiar People* seven years later, "The 'movement' of Rabbi Lichtenstein, of Tapio-Tzele, amounts to next to nothing. Rabbi Lichtenstein appears to be about to have as little influence as Rabinowitz."[460] Nevertheless, his publications in 1886 naturally created much frustration in the Jewish press and the Hungarian community, and the question is of course how he managed to stay in his position for the next six years.[461] Although we do not hear much about local op-

458. Baron, "Rabbi Ignatz Lichtenstein," 257.

459. Gjessing, "Rabbi Isak (Ignaz) Lichtenstein," 174. Gjessing titles Zettler in Norwegian as "katolsk domherre." The equivalent term in English is not clear, but indicates that he was a priest associated with a bishop's seat. I have not been able to identify this person, nor any particular interest towards Jewish converts from any Catholic network in Hungary at the time. Nevertheless, the Catholic Church in Austria-Hungary was to some extent familiar with Jewish mission. In the 19th century some Catholic orders were founded especially to convert Jews; the most famous was the Congregation of Notre Dame de Sion from 1843. The order came to Romania in 1867, where it ran two schools. Pruter, *Jewish Christians*, 39–41; Harling, "Katholische Missionsbestrebungen," 71; and Terray, *Et liv i grenseland*, 73.

460. *The Peculiar People* 6 (1893) 161–67, 166.

461. However, Lichtenstein also refers to some positive reactions; *Judenthum und Christenthum*, iv (referring to the journal *Der Ungarischer Israelit* 31 [1886]). In addition, he must have been read with interest by other progressive Jews, see the letter from *Der Israelitischen Allianz zu Wien* in October 1889, in *Judenthum und Christenthum*, 37. The *Allianz* was founded in 1872 to promote relief and school support for Russian, Galician and Romanian Jews, and it therefore lobbied the Austrian foreign minister frequently. The leaders of the society, who also signed the letter, were Wilhelm von Gutman (1834–1912) and his brother David von Gutman (1825–1895), president of the society. They were financiers and philanthropists, having built a fortune on coal and metal mining, and at the same time founded several orphanages and asylums. Both had been elevated to the Austrian nobility in 1879, and Wilhelm was also a member of the

position to Lichtenstein, we can assume it was there, due to the common attitude to such apostasy. However, as Lichtenstein could not be fired unless this was required by the local congregation, the situation could not have gone on for so long without local support.[462] The Jewish obituary referred to by Baron relates this support to family relations. Moody also confirms the impression that many in Lichtenstein's congregation in Tápiószele were loyal to him: ". . . we were told that on one occasion, a member rose to say, 'We are attached to our Rabbi and wish no other, and if he tells us that we ought to be baptized we shall follow him.'"[463] One missionary reports about the local attitudes to Lichtenstein: 6th of May 1896 Philippus Gordon, who worked for the Swedish Israel Mission, visited Tapio Tzele together with David Baron. Her they met several of the members of the synagogue, both friends and enemies of Lichtenstein. One of the former was the director of the synagogue and a relative to Lichtenstein.[464]

Still, the biggest problems came from the leadership of the Neolog community in Budapest. In spite of the strong acculturation and identification with the Magyar nation among Neologs, Lichtenstein was regarded as an embarrassment. Both Baron and Gjessing report that Lichtenstein was summoned to the rabbinate in Budapest; according to Gjessing he had to meet Chief Rabbi Kohn, Rabbi Kayserling and Dr. Brüll.[465] While Kohn is said to have been emotional and rude at the meet-

---

Austrian Diet. Although probably an attempt at "name-dropping" from Lichtenstein, this reference nevertheless indicates what sort of audience Lichtenstein aimed at with his writings, and probably who read them as well. From the letter from the *Allianz* it is difficult to say whether the society was sympathetic to Lichtenstein or not. Sending him such a list of Jewish deeds may just as well have been a reaction intended to prove how Jewish ethics was well-founded by Judaism and did not need any assistance from Christianity. Landmann, "Gutman, David von," and "Gutman, Wilhelm von," and http://www.jewishencyclopedia.com/view.jsp?artid=332&letter=I.

462. Anonymous, "Rabbi Lichtenstein og hans Omvendelse," 72.

463. Kjær-Hansen, "Isaac Lichtenstein," 3, referring to Moody in *Free Church of Scotland, Report of the Committee of the Conversion of the Jews* (volume not given).

464. Gordon, *På Missionresor*, 10–13.

465. Sámuel Kohn (1841–1920) was a renowned historian and Hungarian rabbi in Budapest from 1866 to 1905, when he became chief rabbi of the *Israelitische Landskanzlei*. He was central during the Jewish Congress in 1868–1869, and was one of the first rabbis to give sermons in Maigyar. Kohn published several works on Jewish history, particulary on the Marranos as well as on the history of the Jews in Hungary. Scheiber, "Kohn, Samuel," 12:264. Meyer Kayserling (1829–1905) was born in Germany, and from 1870 to 1905 he was rabbi in Budapest. He published several works on Jewish

ing, Kayserling and Brüll seem to have been less provoked. Nevertheless, Lichtenstein was only willing to recant a few things, of which Gjessing does not give any details.

Baron's description of Lichtenstein's behavior is slightly more heroic: In the meeting with the assembled rabbinate in Budapest, some in the hall called out "Retract! Retract!" To which Lichtenstein replied, "Gentlemen, I shall most willingly retract if you convince me that I am wrong."[466] Rabbi Kohn eventually proposed a compromise, in which Lichtenstein could believe whatever he liked as long as he kept silent about Christ, and as long as he agreed to sign a document saying his publications had been written during a period of temporary insanity. To this Lichtenstein is said to have answered negatively, uttering that he had just come to his right mind, and would not sign any such document. At this the rabbinate demanded his resignation, saying that he was formally baptized and thus joining a Christian church. Lichtenstein answered that he had no intention of joining any church, as he had found true Judaism in the New Testament. He would therefore stay in his congregation. As Lichtenstein was neither willing to recant nor to resign, the situation appears to have been a deadlock.

When Moody encouraged Lichtenstein to give a public defense to the accusations against him, he declined to do that. Lichtenstein stayed in his position in Tápiószele until 1892, as the Neolog community appears to have been unable to force him away from the post. Traditionally, local Jewish communities in Hungary were largely autonomous entities, and before 1867 most decisions concerning employing a rabbi would be made at the local level.[467] From the obituary in *Jüdische Allgemeine Zeitung* it appears that Lichtenstein's position in the local community made it difficult for the national leadership to do anything with the situation, and it is possible that Budapest was holding back stronger sanctions in fear of the political consequences if they tried to overrule a local community. In addition, perhaps they were considering that Lichtenstein's age would make him retire quite soon anyway.[468]

---

history and literature, particularly on the Marranos. Roth, "Kayserling, Meyer," 12:42.

466. Baron, "Rabbi Ignatz Lichtenstein," 260.

467. Schwarzfuchs, *A Consise*, xi.

468. This does not mean that the Neolog leadership was passive in its attitude towards evangelical influence in the following years. Between 1884 and 1888, leading Neolog editors and school leaders attacked the Scottish Mission for its educational work

In its article about Tápiószele, *Zsidó Lexicon* says that the rabbinate of the community remained vacant until 1923 after Lichtenstein left the town. That the community did not have a rabbi for thirty years after Lichtenstein left is not explained anywhere, but a lack of qualified rabbis may of course be the reason. However, Gjessing and Baron report that after Lichtenstein's resignation, the neighboring rabbi is said to have died in an accident at the railway station when he was on his way to take over Lichtenstein's post. Therefore, after moving to Budapest, Lichtenstein continued to visit the congregation for the next two years.[469] Although not stated explicitly, it is reasonable to believe that Gjessing and Baron considered this event (if it ever took place) an act of divine providence. It is also possible that such an event, in addition to the generally controversial reputation of the Tápiószele community among Hungarian Jewry, made candidates for the post of rabbi there less interested in taking the job.

Although Lichtenstein was not forced to withdraw by the Neolog leadership, he nevertheless resigned in the beginning of 1892, when he was about 67 years old.[470] The move was due to the economic situation of the Jewish community in the town, as it appears to have been exposed to economic sanctions from the national Jewish community. According to Moody the economic losses in Tápiószele took place in 1888–1889.[471] Apparently several members of the community had been ruined due to broken business relations with other Jewish communities in Hungary. This included some relatives of Lichtenstein's wife. According to Baron's reference to the obituary in the *Jüdische Allgemeine Zeitung*, Lichtenstein was forced to leave by the community as a result of these events, something Baron rejects.[472] Nevertheless, although Baron

---

among Jewish children in Budapest, as well as the society's alleged connection to the "swindler" Rabinowitz in Russia. The non-Magyar profile (most of the teachers spoke German) and the offense of encouraging Jewish children to convert to Christianity were central accusations. Kovács, *The History*, 228–37. However, what actually was done and said among and from Lichtenstein's oponents in the efforts to get him away from the rabbinate, is not clear. To find out how a community like the Neolog leadership handled the Lictenstein-affair would be an interesting research topic in itself, not least to better understand the internal dynamics within Hungarian Jewry in this period.

469. Gjessing, "Rabbi Isak (Ignaz) Lichtenstein," 175.
470. Perhaps in April; Baron, "Rabbi Ignatz Lichtenstein," 258.
471. Kjær-Hansen, "Isaac Lichtenstein" 2.
472. Baron, "Rabbi Ignatz Lichtenstein," 264.

claims that Lichtenstein eventually retired voluntarily, he affirms that it was to avoid further problems for the community in Tápiószele. The embargo also made Lichtenstein lose his own fortune, and in addition, his health became worse. Lichtenstein's economic problems are partly explained with the loss of several large sums, partly because he lost an amount of money he was given in compensation for handing over a part of the district to his own brother. The local support for Lichtenstein may also have dwindled. During this period Lichtenstein complained that he received more pity than sympathy among those closest to him, and some in his family declared him insane.[473] He also describes how his wife became despondent and spiritless due to the pressure. Lichtenstein's son Emmanuel, who appears not to have followed his father's new faith, wrote to him that he would support him economically.[474]

During the two years before he left Tápiószele he therefore seems to have been without regular income, and was supported financially by the Jewish-Christian missionary Arnold Frank in Hamburg. Frank offered him a job at the mission in Hamburg, but due to the hints about baptism, Lichtenstein rejected the offer.[475] When Lichtenstein or other sources describe the difficulties he experienced from the Jewish community, it is not always clear if the episodes took place while he was in Budapest or still in Tápiószele. In several of his writings Lichtenstein complains about the attacks from the Jewish community, particularly the other Hungarian rabbis. After the publication of Lichtenstein's last pamphlet, *Ein Geheimnis aus dem Talmud* ("A Mystery from the Talmud") in 1900, one of those who went against Lichtenstein was Kayserling, who accused Lichtenstein of national betrayal: "The person who reveals a secret betrays his people."[476] Gjessing says that in order to stop Lichtenstein's influence, a cultural society was also established, although it appears to have been difficult to find a strategy that would unify his opponents.[477]

473. Lichtenstein, *Judenthum und Christenthum*, iv.

474. Letter dated January 1, 1887, in Budapest, less than three weeks before he died; ibid. Rabbi Lichtenstein's answer from Tapio Tzele on January 8, 1887, is not without wit. Regarding the economy he refers to the Midrash about Jacob being comforted by God about going to Egypt: "A father may indeed care for ten children, yet ten children can scarcely support one father!" ("Zwei Briefe," 5–8, 13).

475. Gjessing, "Rabbi Isak (Ignaz) Lichtenstein," 174.

476. Ibid., 175.

477. Although not saying from where he got this information, Gjessing gives a rather detailed description of what took place at this meeting: Chief Rabbi Kohn made

In addition to the insults against him in the Hungarian Jewish press, Lichtenstein sometimes was harassed physically; he was knocked down at least once, and half of his beard was cut off. However, these examples appear to have been the only events of such character. Nevertheless, the stigma associated with his person continued; in Budapest one owner of a mikve asked him to stay away, otherwise he would be ruined.[478]

In addition to the controversies and economic problems, the Lichtensteins experienced their biggest loss in this period when their oldest son, the above-mentioned Emanuel Lichtenstein, died in his parents' home in Tápiószele on January 20, 1887, soon after his 28th birthday.[479] Shortly before their son's death, the Lichtensteins were visited for the first time by David Baron, who came together with Schönberger, both at the time representing the Mildmay Mission. They stayed with the family during the son's last days and possibly some time after the funeral, trying to comfort both the son and the parents.[480] Probably this visit and the care of the missionaries was an important reason for the lifelong friendship between the Lichtensteins and Baron and Schönberger, which was to last until the rabbi's death.

Hamburg, London, and Budapest

After his resignation Lichtenstein traveled for several months, and before settling down in Budapest early in 1893, he had been in Hamburg and London. In Hamburg, Lichtenstein stayed with the Irish-Presbyterian Mission and the local missionary Frank, from his resignation from Tápiószele in spring 1892 to the beginning of 1893. Frank had supported Lichtenstein economically in the last two years, and the publication of

---

a speech, while Wisburg and Block, the director of the rabbinic seminary, were present. A professor at the mercantile school in Klausenburg, Reti, was cautious about strong sanctions, and said one should not condemn anyone without having heard their opinion first. He also found it legitimate to read the New Testament to learn the weapons of the enemy. ibid.

478. Ibid. Gjessing describes Lichtenstein as a humorous character in some of these episodes: when visiting the synagogue people once asked him, "What is Saul seeking among the prophets?" to which Lichtenstein promptly retorted, "I am looking for the donkeys."

479. Herman, "Den ungarske rabbiner Lichtenstein," 53–59, 72–78.

480. Gjessing, "Rabbi Isak (Ignaz) Lichtenstein," 174; Baron, "Rabbi Ignatz Lichtenstein," 251. Earlier Baron had claimed that the son came to faith in Jesus shortly before he died; Anonymous, "Rabbi Lichtenstein og hans Omvendelse," 68.

Christentum und Judentum was probably sponsored by the mission in Hamburg. Frank also offered him a job as some sort of missionary in Hamburg. The offer said that he did not have to be baptized first, but vague utterings that Frank hoped he would do this, made Lichtenstein reject the offer.[481]

Shortly after the publication of *Christentum und Judentum*, Lichtenstein made his first of three visits to Britain. Wilkinson, the leader of the Mildmay Mission, was behind the invitation, and was apparently encouraged by Baron. At the official meeting that took place in the conference hall at Mildmay in London, Lichtenstein explained his position: He neither could nor would join any mission society. However, if it were possible, he would move to Budapest and be a voice from within the Jewish community there. To do this he needed support. The result of this meeting was that a small council was formed for the support of Lichtenstein and his writings. The group consisted of General Halliday, John Wilkinson, David Baron and five or six others. In addition, C. A. Schönberger seems to have been an important ally for Baron. This group continued its work until Lichtenstein's death.[482]

Budapest and Lichtenstein's Writings between 1893 and 1908

After settling down in Budapest in the beginning of 1893, Lichtenstein lived there the rest of his life.[483] During the following seven years in the Hungarian capital he also wrote most of his publications with the economic support of the committee in London.[484] Lichtenstein does not ap-

481. Gjessing, "Rabbi Isak (Ignaz) Lichtenstein," 174.

482. Baron, "Rabbi Ignatz Lichtenstein," 258. Nothing is said about what happened with the financial situation of Lichtenstein's widow.

483. According to a letter from Lichtenstein, he had left Tápiószele around April 1892; ibid. Other than Hamburg, Budapest happened to be the European city with the largest number of missionaries working among the Jews. In the middle of the 1920s there were about 30 workers stationed in each of the cities. Kjær-Hansen, "Occupation of the Field," 5. The Lichtensteins' street adress in Budapest was Kerület (district) 7, Kiraly u. 9. Marton, "Zsidók útja a világ Messiásához," 51.

484. The following list of eleven published texts is mainly based on Jorge Quiñónez's collection of Lichtenstein's writings, and when in doubt, I have followed his suggestions concerning date of publication. Unfortunately I cannot tell if the list is complete, as none of the sources give any detailed overview of Lichtenstein's publications:
- *Judenthum und Christenthum* (Hamburg: A. Scheibenhuber, year of publication probably 1891 or 1892).
- "Svar på Spørgsmål i Israel: Af et Sabbatsforedrag for Jøder av I. Lichtenstein; med-

pear to have seen any connection between this economic support and a breaking of any Jewish boundaries. In fact he compares himself with the ancient prophets, who also found themselves isolated when they tried to proclaim God's word. According to Baron, the main reason he gives for this choice is to be a witness for Christ within his nation:

> It is a riddle to them that I do not cut my connection with my people, that I still visit the synagogues and frequent Jewish circles, in spite of continual insult and humiliation. They do not see that it is in this very way I obtain the opportunity that I wish for,

---

delt av Pastor Gjessing" ("Answers on questions in Israel: A Sabbath lecture for Jews by I. Lichtenstein; shared by Pastor Gjessing"). In *Missions-Blad for Israel* 67, issue 4–5 (1893) 67.
- "Zwei Briefe oder 'was ich eigentlich will,'" *Saat auf Hoffnung* 30 (1893) 9–36. In "Zwei Briefe" Isaac Lichtenstein gives a summary of the discussion between father and son. The promise to Abraham and the mission of Israel is fulfilled in Jesus. "The Eternal, He is God" may indicate a high Christology. In the following I refer to the English translation, I. Lichtenstein, *Two Letters, or What I really Wish* (London: Hebrew Christian Testimony to Israel, translated by Mrs. Baron, year of publication is unknown).
- "Das Blut Christi, ein Nachklang aus dem Midrasch Echa," *Saat auf Hoffnung* 30 (1893) 229–32.
- *Eine Bitte an die geehrten Leser* (Budapest, 1893 or 1894). In my references, I use the English version: *An Appeal to the Jewish People, by the late Rabbi I. Lichtenstein, Budapest* (London: The Hebrew Christian Testimony to Israel, year of publication unknown).
- "Welche Anknüpfungspunkte findet die evangelische Verkündigung bei den Juden?" in Gustaf Dalman (ed.), *Die allgemeine Konferenz für Judenmission in Leipzig, abgehalten vom 6. bis 8. Juni 1895* (Leipzig, 1896), 40–55 (Schriften des Institutum Judaicum in Leipzig, No. 44–46); for references I use the English version, *The Points of Contact between Evangelical and Jewish Doctrine. An Address by Rabbi I. Lichtenstein (delivered at Leipsic). Translated from the German by Mrs. Baron* (London: Mr. Fegan's Homes, 1908). A Norwegian version is given by Gjessing in *Missions-Blad for Israel* 69, issue 6–7 (1895) 145.
- *Ein Judenspiegel* (Vienna: L. Schönberger, 1896).
- "Ein Weihnachts- und Neujahrsgruß an alle Neugeborenen im Herrn," *Saat auf Hoffnung* 36 (1899) 5–9.
- *Ein Geheimniss aus dem Talmud* (Vienna: L. Schönberger, 1900). When I refer to this work, the pagination is from the original German version, while the English translation in my text is based on the unpublished translation of Monika Ewell from 2004: "A Secret from the Talmud, by Rabbi J. (sic.) Lichtenstein (Budapest, Trommelgasse 52)."
- "Ein Weihnachts und Neujahrsgruß für die auserwählten Kinder des Lichtes," *Saat auf Hoffnung* 37 (1900) 35–40.
- "Ein Neujahrsgruß für die Neugebornen im Herrn zum Heilsjahre 1902," *Saat auf Hoffnung* 39 (1902) 5–8.

and am able to distribute hundreds of New Testaments and other missionary literature, and thus sow the holy seed.[485]

Although nothing is said about the committee in London demanding any mission work in Budapest on Lichtenstein's part, it seems that he at least expected this from himself. In practical terms he functioned like a freelance missionary, particularly as a correspondent with Jewish inquirers. If one believes Baron, being such a witness became a characteristic part of Lichtenstein's personal identity.

Baron describes how Lichtenstein during his first stay in Budapest was quite optimistic about his new opportunities for proclaiming Christ in the Hungarian capital.[486] From the list of publications it is also clear that Lichtenstein was particularly efficient in his writing the three first years in Budapest. During his first month in the Hungarian capital he was also asked to preach in a synagogue. Apparently the meetings awoke much interest and drew many visitors, including Jewish students from the rabbinate seminary in Budapest. The Norwegian article "Svar på Spørgsmål i Israel" in 1893 (see list of publications in note 484), may be minutes from one of the first of these lectures, and is probably representative of both the style and content of his public speeches.[487] Soon, however, the Jewish authorities told the president of the synagogue to keep Lichtenstein away from the pulpit, and scholars from the rabbinate seminary who had attended his sermons, were forced to stop any communication with him. The students' parents were also warned if their son was identified at the meetings.

However, according to Moody's reports from the middle of the 1890s, Lichtenstein's public activity does not appear to have been very significant. In the 1893 report for the Free Church mission work in Budapest, Moody writes that the mission society had started arranging Bible study groups in Hebrew on Sundays. According to Moody, Lichtenstein was usually present at these meetings, but except for giving some comments on the texts with the others, he does not appear to have had a leading role. In addition, there appears to have been a certain condition for his presence, as ". . . he is ready to take part in this meeting as it is not advertised." Kai Kjær-Hansen suggests that this

---

485. Baron, "Rabbi Ignatz Lichtenstein," 261.
486. Ibid., 258-59.
487. Lichtenstein, "Svar på Spørgsmål i Israel," 53-58.

note means that Lichtenstein was poorly motivated to witness about his faith.[488] However, considering his literary production in the same period, it is more reasonable to believe that he was reluctant about being publically associated with the Free Church mission work as such, as that could strengthen the accusations from the Jewish community about his being an agent for the missions. Comparing the narratives of Baron and Moody, it seems that Lichtenstein was quite active (for his age) in relation to the Jewish community as long as he had the opportunity. However, taking part in organized events with the mission societies may have been more problematic for him.

Nevertheless, Lichtenstein continued to attract much interest, and claims he was often questioned about his position by visitors.[489] In Baron's opinion, Lichtenstein's most significant work was his extensive correspondence with many sympathizers.[490] He continued to go to the synagogues and observed some of the Jewish customs, like using the mikve.[491] Neither did he "modernize" his outlook by shaving his beard. (That is, at least not voluntarily; as mentioned above, once half of it had been cut off by some who were offended by him.[492]) Still to be a part of the Jewish people was central for him, as he stated to Baron that it was only from within that he could influence his people.[493] Although violent insults or other aggressive acts by other Jews do not seem to have been a regular occurence, he continued to receive anathemas from both the press and the pulpits. According to Baron he was particularly accused of having sold himself to the English (Anglican) missionaries.[494]

Baptism

The fact that Lichtenstein never let himself be officially baptized probably caused much frustration in the mission societies that in the beginning were encouraged by his writings. The reports about Lichtenstein in the Norwegian *Missions-Blad for Israel* from the 1880s and 1890s, which

488. Kjær-Hansen, "Isaac Lichtenstein," 2.
489. Baron, "Rabbi Ignatz Lichtenstein," 259.
490. Ibid.
491. Gjessing, "Rabbi Isak (Ignaz) Lichtenstein," 175.
492. Ibid.
493. Baron, "Rabbi Ignatz Lichtenstein," 256.
494. Ibid.

are always positive, usually regretfully comment that he still had not been baptized.[495] For Lichtenstein, baptism was the gateway out of the Jewish community, and in 1892/1893 he refused Frank's offer of a post in Hamburg owing to the fact that Frank and his society hoped he would later be baptized. Within the Hungarian context, an official baptism meant that the convert automatically became a member of the denomination of the minister, thus cutting all official bonds to Hungarian Judaism.[496] In his 1887 report, Moody describes his own attempts to convince Lichtenstein to be baptized, and he regrets that the rabbi rejected this.[497] In winter 1887–1888 the Scottish evangelist Andrew Somerville drew thousands of people to his meetings in Hungary, an event that caught much interest.[498] During this journey Somerville also met Lichtenstein, and they discussed baptism.[499] When Baron in his obituary criticizes some of Lichtenstein's positions, he mentions the issue of baptism only indirectly, when describing how he several times tried to persuade Lichtenstein that every (Jewish) believer in Jesus would have to associate himself with other believers.[500] So far Gjessing is the only source I have found that claims Lichtenstein was baptized, or more precisely, that he baptized himself in a Sabbath mikve one Friday afternoon.[501] However, no date or other details are given about this event, but this issue will be discussed closer in the analysis.

Leipzig 1895 and Britain 1896

In June 1895, the 70-year-old rabbi was invited to hold a lecture at the mission conference in Leipzig. This event is striking not only in light of Lichtenstein's repeated refusals to be associated with any mission society, but also due to the controversy concerning the authenticity of his

495. E.g., Herman, "Den ungarske rabbiner Lichtenstein," 77; and "Rabbi Lichtenstein og hans Omvendelse," 73.

496. In *Ein Geheimnis*, 41, Lichtenstein quotes Paul's statement in Romans 9 about how he would prefer to be cut off from salvation if it could save Israel. It is possible that this is also a comment on him not being baptized.

497. Kjær-Hansen, "Isaac Lichtenstein," 3; Moody, "Report of the Rev. Andrew Moody" (1887), 9–12.

498. Sípos, '*Bittet den Herrn der Ernte*,' 39.

499. Kovács, *The History*, 240.

500. Baron, "Rabbi Ignatz Lichtenstein," 261.

501. Gjessing, "Rabbi Isak (Ignaz) Lichtenstein," 175.

conversion. Interestingly, none of these concerns is reflected in the minutes from the conference, which on the other hand give a detailed report about the tensions between Lucky's supporters and opponents later at the same conference, where Dalman even indicates that Lichtenstein was cautious about Lucky's agenda. The background for the invitation is not clear, but it is possible that Baron or other members of the London committee initiated it. By then Lichtenstein had published at least three books and pamphlets in addition to the three published while he was in Tápiószele. In the later publications he not only discusses the relationship between Christianity and Judaism, but also very directly encourages his Jewish readers to embrace Jesus. In light of the general growth of modern anti-Semitism and in particular the pogroms in Eastern Europe since the 1880s, one can only assume that *Das Blut Christi* in particular awoke some interest.[502] His lecture "Welche Anknüpfungspunkte findet die evangelische Verkündigung bei den Juden?" appears to have been welcomed with interest, and was later to be published in mission periodicals as well as translated into English.

In 1896 Lichtenstein went on his second journey to Britain to meet Baron and the rest of the support committee. On his way back to Hungary, Lichtenstein and Baron traveled together in Holland to different meetings arranged by Baroness H. d'Abling. Baron states that the translator at most of the meetings was a certain Mr. Van Os. In Amsterdam he spoke to about 1,500 people in the Free Church of Scotland building. In Hague he spoke in the Nieuwe Kerk, and in Rotterdam in the Princen Kerk to about 2,000 people. In addition, he held speeches at meetings in Haarlem, Utrecht and Leyden, and, according to Baron, many Jews attended.[503] At these meeting Lichtenstein related how he first began to believe that Jesus was Israel's Messiah and redeemer, and that he gives new life as well as revealing God's mysteries.

However, in Budapest his opportunities to preach publically in the Jewish community were increasingly reduced, partly due to resistance from the Jewish community, but also due to his continued refusal to identify himself with any church. He found this development highly

---

502. In 1908 there existed a version of this pamphlet in English, published by Hebrew Christian Testimony. Lichtenstein, *The Points of Contact*, 2.

503. Baron refers to summaries in *The Scattered Nation* 1896; Baron, "Rabbi Ignatz Lichtenstein," 260.

disappointing and frustrating, and Baron recalls that Lichtenstein often said something like:

> Oh, if there were only a Hebrew Christian Church, how gladly I would join it! If I was twenty years younger, I would endeavour myself to form one. In England I feel altogether different; but in the Gentile Churches as they are here I feel out of my element, and they are not a help, but a hindrance to my spiritual life.[504]

In a letter to Baron in 1898 Lichtenstein goes on to describe his agony over his situation:

> The famous philosopher, Hegel, complained on his death-bed that he had but one disciple who understood him, and he had misunderstood him; so I look to the left hand, and none understand me; to the right, and I am still misunderstood. Not alone my enemies misunderstand me, but even true friends of Israel, who themselves rise [sic] the horn of salvation, and call Israel out of darkness and the shadow of death to loose their fetters, in the Name of the Redeemer, who by his own blood has entered in once into the Holy Place, to obtain an eternal redemption—these, my friends, who esteem me and still stand by me in my isolation, do not understand me. It is a riddle to them that I do not cut my connection with my people, that I still visit the synagogues and frequent Jewish circles, in spite of continual insult and humiliation. They do not see that it is in this very way I obtain the opportunity that I wish for, and am able to distribute hundreds of New Testaments and other missionary literature, and thus sow the holy seed—"They who sow in tears shall reap in joy."[505]

In the obituary, Baron states that he did not agree with Lichtenstein's way of distancing himself from the Christian community, as any Jew should follow Jesus outside the camp and associate themselves with other Christians. Still, he wanted to be careful with someone who had a different religious history and environment than his own. Baron understood that Lichtenstein did not feel any attraction to the local churches, and therefore did not feel it right to force him nor to withdraw support.

---

504. Ibid.
505. Ibid.

Lichtenstein's Last Years

The continued dismay from the Christian as well as the Jewish side, in addition to his declining health due to his age, seems to have reduced much of Lichtenstein's activity in the public. After 1900, Lichtenstein does not appear to have published any writings of significance, and in 1903 he went on his third and last visit to Britain with his wife. The stay appears to have been close to a holiday. Baron recalls that they stayed several weeks at the Mission House, and shared discussions and fellowship with Mr. Schönberger and others from Hebrew Christian Testimony to Israel.

According to Harold Sevener, Rabbi Lichtenstein's grandson Emmanuel Lichtenstein claims he was cared for by his grandparents when his own parents died, and sent to a boarding school and later a *gymnasium* (upper secondary).[506] Granting that Sevener is right about his age, Emmanuel Lichtenstein must have been about sixteen when Rabbi Lichtenstein died. As neither Baron nor Gjessing, nor Rabbi Lichtenstein himself, give any information about the relationship to his grandson, it is difficult to confirm. Nevertheless, Sevener's account seems to be confirmed by the Norwegian missionary Gisle Johnson, who arrived in Budapest early in the 1920s. Johnson became personally acquainted with Emmanuel Lichtenstein, and felt confident enough to invite him to meetings on several occasions around 1927.[507] In addition, the name Emmanuel can indicate a connection to Isaac Lichtenstein's oldest son, who died in 1887. If the information about Emmanuel's childhood is correct, it raises a number of questions which the sources do not answer. First of all, it is difficult to say how the old rabbi and his wife would be able to afford Emmanuel's education, considering their economic situation when leaving Tápiószele. None of the sources says anything about who got the income from the publications, but as these needed

---

506. Sevener, *A Rabbi's Vision*, 184.

507. According to Terray, there were several groups of Jewish Christians in Budapest in the period between the world wars; in 1933 there were six of them. In at least some of these groups, the term "Christ-believing Jews" was preffered to "Jewish-Christians." It is possible that Lichtenstein's writings, or the rabbi's memory, had some influence among these groups. In 1925 Johnson's group became members of the local branch of the IHCA. However, at the same time Johnson was involved in intense discussions about the nature of Jewish Christianity, particularly regarding baptism, and in the 1930s his group disintegrated. Terray, *Et liv i grenseland*, 124, 170.

financial support the outcome was probably not significant. Describing Lichtenstein's last months, Baron also mentions another grandson, who was doctor, and other relatives in Budapest, and it is more likely that the orphan was taken care of by these relatives instead of by the old and impoverished—and controversial—grandfather. However, even if this was the case, there is no reason to believe that the grandparents were isolated from the rest of the family, and Emmanuel could very well have had some contact with them. With regard to the economic situation, it is also possible that the support from the British committee was used to support Emmanuel's education together with the rest of the family. Then Baron would probably have known about it, although he might not have seen any reason to report about it.

The Lichtensteins were visited by Baron at least twice after their last journey to Britain, in 1906, when Lichtenstein's health was declining, and in June 1908.[508] On the latter occasion Baron was followed by M. Levertoff and Feinsilber, returning from a mission in Transylvania.[509] Baron found the rabbi's health better than on his visit in Budapest two years earlier.

Only weeks after this visit, in July, Lichtenstein and his wife went to the baths in Vihnye, 150 miles north of Budapest. It is possible that this stay was made possible with support from Baron. In Vihnye Lichtenstein met many Jewish visitors and patients from Hungary and Galicia, and several times he witnessed about his faith. According to Baron he wrote a letter from Vihnye asking for more New Testaments and other Yiddish and Hebrew publications, as he had met much interest and had already given away what he had brought with him.[510] In his letter he describes that he experienced the interest of an old *chazan* (cantor) without office who was leading the morning prayer one Sabbath. After the prayer, the *chazan* had read aloud the entire pamphlet *Sineath Chinom* ("They Hated Me without Cause") by Schönberger, which Lichtenstein had given to him the previous day.[511] This event, as well as the fact that he did not meet any hostilities there, encouraged him a great deal.

The letter was not finished, as the same day, August 13, Lichtenstein fell seriously ill and was taken to Budapest. His (unnamed) grandson,

508. Baron, "Rabbi Ignatz Liechtenstein," 262.
509. Ibid., 263.
510. Baron, "Rabbi Ignatz Lichtenstein," 263.
511. According to Osborne: "Hatred without Cause."

according to Baron a medical doctor in Budapest, immediately sent him to the Jewish hospital in the city. However, Lichtenstein left the hospital after three days due to what Baron calls "the frivolous conduct" of the nurses and doctors. Feinsilber, Hebrew Christian Testimony's representative in Hungary, was with Lichtenstein almost constantly for the following two months.[512] This period appears to have been characterized by conflicts, as Feinsilber seems to have been quarrelling with some of Lichtenstein's relatives about the character of the religious influence at the rabbi's death-bed. Baron says that before Feinsilber turned up the family had taken away all Christian literature, was preventing any Christian influence, and had hired some Jewish nurses. Feinsilber succeeded in replacing the Jewish nurses with two of Christian conviction. One of these was a practicing Baptist who used to read from the New Testament for the rabbi. The last two weeks Lichtenstein was mostly unconscious, but before he became too weak, he was able to thank his wife for their fifty-five year marriage, and asked Feinsilber to tell Baron and Schönberger to "Be no cowards, be not slack in preparing the Kingdom of Messiah Jesus! My whole life has been merely a seed; you will see the fruit of it to the praise of the crucified King of the Jews." He died at 8 AM on Friday, November 16, 1908, and was buried two days later at the cemetery of the Neolog Synagogue in Budapest.[513] The following day the Orthodox journal *Algemeine Judische Zeitung* published its obituary in Yiddish:

> Yesterday the former Reformed Rabbi of Tapio Tzele, I. Lichtenstein—may his name be blotted out!—was buried here. While still Rabbi, he was in the service of the soul entrapping mission. From the Jewish pulpit he proclaimed the foundation doctrines of Christianity, and wrote a pamphlet in which he invited the Jews to recognise the Founder of the Christian religion. Not until the scandal had lasted a long time did the Reformed Rabbinate

---

512. Robert Feinsilber had been associated to Rabinowitz, and before the outbreak of WWI he had become the leader of Hebrew Christian Testimony's work in Hungary, where he ran a relief work. In 1930 he was scandalized due to accusations of embezzlement and expelled from Hungary. Glaser, "A Survey," 121, and Terray, *Et liv i grenseland*, 123 and 126.

513. Baron, "Rabbi Ignatz Lichtenstein," 264. Traditionally Jewish burials were conducted by a *hevra kaddisha* ("holy society") in cooperation with a burial organization. The sources say nothing about if or how Lichtenstein's extraordinary situation was handled in regard to contact with this society or the burial organization. Haumann, *A History of East European Jews*, 158.

of Budapest succeed in inducing the representatives of the community of Tapio Tzele, composed for the most part of relatives or friends of Lichtenstein, to demand his dismissal, in order that he should withdraw from the Rabbinate.

Since that time the old apostate has lived in Budapest from the money supplied to him by English missionary societies, because he lent his name to missionary purposes. He was not, however, formally baptized, and thus this "deceiver and misleader" was buried in the cemetery of the Reformed Synagogue of Budapest. "The name of the wicked shall rot."[514]

---

514. I assume the translation of the text is done by Baron. To the expression "deceiver and misleader" Baron adds in a note: "The same Hebrew terms used about Jesus in Talmud." Marton presents a photograph of Lichtenstein's gravestone at the Jewish cemetary in Budapest (Hungarian: Budapesti Zsidó Hitközség Központi Temetöjében). See Marton, "Zsidók útja a világ Messiásához," 81.

4

Analyzing the Relationship between Jewish Identity and Faith in Jesus

Introduction

In the following five chapters I will discuss selected textual material from Gurland, Lucky and Lichtenstein in relation to the two categories of Jewish identification, namely Jewish tradition and Jewish nationality. Similarly, I will discuss what these texts reveal concerning their relation to Christian doctrines and tradition, the Christian community and mission societies, as well as their relationship to each other and other contemporary leading Jewish Christians. The selected material is from texts written by Gurland, Lucky and Lichtenstein themselves or by people closely connected to them: For Gurland this means the autobiography *In Zwei Welten*, for Lucky the periodicals *Edut leIsrael* and *The Peculiar People*, and for Lichtenstein his German pamphlets from 1886 to 1908. When relevant I will use other material as well.

The Relation to Judaism and the Jewish Tradition

Following DellaPergola's categories for Jewish identity, this chapter investigates Gurland's, Lucky's and Lichtenstein's attitudes to the identification markers related to the national-particularistic category. The topics I will discuss are therefore related to family life, their attitude about being Jewish, and of course major elements in Jewish tradition, like Talmud, Tanak, observance of Jewish holidays and the Sabbath, circumcision, religious burial, and kashrut (the dietary laws). However, as Gurland, Lucky and Lichtenstein dealt differently with these issues, the amount of material as well as the relevance of each element varies. The following discussions try to relate Gurland, Lucky and Lichtenstein to the complex contemporary demographic, social, religious, cultural and political situation of the Jewish people.

Gurland

TALMUD AS A PRISON

We have no sources where Gurland discusses Jewish identity for Jewish believers as such, and it is striking that the material does not reflect more of the debate about key topics like keeping the ceremonial laws, etc., in Jewish mission circles at his time. Still, Gurland often describes and reflects on several of the identification markers listed by DellaPergola, in particular Talmud. As Gurland in many ways is a manifestation of a typical Jewish convert to Protestant Christianity of the period, I also compare him with some Jewish individuals who share many of his own experiences, like Carl Paul Caspari and Leopold Cohen.

From what we know, Gurland took part in at least two public discussions on the relationship between Judaism and Christianity; the improvised debate in a synagogue in Kishinev on March 8, 1864, and the dispute between himself and Rabbi Pucher in Kurland in 1875.[1] While the controversy with Pucher was one of several similar conflicts between Rabbi Pucher and the Lutheran church in the Baltics already from the mid-60s, the discussion in Kishinev appears to have been a single event that ended in the *cherem* (ex-communication) of Gurland. I think it is the event in Kishinev that illuminates the main elements of Gurland's attitude to the Jewish tradition. The discussion in Kurland was focused on the legitimacy of mission activity towards the Jews, and whether Jewish conversions to Christianity were based on materialistic opportunism or motivated by religious conviction. In Kishinev the main issue was the authority of the oral Jewish tradition, in particular Talmud. In addition to the discussion in Kishinev, I also refer to some discourses described in his mission reports.[2]

1. Gurland, *IzW* (1911), "Irrlehren des Talmud," 79–92.
2. Generally the 1911 version of *IzW* (and the English version) tightened the original 1864 text used by Hennings, but also included Gurland's Talmud references in their

In Kishinev, Gurland's criticism of Talmud and Jewish tradition focuses on three points: 1. Talmudic Judaism excludes Jesus as Messiah. 2. Parts of the oral tradition contradict the Hebrew Bible (as well as the New Testament), and it is therefore not valid as the Word of God. 3. The oral tradition also contradicts itself, and contains ridiculous statements.

Most of the narrative is characterized by Gurland's presentation of examples of the material in Talmud he believes is blasphemy, improper anthropomorphism, and cruelty. In sum, Gurland accuses these texts of being devastating for the Jewish people, morally and intellectually, and claims that faith in Jesus as the Messiah is a Jewish value. In other words, to Gurland Jesus has become a marker for Jewish identification. Although a provocative claim in a Russian synagogue, this relationship between Jewish identity and Jesus as Messiah was central for Lucky and Lichtenstein, as well as among other Russian Jewish converts. Georgii Klei, a Jewish convert to the Russian Orthodox Church, claimed in the Russian press in 1868 that he was a "true Israelite," as the Hebrew Bible was fulfilled in the New Testament.[3] In fact, Gurland claims that it is a Jewish obligation to embrace Jesus:

> I asked: "Why do you not believe these innocent ones?" and I was answered: "Because of that rule that stands for us one and for ever: [sic] No true Jew can become a Christian!" "This very sentence should be reversed," I replied, "as it should run: Every true Jew has to become a Christian."[4]

Ralph Hennings places this text within the large production of conversion histories from the mission societies of the 19th century, adding the narrative to the long list of traditional *adversus judaeos* texts.[5] From my

---

full texts, and it is therefore easier for the reader to follow the arguments. While the 1864 text places "Ich:" in front of Gurland's part of the dialogue, other participants in the debate are identified as "NN:" etc. In the *IzW* this is omitted and edited, probably for the ease of the reader. Generally the text of 1864 is longer, as it includes more examples from Jewish tradition and references to Gurland's discussions with his father and grandfather in his childhood; Hennings, "Aus dem Tagebuch," 87.

3. Schainker, "Imperial Hybrids," 92 n. 72.

4. Gurland, *IzW* (1911), 80. "Warum wollt Ihr diesen Unschuldigen nicht glauben?" Fragte ich."Weil wir eine alte Regel haben: Kein wahrer Jude kann Christ sein.""Meine Lieben, diese Regel sollte umgekehrt heisse: ein wahrer Jude muss Christ werden."

5. Hennings, "Aus dem Tagebuch." Hennings uses the original text from *Der Friedensbote* from the autumn of 1864, 105. The lack of a meaningful definition of the concept of adversus judaeos literature makes it difficult to discuss Henning's statement

point of view, it is more appropriate to see the text as a reflection of the contemporary debate in the Russian Jewish community about Judaism.

In Gurland's immediate context of the Russian Empire during the 19th century, anti-Jewish sentiments were characterized by a combination of traditional anti-Judaism, influences from Central Europe, and the various policies of the Russian government from the 1790s to WWI. About the time of the debate in Kishinev, religious Judeophobia was sometimes expressed in the Russian press.[6] In 1862 there was a long-lasting debate in several Russian newspapers and periodicals between Russian and Jewish intellectuals about Talmud and "talmudic fanaticism," where the Jewish participants represented several segments of the Jewish community.[7] A decade later, in 1874, the Jewish leadership in St. Petersburg found it necessary to publish *The World-View of the Talmudists* in an attempt to give a unified defense for the high morals of Jewish tradition.[8]

It is possible that the debate in Kishinev in 1864 reflects the wider debate concerning Talmud from 1862 onward, and the abovementioned debate in the Russian press must have been in the mind of most of the participants. In both controversies Talmud was at stake, and talmudic

---

in a precise manner. The adversus judaeos literature is not one particular genre. Heinz Schreckenberg generally includes all literature where the author has been influenced by traditional church doctrine or church politics on the relationship to the Jews or Judaism. In traditional church literature, the most significant topics were the messiahship of Jesus, the divine rejection of Israel, and the Christians as the new people of God. Schreckenberg, *Die Christlichen Adversus-Judaeos-Texte*, 36. The reason why Hennings categorized the report from the debate in Kishinev as an adversus judaeos text, is probably the fact that it includs topics like the messiahship of Jesus and the attack on Jewish oral tradition.

6. For instance, descriptions of Jews such as, "Outcast, covered with the shame of Christkilling, and stubbornly opposed to the generosity of God" (Professor Ivan Vasilevskii in the monthly journal *Strannik* in 1860); Klier, *Imperial Russia's*, 124.

7. Ibid., 133.

8. In spite of this effort, during the 1870s there was increasing public resentment towards the Jews, particularly related to Talmud. The result of this development was that around 1880, there was significant ambivalence in the situation of Russian Jewry. On the one hand, their legal situation had improved since the takeover in 1855 by Tsar Alexander II. On the other hand, one now found Judeophobia in every political camp in Russia. The Jews and their religion were increasingly regarded as an obstacle to Russification in the wake of public disillusion concerning the assimilation of the Russian Jews. In addition there had, since the 1870s, been increased fear of the imagined *kahal*, the body for Jewish autonomy until its abolition in 1844, and later of rumors about Jewish conspiracy. ibid., 438–39, 453–55.

Jewry was associated with fanaticism. However, the issues that were discussed in the press do not resemble the debate in Kishinev, as the debate in 1862 was concerned with Jewish-Christian relations, and particularly with whether Talmud preached hate towards non-Jews.[9] As Gurland's narrative focuses on the authority of the Talmud in itself, the connection between the narrative and contemporary Russian Judeophobia does not appear very explicit. Considering Gurland's evangelistic approach in the text, it is also striking that his opponents do not associate him with some of the most famous contemporary converts and missionaries to the Jews in Russia, like Alekseev and Brafman. Like Gurland, both of them carried out harsh attacks on Talmud in the public, but nowhere is Gurland associated to them or similar converts.[10] I therefore find it difficult to identify Gurland's accusations against Talmud with the general Russian Judeophobia, at least explicitly.

Considering the use of Gurland's narrative in German mission periodicals, his attitude to the Jewish tradition is probably representative for the Jewish missions, including Faltin's community and network. According to Schreckenberg, pietistic circles would usually be most influenced by the works of Eisenmenger, Wagenseil and Spener. Johann Andreas Eisenmenger (d. 1704) held Talmud to be a destructive force that had made it impossible for the Jewish people to improve themselves or their conditions. The Christian scholar Johann Christoph Wagenseil (d. 1705) in many ways represented the traditional anti-Judaism of the churches, such as supporting the doctrine of supersessionism. However, in contrast to Eisenmenger, he agitated for the civil rights of the Jews. He did not consider the Jewish nation as spiritually and morally hopeless, and consequently he encouraged mission work towards the Jews. Philip Jakob Spener (d. 1705) held that although the exile of the Jewish people

---

9. Ibid., 133–39.

10. Alekseev (b. 1820) tried to discredit the Talmud as well as the rabbinate, but nevertheless defended the Jews in the blood libel trial of Saratov in 1856. He was baptized in 1845 as a cantonist (forced to conscript), and was a missionary for the army until he was discharged in the 1850s for paralysis. Later he published several books on Judaism and Russian Jews.

Iakov Brafman, (b. 1824), converted to the Orthodox Church in 1858, after first having converted to the Lutheran church. Between 1860 and 1866 he was teacher in Hebrew at Minsk Theological Seminary. Later he accused the Jewish community for still being led by a secret *kahal*. Schainker, "Imperial Hybrids," 178–82.

was the divine punishment for their cruelty towards Jesus, one should not prevent them from practicing Judaism.[11]

However, the most influential and widespread book about the fallibility of Talmud in mission circles at the time would probably be the 600-page *Nethivot olam, oder der wahre Israelit*. This work was the 1839 German translation of Alexander McCaul's *The Old Paths*, which, based on the assumption of an absolute disparity between Rabbinism and Old Testament teaching, tries to debunk the Jewish oral tradition.[12] As the volume continued to be published in different translations during the rest of the century (the last German edition was in 1885), it is likely that Gurland's pastor, Rudolf Faltin, would know about it. Consequently, a convert like Gurland would probably have been exposed to McCaul's work if he did not know about it before his conversion. There is at least

---

11. Schreckenberg, *Die Christlichen Adversus-Judaeos-Texte*, 680, 691. Klier claims that for Russian commentators influenced by Eisenmenger's anti-talmudic tract *Entdechtes Judenthum*, the malevolence of the Jews was due to the Jewish religion, particularly Talmud. In Russia, Eisenmenger's views were first available to Russian intellectuals in works by L. A. Chiarini from 1830. Klier, *Imperial Russia's*, 3, 457–58 n. 4.

12. McCaul, *Nethivot olam, oder: Der Wahre Israelit: ein vergleich zwischen dem modernen Judenthum und der religion Moses und der Propheten*. Translation of *The Old Paths: A Comparison of the Principles and Doctrines of Modern Judaism with the Religion of Moses and the Prophets* (London: London Society's Office, 1837); a new edition (2nd) was published in 1880 with a slightlyt changed title (*The Old Paths, or the Talmud Tested by Scripture being a Comparison of the Principles and Doctrines of Modern Judaism with the Religion of Moses and the Prophets*); references are to the 1880 edition. McCaul was an Irish Anglican minister who worked as a missionary for the London Society for Promoting Christianity amongst the Jews, and later became professor at King's College in London. Originally the text appeared in sixty weekly installments, beginning January 15, 1836, later printed in one edition. There were several new editions during the century, published in German as early as 1839 by Wilhelm Küchler in Frankfurt am Main. Primary sources were Jewish liturgies like the Arbah Turim, the Shulchan Aruch and the Yad Hachasakah, but the book also refers to Talmud treatise Pesachim, McCaul, *The Old Paths*, 6. In the latter reference he discusses exactly the same text as Gurland, namely Talmud treatise Pesachim fol. 49, col. 2, where Rabbi Elazar discusses with his disciples the treatment of the amhaaretz. On the same occasion he also uses the examples of "render an amhaaretz like a fish" and the prohibition to marry any amhaaretz, see ibid. McCaul's work was not only known in Eastern European mission circles, but also among Russian Jewish intellectuals in the 1860s, as it was repudiated in Isaac Baer Levinsohn's *Ahiyah Shiloni ha-hozeh: kolel bitul taanotav shel sefer Netivot olam (bameh she-nogea le-dat Yisrael)* (1864); Feiner, *Haskalah and History*, 162; and Jocz, *The Jewish People and Jesus Christ*, 215, 390. See also Quiñónez, "The Doyen," 75.

one clear example in the narrative from Kishinev where Gurland uses the same arguments as McCaul, namely on the rabbis' view on *amhaaretz*:[13]

> "Dear brethren! Why don't you examine yourselves the teachings of the Chachamim as to whether they agree with the Holy Writ?! Take for instance, the 5th commandment! In Pesachim, page 49 column 2, Rabbi Eleasar says: It is permitted to tear open the nostril of an Amhaaretz (unlearned person) even on the day of Atonement when it falls on a Saturday. And to this his disciple is reported to have answered: Rabbi, perhaps you better say, it is permitted to slaughter the man, and the rabbi is said to have answered: This would make it necessary to say a special blessing, and this should be avoided! Now, tell me please, how can this be consistent with the commandment love thy neighbour?! And regarding anyone who is not a learned man the Talmud has only words of mockery and disdain and says moreover: An Amhaaretz (unlearned person) may be torn like a fish, and for those rabbis the word Amhaaretz means those who though having studied The Old Testament did not study Gemara (Talmud)! Rabbis have declared, that no exception can be made with regard to the inhibition to marry such an unlearned man's daughter who would be no better than an animal..."[14]

However, in spite of this parallel concerning the *amhaaretz*, the rest of Gurland's accusations and arguments against Talmud do not seem to resemble either McCaul or the pietistic literature.[15] My thesis is that

---

13. The term *amhaaretz* (*am ha'aretz*) means a person of the land, a commoner, but within Jewish tradition it also relates to a Jew without knowledge of Judaism or who does not want to observe the Torah; Schainker, "Imperial Hybrids," 161.

14. Gurland, *IzW* (1911), 89. "Brüder, prüft doch selbst nach Gottes Geboten die Lehre der Chachamim. Nehmt das 5. Gebot. In der Lehre Pesachim Fol. 49, Col. 2 sagt Rabbi Eleasar; Es ist erlaubt, einem Amhaarez (Nichtgelehrten) die Nasenlöcher aufzureissen, sogar am Versönungstage, der auf den Sabbat fällt. Da sagen die Schüler zu ihm: Rabbi, sage lieber, dass es erlaubt sei, ihn zu schlachten. Er antwortete: Dieses würde einen Segensspruch erfordern, der so nicht nötig ist! Wo bleibt da das Gebot der Liebe? Nur Spott und Verachtung kennt der Talmud gegen der Nichtgelehrten, von dem er sagt: Es ist erlaubt, einen Amhaarez zu zerreichen wie einen Fisch! Amhaarez heisst aber der, welcher wohl die Schreift studiert hat, aber nicht Gemara (Talmud). Es ist ohne Ausnahme verboten, eines solchen Mannes Tochter zu heiraten, den sie sei nicht besser als ein Tier." For a text reference, see http://juchre.org/talmud/pesachim/pesachim2.htm.

15. If Gurland based his arguments on the narrative in Christian sources, it must also be taken into account that the influence from German-speaking Jewish mission circles could go in different directions. One of the most famous evangelistic works designed for the Jewish mission in German Protestantism was Johann Müller's "*Licht*

the arguments in the debate reflect the contemporary internal Jewish controversy between Russian *maskilim* and traditionalists, and not controversies between Jews and Christians. In his biography on Gurland, Le Roi explicitly places him within the *Haskalah* movement.[16] From the reactions in Gurland's audience it appears that Gurland was, more than anything, associated to the Russian *Haskalah*, the Jewish version of the Enlightenment that in Galicia and Russia lasted for most of the 19th century:[17]

> At this point all the Jews present cried out: "You impudent fellow, you dare to blaspheme our holy faith! But you are not the first and only one; Israel had more of such perverters but Israel also outlived them, such as Erter, Ginsburg, Lebensohn and others more! Israel will be faithful to his faith, but the perverters will go to their perdition!"
>
> "My dear friends," I answered, "I am in no wise making fun of you or mocking you! This matter is much too serious to me! My heart bleeds because my brethren go astray. Do not consider me one of those critics who not only reject the Talmud but also contest all foundation of Scripture and are solely in favour of materialism and rationalism."[18]

The persons mentioned by the audience were all leading representatives of the Russian *Haskalah*. Ginzburg (Gunzburg) was one of the leading Hebrew writers in Vilna, who was devoted to reform and modernizing the Jewish way of life. Ginzburg and his sympathizers supported and encouraged the attempts of the Russian government to

---

am Abend." Müller's work from 18th century Pietism was one of the classics among the friends of the Jewish mission in the German speaking countries, and Faltin would almost certainly know about it. Müller tried to show how even the Jewish oral tradition points towards Jesus as Messiah, an approach which is similar to Isaac Lichtenstein's, but which is totally absent in Gurland's narrative. Skarsaune, *Israels venner*, 21.

16. Le Roi, *Rudolf Hermann Gurland*, 4.
17. Dubin, "The Social and Cultural Context," 636–59, 649.
18. Gurland, *IzW* (1911), 86. "Da schreien die Juden: "Nein! So frech sind Sie! Unseren heiligen Glauben zu lästern!! Aber Sie sind nicht der Erste, Israel hat solcher Verderber viele gehabt, aber auch solcher Klugen viele überlebt, wie Erter, Ginsburg, Lebenson [sic.] und andere mehr! Israel bleibt seinem Glauben treu, aber die Spötter vergehen!" "Sie täuschen sich, liebe Brüder, ich treibe keinen Scherz und Spott, viel zu ernst und heilig ist mir die Sache. Mein Herz blutet, weil meine Brüder in der Irre gehen. Auch bitte ich, mich nicht zu den genannten Kritikern zu zählen, den diese haben nicht nur gegen den Talmud getritten, sondern auch jeden Glaubensgrund an die Schrift untergraben und dem Materialismus und Rationalismus Tor und Tür geöffnet."

integrate the Jewish population in the Russian state. Both his support for the Tsar and his own attempts to reform his Jewish community made him very unpopular among the majority of traditionalists, and as shown by the debate in Kishinev, these persons were regarded as apostates.

Traditionally, *Haskalah* has been associated with various phenomena that happened at the same time, especially the assimilation process. Due to this, *Haskalah* has been regarded as an ideology that made possible a disintegration of the Jewish people as such. The *maskilim* claimed that all knowledge should be grounded in rational arguments and common reason, which necessarily led them into fierce criticism of their religious leaders. According to the *maskilim*, traditional rabbis—whose authority came from their knowledge of halakah—did not live up to the new cultural ideal. These rabbis were depicted as narrow-minded, obscurantist, superstitious, and not very useful even for their own society. Some of the *maskilim* not only challenged and criticized Rabbinism, but even questioned the right of the Jewish communities to live as autonomous corporate bodies enforcing their own laws upon their members.

Among the *maskilim* there were moderates and radicals in Russia, Germany and Galicia. While moderates sought to create a fashionable Judaism that would fit well into the general framework of the Enlightenment, the radicals tended to dismiss halakic observance as unnecessary and outmoded, and even as a hindrance to the full development of human potential. There are different opinions concerning how the Russian *maskilim* placed themselves in regard to the Jewish tradition. While Isaac Ber Levinsohn publically defended Talmud against Christian accusations and stressed the historical continuity between ancient Judaism and contemporary *Haskalah*, Mordechai Aaron Guenzberg held that *Haskalah* was a radical break with several elements in the Jewish tradition, and attacked traditional rabbis for deluding the Jewish population.[19] Concerning the movement in Russia, Klier suggests a distinction between different groups of Jewish intellectuals: 1. The pioneers of the Russian *Haskalah* ("the Old *Maskilim*"), including men like Isaac Baer Levinsohn, who with the support of the Russian government tried to establish progressive Jewish schools from the 1820s. 2. The next generation ("the Young *Maskilim*"), who graduated from these schools and took posts as teachers and controversial positions as state rabbis. 3. In contrast to these, who were inwardly directed

---

19. Feiner, *Haskalah and History*, 178–86.

in their efforts to reform Jewish society, there was the group Klier calls "the Russian Jewish intelligentsia" who considered themselves more a part of Russian society, speaking Russian and partaking in Russian culture, and speaking mainly for a Russian public. 4. Lastly he mentions "the Total Assimilationists," who generally ignored their Jewish background and the Jewish community until they returned to this community in the wake of the pogroms in 1881–1882. Many of them converted to Christianity for career reasons, like Professor Daniel Khvolson in St. Petersburg.[20]

The *maskilim* usually held positions where they had opportunities to proclaim their views. Gurland's years as tutor before and after Wilkomir were periods when he could be seen as a typical *maskil*, as many of them worked as teachers in new Jewish schools and tutors in private households. Others were employees in the Hebrew printing trade, founders of and contributors to *Haskalah* periodicals or members of voluntary associations devoted to cultivating the Hebrew language or spreading enlightenment. With its interest in ancient Judaism and the Hebrew language, the *Haskalah* movement was crucial for the development of Modern Hebrew/Ivrit.[21] The *maskilim* wanted to make the rabbinic form of Hebrew as it had developed during the Middle Ages into a secular and anti-rabbinic language, able to express new ideas with the elegance of the Bible. During the 19th century, the supporters of Modern Hebrew had to fight for its survival against the national languages that surrounded every Jewish community, and also the established (*Ashkenazi*) Jewish language itself: Yiddish. At the beginning of the 1880s, the conflict between Enlightenment ideals and Jewish continuity, the threat of assimilation, and not least the increased pogroms supported by the Russian regime became apparent, and the *Haskalah* ceased to exist as a movement.[22]

However, in 1864 the Russian *Haskalah* was still a vital force and a highly controversial factor in the Jewish community. Gurland's audience

20. Klier, *Imperial Russia's*, 26–28, 135.

21. Slouschz, *The Renascence*, 9; and Feiner, *Haskalah and History*, 4.

22. From the 1880s to WWI Yiddish folklorists and intellectuals in Russia and Galicia collected and spread much Yiddish material, particularly songs and expressions. This work was not only a parallel to similar cultural movements in Eastern Europe at the time, but was a competitive force against Zionists as well as assimilationists. A significant characteristic of the Yiddish movement was its abandonment of Jewish tradition. Gottesman, *Defining the Yiddish Nation*, xii–xiii, xx, 174.

in Kishinev recognized his viewpoints as arguments from the *Haskalah*, placing him together with the other Russian and Galician *maskilim* of the period. We have no other information in the text about their reason for this conclusion other than Gurland's own arguments in the debate, in addition to his own reference to the former conflicts in Wilkomir. Still, from his *yeshiva* years his thoughts about the oral tradition had been quite similar to the views of the *maskilim*, who regarded Talmud and Kabbalah as unreasonable and irrelevant. *Haskalah* literature was of course forbidden in the Russian *yeshivot*, but the new ideas nevertheless leaked in, and some students became *maskilim*.[23] Since Russian *maskilim* sought a synthesis between European culture and Jewish tradition they were highly literate, learned in biblical and rabbinic literature. Their writings ranged from Hebrew poetry, philosophy, prose and science to Yiddish fiction, and it is not surprising that *yeshiva* students were exposed to this literature.[24] A *yeshiva* like Volozhin could, therefore, in the late 1840s become a nest for *Haskalah* thought, as many of the students had motives for attending the school other than to study Torah, like finding a wife or escaping from home.[25] The *maskilim* had condemned the yeshivot for years as being centers for obscurantism whose strict regimes, physical dilapidation and intensive study of useless material were destroying the psyche of young Jews.[26] Considering Gurland's difficult experience with education, this criticism would probably have won sympathy with him. Already in his letters before he became a rabbi in Wilkomir, Gurland expressed his feeling of spiritual claustrophobia and deep-felt doubt on the validity of Talmud and Kabbalah, and he comes close to patronizing his co-believers when he describes how they deal with religious practice.[27] In his childhood narratives, the descrip-

---

23. Helmreich, *The World of the Yeshiva*, 9. This process is described in Jewish literature. In his autobiography, Simon Solomon (b. 1895) describes his life as a Belarusian yeshiva student who struggled with the relationship between science, modern ideologies and traditional Judaism. Solomon, *In the Thicket*; Gordon, *Between Two Worlds*.

24. In particular, scientific literature won much popularity; Zalkin, "Scientific Literature," 249–71, 269.

25. Shapiro, *Between the Yeshiva World and Modern Orthodoxy*, 2.

26. Ibid., 30.

27. On one occasion Gurland describes attending a public meeting with a renowned rabbi who sold his spiritual merits to the one in the audience who was willing to pay 2,000 rubles. In another letter he describes his mother's joy when he had become a rabbi, believing that her son now could open up paradise for her. Gurland, *IzW* (1911),

tion of his education with his father as well as in the *yeshiva* resembles the general maskilic rhetoric about the anomalous occupational profile of traditional Jewish society in Russia.

The correspondence between the *maskilim* was important for them as a means to escape their isolation as well as a tool for expressing their ideas, and to some extent the correspondence between Samuel and Gurland conforms to this pattern. It is also possible that Gurland met *maskilim* in person, as these generally targeted *yeshiva* students to introduce them to a scientific way of thinking.[28] In general, Gurland's biography resembles the traditional *maskil* life story and contains the hallmarks of a *maskil* autobiography, very precisely expressed in Mordecai Plungian's biography of Rabbi Manasseh ben Joseph of Ilyda (1767–1831): "A brilliant scholar from Lithuania, whose tendencies to broaden his horizons were blocked from an early age; a youthful marriage that ended in divorce; religious scholarship that rejected *pilpul* and adopted a critical approach."[29] This summary could easily be used for Gurland as well.

When Gurland converted, he had been working on a book about reform attempts within Judaism, and his aspiration for a Judaism based on the *Tanak* must have been well-known in his audience. It is therefore not surprising that the participants in the debate in Kishinev regarded Gurland as a *maskil*, not bothering to associate him with Christian missionaries or infamous converts like Alekseev.[30] Still, having in mind the general controversy about Talmud in the Russian public in the two years before Gurland's conversion, it is striking that none of the participants at the debate made any attempt at a scholarly defense of Talmud like that in the Russian press. Considering Gurland's background, he must have been aware of these arguments himself. Granted that Gurland's narrative is not fiction, it is possible that such apology was omitted to underscore the stereotypical fanatics in Talmudic Judaism. On the other hand, it is quite possible that such apologetic arguments were known among the

---

38–42. According to Zalkin, the *maskilim* also considered Torah studies outright unhealthy due to the lack of activity, which corresponds to how *IzW* stresses exactly this experience for Gurland; Zalkin, "Scientific Literature," 257.

28. Feiner, *Haskalah and History*, 77.

29. Ibid., 225.

30. From Jewish traditionalists' point of view the difference would not be too big anyway; the consequences of both, as the traditionalists saw it, were that these individuals were lost to the Jewish community.

participants, but that they were not regarded as legitimate. Probably this would include an interpretation of some of the Talmudic texts as metaphors, which traditionalists would be reluctant to do.[31] After all, although the Jewish community in Kishinev was one of the havens for the Russian *Haskalah*, the circle of local *maskilim* could not have been very big. From the 1840s and onward, in each of these communities their numbers varied from a few individuals to some dozen, and mainstream members of the Kishinev Jewish community would probably not accept their way of thinking.[32] Instead, connecting Gurland to the most famous Russian and Galician *maskilim* could very well be a way to discredit the local *Haskalah* circle, as associating them with converts to Christianity was a common traditionalist strategy.[33]

However, Gurland did not accept being categorized with the leading *maskilim*, and he apparently refused any ideological connection with them. From Gurland's point of view, these persons represented unbelief toward not only the oral Jewish tradition, but the scriptural as well.[34] Gurland's need to distance himself from the *Haskalah* movement is also expressed later in *IzW*, where he expresses both sympathy and ambivalence to Zionist ideology as well as to the contemporary awakening of the Hebrew language.[35] For Gurland, the phenomenon was interesting. Still, when Hebrew and the Jewish nation became objects of interest in themselves and not just as means to lead people to an encounter with the biblical message, his attitude became somewhat ambivalent.

In other words, Gurland describes himself as combating Talmud *and* defending the divine revelation of the Tanak at the same time.

---

31. See Rabbi Isaac Lichtenstein's discussion of McCaul in *Der Talmud auf der Anklagebank*.

32. Feiner, *Haskalah and History*, 159. It is possible that the existence of such a circle of *maskilim* was one of the reasons Gurland moved to Kishinev.

33. Ibid., 184–85.

34. Although this appears to be a correct description of several of the Galician and Russian *maskilim*, Gurland is rather bombastic in his views. As Feiner points out, there were significant controversies on the adherence to Jewish tradition in these circles. In the 1850s the leading Galician *maskil* Rapoport defended Jewish tradition to such an extent that he was accused of having turned Orthodox; Feiner, *Haskalah and History*, 156. However, other Russian converts were just as suspicious as Gurland about progressive Judaism. In 1872, Alekseev, a convert to the Russian Orthodox Church, warned Jewish converts against progressive Judaism, as it undermined messianic expectations; Schainker, "Imperial Hybrids," 252.

35. Gurland, *IzW* (1911), 196.

He claims that the Tanak is the only word of God compared with the oral tradition, but thinks the *maskilim* undermine the authority of the scriptural revelation as well as the oral. A similar view against Talmud is repeated several times in the sources, particularly in reports of his discussions with other Jews. One example is the encounter with some Jews on a train journey in Russia sometime after 1887. Involving himself in a discussion between a group of Russian Jews and a progressive German Jew, Gurland supports the Russian Jews against the materialist German, presenting himself as a "Ben Israel" (a son of Israel). In this discussion Gurland repeats his antipathy towards a secular worldview, and claims his loyalty to the Hebrew Bible: "I have not abandoned the faith of our fathers, I believe everything that Moses and the prophets taught us."[36] On another occasion, when Gurland was in a dentist's waiting room, he took the opportunity to discuss the Old Testament concept of suffering (!) with the Jews present.[37] Gurland states his disagreement with some of them about the availability of help from the Talmud. Gurland refers to Jesus as the Messiah who can heal the Jewish people. When referring to Isaiah 53, an old Jew answers that it is prohibited to think about this, stating, "Die Geheimnisse Gottes ergründen zu wollen, macht die Menschen meshuge (verrückt)."[38]

Hennings describes Gurland's distinction between the oral and written traditions as alien to Judaism, and considers the narrative to be an echo of missionary rhetoric. However, although this separation is uncommon within rabbinic Judaism, it is not unheard of. As already mentioned, Gurland was not alone in this view, as it was shared by many *maskilim*. In Western Europe there were also examples of non-Reform Jewish communities that distinguished between the Hebrew Bible and Talmud. In addition, Steven Singer describes how the Jewish community in London in the 19th century was characterized by a distinguished neo-Karaite position in relation to the oral tradition, even among the conservative Jews.[39]

---

36. Gurland, *Erlebnisse*, 18–23. The year of publication is unknown, but due to a reference in the text to Gurland handing out Bibles, it is probably after 1887, when Gurland began assisting the Mildmay Mission with the distribution of Hebrew Bibles.

37. Ibid., 6.

38. Ibid. "To investigate the secrets of God would lead people to madness."

39. Singer, *Jewish Religious Thought*, 204. The Karaites are a Jewish community who reject Talmud's authority.

To summarize, there is no doubt that Gurland had a strong antipathy to the post-biblical Jewish tradition, and in particular Talmud. The question is whether Gurland was arguing as a traditional Jewish-Christian apostate, or if his views were an echo of the internal Jewish debate following the modernization of the Jewish society. His opponents place him among the *maskilim*. Aside from Gurland's rhetoric about the legitimacy and obligation for all Jews to embrace Christianity, most of the narrative from Kishinev appears to reflect the internal strife between Jewish traditionalists and agitators of the *Haskalah* in Russia in the middle of the 19th century. However, Gurland's new Christian interpretation of the Hebrew Bible is the foundation for his rhetoric, in Kishinev and in his later material. Not only is the Hebrew Bible confirmed as Holy Scripture, but these writings also confirm the messiahship of Jesus.

In relation to Gurland's attitude to Jewish tradition versus his Christian understanding of the Old Testament, there are also parallels to other famous Jewish Christians. One of them was Delitzsch's old friend Carl Paul Caspari, who after his conversion became a professor of Old Testament at the University in Oslo. In mission circles both Gurland and Caspari were held in high esteem, and at least in retrospect some found it natural to compare these two and their ethnic identities.[40] Although Gurland and Caspari agreed that neither traditional nor progressive Judaism were authentic expressions of the Old Testament, there were significant differences between their views before their conversions.[41] In contrast to Gurland, Caspari had much sympathy for Jewish rationalism, particularly in the tradition of Moses Mendelsohn and Immanuel Kant. Unlike Gurland, he did not come from a religious family, and regarded himself as a Deist. According to Skarsaune, it was when Caspari became a Christian, that he first felt like a Jew, as it was then that the Old Testament came back to him as a theological document.[42] For Gurland there was never a time when he did not identify himself as Jewish. A comparison between Gurland and the convert Leopold Cohen shows fewer differences on this topic. Both of them claimed a rabbinic background, and although Cohen does not refer to any struggle about the relationship between Talmud and the Hebrew Bible, like Gurland he accepted the divine inspiration of the Bible before his conversion.

40. Fauerholdt, "National-Jüdiches Christentum," 23.
41. Skarsaune, "En Lærd af Guds Naade," 55.
42. Ibid., 81.

However, a significant difference is that while Gurland ceased any regular observance of Jewish customs after his baptism, Cohen appears to have continued, and encouraged some maintenance of Jewish customs, at least in private circles.[43] This brings us to a closer look at Gurland's private sphere and family life.[44]

Gurland's Relations to His Family and the Jewish Community

After the *cherem* (ban) was issued on Gurland in spring 1864, he did not share any communal life with Jewish society according to *IzW*. Following the title of his autobiography, he now had moved into another world, the society of German (Lutheran) Christianity and the Jewish mission societies. How radical this situation could be is illustrated by the little story about Gurland getting in touch with his daughter from his first marriage, when the 16-year-old girl refused to have any contact with a "Goj" (non-Jew).[45] Gurland's assimilation process reached its peak when he married Baronesse Helene von Drachenfels in 1878. It probably says much about the consequences of the ban that the biography of their son Rudolf Gurland (1885–1947) almost never refers to Jews. Even when he speaks about the time in cosmopolitan Odessa, it is the holidays in Kurland that come to his mind.[46] It therefore seems that their Jewish heritage did not have a central role in the ex-rabbi's own family.[47]

There is little doubt that Gurland knew what he was doing in this respect when he married into the Baltic German nobility. At the conference in Leipzig in the summer of 1895, the issue of marriage between Jews and non-Jews was touched upon in discussing the challenges from

---

43. Ariel, *Evangelizing*, 33.

44. See DellaPergola's way of structuring Jewish identification, where the variables "Circumcise male children," "Observe kashrut at home," "Form a family and honor parents" and "Not to marry with non-Jews" are located under a particularistic identity; see introduction.

45. Gurland, *IzW* (1911), 66.

46. Bitter and Gurland, *Unsichtbare Kirche*, 29. However, the context of the text should be taken into account. Although the memories are told in the context of speeches held at private occasions, these took place under the Nazi regime, and as Rudolf Gurland had already been fired as pastor in the Hannoverian church due to his "bastard" family background, it would be surprising if Jews played a role in a speech by him at that time.

47. Which is confirmed by Gurland's grandson, Pastor Hans-Heinrich Gurland, in a letter to me, dated November 25, 2004.

the circle around Christian Theophilus Lucky/Chaim Jedidjah Pollak. There Lucky's Jewish-Christian opponents (most probably Gurland was among these) explained that as long as some of the believers from Israel were married to non-Jewish spouses, their children would not be accepted as Jews by Jewish society. In other words, Gurland's conversion to Lutheran Christianity led him down the road to cultural assimilation, at least for his children. The combination of assimilation and conversion/apostasy is well known in Jewish history of the period, and in that respect Gurland's situation seems to fit well into an ordinary demographic scheme. However, the sources seem to indicate that in spite of the lack of Jewish identification in his Baltic German family, Gurland does not seem to be described as someone who closed all doors behind him. In spite of Gurland's antipathy towards Talmud and his marriage to a non-Jew, there are also factors in Gurland's life that show he did not want to turn away from either the Jewish people or his national background as such.

First of all, Gurland includes himself in the Jewish people, e.g., by using "we" or "my people" and other similar expressions to describe himself as a Jew. These expressions occur all the way until his death, both in his autobiography and in his articles in mission periodicals.[48] Within the framework of DellaPergola such expressions are a clear statement of self-identification with the Jewish people, independent of what the judgment of the Jewish community would be.[49] Although Gurland's conversion in Kishinev apparently cut him off from the Jewish community, the picture of his relationship with other Jews is more complex. The events around his daughter Sophie moving in with him show that he was still able to operate within Jewish circles, regardless of his new life as a missionary and Lutheran pastor. When he began his missionary work in the Baltic, he likewise had some opportunities to visit institutions and individuals in the Jewish community. Several of his anecdotes from the Baltic provinces reflect the ambivalence found among other Jews when dealing with Gurland, like the story about his encounter with his first Talmud teacher, whom he had not seen for decades, on the street in Vilnius. While the teacher greets Gurland with enthusiasm, the 74-year-

---

48. Gurland, *IzW* (1911), 202; Gurland, *Erlebnisse*, 6–8, 18–20.

49. The same expressions were also used by, e.g., Hannah Arendt. Kohn, "Preface," xxiii.

old rabbi's son tries to protect his father from the *talmid rosche*.⁵⁰ The son's attitude, however, did not prevent them meeting again on several occasions. When, at the teacher's deathbed, Gurland was asked to swear that he really believed in the Old Testament, Gurland put the rabbi's *talith* over his shoulders as a sign of the oath.⁵¹

The story of Gurland's mother's visit to the rectory in Mitau is possibly colored by Helene Gurland's wish to harmonize family relations, but nevertheless the same ambivalence seems to be present. That Gurland began sending money to her after his father's death in 1862 at least indicates that he wanted to maintain a connection with his family. While Helene Gurland claims that his mother had to visit them in secret, they were nevertheless able to keep in touch by correspondence later. We can only imagine how her stay in Mitau in 1879 was looked upon by the local Jewish and Christian communities. Not only did the minister's mother visit the local synagogues in Mitau frequently, but Gurland had also arranged for a Jewish servant to serve her kosher food in the rectory. Although not stated explicitly, it is possible that the reconciliation between Ida Gurland and her son had influence on other parts of his family. In one of his reports about the mission work in 1897 in Odessa, Gurland writes that he met an old aunt whom he had not seen for a very long time. She seems to have been very pleased to see him, and Gurland visited her several times.⁵²

Considering the traditional understanding of the dramatic social consequences of conversion to Christianity, it is striking that Gurland was both willing and able to maintain contact and some trust in the Jewish community. This phenomenon fits well into the pattern explained by Schainker on how Jewish communities and individuals in 19th-century Russia dealt with converts. Referring to church and court archives as well as Yiddish authors like Chaim Zhitloskii, Sholem Aleichem and Sholem Asch, Schainker gives a nuanced description of the relationship between Jews and the 84,500 Jewish converts to Christianity in the Russian Empire in the 19th century. Despite the emotional stress that often was involved, converts were not necessarily cut off from their families and their old Jewish community. Some of them continued to

---

50. Gurland, *Bericht*, 16.

51. Ibid., 18. However, Rabbi Pucher claims that this story is fabricated; Pucher, *Offener Brief*, 6.

52. Le Roi, *Rudolf Hermann Gurland*, 41.

function in Jewish society despite officially leaving the synagogue, as conversion was not necessarily grounded in a wish to leave Judaism or the Jewish community (which nevertheless was the case for many). For Gurland, the religious discontinuity in the wake of his conversion was not complete, and on some occasions there were elements of continuity between his Jewish upbringing and his practice of the Christian faith. Parts of this pattern, for Gurland and for many other converts, can possibly be explained by Hunsberger's theory about atypical converts. In his study on people whose religious decisions took the opposite direction of what was commonly expected, Hunsberger concludes that in most cases the "socialization anomalies" were not an expression of anomaly at all.[53] For the category "Amazing Apostates" (in Hunsberger's study usually people with a strong religious background who became atheists or agnostics), the apostasy was usually the result of an intellectual process that, considering what they had experienced, was quite understandable. Paradoxically this would not mean that their religious training by their parents had failed, but rather that this training made them care deeply for truth and integrity. Following Hunsberger, it is interesting to see how Gurland dealt with his Jewish family after his conversion, particularly with his mother.

Lucky

FAITH IN JESUS AS A JEWISH VIRTUE

Lucky's most characteristic feature was his loyalty to the Jewish tradition combined with his faith in Jesus. This was expressed most explicitly by his habit (at least when living in Stanislau from 1890 to 1914) of attending the synagogue on the Sabbath and Christian services on Sundays.[54] This leads Kurt Hruby to describe Lucky as *ein Talmudjude*, associating him with those Eastern European Jews who stuck to traditional Judaism and the Babylonian Talmud.[55]

---

53. Hunsberger, "Swimming," 233–48, 245. The continuity between converts' old and new worldviews is also underlined by Rebecca Sachs Norris in her article "Converting to What?," 171–82, 179.

54. Zöckler, *Gott hört Gebet*, 13; *Missions-Blad for Israel* 66 (1892) 123; and Weidauer, "Erindringer," 209. The sources do not say if he followed this practice in the USA or during his last years in Holland.

55. Hruby, "Zur Problematik," 80.

Many of Lucky's writings focused on different aspects of the relationship between the Christian and Jewish traditions and on how Lucky himself related to these. Basically, Lucky regards the distinction between Christianity and Judaism as two different religious bodies as "foolish."[56] In Lucky's opinion anyone who seeks eternal life should pay heed to the *Tanak*, the rabbinic tradition, and Christ. The New Testament and the Christian cardinal doctrines were the perfection of Judaism and the Jewish tradition, and this relationship should be reflected in traditional Torah observance among Jewish believers:

> I am a Hebrew, and the God of heaven I fear. I am a Jew and observe the Torah. Both the written and the oral Torah are Torah in my eyes, and to the Messiah Yeshua my soul has cleaved exceedingly. He is my life and my spirit because he is my king and my saviour, whom God sent to be the resurrection of the soul of every person and to give us eternal life. I am an Israelite and I am also a Messianic, a disciple of Moses and the men of the Great Assembly and a disciple of Yeshua the Messiah and his apostles alike.[57]
>
> People are mistaken when they say that a Jew cannot walk in the ways of Yeshua. On the contrary. It is because I am a Jew that I must cleave to the Messiah . . . If only our brethren from within Israel had cleaved to Yeshua, now everything the prophets saw in visions of the spirit would have been in front of their eyes. . . . But Israel was contemptuous of the life of the world and thus sits in darkness and the shadow of death, and the kingdom of heaven has not been fully established on earth.[58]

In other words, faith in Jesus was mandatory for every Jew, and embracing Jesus as Messiah became a core concept for Jewish identity. Lucky was not the only Jewish believer in Jesus who had this practice and these opinions, but he probably had the most controversial position regarding the continuity between Judaism and Christianity among Jewish-Christian theologians of his time.

---

56. "The Watch of HaEduth," *HaEdut* 4/2 (1897) 1–3.

57. Ibid., 3. "The men of the Great Assembly" refers to the 120 elders who followed Ezra from exile and who worked out new rules to strengthen Torah observance. See Danby, *The Mishnah*. 446 n. 5.

58. "The Watch of HaEduth," *HaEdut* 4/4 (1897) 1–10; 1.

The Tanak, the New Testament and Talmud

Lucky was eager to state that he was no *exelyt* (someone who had left the synagogue), as he had left neither his people nor the synagogue. It was fundamental for Lucky that Jesus did not come with new doctrines or a new covenant, but instead confirmed the already present gift given in the Hebrew Bible.[59] In contrast to his German friends, Weidauer says, Lucky therefore usually based his theological statements on Old rather than New Testament texts. Basically, the people of God in the Old Testament shared the treasures of salvation with the people of the New Testament. This idea was something that he found expressed in the Psalms and the prophets, e.g., in Jeremiah. However, for Lucky the New Testament was not only the fulfillment of the Tanak, but also confirmed the main teachings of the rabbinic tradition.

Among the mission societies, Lucky's positive attitude to Talmud was not regarded as the most significant problem.[60] The reason was probably that using rabbinic tradition as a bridge between Christianity and Judaism was a method with which some of them already were familiar. Many of Lucky's sympathizers as well as those who were more skeptical of him preferred this approach. However, among Christian theologians with a positive view of Talmud there were also significant differences about its practical consequences. Naturally, Lucky's views on the relationship between Christianity and Judaism evoked interest as well as dismay.

The question was given much attention in *Edut leIsrael/HaEdut*, and to some extent also in *The Peculiar People*. In an article in *Saat auf Hoffnung* in 1892 and 1893, Zöckler focuses on four topics he found repeatedly discussed in the Hebrew journal: the relationship between the Torah and the New Testament, the relationship between the oral and written Torah, the covenant with Israel vs. the new covenant, and Jesus' conflicts with the Pharisees.[61] The following sections A–D are struc-

---

59. Weidauer, "Erindringer," 172.

60. The criticism against Lucky from the mission societies was seldom related to his own Torah observance. What mainly caused controversy was his claim that modern Jewish Christians should observe Jewish customs (see the chapter about his relationship to Hebrew Christianity).

61. Zöckler, "Judentum und Christentum." At the time Zöckler wrote his article in the early 1890s, Lucky's previous co-editor Moses Löwen and the Berlin Society had just ended their cooperation with Lucky. Due to the tensions in relation to this,

tured according to Zöckler's outline of these topics, but the discussion is my own, based on the material from Zöckler's article, Le Cornu's translations of contemporary and later publications of *Edut leIsrael/HaEdut, The Peculiar People*, Weidauer and Wiegand. The quotations in German are excerpts from Zöckler's translation of *Edut leIsrael*, and when necessary I comment on Zöckler's use of the excerpts and his own position regarding some of the issues. When I refer to *Edut leIsrael/HaEdut*, I identify the actual text with Lucky's position.

THE RELATIONSHIP BETWEEN THE TORAH AND THE MESSIAH/THE NEW TESTAMENT—As editor of *Edut leIsrael/HaEdut*, Lucky spent much time and space on the relationship between the Torah and the New Testament. One of the things that made a handful of German and Scandinavian ministers appreciate their friendship with Lucky so much was how his insights into the Jewish tradition were fruitful for their own reading of the New Testament. This was fully in accordance with Lucky's own intentions, and was one of his reasons for stressing the continuity between Talmud and the Christian Bible: "Because if the eyes of the nations are opened they may see that the books of the Talmud are flesh of the flesh of the books of the NT, through the books of the Pharisees and Sages we will better understand, interpret, and exegete the books of the Gospels as the Apostles."[62] However, Lucky's identification with the Jewish tradition went deeper than pure instrumental purposes. The most characteristic feature of Lucky's theology, according to Weidauer, was his belief that the prophets and the believers in the Old Testament in reality had met Christ. The salvation provided by Christ was not something new but had been present in the Old Testament all the time. Christ's sacrifice and

---

Zöckler's article was probably read very carefully by people with good knowledge of the Hebrew original. Regarded as one of Lucky's friends, Zöckler clearly does not want to give the impression that he always supports the concepts in the journal. Several times he questions *Edut*'s point of view, although he supports the main ideas. However, Zöckler's article is probably colored by the author's own ideas and purpose. I have not found the same systematical approach to Lucky's ideas in *The Peculiar People*. As Lucky did not edit the American periodical himself, one cannot expect the two journals to have shared the same views in every detail, although they had most ideas in common. The denominational background must also be considered, as the editorial staff of *The Peculiar People* were representatives of the Seventh Day Baptist church, while Zöckler was influenced by Lutheran neo-Orthodoxy and revivalist ideas. Neither is it absolutely clear whether, or to what extent, the profile of *Edut leIsrael* from 1890 to 1892 was influenced by Löwen, Lucky's co-editor during this period.

62. "Book review: Lichtenstein's commentary on the New Testament," 15.

resurrection were the perfection of this gift, a divine guarantee.[63] This does not mean that pious Jews did not need Jesus. Referring to Acts 4, *Edut* claims that there is no other way for the Jewish people to repent than through Jesus as Messiah.[64]

In spite of his focus on the continuity between Jewish tradition and the New Testament, Lucky nevertheless gave the Christian Bible a certain spiritual priority. Hence, when discussing the transfer of the Sabbath from Saturday to Sunday, Lucky refers to "The two books of the Torah," i.e. the Tanak and the New Testament.[65] Lucky also follows the traditional Christian interpretation of the Hebrew Bible on the Messianic question, e.g., describing Joseph as the prototype for Jesus.[66]

Nevertheless, aiming at a Jewish audience, *Edut* is generally more concerned with problems connected to the traditional ideology and practices of Christian mission work towards Jews. In particular, the journal deals with the claim often found in traditional Christianity: as Jesus is the Messiah, Judaism is no longer valid. This claim only serves to maintain the distance between non-Christian Jews and converts. However the limitations of the Torah are defined or argued among Jewish Christians, the observant Jew will ask how it can be that the Torah of God is broken by Messiah, as the Messiah would not abolish the law.[67] One of the main traditional Jewish accusations against converts is that they become "lawless," and it is essential for Lucky to prove that this is not a New Testament doctrine. A Jewish believer instead has a new and more intense desire to live according to the law:

> God wanted to give us righteousness, and therefore he made the Torah great, to enlighten our souls, to lead us in his truth and to lead us to Messiah, that we should be made righteous by faith. And Rabbi Simlai says (ibid., 24a): "Habakuk came and placed the whole Torah on one sentence: The righteous shall live by faith (Habakuk 2:4)." Likewise this is the meaning of the holy Saul. All the teachers of Israel held that the goal of the Torah is faith, repentance, sanctification and eternal righteousness, and therefore the holy Saul says: "Messiah is the goal of the Torah

---

63. Weidauer, "Erindringer," 174.
64. "Letters from England," *Edut leIsrael* 1/4-5 (1888) 73.
65. "The Sabbath Day," 1.
66. "Joseph's Explanation," 93–94.
67. "Wie kann Gottes Thora gebrochen werden?" Zöckler, "Judentum und Christentum" (1892) 249.

(Rom 10:4)." Do we, then, destroy or make the Torah nothing by faith? Far from it. More, we lift up the law (ibid., 3.21). The Torah is holy, good and right. Then it is a Torah of the Spirit of life, and therefore we live and work in it according to the Spirit and not according the letter, as it is our life and the length of our days. And our sages, of blessed memory, have even mentioned such a doctrine.[68]

For Lucky, Jesus' loyalty to the Torah was essential. In *Edut* he points out several incidents that show how Jesus clung to the Mosaic regulations, e.g., sending the healed leper to the priests in accordance with Leviticus and forcing the demons from the possessed man into pigs so they died, "because the Gadarenes transgressed the Torah by breeding them.... So Yeshua did not have mercy on the unclean property of the pagans, even though in all other things he did good to the sinners and showed them mercy."[69]

Zöckler emphasizes that Lucky believed Paul himself affirmed the Torah: Paul's point is not to attack life under the law, but life under the law without Christ. Paul does not attack the law of life, but a piety that is not motivated from the heart. Paul's enemies are not Jews who want to observe the law, but hypocrites: "They don't bring the Torah to the inner chambers, don't give it to their 'abschliessenden' knowledge, they don't do the works of the law according to the Spirit, only the letter."[70]

---

68. Zöckler, "Judentum und Christentum," (1892) 254. Gott gefiel es, uns Gerechtigkeit zu geben, und darum machte er Groß die Thora, unsere Seelen zu läutern, uns in seiner Wahrheit zu leiten und uns zum Messias zu führen, dessen Bestimmung es war, eine ewige Gerechtigkeit zu bringen, auf das wir gerecht würden durch glauben. Und R. Simlaï legt aus (ebenda 24a [referring to *Makkoth*]): es kam Habakuk und stellte sich die ganze Thora auf einen Satz: "Die Gerechte wird seines Glaubens leben (Habakuk 2,4)." Und ebendies ist die Meinung des hl. Saul. Kurz alle Lehrer Israels behaupten, das Ziel der Thora sei Glaube, Buse, Heiligung und ewige Gerechtigkeit und darum sagt der hl. Saul: "Das Ziel der Thora ist der Messias (Röm.10,4)." Brechen wir den nun oder vereiteln wir die Thora durch den Glauben? Das sei ferne. Vielmehr wir richten das Gesetz auf (ebenda 3,21). Die Thora ist heilig, gut und recht. Denn sie ist eine Thora des Geistes des Lebens und darum leben und weben wir auch in ihr nach dem Geist und nicht nach dem Buchstaben, denn sie ist unser Leben und die Länge unserer Tage. Und eben ein Lernen der Thora in diesem Sinne nannten unsere Weisen, i.A.i.S. ["ihr Andenken in Segen"

69. "The Watch of HaEduth," *HaEdut* 4/4 (1897) 5.

70. Zöckler, "Judentum und Christentum," (1892) 255: "Sie bringen nicht in der Inneren Kammern der Thora ein, sie gelangen nicht zu ihrer abschließenden Erkenntnis, sie thun nicht des Gesetzes Werke nach dem Geist, sondern nach dem Buchstaben."

However, it is wrong to accuse all the teachers in the Talmud of this, as they usually encourage readers to find the inner side of the law themselves. In fact, they agree with Paul that the perfect fulfillment of the law is found in faith. Therefore the Torah is a teacher of faith. On this foundation *Edut* builds, that there is no *new* law for the reborn; the first law is still valid:

> The Torah of truth is only one, namely the one the almighty God gave to his people Israel by the mouth of Moses in the fire on the mountain . . . and the nations that believe in the gospel have not another Torah, only the Torah of God, which is first revealed hidden by the curtain by the mouth of Moses, and later the glory was revealed the day the curtain was ripped in two parts, and the earth was shaking and the mountains were torn apart.[71]

To come to terms with Protestant doctrine on salvation by grace vs. salvation by works, Lucky distinguished between the moral law (the Ten Commandments) and the ceremonial law. The last is only valid for Israel, as a remembrance of the saving deeds of God during history: "But then . . . when the upbringing has reached its goal . . . when the faith is fulfilled in us, why do we still need the staff? Or will we throw away our staff? Far from it! We want to honor it and hold it dear."[72] Jews who believe in Jesus will therefore not observe the Jewish customs as a way to be saved, but out of respect for how God has saved Israel. Lucky, according to Zöckler, was aware that this may be seen as a doctrine of salvation built on works, and explicitly rejects this doctrine: "Yes," our author replies, "if we want to earn righteousness by it! It is true: Those who will be righteous by the Torah fall out of grace."[73]

---

71. For Zöckler, this way of thinking corresponds to the Lutheran creed *The Form of Concord,* paragraph 6. ibid., 256: "Die Thora der Wahrheit ist nur eine, nämlich die, welche der allgütige Gott seinem Volke Israel durch den Mund Mosis auf dem Berge aus dem Feuer heraus gab. . . . Und nicht haben die Völker, welche an das Evangelium glauben, eine andere Thora, sondern nur die Thora Gottes, welche offenbart worden ist zuerst Israel unter der Decke durch Moses Mund, und deren Herrlichkeit dann offenbar geworden ist an dem Tage, da der Vorhang in zwei Stücke von oben bis unten zerriss, und die Erde erbebte und die Felsen zerrissen."

72. Ibid., 257: "Wenn nun aber . . . die Erziehung ihren Zweck erreicht . . . , wenn der Glaube in uns vollendet ist, was brauchen wir noch den Stab? Aber sollen wir unsern stab wegwerfen? Das sei ferne! Wir wollen ihn ehren und hochhalten."

73. Ibid., 257: "Es ist wahr: wer gerecht werden will durch die Thora, der fällt aus der Gnade."

Although the Torah is only one, namely the Mosaic law, it is applied differently to different people. On this point Lucky would meet opposition from Zöckler and other German friends, who found this distinction both inconsistent and unbiblical. As Zöckler sees it, the moral law sometimes goes further than the Decalogue, and even the Ten Commandments have ceremonial elements (e.g., the commandment about the Sabbath). In addition, he finds that *Edut leIsrael* is not consistent in the use of these terms.[74]

Along with the hermeneutical issues related to the relationship between Judaism and the New Testament, the topic of Christology is also highlighted. Generally, *Edut* as well as *The Peculiar People* say very little explicitly about Christology, although Jesus' divine status is taken for granted, as is his position as the promised new Moses and Messiah.[75] Particularly when explaining passages in the New Testament that deal with Jesus as a teacher, there are references to the divine authority of Jesus, e.g., when explaining the Sermon on the Mount in Matthew 5–6: "A prophet like Moses arose before them. He speaks God's word and he will answer us. Yeshua's voice was the voice of God to them. . . ." Talking about when the Pharisees accused the disciples of transgressing the Sabbath by eating grain in the field, Lucky defends the disciples: "The disciples didn't do anything they shouldn't have. What could they have done? Had they not gone to listen to the words of Torah from the mouth of the priest-Messiah?" The answer from Jesus is paraphrased: "One who is greater than the temple is here. Here before you the Torah is clothed in human flesh, and these disciples have come to listen to it and to serve in the house."[76]

---

74. Ibid., 262. The year before Zöckler's article, Dalman had commented on this distinction of the law. Dalman disagrees with this distinction, due to the nature of the Sabbath commandment and Exod 24:7–8. See Dalman, "Theorie und Praxis," 109–10. In connection to this, Zöckler says that the thoughts in *Edut leIsrael* as well as those of Rabinowitz in Kishinev have been influenced by Yechiel Lichtenstein. As Lucky and Rabinowitz appear to have rather different views on law observance, this is a question that will need further research (Zöckler, "Judentum und Christentum," [1892] 263). For Zöckler, the whole issue is a matter of Christian liberty; no one can forbid Israel to fulfil the law of its own free will: "Denn wir stehen in der Freiheit des Messias; wer aber frei ist, kann thun oder lassen, sonst ist er nicht wirklich frei" ("As we stand in the freedom of Messiah, and as someone who is free to observe the law or let it be, otherwise he is not really free"). ibid., 257.

75. Anonymous [H.G.R.], "Israel's Salvation," 109.

76. "The Watch of HaEduth," *HaEdut* 4/4 (1897) 5 and 8. In the late issues of *Edut*,

For *Edut*, all of the Christological problems and controversies, like Jesus' relation to God, are summed up in one question: Is Jesus the Messiah? For *Edut*, this is the key issue between Judaism and Christianity, and if it is settled, the other fundamental elements in Christian doctrine will fit in automatically: The necessity of the virgin birth and of the suffering and death of Christ, as well as his position as Son of God.[77] This point is made clear by this answer to a Jewish opponent:

> What do you want; is this not pure Jewish doctrine? Does it not say what both the Holy Scripture and our wise of blessed memory say? . . . And if he is the Messiah, then also he is the Son of God, and we do not need to speculate about this term, as this term is not foreign to us![78]

Jesus not only supported the Torah, but also had renewed it, and this is what Lucky wants to show the Jewish people. The road to salvation goes through the law to Christ.

THE RELATIONSHIP BETWEEN THE ORAL AND WRITTEN TORAH— According to Wiegand's account of Lucky's conversion, during his studies in Berlin Lucky was very concerned about the status and function of divine revelation. That he studied at Geiger's progressive *Hochshule* as well as Hildesheimer's seminary is probably an expression of his struggle with this issue. According to Wiegand, when the young Pollak first concluded that the Torah was God's revelation (apparently in the sense of verbal inspiration), the next step was accepting Jesus as Messiah.[79] For Lucky it was a logical consequence that if the Torah in its fixed form was somehow God's word, then the New Testament would have the same status.[80] However, this issue is never explained systematically.

---

there can also be found more examples of traditional Christological terms: "The Torah took on flesh and was revealed before the eyes of all human beings." See "The Watch of HaEduth," *HaEduth* 5/2 (1898) 25.

77. "Zöckler, "Judentum und Christentum," (1892) 263.

78. Ibid., 264: "Was willst Du? Sind das nicht lauter jüdische Lehren? Entsprechend das nicht alles dem, was die hl. Schrift und unsere Weisen, i.A.i.S., gelehrt haben? . . . Und wenn er der Messias ist, so ist er auch Gottes Sohn, und wir brauchen diesen Begriff nicht zu philosophieren, denn dieser Begriff ist uns nicht fremd!"

79. At least for the American periodical, the validity of the gospel and belief in verbal inspiration were connected; the discussion about Yom Kippur, "The Feast of Tabernacles," 67.

80. Wiegand, "Chajim Jedidjah Lucky," 44.

The question that *Edut* and *The Peculiar People* discussed more thoroughly was the continuity and divine coherence between the Hebrew Bible and Talmud. In both journals Talmud and Jewish tradition are given much importance, a position Lucky always appears ready to defend against Christian as well as progressive or secular Jewish opponents. When discussing the situation of Jewish individuals who want to convert to Christianity, Lucky rejected the traditional claim that converts should leave the rabbinical traditions altogether: Why should Gentile Christians demand that Jews leave the law in favor of (non-Jewish) laws that are not grounded in the Bible, like celebrating Christmas, Sunday, etc.? Why should Jewish Christians regard rabbinical ethics as something inferior, and stick to so-called Christian ethics, similarly connected to the laws of the Old Testament?[81]

In addition, Lucky also felt it necessary to defend *Edut*'s position against Jewish charges. Apparently Lucky was ridiculed for his attitude to Talmud. Why would *Edut* be attacked by Jews for its support of observing Talmud? At least two explanations seem plausible.

1) *Edut*'s position was probably just as original and confusing for Jews as it was for Christians—and just as suspicious. *The Peculiar People* was accused several times of being an undercover agent for missionary purposes.[82] It would be strange if the same charges not had been directed against *Edut leIsrael*.

2) For Jews with progressive or neo-Karaite sympathies, *Edut*'s adoration of Talmud was probably regarded as anachronistic. For many of these, the devaluation of the oral tradition was not only necessary for the intended assimilation of the Jewish population into European society, but also expected to be the best way to reach a better understanding between Judaism and Christianity. When a Jewish convert to Christianity now agitated for a return to Torah observance, it is understandable that some suspected this to be just another trick by Christian missionaries without any real loyalty to the Jewish tradition.

According to Zöckler, *Edut* talks about the Torah in the Orthodox meaning of the word, regarding the written text (the Tanak) and the

---

81. Ibid., 48.
82. *The Peculiar People* 2 (1889) 2. The article has no title.

oral tradition (*Torah she-baal pe*) as a unity.[83] I find it difficult to verify Zöckler's understanding of Lucky on this. As far as I have read, Lucky and the journals never seem to stress the oral tradition as a *divine* revelation in the same sense as the (Hebrew and Christian) Bible. The Torah is, according to *Edut*, the revealed Word of God, but *Edut*'s position was in practice ambivalent on this question. Not all rabbinic teachers of Israel are regarded as always being carriers of the Word of God. Already in the first issues some of the messianic expectations found in Talmud are characterized as "whimsies."[84] The Talmud contains good as well as bad parts, as the sages were only human.[85] Still, the work of the rabbis in the Talmud is of great importance for Lucky, in spite of their opposition to Christianity. Sometimes *Edut* described the Talmud and the Jewish literature as the Word of God, apparently in the same way as the Bible, while on other occasions it describes it as parallel to the role the early church fathers and Christian theology would have for non-Jewish believers. Early church fathers like Ambrose, Augustine and Irenaeus would, from this point of view, have their counterparts in individuals such as Rabbi Akiba, Rabbi Meir, Baal Shem and Rabbi Pinchas, while the reformers and more modern theologians would likewise have their parallels in Rappoport, Luzatto and Krochmal. The major flaw in the Jewish tradition is Talmud's rejection of Jesus, leading *Edut* to lament, "If only our sages . . . had become wise."[86] Consequently, it is claimed that neither traditional nor Hasidic Judaism represents the true Israel.[87] Nevertheless, Talmud is regarded as "a prosperous tool" in the revival of Jewish spiritual life.[88] This ambivalence towards the Jewish tradition is found in the both the American and Hebrew journals from the beginning to the end of their publication.

In its teaching on Christian doctrine, *Edut* would affirm the traditional Protestant idea that the way to Jesus goes via the law to the

83. Zöckler, "Judentum und Christentum," (1892) 250.
84. "Book review," *Edut leIsrael* 1/3 (1888) 57 n. 17.
85. Letters from Galicia," 69.
86. "Letters from England," 105.
87. Anonymous [J. D. N.], "Testimony in Jacob," 152, 155. I assume Lucky might have been the author, and in any case he would probably not have printed this without approving the content of the article. As far as I know, this is one of the very few places where Lucky or *Edut* refers to Hasidism.
88. Anonymous [H. G. R.], "Israel's Salvation," 125.

gospel. The significant difference from traditional Christian tradition is that "the law" includes Talmud, which for Lucky would be one of the building stones for the Christian Israel of the future.[89] This of course raises the question of whether Jewish Christians are obliged to observe the Talmud; Lucky thinks they should. However, this should not be as a result of coercion, but only in freedom and voluntarily. Still, *Edut* had to say something about outdated laws or those that could only be observed in *Eretz Israel*. According to Zöckler, Lucky not only wanted to follow the orthodox interpretation and practice on these issues, but was also convinced that his views fit with Paul's reflections about the law. The Talmud and Paul are based on the same spiritual source, and the goal of both is not external deeds but inner change of mind, repentance and sanctification.[90]

According to Lucky, both Talmud and Paul teach repentance from sin and justification by faith. It is therefore a mistake for Jewish Christians to regard the Talmud as an enemy of the New Testament; the result is alienation from Jewish traditions as well as a poorer spiritual life as a believer in Jesus. In 1892 *The Peculiar People* printed a letter which was first printed in *Edut leIsrael*. Based on what Wiegand and Löwen say about Lucky's use of pseudonyms, the author is probably Lucky himself:

> I am a Hebrew, and I have always feared the God of heaven. From my youth on my father brought me up in the lap of a pure and refined faith, the faith of our holy law, which was given us from God through Moses, the faithful shepherd, and which is explained to us by our sages of blessed memory, those giants of spirit who lived in the land of Israel and Babylon. Thanks and blessings be to the God of my fathers that I am still clinging to the law, the written as well as the oral law, and it is the crown of my head and my glory in life, and in its words has been all the life of my spirit and my soul to this day.[91]

Edut leIsrael also distinguishes between the eternal validity of the Mosaic Law in contrast to the teaching of the Rabbis.[92] Just like non-Jewish

---

89. Zöckler, "Judentum und Christentum," (1892) 251.

90. Ibid., 252.

91. "An Israelite Indeed," 273. The origin is said to be "a frequent contributor." As this term is used several other times in the American journal, it is possible that Lucky is the author other times as well. The translation is said to be based on a text from *Edut leIsrael* 3/1 (1891).

92. Zöckler, "Judentum und Christentum," (1892) 259.

Christian customs change over time, so is the ceremonial law fluid and under constant development:

> The Torah is like living water. Water that is not alive does not move and it is therefore destroyed. The living water however, flows and flows over. As life changes to different forms, soon to this, and soon to another essence, so several parts of the Torah of Moses have changed since the days of Moses, the Torah of Moses is a living Torah, and therefore the oral Torah came and changed several parts of the Torah of Moses according to life; our wise, of blessed memory, the origins of the oral Torah, saw this as the purpose of the Torah.[93]

In this quotation, the written Torah is special because it was the first to come. The oral Torah is open to be changed over time, according to contemporary circumstances. In itself this is a traditional rabbinic perspective on the Torah, and is not necessarily an attempt to draw the attention of modernized readers who want religious reform of Judaism.[94] What is different is that Lucky thinks there is a connection between the Torah and the New Testament.

THE ETERNAL COVENANT WITH ISRAEL—If the relationship between Judaism and the New Testament is this strong, it was meaningless for Lucky to speak about the old and new covenants as if they were two distinct entities. Where there is only one Torah, there is only one covenant, the Sinai covenant. For Lucky, one of the crucial things about Jesus is that in and by him the covenant between God and Israel is made new again.

> At that time the Lord made a covenant, an eternal covenant, and this covenant was made for everything that can be called human. The Torah is the Torah of the covenant, the covenant of the testimony tablets that Moses held when he came from the mountain, and which was in the covenant camp. This covenant was then

---

93. Ibid., 253–54: "Die Thora ist gleicht lebendigem Wasser. Das Wasser, welches nicht lebendig ist, das steht still und seine Stätte ist Schilf und Vinken. Das lebendige Wasser aber fließt und fließt über. Denn das Leben nimmt in stetem Wechsel bald diese und bald jene Gestalt an. Viele Stücke in der Thora Mosis haben ihr Aussehen seit Moses tagen bis heute verändert, denn die Thora Mosis ist eine lebendige Thora, und daher kam die mündliche Thora (thora-sche-baal-pe) und veränderte viele Stücke in Mosis Thora entsprechend dem Leben, denn unsere Weisen, i.A.i.S., die Urheber der mündlichen Thora, Saat auf Hoffnungen eben auf das Ziel der Thora."

94. Melchior, "Jødedommens historiske fundament," 40.

made young and new by Jesus the Messiah the true redeemer. Thus God then renewed his covenant by the sacrifice of Jesus and gave admittance to all the other nations in the world.[95]

The new covenant is not new in the sense that the old one has been discarded. Instead it has been intensified and made available to non-Jews as well. It is the same covenant, but now the nations can have a part in it until the national conversion of Israel. In response to a (fabricated?) letter from a German Catholic woman, Lucky explains this view:[96]

> At Sinai God made an eternal covenant with our fathers, although not only with our fathers, but also with us who live today. The covenant was made for me and you, and for all who are named humans. But first the Torah was given to the children of Israel, as they are the root of the holy tree, and all the nations were in the darkness and exchanged the glory of the eternal God with the image of mortal men. . . . But then came the time of mercy also to the rest of the nations. Forty years before the destruction of the temple the Lord gave mercy to all the children of men and sent his only begotten Son, Jesus Christ, the Son of God in power and glory, and gave him as a sacrifice, to do away with sin, to sentence for guilt and to bring forth righteousness. By this sacrifice God renewed the covenant with his people Israel and opened the door that all believers can pass from all the nations.[97]

---

95. Zöckler, "Judentum und Christentum," (1892) 260: " Damals schloss der Herr einen Bund mit unsern Vätern, einen ewigen Bund, und dieser Bund wurde geschlossen um aller willen, welche mit dem Namen Mensch genannt werden. Die Thora ist die Thora des Bundes, des Bundes der Zeugnistafeln, welche Mose in der Hand hielt, als er von dem Berge kam, und welche dann in der Bundeslade waren; und diese Thora ward wieder jugendlich neu durch Jesus den Messias, den wahrhaftigen Erlöser. Denn Gott erneuerte seinen Bund damals für sein Volk Israel durch das Opfer Jesu und verschaffte damals auch allen übrigen Völkern auf der Welt Zugang."

96. The terms "old" and "new" covenants refer to the New Testament statement that the death and resurrection of Jesus is the fulfillment of Jeremiah 31. In traditional anti-Judaic church doctrine, this meant that God's covenant with the people of Israel has been annulled since the days of Jesus and has been replaced with a new covenant between God and the Christian church. In Jewish thought, Christian anti-Judaism has been particularly associated with the Roman Catholic Church. If the correspondence between *Edut* and this woman was fabricated, it is probably not a coincidence that the journal gave the role of an adherent to traditional Christianity to a Roman Catholic.

97. Zöckler, "Judentum und Christentum," (1892) 260–61: "Am Sinai Schloss Gott mit unsern Vätern einen ewigen Bund, aber nicht allein mit unsern Vätern, sondern mit uns allen, die wir heute leben. Der Bund wurde geschlossen um meinet- und um deinetwillen, und um aller willen, die sich Menschen nennen. Aber zuerst ward die Thora den Kindern Israel gegeben, denn sie sind die Wurzelzweige des hl. Baums, und alle

These examples make Zöckler ask a critical question: How is this "one covenant" theology to be understood in light of the Letter to the Hebrews? Obviously Zöckler refers to how this New Testament letter discusses the relationship between the old and new covenants, arguing that the new has replaced the old. Zöckler's question is a very relevant one. In fact, as far as I know, this New Testament letter is never commented on by Lucky. The Letter to the Hebrews is one of two letters in the New Testament that distinguish clearly between the two covenants; the other is the Letter to the Galatians. The latter stresses the liberty to observe Torah versus "Judaizers," but apparently neither *Edut* nor *The Peculiar People* takes up these New Testament letters in their discussions on the covenant issue, at least not explicitly.

Except for Zöckler's question above, the sources are silent on this, be they Lucky's friends or Christian opponents. For Lucky and his friends, the reason may of course be that these letters complicated Lucky's agenda. On the other hand, his motives could be pedagogic; Lucky did not ignore other parts of the New Testament that called his ideas into question. In particular, narratives from the Gospels and Acts are described and commented on, as seen in section D below. However, Hebrews and Galatians are more like systematic sermons than the narratives in the Gospels, and would be regarded as rather heavy reading, even by Protestant laypeople—not to mention (Jewish) readers of *Edut* who would be unfamiliar with the New Testament.

JESUS' CONFLICTS WITH THE PHARISEES—However, if the relationship between the New Testament and Judaism is characterized by continuity, why do the Gospels dwell so much on the hostility of the Pharisees towards Jesus? As Zöckler sees it, for *Edut leIsrael* the disagreements between Jesus and the Pharisees come down to basically one question, namely the chronology of how Israel will be saved. In one of the last issues, *Edut* converses with a Jewish correspondent who points to the

---

andern Völker waren verfinstert in der Erkenntnis und vertauschten die Herrlichkeit des ewigen Gottes mit dem Bild sterblicher Menschen. . . . Aber dann kam die Zeit der Erbarmung auch für alle übrigen Völker. Vierzig Jahre vor der Zerstörung des Tempels erbarmte sich der Herr über alle Menschenkinder und sandte seinen eingeborenen Sohn, Jesus Christus, den Sohn Gottes in Machtherrlichkeit und gab ihn zum Opfer dahin, um die Sünde abzuthun, die Schuld zu sühnen und ewige Gerechtigkeit zu beschaffen. Durch dieses Opfer erneute Gott den Bund mit seinem Volke Israel und öffnete auch allen übrigen Völkern die Thore, durch welche die Gläubigen eingehen."

traditional Jewish reason for not accepting Jesus as Messiah: the Jews expect that the Messiah will liberate them from the yoke of their Gentile rulers, but Jesus has done nothing to ease the burden of the yoke of alien nations. *Edut* responds:

> I do not understand the question. Should not the Jews, who were those who heard the word of God, as God had spoken through Moses and the prophets to them, by uncountable miracles and signs, not know what God wanted of them? It is far from you to judge our fathers like that, those who were scholars of the Torah. They went wrong, yes, but not the way you think. They knew that the Messiah would come to do away with sin, to atone for guilt and to bring forth an eternal righteousness (Daniel 9:24), and Isaiah had preached the same long before Daniel. God's gracious thoughts for us, to atone for sin and do away with the sin of the first men, are clear and obvious in the whole history of our people. But our fathers in the days of Jesus went wrong, as they believed that the Messiah first would restore the kingdom of Israel and then liberate them from their sins . . . when the order of things really was the opposite.[98]

Generally, Lucky claims that the apostles as well as Jesus himself followed all of the traditions of the scribes and Pharisees. The Pharisees' hostility towards Jesus is explained on the background of the theological and political disputes of the time: "Because of the struggles of the scribes and the Pharisees against the Sadducees and Boethuseans, they were like wild beasts and knew no mercy.[99] They guarded their order and

---

98. Zöckler, "Judentum und Christentum," (1893) 48–49: "Diese Frage verstehe Ich nicht. Die Juden, welche Hörer des Göttlichen Worts waren denn zu ihnen hat doch Gott durch Mose und die Propheten geredet, und durch unzähligen Wunder und Zeichen, die sollten nicht gewusst haben, was Gott von ihnen verlangte? Fern sei es von dir, solch ein Urteil über unsere Väter zu Fällen, welche Forscher in der Thora waren. Sie irrten freilich, aber nicht so, wie du meinst. Sie wussten, dass der Messias kommen würde, abzuthun die Sünden, zu sühnen die Schuld und zu bringen ewige Gerechtigkeit (Dan. 9.24), und Jesaja hatte da lange vor Daniel gepredigt. Der gnädige Gedanke Gottes über uns, die Sünde zu sühnen und die Sünde des ersten abzuthun, ist sichtbar und offenkundig in der gesamten Geschichte unseres Volkes. Aber unsere Väter in den Tagen Jesus irrten, indem sie dachten, dass der Messias zuerst das Reich Israel wiederbringen und dann sie von ihren Sünden entkündigen würde . . . während in Wahrheit die Ordnung umgekehrt war."

99. "Boethuseans" is, in rabbinical terminology, synonymous with Sadducees. See Danby, *The Mishnah*, 506 n. 1.

regulations as the apple of their eye."[100] Often *Edut* argues in the form of paraphrases of relevant passages. In fact, on some occasions Lucky's paraphrases seem speculative rather than the result of serious exegesis, e.g., when he explains why the disciples did not wash their hands (Mark 7:2) before a meal. *Edut* explains that the reason was quite simply that they lacked water.[101]

Jewish Mysticism

According to Lucky, the Talmud and the New Testament express basically the same ideas when it comes to questions of the Torah and Messiah—with the significant exception of whether Jesus was the Messiah or not. However, when describing the common ideas in Jewish and Christian tradition, it is striking that Lucky does not refer to Jewsh mysticism. Many of the previous as well as contemporary attempts to link Christianity with Judaism had been done by comparing elements from, e.g., Kabbalah with Christian doctrine. Hasidic ideas about the godhead have been seen as interesting links to the Christian doctrine of the Trinity, and have inspired other Jewish Christians with a strong Jewish identification, like Paul Phillip Levertoff and Herschensohn-Lichtenstein (Yechiel Z. Lichtenstein).[102] In spite of *Edut*'s enthusiasm about Herschensohn-Lichtenstein, there is no trace of his Hasidic ideas in *Edut*. Herschensohn-Lichtenstein's enthusiasm for Jewish mysticism is not even mentioned in the journal, which—if nothing else—gives the impression that this aspect of Jewish tradition was not very important to Lucky. This lack of Hasidic-inspired material is striking when considering Lucky's Galician background.[103] If Wiegand is correct, Lucky had even been involved in a Hasidic group in his youth.[104]

The reason might be that Lucky felt this approach was alien, and probably some of the explanation can be found in his education. At the rabbinic seminaries, Jewish mysticism was apparently not regarded as very helpful in building a modern Jewish Torah-observant society, and

---

100. "The Watch of HaEduth," *HaEdut* 4/4 (1897) 8–9.

101. Ibid., 9.

102. Jocz, *The Jewish People and Jesus Christ*, 209. See also Quiñónez, "Paul Philip Levertoff," 21, 27.

103. The same could be said about Rabinowitz, who also had come from a Hasidic background. Zipperstein, "Heresy," 209.

104. Wiegand, "Chajim Jedidjah Lucky," 42.

certainly not at the *Hochschule*.[105] It is possible that some of the same tensions in the Jewish community in Galicia can explain Lucky's silence on the issue. Lucky's background would probably make him regard Jewish mysticism as irrelevant for Jewish life altogether. In addition, Hasidism had lost much of its previous influence and authority in the Galician Jewish population in the last decades before WWI. It would therefore not be natural for Lucky to integrate Kabbalah and Hasidic speculations into his own arguments.

Jewish Identity in Exile: Law Observance and Jewish Family Life

Torah Observance as a National Obligation—A natural consequence of Lucky's embrace of the Jewish oral tradition was that he felt obliged to observe halakah.[106] When he began to believe in Jesus he had already left many of the secular ideologies and returned to a position where Torah observance and Jewish identity were significant, and the Jewish religious customs and their spiritual meaning were dear to him. His conversion to Christianity did not change this view. It was the same God who had spoken to Israel through the prophets and who had revealed himself through his Son. Although Jewish customs were seen in the new light of Jesus, Lucky maintained a Jewish lifestyle after his conversion. As late as in 1900, his main New Testament reference for this position was the word of Jesus in Matthew 23:1–3,[107] which for him justified the observance of not only biblical regulations but the oral tradition as well.[108] Although he accepted the doctrine of Christian liberty, he did not think that this liberty demanded that a Jewish believer should leave his or her Jewish identity behind: "Jesus didn't die so the Jews could eat pork," Weidauer recalls Lucky saying. Weidauer compared Lucky's view with the Blue Cross organization, which based on solidarity with alcoholics preached that Christians should keep away from using alcohol,

---

105. In Galicia before 1850, the *maskilim*'s strongest enemies had been the *Hasidim*; Feiner, *Haskalah and History*, 78.

106. Zöckler, "Judentum und Christentum," (1892) 251.

107. "Then Jesus said to the crowds and to his disciples, 'The scribes and the Pharisees sit on Moses' seat; therefore, do whatever they teach you and follow it; but do not do as they do, for they do not practice what they teach." (NRSV).

108. "Judenschristlichen Gedanken und Hoffnungen." According to Weidauer, the author is Lucky (Weidauer, "Erindringer," 172).

although there exists no biblical prohibition on drinking. In the same way, Lucky wanted to use Christian liberty to identify himself with the Jewish people. Thus he sought to avoid being regarded as a *meshummad* in the Jewish community. This attitude had its price: according to Weidauer, Lucky often felt much grief due to his non-Jewish friends' lack of understanding.[109]

However, in his own writings Lucky tried to promote his view, based not on the doctrine of Christian liberty but on specific texts in the Gospels and Acts. When commenting on these New Testament writings, he is particularly concerned about the Jewish believer's attitude to keeping kosher. Lucky rejects the interpretation of the apostolic authority to loose and bind (Matthew 18:18) as an authorization to debunk Jewish oral tradition. Paraphrasing Peter's encounter with Cornelius, and Paul and Barnabas' mission experiences in Acts 10–11 and 13–14, he tries to explain the view of the Pharisees who believed in Jesus but struggled with Paul over letting non-Jews into the church without circumcision. They did not believe that the *shekina* (God's divine presence) could dwell on uncircumcised people, and found it difficult to accept that the martyrdom under the Greeks described in the Books of Maccabees was in vain. According to Saul and Barnabas, "the yoke of the Torah had been placed upon the neck of the children of Israel, not on the neck of another people." In fact, their mission narratives described how the *shekina* rested upon the Gentiles who believed in Jesus. In Acts 15, the leaders of the Jerusalem congregation accepted this. However, according to Lucky, this solution was not meant to last forever: their intention was that the Gentile believers would eventually choose to follow their Jewish brethren after listening to Torah readings: "That which the elders of the community of the Messiah permitted, they did so not to us but only to the Gentiles."[110]

Basically, Lucky held that the decree in Acts was given for the sake of continued fellowship between Jewish and non-Jewish believers in Jesus; for instance, referring to the narratives in Acts 10–11, he said, "God showed Simon Peter that a Jew could associate with a Gentile, to eat bread with him."[111] As seen in the biography, Lucky apparently had no problem visiting non-Jewish contacts, and even cultivated friendship

---

109. Weidauer, "Erindringer," 172.
110. "The Watch of HaEduth," *HaEdut* 5/2 (1898) 33.
111. Ibid.

with many missionaries and their families. Still, his observance of Jewish food regulations made these visits difficult for some of the non-Jewish housewives. To associate with non-Jews and eat with them did not mean that he abandoned kosher: "But that which was forbidden him to eat he did not eat. He didn't eat in Cornelius' house anything which was forbidden to us, as the vision demonstrates to us."[112] According to Lucky, in Acts 15 the Jerusalem congregation acknowledged the Gentile believers as authentic members of the assembly. "They [the elders and the apostles] did not act as the houses of Hillel and Shammai. Their decision was not like the halakic ruling."[113] Lucky supports the decision of the apostles because he considers it in accordance with Judaism: "And is not this the whole witness of the teaching of the Sages? . . . They are our brethren; they are like Jews, because everyone who rejects idolatry is considered as a Jew."[114]

However, for Jewish believers the situation is somewhat different:

> But the elders of the community of the Messiah did not permit us Jews to turn from the Torah of Moses. For us, the Torah of Moses is the Torah. It is our heritage, and in its paths we shall walk, because its paths are paths of peace and its ways are ways of pleasantness, ways of immortality, the ways of the Messiah, the Prince of Peace.[115]

Aside from dealing with the decree and the narratives from Acts, Lucky also needs to explain to his Jewish readers the views in the Gospels on this issue. According to him, the gospels describe how "our Lord Yeshua penetrates the thought and spirit of the Torah and finds its true depth and reveals meanings in it which had never been revealed until his day." To prove that the New Testament does not prohibit Torah observance, Lucky paraphrases Jesus (rather freely) in the Sermon on the Mount (Matthew 5):

> I have not come to abolish the Torah but to fulfill it. I have not come to destroy but to establish and to strengthen the whole of the Torah. Behold, the House [Temple] of the Torah stands before you in all its glory: its rooms are spacious and its attics rejoice the heart. But people have yet not attempted to enter within

112. Ibid.
113. Ibid., 34.
114. Ibid.
115. Ibid.

the House but only gather in its courtyard (the people of Israel). Even the scribes and Pharisees, the teachers of the Torah to their people and their guides, even they have still not entered into the holy of holies. So I have come to lead you into the inside of the House and to fulfill the words of the Torah as it arose in God's thought when He gave it. For truly I say to you, until heaven and earth pass away, not one jot or tittle will pass away from the Torah until it has all been fulfilled.[116]

For example, Lucky does not believe that Jesus overturned the regulations concerning Jewish fasts in Matthew 6:

> Yeshua is not speaking here of public, communal fasts. Because on a communal fast day, it is forbidden to wash or anoint your hair, and all the community wails and laments and beats their breasts and heads. Anyone who doesn't participate in such a fast is considered a traitor among his people because he has removed himself from the community. . . . Only in an individual, private fast, where a person truly fasts and afflicts himself, can there be any hypocrisy if he puts on an appearance so that everyone who sees him knows that he is fasting. . . .[117]

Lucky's insistence on Torah observance often made people believe he claimed that Jewish believers were obliged to follow Jewish customs and Talmud. This was denied several times by both Lucky and his German friends.[118] Observance of the Torah should be voluntary and based on an independent decision, and keeping the ceremonial law was not necessary for the sake of salvation.[119] Lucky's point was that it was impossible

---

116. "The Watch of HaEduth," *HaEdut* 4/4 (1897) 2.

117. Ibid., 5.

118. Zöckler, "Judentum und Christentum," (1892) 252.

119. What, then, is the purpose of observing the law? At this point in his article, Zöckler gives his own understanding of *Edut*'s position, without referring to any given text from the journal. Zöckler claims that *Edut*'s fundamental position is that religious and Christian life is not possible without a public lifestyle. This is done by all the nations, and is colored by their national characteristics. It is therefore only natural that Jewish Christians should stick to a way of life that is connected to customs and institutions related to Jewish ceremonial laws. For the Jewish Christian this is an act of faith, whereby he publicly proclaims the faith for the future of Israel. Without this observance of Jewish customs, there will never be any national conversion of Israel, but only "Poles converted to Christ." In this light, observance of the ceremonial law is self-evident: When the sons of Israel who believe in the Messiah give up the signs of nationality and do not keep or observe them (first of all circumcision, Sabbath and the festivals), will not Israel disappear into the other nations? Who should then inherit the promise to

to have a Jewish identity without Torah observance, particularly as the Jewish people were without its own land.[120]

Torah Observance, Festivals, and the Family—Lucky did not present a differentiated system for Torah observance until his last years (see the chapter on Hebrew Christianity), but one key factor for the continuity of Jewish identity had been central for him: Jewish family life. Although Lucky shared Rabinowitz's vision of creating congregations or fellowships of Jewish believers, he seems to have found the question of a "pure" Jewish family life more significant for the sake of Jewish identification than fellowships of individuals claiming a Jewish identity. At the mission conference in Leipzig in 1895, Dalman refers to the resistance against Lucky's ideas being connected to the fact that many of the Jewish Christians present had non-Jewish spouses. According to Jewish Orthodoxy, one needs to be born of a Jewish woman to be counted as Jewish. Consequently, Dalman states, to achieve the continuity of the Jewish Christians' Jewish nationality, only a prohibition of mixed marriages would have the effect Lucky (and Wiegand) sought.[121]

Dalman hardly exaggerated Wiegand and Lucky's position. Löwen describes how Lucky already in New York sent some of his Galician sympathizers back to Galicia with the purpose of leading them into Jewish marriages. During their work on *Edut leIsrael* in Stanislau and Lemberg, Lucky even encouraged Löwen to let his German wife be "Judaized." Likewise, one of the reasons for the tensions between Yechiel Lichtenstein and Lucky in 1889 was the fact that Lichtenstein had married a non-Jewish woman. After 1895, the controversy about non-Jewish wives and husbands does not seem to have been discussed openly, but in his obituary in 1917 Wiegand revisits the topic: "They [the Jewish Christians] stand outside their people. That is something the non-Jewish wives they marry take care of. And later the children are surely not Jewish

---

the fathers? In other words, Jewish Christians should make the survival of the Jewish nation part of their own way of life, not only for the sake of the Jewish people as such, but to help bring the prophecies to fulfillment. Ibid., 258.

120. Ibid. Lucky attacks I. T. Reichardt, who wanted to have a Jewish identity without the Mosaic laws, and did not believe this would make Israel disappear into the other nations. According to Dalman, Reichardt thought that Torah observance for Jewish Christians had to be suspended until Israel's return to Palestine and the millennial kingdom, as this observance was only possible in the land of Israel under the regime of Christ. Dalman, "Theorie und Praxis," 108–9.

121. Dalman, *Die Allgemeine Konferenz für Judenmission*, 20.

any longer."[122] The problem of non-Jewish wives was not a matter of race, but was related to the fact that the children of these mixed marriages were socialized into a Gentile culture, normally without any connection to their Jewish background. More than anything, Lucky feared the assimilation that followed in the wake of mixed marriages. True enough, traditional mission methods usually led converts to leave their Jewish origins, but for Lucky the New Testament contained so much affection for the Jewish nation and Jewish tradition that it could, to some extent, balance the assimilation process. In some cases it could perhaps even lead Jews alienated from their own people back to their national roots. Mixed marriages, however, would only ensure that Jewish identity disappeared after the first generation of believers.[123]

In addition to the issue of intermarriage, Lucky was also very concerned about Sabbath observance, on which he shared views with Seventh Day Baptists. Lucky claims that Jesus never abandoned observance of the Sabbath, and that his controversies about the Sabbath were related to the practice of the Pharisees:

> And from the day on which the vision was sealed in Israel until the revelation of Yeshua the Messiah before mankind, the commandment of Shabbat increased greatly. The scribes and Pharisees highly elevated it because they added fences of hundreds and thousands and many stringencies, until it became a heavy burden and a great trouble on the shoulders of the people. They also brought great evil on the people in their nitpicking regarding the observance of this most precious of commandments. ... The devout Jews kept the Torah of the scribes and chose to give their backs to those who struck them and their lives as martyrs rather than to touch the blade of a sword or a javelin or a spear on Shabbat. They didn't do this out of wisdom, because the scribes did not wish them to do this, and so the scribes added additional regulations afterwards, saying that in order to fight against the enemies of the Lord it was permissible to fight on Shabbat. But all this is evidence that the holiness of Shabbat was embedded deeply in the Jews, in their whole heart, soul, and strength. ... The controversy between him [Jesus] and the teachers of the

---

122. Wiegand, "Chajim Jedidjah Lucky," 45.

123. Lucky's attitude to mixed marriages did not mean that he was uncritical of Jewish practice and tradition in all aspects of Jewish marriage. Particularly when it came to divorce, he was very negative about it, as when commenting upon Matthew 5. "The Watch of HaEduth," *HaEdut* 4/4 (1897) 4.

people at that time was not about keeping Shabbat per se but about how to keep it—what is permitted and what is forbidden on Shabbat. Because the scribes and Pharisees in those days magnified this question [without] end and thereby increased the laws of Shabbat without number.[124]

This controversy between Jesus and the scribes was not limited to his own age. As the scribes belonged to the environment that was behind *Mishnah*, Lucky conveys a more critical view on talmudic regulations as well:

From all the passages we have looked at above, clear evidence arises that our Lord Yeshua honoured the seventh day and sanctified it to rest and cease from work on it according to the spirit of the Torah of Moses and the Prophets. He only removed from it all the foreign additions and strange ideas with which the authors of the mishna surrounded it.[125]

Lucky claims that during the first decades after Christ, "Messianic" Jews observed the Sabbath, and the Gentile believers did as well. The transfer of observance from the Sabbath to Sunday was due to Gentile church fathers. He refers to how many "Messianics" in addition to other Jews observed the seventh day, like the Copts and the Ethiopians. Later, Greeks and Romans changed their mind, and adopted the pagan elevation of Sunday. This became one of the reasons for the increasing separation between Jewish and Gentile believers:

At that time, the link of fellowship between them was broken, the Jewish believers separated from the gentile believers, turning their back rather than their face to them, and returned to their teachers, the Pharisees. The gentile believers wanted both sides of the fence, and from the Mount of Olives danced as deer to Mount Olympus.[126]

Lucky attacks Luther, among others, for classifying the Sabbath as for the Jews alone. Lucky thought not only that Sabbath observance was for Jewish believers, but that a pure Christian doctrine included Sabbath observance for Gentile Christians as well. Seventh day observing churches were therefore preferred:

124. "The Sabbath Day," 6.
125. Ibid., 10.
126. Ibid., 14.

> Let us forsake the day of the sun, because this is not our rest, and let us establish the Day of the Lord, the seventh day, to find in it rest for our souls. Not only we in Israel bound ourselves to this Shabbat but all those who believe in Yeshua. They, too, who have been quarried from the rock of the Gentiles are called to sanctify Shabbat, the Jewish Shabbat, because thus God spoke by the mouth of His prophet Isaiah: "Everyone who keeps from defiling Shabbat and holds fast My covenant, even them I will bring to My holy mountain and make them joyful in My house of prayer" (Isa. 56:6–7). Yes, many will fall away and walk in error to the day of the sun, but God also chose from amongst them a remnant who is devoted to Shabbat in America and England, etc.[127]

Lucky also appears to have celebrated the Jewish festivals, and the most important Jewish festival according to him is Shavuot. This festival is a time to praise God for the wonders of nature, the history of Israel, and the covenant at Sinai. That the outpouring of the Holy Spirit took place at Shavuot indicates a fulfillment of the Passover events. The seven weeks were fulfilled in the days of Jesus.[128] Lucky sees the events related to Jesus and the Holy Spirit as a divine confirmation and renewal of God's promises and his covenant with Israel.[129] This is the background for his article on the Book of Ruth in one of the late issues of *Edut*.[130]

Lichtenstein

Jewish Identity and Family Life

Lichtenstein did not accept the label "former Jews" for Jewish Christians:[131] "'Jewish-Christians'? You must accustom yourself to the expression. There are Jews who are Christians also; Jews who believe in Christ, not in

---

127. Ibid., 15. This paragraph is followed by a statement in regard to Christian observers of the Sabbath: "The Gentiles who observe the seventh day in England are not many in this generation, but in the previous century, when the Spirit passed through the body of the Messiah and cleansed it, righteous men arose there to restore the holiness of Shabbat to the seventh day. Because this is the day that the Lord blessed. The churches which sanctify the seventh day in America are their descendants."

128. "Shavuot—By a Faithful Celebrant," 13.

129. Ibid.

130. Ibid., 14–21. It is also possible that Lucky was interested in this book for personal reasons: The article is signed "by a Bethlehemite," and according to SDB sources Lucky was of the tribe of Benjamin; see Randolph, "Christian Theophilus Lucky," 207.

131. Lichtenstein, *Ein Geheimnis*, 12–16.

spite of, but because they are Jews, and have found in Jesus the Messiah of Israel."[132] According to Lichtenstein, these Jews should not cease to be Jews, especially not in a time of tolerance and progress.[133] This view is the background for his social and religious position after 1886. Lichtenstein's fear of being cut off from his people made him avoid a public baptism his whole life, and eventually made it possible for his family to have him buried at the Neolog cemetery in Budapest.[134] Although he was regarded a traitor by the Jewish community, his official identity as a Jew could not be denied or ignored. This situation was not regarded only as a formality, either by him or by the Neolog leadership. The alleged impossibility of his position even led representatives from the Neolog community to request that he withdraw his title.[135] For Lichtenstein, this was never an option.

However, in his publications, Lichtenstein does not dwell upon his own feelings of being Jewish. Instead he is intensely concerned about the lack of Jewish feeling among the Jewish people of his day. When dealing with family life, Lichtenstein is particularly worried about the spiritual decline and religious indifference of the younger generation, something that also worried Lucky.[136] In contrast to Lucky, however, Lichtenstein does not appear to have been very worried about intermarriage. In fact, intermarriage is never an issue in Lichtenstein's writings, just as he never mentions Zionism or Jewish nationalism. This does not mean that he was indifferent to the question, but possibly that he considered other problems more crucial. For him the threat against the Jewish people was not so much their choice of spouses as the disintegration of their religious life and observance.

Lichtenstein's enthusiasm for Jesus is partly due to his belief that the embrace of Jesus by his people would revitalize their spiritual life as well as strengthening observance of the law. Particularly in his early writings, Jesus is understood not so much as a savior who redeems

132. Lichtenstein, *A Jewish Mirror*, 7.
133. Lichtenstein, *Ein Geheimnis*, 1.
134. Anacker, "Meine Reise nach Galizien," 89.
135. Gjessing, "Rabbi Isak (Ignaz) Lichtenstein," 174.
136. Soon after his return to Europe, Lucky complained, "Although the city (Stanislau) has changed for the better in the last decade, the house of Israel has changed for the worse. They are going backwards daily in their morals and ethics." "A Letter from Our Writer in Stanislawow," 6.

the individual from sin and eternal punishment, but as a redeemer of Judaism, the Jewish people as Jewish, and Jewish spiritual life. If Israel in the future should come to believe that God has visited them and sent the Counselor, they need to hear that they will not cease being Jews by becoming Christians. Instead they are becoming true Jews, spiritually speaking:

> You need not, like withered leaves, fall away from your ancient stock, or deny parents or nationality; you need not be unfaithful to the God of your fathers, on account of reverence rendered to the Son, for only when you do Him homage are you a true Jew, a genuine son of Abraham, not only after the flesh, but after the Spirit.[137]

Adherence to the Torah and the Talmud

This revitalization of Jewish virtues is not only connected to the Hebrew Bible, but to Jewish tradition as a whole. Like Lucky, Lichtenstein claims to hold Jewish tradition, first of all the Hebrew Bible and Talmud, in high esteem, and he insists that there is a spiritual connection between the gospel and the Talmud:

> Many imagine the Talmud to be the iron wall which separates Israel from the Gospel; but daily experiences prove that in this they are mistaken. Talmudists, who by the grace of God have received the knowledge of the truth, worship the Lord Jesus with all their heart, and cleave to Him with every fiber of their heart.[138]

From the start of his publications in 1886, Lichtenstein underlines the spiritual unity and coherence between Judaism and Christianity, the Jewish tradition and the New Testament. In most of his writings he refers to the Talmud and other Jewish literature as an authority apparently on the level of the New Testament when arguing for his views. His positive view of Jewish tradition is most explicitly found in his first booklet from 1886, *Der Talmud auf der Anklagenbank*. The main purpose of the book is to defend the Talmud against the missionary and Professor Rev. Alexander McCaul's book, *The Old Paths*, which I already have presented in relation to Gurland's narrative about the debate in Kishinev

---

137. Lichtenstein, *The Points of Contact*, 13.

138. Considering that Lichtenstein was addressing mission leaders in Leipzig in 1895, it is possible that one "Talmudist" he had in mind was Lucky. Ibid., 8–9.

in 1864.[139] McCaul ridicules Talmud for the way it contradicts common sense and the Old and New Testaments, and says it has kept the Jewish people under the yoke of the rabbinic tradition. According to McCaul, this would become obvious if one made Talmud available to the public; the translation of Talmud into European languages would be "the most fatal attack that can be made on its authority. It needs only to be seen as it is, in order to be rejected."[140]

McCaul does not succumb to anti-Semitism in the sense of believing the Jews are degenerate, and sometimes he points to the existence of Jewish virtues. However, all good virtues in the Jewish people are due to the Old Testament, while the oral tradition corrupts the Jewish mentality as well as the Jewish community. In his work he therefore encourages the Jews to get rid of the legends of the oral tradition, as then the genius of the Jewish nation will be revealed to the nations.[141] Generally, McCaul believes that texts from the Talmud are meant to be understood literally, for example when describing Talmud texts that appear to encourage cruelty, and he rejects claims from Jewish representatives that these texts were meant figuratively.[142]

Lichtenstein is not only concerned about McCaul's book, but takes the opportunity to defend the Talmud generally against similar attacks, from Christians as well as Jews, and from his son Emmanuel.[143] In his pamphlet, Lichtenstein dwells on three of McCaul's accusations:

1) *Talmud encourages cruelty*. Lichtenstein rejects McCaul's idea that Talmud encourages the killing of *amhaaretz*. In particular he refers to

---

139. After its first publication in 1838, the book was reprinted a number of times, which made it quite natural to comment upon as late as 1886.

140. McCaul, *The Old Paths*, v.

141. Ibid., 143.

142. McCaul holds the number of legends in the Jewish tradition as proof that the tradition is not from God, although he is well aware that many European Jewish scholars explained them as part of the Haggadah and as allegories. He rejects this interpretation because these legends are verified by their function in the Jewish prayer book. ibid., 136.

143. I do not know if Lichtenstein, in 1886 or later, was familiar with the narrative about Gurland's discussion in the synagogue in Chisinau in 1864. In *Zwei Briefe* Lichtenstein defends the role of miracles in the Jewish tradition. The history of Israel is full of miracles, but they are usually tools for the divine message. To mock these histories, he says to his son, would be like patronizing the sages from Hungarian history. Lichtenstein, *Two Letters; or What I really Wish*, 17; also Lichtenstein, *Zwei Briefe*, 16.

Pesachim 49.2, one of the same texts that Gurland discussed in Kishinev in 1864. Lichtenstein believes that taking this text as a general proof of the content of Talmud is wrong. It is correct that Talmud condemns the *amhaaretz*, but only understood as nihilists and people who have no respect for God. Anyway, he points out, the Jewish literature gives no example of any *amhaaretz* who was killed, and to the contrary, the Talmud prohibits capital punishment.[144]

2) *The legends.* In discussing the liturgy for the Feast of Pentecost, McCaul refers to the Talmud narrative about how God killed Leviathan and gave the body to the righteous, but according to Lichtenstein this story is a parallel to the narrative found in Revelation 19 in the New Testament.[145] These narratives are not to be taken literally, but are stories about how tyrants and oppressors of God's people fell (Psalm 68).[146] Finally, Lichtenstein responds to McCaul's description of the idea that every Jewish man returning home to the Sabbath table from the synagogue is followed by two angels.[147] This story is also not meant to be taken literally, but is about the spiritual and moral struggle that goes on in most people. Lichtenstein finds this story to be a good parallel to the Parable of the Ten Virgins in Matthew 25:1–12.

3) *Superstition found in Talmud.* McCaul accuses Talmud of encouraging superstition, like the practice of magic, wearing amulets, and belief in other things like healing and demons. Lichtenstein explains these examples as mostly related to the Essenes, claiming that mainstream groups like the Pharisees warned against magic.[148]

In other words, in his early writings Lichtenstein is concerned with defending Talmud against patronizing assaults, particularly regarding its anthropomorphisms and legends. Lichtenstein defends these stories partly by explaining them metaphorically (in spite of McCaul's rejection of this approach) and partly in the light of the New Testament.

---

144. Lichtenstein, *Der Talmud*, 10–12.
145. McCaul, *The Old Paths*, 128.
146. Lichtenstein, *Der Talmud*, 10–12.
147. Lichtenstein and McCaul refer to the description of the arrangement of the Sabbath table, and the two angels that follow the man home after the synagogue service. Lichtenstein, *Der Talmud*, 16–18.
148. Lichtenstein, *Der Talmud*, 15.

For the next fifteen years, Lichtenstein continues to use the metaphorical approach in his writings. Unlike McCaul or Jewish readers with neo-Karaite leanings, Lichtenstein refuses to read the whole set of rabbinic texts literally. Particularly the narratives of the Haggadah are regarded as parables or even allegories that describe spiritual truths, as in his pamphlet *Das Blut Christi* (1893). This was probably what he thought was the best way to rescue the values of the Hebrew Bible in the Jewish people.[149] Finally, this reading also made it possible for him to regard Talmud, the midrashic literature, and the New Testament as religious texts that are coherent with each other.[150]

Using Talmud and other Jewish literature to confirm Christian doctrines was not something new in the Christian mission to the Jews. The Jewish-Christian "dialogue" in 1263 in Barcelona was the scene of one of the first attempts to do this, led by the Jewish convert Friar Paul of the Dominicans.[151] This approach was also used by missionaries in the German-speaking regions of Europe; the most famous example was Johann Müller's *Licht am Abend* from the 18th century.[152] However, in spite of the similarities between Lichtenstein's reading of the Jewish and Christian texts and this Christian tradition, Lichtenstein's approach does not regard the Jewish tradition as merely a stepping-stone to Christianity. For him, Talmud continues to be a spiritual authority also for the believer in Jesus. The reason is that Lichtenstein believes the Talmud and the Gospels to be connected in spirit; in fact, he believes that the essence of Judaism is the essence of Christianity.[153] In fact, even the doctrine of the Trinity, one of the main theological differences between Judaism and Christianity, seems to have been suggested in the Jewish tradition. For Lichtenstein, the Jewish concept of *shekina* is a central meeting point

---

149. Lichtenstein, *Judenthum und Christenthum*, 29.

150. Lichtenstein, *Der Talmud*, 19–20.

151. Paul tried to demonstrate from both the Bible and the Talmud that: 1. The Messiah had come; 2. This Messiah was supposed to be human as well as divine; 3. He should suffer and die; and 4. The advent of Messiah would eventually make the Jewish law lose its force. Chazan, *Jewish Suffering*, 18.

152. Skarsaune, *Israels venner*, 21.

153. "Was wohl kein ehrlicher Sachverständiger bestreiten kann, dass die Talmudisten und Evangelisten Geistesverwandte, Geistesbrüder waren. Wie konnte dies auch anders sein?" (Lichtenstein, *Die Liebe*, 29); also Lichtenstein, *Ein Geheimnis*, 23.

between Judaism and Christianity, as it leads to a concept similar to the Trinity:[154]

> Again, I will not speak of the Holy Spirit or the Christian doctrine of the Godhead—Father, Son and Spirit—although our Chassidim, who claim to be successors of the heroes of the Talmud, and with whom the orthodox in Judaism now go hand in hand, believe in a tenfold godhead, in ten emanations, who with En-Sof (the Eternal) form one absolute, inseparable unit, with ten sides and ten faces. These say "As the fire with its flames and its sparks is but one, so the Eternal with the Sefirot radiating from him is one in being."[155] Many also of our most advanced Rabbis cannot think of God without the Schechina (glory) and the Ruach Haqadosh, Holy Spirit.[156] Neither will I here represent Christ as the Lamb of sacrifice whose death was an atonement, although our Talmudists often repeat [text in Hebrew] "The righteous bear the sins of their generation." [text in Hebrew] "As the death of the red heifer is an atonement, so also the death of the righteous is atoning."[157]

For Lichtenstein, Talmud was not a wall to protect Jews from Christian teaching, but rather a sea of knowledge: "I say from the 'sea', for certainly some theses are to be found in Talmud, in which the salt is without savor, and worthless, but the salt of the Covenant is also there."[158]

In his defense of Talmud and Judaism against the neo-Karaites, Christian missionaries and Jewish apostates, Lichtenstein seems to have been influenced by the hermeneutics of progressive Judaism, particularly when it came to interpretation of anthropomorphisms in the Jewish literature. However, it must be noted that this insistence on the coherence between Judaism and Christianity was not parallel to the

---

154. Lichtenstein, *Points of Contact*, 7.

155. It is possible that Lichtenstein refers more to the Kabbalist idea of *shekina* than that within the rabbinic framework; see the article "Sefirot," 618–19.

156. Lichtenstein's footnote: *Shekinah* [in Hebrew] Protocol of the first Assembly of Rabbis at Braunschweig, June 1844. Third edition, page 105.

157. Lichtenstein, *An Appeal*, 15. Except for the case of *shekina*, Lichtenstein appears to avoid developing Hasidic ideas and elements further in his polemics. This is in contrast to Yechiel Lichtenstein and his successor at the Institutum Delitzschianum in Leipzig, Paul Levertoff, who both were Jewish believers in Jesus influenced by Hasidic thinking and piety; Quiñónez, "Paul Phillip Levertoff" and Anonymus, "Jechiel Zevi Lichtenstein," *Missions-Blad for Israel* 86 (1912) 122–27.

158. Lichtenstein, *Points of Contact*, 9.

widespread ideas among many 19th-century Jewish reformers about the modernization of Judaism. In these circles, one expected a development in which Judaism would lose its supernatural character and become a religion of morality, based on rationalism and tolerance, similar to or even better than Christianity.[159] Although Lichtenstein several times praises the progress and political tolerance of his day and appeals to reason, his main concern is not only to show how the New Testament and the Jewish tradition confirm each other, but also to convince his readers that Jesus is the Messiah.[160] In addition, in spite of his metaphorical reading of the Jewish tradition, Lichtenstein refrains from rationalizing the gospel narratives about miracles.

An important aspect of Lichtenstein's attitude to the Neolog agenda is that there are no indications in the sources that Lichtenstein wanted to reform the liturgy, which was an essential dimension of the progressive reforms of Hungarian Jewry. Instead he experienced traditional Jewish worship as another expression of the continuity between Christianity and Judaism, as Jewish prayer always underlines that God is both merciful and just, and that his purpose is the salvation of the world, not only Israel.[161] In a lecture about the relationship between Sukkot and the Christian Pentecost, Lichtenstein also uses these festivals to show how Jesus is the end of the law and how all believers have the Holy Spirit.[162]

Nevertheless, in spite of his positive attitude to Talmud, there are certain indications that he thought the oral tradition was of limited value from the perspective of salvation history. This he believes to be in accordance with the Jewish tradition itself, referring to Rabbi Simlai's thinking on the development of the 613 commandments after Sinai: Psalm 15 and Isaiah 33 talk about six commandments, Micha about three, Isaiah 56 about two, and Amos 5 about one; then finally comes the reference to

---

159. Illmann and Harviainen, *Judisk historia*, 146–50. Some radical reformers would even abolish circumcision and argued for Sunday observance. In the USA there was also some sporadic contact between Jewish reformers, liberal Protestants and Unitarians, which could give the impression that Reform Judaism sought some sort of confluence between Christianity and Judaism. See Freehof, "Introduction," xv–xvi; and Meyer, *Response to Modernit*, 289.

160. Lichtenstein, *Die Liebe*, 7.

161. Lichtenstein, *Mein Zeugnis*, 5, 11–12.

162. Lichtenstein, *Points of Contact*, 3–4.

the righteous living by faith in Habakkuk 2:4—which is one of the main references in Paul's letter to the Romans, in chapter 3.[163]

More importantly, at least in his late writings, Lichtenstein believes that the Old Testament (which is the term he usually uses for the Hebrew Bible) must be understood in light of the New Testament. Although Lichtenstein believes the Talmud is related to Christianity, it is the New Testament that primarily casts light on the Old Testament: "The New Testament rises over the Old Testament, like a dove over the water, and God said: Let there be light."[164] In one of his last writings, he argues for the relationship between these Scriptures by referring to Matthew 6:22, Proverbs 4:25, and Galatians 5:22: The revelation of Sinai is the sun, and Christ is the light of heaven that enables people to see this light.[165] In his last pamphlet, *Ein Geheimnis aus dem Talmud* (1900), Lichtenstein claims that Talmud predicts the end of the Babylonian and Palestinian Talmuds as a part of the messianic kingdom, as well as connecting Jesus as Messiah with the fate of Talmud:

> What then is the situation for the Jewish Talmud, which has so many fine pearls of morals and customs, but in its belief and justifications opposes the Gospel? What then should happen to the honourable Talmud? Well, I want to tell you a secret out of the Talmud, it is found in Sanhedrin 38a: Judah and Hezekiah, the sons of R. Hiyya once sat at the table with Rabbi and uttered not a word. Whereupon he said: "Give the young men plenty of strong wine, so that they may say something." When the wine took effect, they began by saying: "The Son of David cannot appear ere the two ruling houses in Israel shall have come to an end, the Exilarchate in Babylon and the Patriarchate in Palestine, for it is written: And he shall be a Sanctuary, for a stone of stumbling and for a rock of offence to both houses of Israel." (Isaiah 8.14). Whereupon he (Rabbi) exclaimed, "You throw thorns in my eyes, my children!" At this, R. Hiyyah (his disciple) remarked, "Master, be not angered, for the numerical value of letters of יין (wine)

---

163. Lichtenstein, *Der Talmud*, 19–21. *m.Makkot* 23:2 and 24:1. Lichtenstein calls him Rabbi Simlui.

164. Lichtenstein, *Ein Geheimnis* (transl. Monika Ewell, *A Secret from the Talmud*), 23.

165. Lichtenstein, "Ein Weihnachts- und Neujahrsgruss für die auserwählten Kinder des Lichtes," 35–40.

is seventy, and likewise the letters of סיד (mysterious secrets). When yayin (wine) goes in, sod (secrets) comes out."[166]

Although Lichtenstein leaves several questions unanswered, he seems to think that the Talmud, both the Babylonian and the Palestinian, has lost its traditional function in light of Jesus as Messiah. Still, it is not entirely clear whether he relates the subordination of Talmud to the first coming of Jesus or to the situation of the Jewish people in modern times.

Faith in Jesus as a Jewish Virtue

Lichtenstein's major break with the traditional faith of the synagogue is that he embraces Jesus as the Messiah, a fact he is aware of:

> I have penetrated far into the Holy of Holies, I have boldly—my enemies say madly—crossed the Rubicon. . . . I have paid homage to the founder of Christianity, and rendered him praise as the Redeemer of the World, the Saviour, the long-expected Messiah of the Jews.[167]

However, for Lichtenstein this move was the opposite of leaving Judaism. As the quotation from *Ein Geheimnis* above demonstrates, the Jewish tradition is in the hands of Jesus as the Messiah. For Lichtenstein, therefore, the messiahship of Jesus is a key not only to understanding Talmud and the Scriptures, but a crucial factor for living an authentic Jewish life as well. However, in contrast to Gurland's "Every true Jew has to become a Christian," Lichtenstein claims that faith in Jesus will lead to a stronger identification with the Jewish tradition. In the terms of DellaPergola, Lichtenstein makes faith in Jesus a key Jewish identification marker. Jesus is Jewishness in concentrated form, so that Jesus' reference to the love of God and neighbor being the greatest commands (Mark 12:28–31) is not only an assertion of the Jewish creed, but also a description of Jesus.[168] Jesus' claim of being divine melds with the love, mercy and compassion he preaches and demonstrates in his own life.[169]

---

166. Lichtenstein, *Ein Geheimnis*, 23. There is no Hebrew in the English translation; the two Hebrew words towards the end of the quotation are brought in from the German version.

167. Lichtenstein, *An Appeal to the Jewish People*, 3–4.

168. Lichtenstein, *Ein Geheimnis*, 17.

169. Ibid., 8.

One of the church's main proof texts for Jesus being the Messiah is the prophecy about the Lord's servant in Isaiah 53; the dominant Jewish response is that this text is about the people of Israel. For Lichtenstein, Isaiah 53 testifies about the Messiah and Jesus. He says that the Servant of the Lord cannot be Israel, because according to the prophets the Jews suffer only for their own sins. Additionally, according to the Jewish tradition there is no *tzaddik* (righteous person) without sin. Further, the traditional Jewish concept of two Messiahs is not plausible; it is but a poor solution for coming to terms with the images of a simultaneously victorious and suffering king. The Hebrew Bible, however, knows only one Messiah.[170] In any case, the Jewish nation's inability to see Jesus as Messiah is easily understandable for Lichtenstein. Even Jesus' own disciples did not understand the idea of a suffering Messiah until after his death and resurrection. In addition to the traditional references to the Old Testament, Lichtenstein believes that references to Jesus as the Suffering Servant can be found in the Talmud as well, like the rabbinic references to Hezekiah, who was healed on the third day.[171]

Lichtenstein's argument for Jesus as Messiah is based partly on his resurrection, after which he once appeared to 500 people (1 Cor. 15:6), and partly on his life, which proves that he is Messiah. The main traditional Jewish argument against Jesus' messiahship is that he did not bring peace on earth. Lichtenstein counters this argument in two ways.

First, Jesus *did* change the world, as proven by the establishing and spread of modern civilization. The Jews must turn to Jesus, who has

> made fruitful the spirit of the nations, who has averted the deathblow from the human victim of degraded heathen sacrifice, who has given a new direction to thought and manner of life, and a new existence to nations and states. . . . Certainly He has effected that which was prophesied of the Seed of David, His work has been that of the predicted Messiah and the true Seed of Abraham, through Him all nations of the earth are being and will yet be blessed.[172]

It is fundamental for Lichtenstein that the grace and truth of Jesus are the source of progress in European civilization. For Lichtenstein, the only reason he could subdue all the heathens is that he is the Redeemer.

170. Lichtenstein, *Svar på spørsmål i Israel*, 53–58.
171. Ibid., 54.
172. Lichtenstein, *An Appeal*, 16.

This conquest of the world was not by the sword, like Islam's conquest, but with the sword of the Spirit, the word of God.[173] In fact, when non-Christian nations, including the Jewish communities, establish humanitarian institutions like hospitals on their own, it is basically an imitation of Christianity and initiated by the Parable of the Good Samaritan in Luke 10. As all nations are blessed through the Son of David, the Jewish people should "pay homage to the son" and will eventually have 1,000 years of peace.[174] Lichtenstein finds it strange that the rejection of Christianity can be combined with a strong focus on the Shema (the Jewish creed), which the contemporary (progressive) rabbis believe is the essence of Judaism. Lichtenstein finds this idea very close to Jesus' statement about the two greatest commands in Mark 12 and its synoptic parallels.[175]

Second, the peace Jesus has brought to earth is primarily an inner peace, which is available to everyone who will submit to Christ. However, ultimate peace on earth still awaits all people, and the national conversion to Christ is central here. When Israel eventually turns to Christ, Jesus will return and establish his earthly kingdom in Jerusalem. The blood in the Communion not only takes away sins, but also creates a new covenant. According to Lichtenstein, this explains why Isaiah 55 speaks about a covenant. For Lichtenstein it is essential that salvation from sin must come before earthly redemption, otherwise sin will come between God and his people (Lichtenstein here refers to Ezekiel 36:33). When the time comes that "Joseph-Jesus" is recognized by Israel, an epoch will begin in which the kingdom of God is established on earth: "once more shall Jacob . . . pass through a night of wrestling, when his eyes shall be opened."[176]

From a traditional Christian perspective, Lichtenstein's Christology (his view on Jesus) in his first three booklets is not complete. Although Lichtenstein describes him as "Son of God" (*Gottesohn*), Jesus is mainly depicted as a martyr for progress and truth as well as Israel's spiritual king and the agent of God; concepts like the Trinity and the Incarnation are not mentioned.[177] Likewise, Lichtenstein does not say much about

173. Ibid., 19.
174. Lichtenstein, *Ein Geheimnis*, 6.
175. Lichtenstein, *A Jewish Mirror*, 8.
176. Ibid., 20.
177. Lichtenstein, *Die Liebe*, 27.

the death of Jesus as an atoning sacrifice. At least in his first writings, Lichtenstein appears to think the murder of Jesus had many similarities to the fate of other famous persons with provocative and progressive ideas, also in the history of Israel. Jesus encountered the same reaction as Zechariah in the temple, Jeremiah and Isaiah.[178]

In his later writings, Lichtenstein seems to present a more traditional Christian Christology, where Jesus is described as a miraculous and divine person, "who is the sun around whom the Prophets circled like planets."[179] In describing Jesus as divine, Lichtenstein is eager to use terms and metaphors from the Jewish tradition. In the booklet *Judenspiegel* (1896), Lichtenstein refers to the discussion between a rabbi and a schismatic, who seems to react to biblical anthropomorphisms. When the latter asks how God could live in the tabernacle, the rabbi explains that the sanctuary of God is like a mirror for a man, as a mirror contains the whole form of a much bigger person. For Lichtenstein, Christ "is the true Sanctuary, the Tabernacle where the majesty of God is enthroned ... A Crystal mirror of the Divine greatness, and power, and victory, full of beauty and glory, is Jesus Christ."[180] The divine attributes of Jesus are usually described in terms of the Hebrew Bible and the New Testament. Jesus is described as *the new Jacob's ladder, the Lamb, the fire without consuming* [sic.], *the seven-branched candlestick, the High Priest, the king* and *the prophet*. By the term *prophet*, Lichtenstein means that Jesus is the successor of Moses prophesied in Deuteronomy 18. The temptation by Satan in the desert shows that Jesus has a unique relationship with God, like two silver trumpets hammered out of one piece. According to Lichtenstein, the work and teaching of Jesus is always related to Moses:

> Like the Bee sucks the honey out of the roses, Jesus also draws out of the depth from Moses, the Prophets and the Psalms, the therein hidden Spirit of Life and outs it into the light so that his Apostle now can teach.[181]

---

178. Lichtenstein, *Points of Contact*, 11.
179. Ibid. This development may well be the result of influence from Baron and others, something Baron indicates in his obituary; Baron, "Rabbi Ignatz Lichtenstein," 256.
180. Lichtenstein, *A Jewish Mirror*, 7.
181. Lichtenstein, *Ein Geheimnis*, 25.

> The Jews should consider how the Old Testament and the New Testament grew out of her history, and that Jesus' blood is the realization of Moses and the Prophets.[182]

In his humanness, Christ appears to be a *Son of Abraham*, a *Son of David*—and yet at the same time is the Salvation of God unto the ends of the earth:

> In Jesus is Israel's mission put into effect. He blessed all Nations, and all Nations are blessed in him. . . . Israel's election and upbringing carries this end in view, that it happened through Jesus: He is in person the incarnate Salvation of God for Israel, and from there to the nations.[183]

In other words, not only is Jesus in continuity with the Jewish tradition, but he has also accomplished the mission of Israel in the world. The Mosaic religion with its ceremonies and festivals is a Jewish religion conducted by priests. However, the world religion founded by Christ is the Jewish faith expressed in the Shema.[184] It is possible that Lichtenstein here relates to the part of Jewish tradition that sees Christianity (and Islam) as divine tools to bring the world to worship the God of Israel and to prepare for the coming of the Messiah (*preparatio messianica*). The most famous expression of this view is from Maimonides, who claimed that Christianity and Islam had served "to prepare the whole world to worship God with one accord" by spreading the Hebrew Bible, the commandments and the knowledge of the messianic age.[185]

While Lichtenstein in his writings focuses heavily on Jesus and his works, the role of the Holy Spirit—the third person in the Christian Trinity—plays a minor role. The few references usually focus on the work of the Holy Spirit more than its divine character as such. However, it is always related to God's or Jesus' activity, and regarded as a continuing force in Jewish as well as salvation history, as when he refers to Isaiah 11. The same spirit worked in Eden, as well as within Abraham and Moses.

---

182. Ibid., 37.

183. Here he refers to Rom 10:4 and Hos 2:19–20. ibid., 35.

184. Here he refers to John 1:17; Isa 21:11–12: and Ps 106:48. Lichtenstein, *Mein Zeugnis*, 13.

185. Sacks, *One People?*, 222; and Talmage, *Disputation and Dialogue*, 257–58.

This spirit was not only behind the two chief commandments, but is the force that still enables people to love their enemies.[186]

From what he writes, it appears that Lichtenstein's Christology not only gave him a hermeneutic tool for interpreting Jewish tradition as well as Jewish history, but also implied an existential imperative for the Jewish people. For Jews it is not only legitimate to believe in Jesus, but a divine call:

> Should not the Jews study the New Testament to learn to know Christ? Indeed! The one who loves him must love him, the one who loves him must honour him, the one who honours him must worship him, and the one who worships him understands him when he says: I and the Father, we are one.[187]

Lichtenstein's Attitude to Torah Observance

A central issue in understanding Lichtenstein and the Jewish community in Tápiószele is his connection and relationship to Hungarian Jewry, particularly the Neolog community. As described in the biography, Lichtenstein was under the supervision of the Reform Jewish community in Budapest, and was buried at its cemetery there. Consequently, one can expect that Lichtenstein held progressive views on Jewish customs like Sabbath observance and the dietary laws, which is indicated by Gjessing.[188] Baron, however, claims that in spite of the fact that he was buried at the Neolog cemetery, Lichtenstein was "orthodox."[189] Unfortunately, Baron does not explain what he means with this statement, but one can at least assume that he found it difficult to associate Lichtenstein with a very liberal Jewish practice or strong assimilationist tendencies.

As we do not have any material on Lichtenstein's position on these matters before he became a Christian, we can only turn to the writings of the Christian rabbi after 1886. In these publications, however, he does not discuss law observance as such explicitly, as his main goal is to convince his readers that Jesus is the Messiah. Consequently, the sources

---

186. Lichtenstein, *Two Letters, or What I really Wish*, 30–31.
187. Lichtenstein, *Judenthum und Christenthum*, 97.
188. Gjessing, "Rabbi Isak (Ignaz) Lichtenstein," 174.
189. Baron, "Rabbi Ignatz Lichtenstein," 265, first note.

give little information on how he told his community in Tápiószele to relate to kosher laws, etc.[190]

Instead, Lichtenstein pays most of his attention to what he feels is a dramatic spiritual decline for the Jewish people, which he finds to be partly the Neolog leadership's fault. In his third pamphlet from 1886, *Die Liebe und die Bekehrung*, Lichtenstein gives a very pessimistic diagnosis for the Jewish people due to the spiritual disintegration in Israel. This is especially the case among the young, who have abandoned the old Jewish religious beliefs and lifestyle. Religious enthusiasm has cooled down, and his letter to his son describes the situation as a disease for the Jewish people.[191]

Lichtenstein did not have much sympathy for contemporary Reform Judaism. In his early writings he gets rather sarcastic about the leaders of the movement: "Zum Gluck aber haben wir Doktor-Rabbinen, diese sollen die Secirmesser schärfen, mit kühner Hand alle Glieder, die uns belasten, entfernen."[192] For Lichtenstein, the permission to eat pork or to smoke on the Sabbath—not to mention to refrain from the circumcision of Jewish boys—is against common sense. Even if a rabbi has come to the conclusion that these regulations are outdated (it is unclear whether Lichtenstein is admitting that this is his position), to accept this would be a betrayal of the basic doctrines of his people, as the religion demands that its people be perfect (Gen. 17:1). To abandon some of the Jewish customs for the sake of convenience is not a legal way of dealing with the law. The only outcome of these reforms is confusion among Jewish youth, who only learn hypocrisy from this practice. Lichtenstein thinks that the decisions and practices of the reformers are against both the Hebrew Bible and the New Testament. Ironically, by their practice and teaching, the Jewish reformers come very close to a Christian view of the law, but without being consistent about it. To Lichtenstein this

---

190. Lichtenstein, *Points of Contact*, 3. Sometimes it is indicated that he observed the festivals, as when he points to the connection between Shavuot and Pentecost.

191. For Lichtenstein it is the lack of spiritual enthusiasm which makes law observance difficult; see his comments in Leipzig against Wiegand in 1895 (Dalman, *Die allgemeine Konferenz für Judenmission*, 19).

192 Lichtenstein, *Die Liebe*, 13. "Luckily, we have the Doctor-rabbis, who will sharpen the *Secirknives* [sic. I have note found a better word for this ritual knife] and with a steady hand cut off all the parts that oppress us."

seems pointless without accepting Christ as well. Their efforts to rescue Judaism present an illusion: a "Christenthum ohne Christ."[193]

Lichtenstein argues that it is the inconsistency of the reforms that threatens Hungarian and European Jewry with spiritual disintegration, and he therefore asks his readers to take the logical step and accept the gospel—for the sake of Judaism! For his purposes, Lichtenstein quotes key paragraphs from the New Testament, such as Matthew 15:11, Mark 2 and Romans 2. While the Matthew reference explains that it is what comes from within that makes people unclean, in Mark Jesus claims his supremacy over the Sabbath. When he comes to the Letter to the Romans, Lichtenstein's point gets clearer: Anyone who keeps even most of the law, but fails to observe only a small part of it, has failed the whole law. Israel is, in other words, supposed to keep the whole law, but is not able to, and there is no help in Reform Judaism.[194] In other words: The only legitimate way a Jew can feel free from observing the law is by embracing Jesus.

The question is whether Lichtenstein finds the problem to be related to modernity, or if it is of a more essential nature. The way Gjessing understands *Die Liebe*, Jewish religion and modernity cannot be combined.[195] Gjessing's understanding of Lichtenstein may be from a comment in *Die Liebe*, where Lichtenstein explains why he does not use every moment to instruct the law breakers despite being so upset by the situation. Lichtenstein's answer is that in the era of modernity, it is only the gospel which can help the Jewish nation.[196]

However, when lamenting the situation of European Jewry, it is not the modern age as such which appears to be the problem for Lichtenstein, but the Jewish people itself: "Ja! Es ist etwas faul in Israel," Lichtenstein once exclaims.[197] The virtues of the patriarchs, the humble satisfaction, Jewish solidarity and a fresh spirit of mind—all of it has left the Jewish community. The law is too heavy on everyone. The Hungarian Jew does

---

193. Lichtenstein, *Judenthum und Christenthum*, 35. "A Christianity without Christ."

194. Herman, "Den ungarske rabbiner Lichtenstein," 73.

195. Ibid. In addition to his reading of *Die Liebe*, this conclusion may be based on supplementary information from Gjessing's encounter with Lichtenstein in Budapest, where they both lived at the time.

196. Lichtenstein, *Die Liebe*, 30.

197. "Indeed! There is something rotten in Israel." Lichtenstein, *Judenthum und Christenthum*, 29.

not live like a Jew, feel like a Jew or act like a Jew. All attempts at reform are therefore futile. As long as the reformers introduce religious Christian thoughts to Judaism and imitate the Christian way of worship without mentioning the true source of it, this cannot bring redemption to Judaism, there is no blessing from it:

> Why are you content with an illusion, without body, without soul, with a sun without warmth, a shadow without any ideal—Christianity without Christ! Why do you not work to bring the redemption of Israel closer? Why do you not tell this extract of the doctrines of Talmud in his name who has taught it, who has given it validity by his passion, who has sealed it with his life, his blood? Why do you steer away from mentioning the great teacher, the faithful shepherd by his right name, he who invites everyone who labours and is loaded with burdens to find life and rest for their souls? Why do you lack the moral courage to publically proclaim: The law is given by Moses, the mercy and truth has come with Jesus Christ?[198]

Israel needs a radical cure for its disease, and the only way to prevent the disintegration of Jewish religious life is to accept Christianity. The modern Jew does not follow God or Jewish tradition. Against this development as well as the "new Goliath," the anti-Semites, only Jesus can help: "The true balm of Gilead for Israel lies in the hand of Jesus."[199] Christianity is a moral lifeline for those who feel the Jewish law is too heavy, and Lichtenstein therefore claims that true Jews should accept Christ:

> . . . . the curse is lifted, the ice melted, the load that has crushed our heart is broken, the ropes that have pressed on our chest have opened up a bit . . . we are no longer split, are no longer in deep

---

198 Lichtenstein, *Judenthum und Christenthum*, 35. ". . . warum begnügt Ihr Euch mit ein Illusion, ohne Körper, ohne Seele, mit einer Sonne ohne erwärmende Strahlen, mit einen Schattenbilde ohne Ideal, mit einem Christenthum ohne Christ!—Warum beschleunigt Ihr diese Erlösung nicht, warum theilt Ihr den Extrakt dieser Lehre des Talmuds nicht mit, im Namen dessen, der sie vorgetragen, der sie durch Leiden zur Geltung gebracht, der mit seinem Leben, mit seinem Blute erkauft, besiegelt hat? Warum scheuet Ihr Euch, den grossen Lehrer, den treuen Hirten beim rechten Namen zu nennen, der, die mühselig und beladen sind, zu sich rief, um sie zum erquicken, damit sie Ruhe finden für ihre Seele? Warum fehlt es Euch an moralischen Muth, offentlich zu verkünden: Das Gesetz ist durch Moses gegeben, die Gnade und Wahrheit durch Jesum Christum geworden!"

199. Lichtenstein, *Ein Geheimnis*, 33.

conflict with our creed, do not have to blame ourselves every day and hour for being people who break the Religion.[200]

Lichtenstein does not appear to propagate a Jewish anti-nominalism, but rather a revitalized Jewish life where law observance is included, but under Jesus' commandment of love and free from any hypocrisy:

> And now, my dear ones! In accordance with [how] the Jew as a chosen people received the law on Sinai, which was carried with joy, bravery and patience through all the Nations, countries and continents, and who with his life and hot heart-blood has sealed the Covenant, now continue for a second time: "Everything which God has said, we will do and follow." With a will of new life, a will of new efforts, a firm will, unbreakable, without fraudery, without falseness, with body and soul, with heart and spirit, with cheer and enthusiasm, with our Semitic, Abrahamic blood, with the blood of Jesus from the royal tribe of David, with the word: "Hear O Israel, the Lord our God is one God." . . . And: "You shall love your neighbour as yourself," [. . .] in the new Covenant, because its yoke is easy, its burden is gentle and its crown of thorns—the Love.[201]

It is fundamental for Lichtenstein that the Christianity he is talking about is not alien to Judaism. "Pure" Christianity, understood as the message found in the New Testament, is not only the way to God, but has taken over as being a carrier of the Jewish virtues, bringing the Word of God to the world. With his teaching, Christ has cleansed Judaism and now he reveals the gold.[202] Many seem to have understood this as meaning

---

200. Lichtenstein, *Die Liebe*, 16–17. ". . . der Bann ist gelöst, das Eis geschmolzen, die Kreuste die unser Hertz beengt hat, gebrochen, die Fesseln, die unsere Brust gedrückt, gelockert . . . den wir sind nicht mehr zervallen mit uns selbst, stehen nicht mehr im krassesten Widerspruche mit unserem Glaubenbekenntniss, müssen uns nicht mehr täglich, stündlich, als Religionsübertreter, Religionschänder anklagen . . ."

201. Lichtenstein, *Die Liebe*, 28. "Und endlich, meine Theuern! So wie der Jude als auserwähltes Volk, das Gesetz von Sinai empfangen, es freudig, kühn, ausdauernd durch alle Völkerländer und Welttheile getragen, mit seinem Leben, mit seinem warmen Hertzenblute den alten Bund besiegelt hat; also wiederholet zum zweitermal: "Alles, was Gott gesprochen, wollen wir thun und befolgen." Wollen mit neuem Leben, mit neuem Streben, wollen fest, unerschütterlich, ohne Trug, ohne Falsch, mit Leib und Seele, mit Hertz und Geist, mit Jubel und Begeisterung, mit unserem semittischen, abrahamitischen Blute, mit dem Blute Jesu, aus dem königlichen Stamme David's mit der Devise: "Höhre Israel, der Herr unser Gott ist ein einiger Gott." . . . Und; "Du sollst deinen Nähcsten lieben, wie dich selbst," einziechen in den neuen Bund, denn sein Joch ist leicht, seine Last ist sanst und seine Dornekrone—die Liebe."

202. Lichtenstein, *Judenthum und Christenthum*, 36–37.

Analyzing the Relationship between Jewish Identity and Faith in Jesus 235

that Jewish ethics and religious life needed Christian stimuli to go on. The Magyar Jewish lexicon from 1929 reflects this when it summarizes Lichtenstein's position as "Kinek a zsidó vallás nehéz, keresse üdvét Jézus kebelén."[203] In *Judenthum und Christenthum* (1893), Lichtenstein takes the most systematic approach we know of other than in *Der Talmud auf der Anklagenbank*, where he discusses the validity of the Jewish law. Here he discusses a letter from the Austrian society *Der Israelitischen Allianz zu Wien*, dated October 9, 1889. The *Allianz* has presented a list of Jewish doctrines and ethics, which Lichtenstein is asked to support with his signature. Lichtenstein uses the list to compare Judaism with Christianity[204] in his answer to Vienna. In this letter (dated Oct. 13), he seeks to prove that a Christianity in accordance with the spirit of Christ is a reformed Judaism, and thereby the essence of a world religion. According to Lichtenstein there is continuity between Judaism and Christianity, which he seeks to highlight for Jewish readers as well as for anti-Semites/anti-Judaists.[205]

---

203. "For whom the Jewish religion is too difficult, should seek salvation in the bosom of Jesus" Anonymous, "Tápiószele," 881.

204. Lichtenstein, *Judenthum und Christenthum*, 42–97.

205. Lichtenstein's comments on the different paragraphs is summarized below, *Judenthum und Christenthum*, 52: Love your neighbor is the foundation of both the Christian and Jewish religions. Lichtenstein claims that universal love is central for Talmud, and a key characterization of a Christian (1 John 4).

Page 56: Both religions respect the life and property of others; Lichtenstein refers to Genesis 9:6 and Rabbi Nachum Isch Gamsu who punished himself for not helping a beggar fast enough, and compares this with Luke 10:25–31.

Page 59: Both religions respect the honor of others, Deuteronomy 25:2–3, 21–22 and Romans 12:1–10.

Page 63: Both religions respect religious convictions, in the sense that they respect all respectable deeds, but never idolatry. Lichtenstein refers to an anecdote where Landesrabbiner Mordechai ben Ed refused to have a driver who did not respect the cross, and also Romans 14:1–23.

Page 69: Both religions command that one seek to comfort those who mourn and hunger.

Page 72: Both religions respect decent work, Job 5:7, and at this he refers to how the Talmudists and Paul worked with their hands.

Page 75: Both religions command to speak the truth.

Page 76: Both religions value humbleness for God and men.

Page 78: Both religions encourage answering evil with good.

Page 80: Both religions honor marriage.

Page 84: Both religions command respect for the government.

Page 85: Both religions command to work for the good of the neighbor.

However, not a word is said about the relevance of the social dimensions of the Jewish law (or what traditional Christian terminology characterizes as the ceremonial law), such as Sabbath observance. This is probably not to be expected, as it is not mentioned in the letter from the *Allianz* in the first place. Nevertheless, it is evident that Lichtenstein in his writings did not pay much attention to the practical dimensions of law observance. This does not mean that Lichtenstein, be it before or after his spiritual reorientation, was indifferent to whether Jewish law observance was wanted or not, and in what form. As pointed out by Gjessing, the political developments after 1867 had made Lichtenstein less strict about the Jewish dietary laws, at least when it came to Jewish soldiers in the Hungarian army.[206] Still, none of the sources describes Lichtenstein as anything other than a Jew with a strong loyalty not only to his people but also to Jewish tradition.[207] This would partly explain his accusations against the reforms of the Jewish way of life and worship. Lichtenstein's reference to Joshua in *Die Liebe*—"Everything that God has said, we will do and follow"—suggests that law observance was included in his adherence to the Jewish tradition.[208] Lichtenstein's ambivalence to the reform efforts may explain Baron's objection to associating him with the Neolog camp. Although he and his congregation belonged to the Neolog community, his adherence to the Jewish tradition created a distance between him and the mainstream tendency within the national community.[209]

In this way, the discussion on whether Lichtenstein could be regarded as "Neolog" (Gjessing) or "Orthodox" (Baron) may in part also explain his conversion. His increasing frustration over the effects of the Hungarian Jewish reforms on the Jewish community may have made him more open to "Christianity with Christ," particularly if he thought

---

Page 89: Both religions command to love the fatherland, *Sotha* 44 and Romans 13:1–7.

Page 91: Both religions command to hallow the name of God by our work for others.

206. Gjessing, "Rabbi Isak (Ignaz) Lichtenstein," 173–74.

207. This was in contrast to, e.g., Rabinowitz, who in spite of his identification with the Jewish people did not observe all the Sabbath regulations; Kjær-Hansen, *Joseph Rabinowitz*, 149.

208. Lichtenstein, *Die Liebe*, 28.

209. As Lichtenstein in his first writings appears rather optimistic in his expectation of gaining support from his readers, he seems to expect that other Neologs shared his frustration over the effects of Neolog reforms.

that this solution also confirmed and strengthened Jewish values and the essence of Judaism, something the Neologs had lost on the way.

At the mission conference in Leipzig in 1895, the 70-year-old rabbi not only held a lecture about the points of contact between Judaism and Christianity, but also participated in the debate following Wiegand's proposal about continued law observance for Jewish believers in Jesus. The brief reference to Lichtenstein's attitude to Wiegand's proposals may explain the rabbi's position: "Also Rabbi Lichtenstein would only hear about a keeping of the law in a spirit of humbleness, devotion and love."[210] The fact that the minutes mention Lichtenstein's position in particular probably reflects the fact that the participants at the conference found it striking that Wiegand (and Lucky) did not find more sympathy from the unbaptized rabbi on this question. Further, this note confirms the impression that Lichtenstein was not interested in issues of law observance as such, but rather the right motivation for this observance. In other words, for him the spiritual life of the Jewish people is connected to a life in accordance with the Jewish tradition, but only in the light of the New Testament and the love of Jesus. Law observance for Jews who believed in Jesus would only be relevant or adequate as long as they were motivated by love from him. Otherwise such practice would be invalid and inauthentic. While most Jewish believers in Jesus saw Christianity as the road to liberation from the Talmud, Lichtenstein seems to have been reinforced in his adherence to the Jewish tradition by reading the New Testament. This does not mean that he paid much attention to practical issues related to law observance. That faith in Jesus revitalized his spiritual experience and motivation was more important.

---

210. Dalman, *Die allgemeine Konferenz für Judenmission*, 19. "Auch Rabbiner Lichtenstein wollte nur von einer Erfüllung des Gesetzes im Geiste der Demut, Ergebung und Liebe etwas wissen."

The Relation to the Jewish People

Having looked at the identification with Jewish tradition, the following section will survey the relation Gurland, Lucky and Lichtenstein had to the Jewish people. In terms of DellaPergola's second category for Jewish identity, this means identification with the national community, covering the core concepts "Help the needy/love your neighbor," "Hebrew" and "Yiddish," "Zionism" and "Jewish nationalism," and "peace among Jews." To give an adequate understanding of several of the variables and their effect on the three individuals, I will first give a short introduction to the cultural, political and social situation of Eastern European Jewry in the last decades before WWI.

The Transformation of Jewish Identity in the Nineteenth Century

Due to the general transformation and modernization of Jewish identity that took place in Europe during the decades before WWI, Jewish identification increasingly became a more complex issue. According to Meyer, the forces that shaped modern Jewish identity more than anything were the Enlightenment, which drew Jews to identify with the world beyond the boundaries of Judaism; anti-Semitism, which both strengthened and weakened Jewish ties; and Jewish nationalism, which drew modern Jews together around a common goal and made them reevaluate their Jewish self-definition.[211] It was often in the border regions of Jewish identity that these forces could reverse the trajectory for many individuals. In addition, religion itself could play a role in this reorientation, with an awareness that fully integrated enlightenment left no room for what was particularly Jewish. Anti-Semitism also had a divisive effect, as it made many Jews of various backgrounds look for scapegoats, like Ostjuden and the Orthodox.[212]

Some categories of identification with the Jewish people were consistent with traditional values, like loyalty to the family, solidarity with the Jewish people, use of Yiddish and Hebrew, and adherence to a common cultural and historical heritage. Nevertheless, masses of Jews began to develop a Jewish identity that was increasingly distinguished from the traditional one tied to the synagogue and religious observance. For

---

211. Meyer, *Jewish Identity*, 8.
212. Ibid., 29, 50.

many European Jews, a relationship to the religious Jewish tradition was no longer the key element in their national identity, and in some cases it even became irrelevant. To some extent, Jewish identification became secularized, and an increasing number of Jewish individuals and networks saw themselves as Jewish regardless of their religious convictions. Central to this development was the new Jewish nationalism, which today is mostly associated with Zionism, but then was expressed in several competing ways. Just as important were increased assimilation and the appearance of modern anti-Semitism. In different ways Gurland, Lucky and Lichtenstein had to deal with these movements and changes like all other Jews. That Jewish individuals who distanced themselves from traditional Judaism, continued to claim a Jewish identity encouraged others to claim a Jewish as well as a Christian identity. By accepting Christianity, they would have broken one of the most significant taboos in the Jewish consciousness, but now some could see a legitimate reason to cooperate with missionaries and still be a faithful Jew. Indeed, some would claim that their Jewish identification had become stronger due to their faith. For these, their attitude to the Christian churches, mission societies and other Jewish Christians would match their perception of Jewish identity.

Jewish Assimilation and Anti-Semitism

More than anything, the modernization of the European Jewish population is related to the emancipation processes that followed the Enlightenment period. Generally, the emancipation of the European Jews began in Western Europe and moved eastward, and from about 1800 the German states and the Austrian Empire increasingly gave civil rights to the Jews. From the 1860s until the murder of Tsar Alexander II in 1882 the Russian Empire showed signs of following the same course, although more ambivalently. However, from the authorities' perspective, the goal of this new policy was the assimilation of the Jews into the general European population as part of the modernization of the states. While parts of the Jewish communities were alarmed by this prospect, many embraced the new opportunities. However, most of them also found that in the end the new civil rights were limited, and that the way to these opportunities also included conversion to Christianity due to career restrictions or for higher social acceptance. Thus leading to an increase in Jewish conversions and baptisms, the emancipation process also disturbed the non-Jewish community. Friends of the mission towards the Jews were ambivalent about the new willingness among Jews to be baptized, and many felt this process was a cultural and socio-political threat.[213] Some in the mission societies saw these nominal conversions as a legitimate goal of mission work, while others preferred conversions based on religious conviction.

Not least, the emancipation of the Jews was regarded as a major threat by the anti-Semites, who held that baptism could not change what they considered racial realities; baptized Jews would, rather, undermine European civilization. Giving civil rights to Jews would lead to a decline of the European races, as well as strengthening "Jewish" values like capitalism, socialism, liberalism, secularization etc. Because of these sentiments, modern anti-Semitism became a mass movement from the 1870s; it used traditional accusations against the Jews in combination with more "modern" issues like Social Darwinism. The beginning of the movement is particularly associated with the Austrian professor August Rohling. In 1871, Rohling published his book *Der Talmudjude*, which greatly influenced the increasing anti-Semitism in Central Europe.[214]

Jewish Nationalism

The setback for Jewish integration into European society that was expressed in anti-Semitism and the continued exclusion from the European community were an immense disappointment for many Jews, and increased their feeling that the emancipation was a fiasco. The situation in Russia was particularly critical. Around 1880, the Russian *Haskalah* lost its influence as hopes for the assimilation of the Jewish people faded away. Particularly important for this change of view were the pogroms following the assassination of Tsar Alexander II, but even before that, the Jewish population experienced increasing pressure from the Russian government following the defeat in the Crimean war in 1855. Odessa, with its huge Jewish population, now became the seat of disillusioned *maskilim*. They not only changed their attitude to the Jewish people from sarcasm to solidarity, but sought a way back to the Jewish commu-

---

213. See Pastor Müller's articles in the 1860s about mission work as a substitute for emancipation in the Russian Empire: Müller, "Ueber Judenmission," 99 and 107; and Müller, "Zur Characteristik des modernen Judenthums," 483–99.

214. Wagner, *Franz Delitzsch*, 411.

nity as well.²¹⁵ Jewish communities experienced a new need for Jewish identification, something Jewish nationalism was able to provide.²¹⁶

The new Jewish nationalism focused on two issues: the restoration of a Jewish language (whether Yiddish or Hebrew) and some sort of political autonomy, be it in Palestine, Europe or elsewhere. The restoration of Hebrew was central for the Zionists. Although it had ceased to be the language spoken by most Palestinian Jews at the end of the biblical period, written Hebrew had not been forgotten.²¹⁷ Instead it had survived during the Middle Ages as the sacred tongue, used mainly in religious literature. Like Latin for Western Christianity, Hebrew had become a lingua franca for the best educated among the Jewish people, which meant that the vast majority of the people used either Yiddish or one of the Gentile languages. The *maskilim* wanted to turn written Hebrew into a secular language as well, an idea that provoked the traditionalists. At the same time, in the 1880s, Eliezer Ben-Yehuda began the restoration of Hebrew as a spoken language in Ottoman Palestine/Eretz Israel.²¹⁸ However, the vast majority of Jews spoke Yiddish, a language that for Zionists represented the exile, and consequently the use of these two Jewish languages was characterized by intense rivalry until 1939.²¹⁹

Today Jewish nationalism is mainly associated with Zionism, which emerged in the last decades of the nineteenth century. Most scholars of Jewish studies explain that Zionism was a response to the nineteenth-century double bind that modernity imposed on European Jews. These two aspects are well described in Max Nordau's speech to the first Zionist Congress in Basel in 1897:

> [The] Emancipated Jew in Western Europe has abandoned his specifically Jewish character, yet the nations do not accept him as a part of their communities. He flees from his Jewish fellows, because Anti-Semitism has taught him . . . to be contemptuous to

215. Hannah Arendt and Jean Paul Sartre have pointed out how anti-Semitism and nationalism forced Jews to regard themselves as Jews. Banik, *Solidaritet og tilhørighet*, 272.

216. Banik, *Solidaritet og tilhørighet*, 66.

217. Hoffman, *In the Beginning*, 182.

218. Eliezer Ben-Yehuda (1858–1922) was a Russian Jewish linguist who settled in Jerusalem in 1881 to establish Hebrew as the everyday language of the Jewish population in Palestine. Hoffman, *In the Beginning*, 312.

219. Jacobs, *Jewish Politics*, 101. However, as Feiner points out, several of the Russian *maskilim* wrote in Yiddish as late as the 1880s. Feiner, *Haskalah and History*, 241.

them, but his Gentile compatriots repulse him as he attempts to associate with them. He has lost his home in the ghetto, yet the land of his birth is denied to him as his home.[220]

More than any other person, the movement is associated with Theodor Herzl and his *Der Judenstat* (1896) and intense political activism over the next eight years. However, the increasing consciousness of cultural unity found political expression already in the 1860s, when persons like Peretz Smolenskin (1842–1885) and Moses Hess (1812–1875) defended the legitimacy of Jewish nationalism and argued for a Jewish state. These ideas did not become part of a movement until the violent pogroms in 1881–1884, events which were highly suspected to be supported by the Russian authorities. This gave birth to a national movement that became increasingly more structured during the 1880s, as small groups of *Hovevei Zion* ("Lovers of Zion") increasingly attached themselves to the national *Hibbat Zion* ("Love of Zion").[221] The first Palestinian colony was founded in 1874, but the work did not commence in earnest until 1879. The result was the founding of various colonization societies, not only in Russia but also in Germany, France, England, and America, promoting Jewish settlement in Palestine. At the conference of Hovevei Zion and other societies, held at Kattowitz on November 6, 1884, no less than fifty groups were represented. This activity was made possible by a combination of the fragile position of the Ottoman Empire in Palestine and the financial support of Jewish philanthropists like Baron Rothschild.

The term "Zionism" was not used until it was first presented in 1890 by Nathan Birnbaum in Vienna. He was inspired by Leon Pinsker, a Jewish doctor in Odessa (1821–1891), who in 1882 had published the pamphlet *Autoemnzipation*, the first attempt to awake some consciousness about a Jewish state that found an audience.[222] Pinsker described anti-Semitism as a "hereditary psychosis," and claimed that traditional Judaism was part of the problem, as its religious messianism had crippled all human action and initiative to better conditions for the Jewish people.[223] Jewish nationalism in Eastern Europe was not homogenous; between 1896 and 1907 the main Jewish national groups were estab-

---

220. Omer-Sherman, *Diaspora*, 6.
221. Haumann, *A History of East European Jews*, 167.
222. Harket, *Historien om en moderne idé*, 109.
223. Jacobs, *Jewish Politics*, xix.

lished and they competed for followers among the Jewish population. There were three different factions:[224]

1) *Diaspora nationalism.* Representatives of this faction, like Chaim Zhitlovsky, the (Socialist) *Bund* and Simon Dubnow and his *Volkspartei*, fought for a democratic and federal Russia that would grant the Jews national cultural autonomy applied to the Jews as individuals and not based on territory. The *Bund*, established in Vilna 1897, had many more adherents in the Jewish communities than the Zionists, but disappeared due to the Holocaust and Soviet suppression.[225]

2) *Territorial nationalism.* This faction wanted an independent national state for the Jews, but not necessarily in Palestine. Both Birnbaum and Herzl followed this line. Herzl's opinion was that the choice was between Argentina and Palestine.[226] After the pogrom in Kishinev in 1903, the British considered Uganda for Jewish colonization, which stirred much debate.[227] However, by the 1920s the Diaspora and territorial groups had come to a dead end, in the early 1940s the *Bund* was exterminated by the Nazis, and at the end of WWII Zionism became the sole mass political power in the Jewish world and was regarded as the "owner" of Jewish nationalism. When Gurland, and in particular Lucky, relate to Jewish nationalism, it is the Palestinian Zionism that is in focus.

3) *Palestine as the homeland.* The majority of Zionists and participants in Hovevei Zion in Russia and Eastern Europe had no alternative but Palestine. Still, the ultimate political goal of the settlements was not clear. Some Zionists, like Ha'am, looked for cultural quality more than a

---

224. Dieckhoff, *The Invention of a Nation*, 5, 9. However, Harket describes the three branches within the Zionist movement slightly differently: 1) The religious Zionists who followed Herzl's political Zionism, without sharing his view on the content of that state. 2) Practical Zionists, among them Moshe Leib Lilienblum, who held that what gave the movement legitimacy was the need to give Jewish refugees a home in Palestine. 3) The radical cultural Zionists, following Ahad Ha'am in promoting a cultural revival among the Jewish people. This faction consisted mostly of students from Russia and Western Europe. Harket, *Historien om en moderne idé*, 213.

225. Jacobs, *Jewish Politics*, xix. While the Russian government at times tolerated Zionists, as they encouraged Jews to emigrate, the Bund was regarded with more suspicion. Roshwald, *Ethnic Nationalism*, 25.

226. Herzl, *Jødestaten*, 41.

227. http://www.jewishencyclopedia.com/view.jsp?artid=132&letter=Z&search=Messianic%20Judaism#328.

large Jewish population in Palestine, and their support for a bi-national Jewish-Arab state was due to their tendency to counterbalance politics with morals.[228] Ahad Ha'am claimed that it was typical for Judaism and the Jewish national character to disdain physical force and revenge. These ideas, however, did not find many followers.[229] In the end, Zionist leaders could not overlook the orientation towards Palestine in the Russian Jewish community. However, the vision of a Jewish homeland did not create a mass migration to Palestine. At the beginning of the 20th century, only approximately 5,000 colonists had settled in Palestine, in 25 agricultural colonies. The streams of emigrating Jews were heading west to Austria, Germany and America.[230] Still, in spite of the internal tensions, the competition of mass emigration to America, and intense opposition from parts of the Jewish community, Zionism was able to show results: between 1904 and 1914 about 35,000 Jews immigrated, and in 1919 the Jewish population of 57,7000 composed 9.7 percent of the total population of Palestine.[231]

Traditionalist Opposition to Zionism

According to Zvi Gitelman, Zionism—like other modern Jewish movements in the last decades before WWI—represented a cultural innovation, and in practice created a kind of counterculture and even countercommunity to traditional Judaism.[232] Most traditionalists in the Jewish communities therefore opposed Jewish nationalism, and Zionism in particular caused much controversy, since it was about resettlement of the Holy Land itself. Although Zionism was based on Jewish tradition and included elements of messianism, the movement also introduced something new in Jewish history.[233] Zionism was seen as a revolutionary break from the traditional attitude to a Jewish return to the Land of

---

228. Ahad Ha'am (Asher Ginzberg, 1856–1927), a leading cultural Zionist who thought that Palestine would never be able to accommodate the millions of Jews worldwide, and therefore a Jewish nation would best serve international Jewry as a cultural and emotional center. Roshwald, *Ethnic Nationalism*, 141; and Shapira, *Land and Power*, 23.

229. Dieckhoff, *The Invention of a Nation*, 4.

230. Dawidowicz, *The Golden Tradition*, 53.

231. Shapira, *Land and Power,* 62; Butenschøn, *Midt-Østen*, 175.

232. Gitelman, "A Century," 18.

233. Haumann, *A History of East European Jews*, 170.

Israel: that it should only happen when the Messiah came. Jewish opposition to Hovevei Zion and later Zionism was leveled first and foremost at the secular profile of the ideology. In addition, traditionalists regarded the ideology not only as deluded and unrealistic, but also as an attack on the theological interpretation of Jewish history.[234] Traditionally, messianic expectations held that Israel could not save itself, but was dependent on a "cataclysmic intervention of a divinely endowed being . . . [that] could destroy the wicked powers which oppressed it, restore the people, cleansed by suffering, to its ancient glory and rebuild the broken harmonies of the world."[235] Almost all the Jewish prayers and liturgies include the messianic hope, which includes hope for the restoration of Jerusalem and the temple.[236] However, following disastrous experiences with false messiahs, with the Sabbatarian movement (1648 and 1666) as the peak event, at the beginning of the 19th century messianic expectations receded into the background of Jewish religious life and consciousness and were partly replaced by assimilation and Jewish nationalism.[237] The experiences of the Exile had reformed Judaism, making it a religion disconnected from the need for territory, and many Jews felt that to establish a Jewish state in Palestine would be to make the Jewish religion more primitive. In addition, a massive return to the Holy Land was regarded as a religious trespass. The traditional Jewish reluctance to make mass *aliyah* was particularly expressed in the talmudic concept of the so-called "three oaths," which tells the people of Israel to accept the yoke of exile and not to "force the End." Therefore messianic movements, in particular the one after Sabbatai Zevi, were not only transgressions of the oaths, but were even demonic expressions.[238] According to Ravitzky it was among the *Hasidim* in Eastern Europe that the castigation of the ideology was strongest. Here the traditional fear of "forcing the End" was deep and widespread; here Zionism was examined in the

---

234. Ravitzky, *Messianism*, 13.

235. Silver, *A History*, ix.

236. Groth, *Jødedommen*, 95. According to Neusner, Mishnah is only concerned about the law, while any eschatological dimension is neglected. In Talmud, Messiah is described as a priest who gives Israel the law. When Israel keeps the law, Messiah will come. Neusner, "Mishnah and Messiah," 278–81.

237. The movement made an impact also on Christian observers. Silver, *A History*, xviii and 182.

238. Ravitzky, *Messianism*, 229.

light of messianism and the disastrous Sabbateanism.[239] Of course, there were Hasidic settlements in Palestine, one for each Hasidic dynasty. Nevertheless, mainstream *Hasidim* would avoid any active attempt for a national return to Palestine.[240] Instead, many Jewish Orthodox leaders worked for emancipation to prevent any initiative for mass *aliyah*. Even Jewish inhabitants of Palestine should live according to the edict of exile.[241] Before WWI, most Hasidic Jewish communities excoriated families and young people who joined Zionism.[242] Although the movement did not attack Hasidism explicitly, the very existence of Zionism undermined Hasidism as an ideological alternative.[243] The anxiety of the Jewish (and Christian) leaders derived more from the loss of clear boundaries than from the existence of an alternative.[244]

Still, some traditionalists supported the initiative for a Jewish return to Palestine/Eretz Israel. For them, the emancipation and the development of a new attitude to freedom were felt as a call of Divine Providence; it was the End that was forcing the Jews, not the opposite.[245] While "the three oaths" traditionally placed a barrier between the people and its land, writers like Kalischer and others not only tried to neutralize the doctrine of passivity, but to use the oaths for a new purpose.[246]

Gurland

Identification with German culture

In his article about Islamophobia, Ottar Brox points out the danger that carriers of "legal" and moderate criticism of a religion, e.g., Islam, can end up in the Islamophobic camp. This is not necessarily a situation that is wanted by the individual, but has been forced upon him or her due

---

239. Ibid., 14.
240. Shazar, "The Idea of Redemption," 414.
241. Ravitzky, *Messianism*, 230.
242. Rosen, "Hasidism," 219.
243. Ibid., 213.
244. Ibid., 225.
245. Ravitzky, *Messianism*, 27.
246. Ibid., 31. However, in Eastern Europe several traditionalists would support the early Hibbat Zion, in spite of the irreligious character of the movement. One of the most prominent of these was Naftali Zvi Yehuda Berlin (1817–1893), headmaster of the Volozhin yeshiva. Not only did he regard the Zionist movement as a legitimate part of Jewish identity, but he also supported settlement in Palestine. Sacks, *One People?*, 71.

to the dynamics of the discourse, where the person gradually adapts herself to the environment where her point of view is more than welcome.[247] Assuming that there are certain parallels between the present-day debate Brox is referring to and "the Jewish question" in the decades before WWI, it is natural to look for the same dynamic with Gurland, particularly because he saw the rise of Jewish nationalism as well as anti-Semitism. In this light, it is significant to see that Gurland sometimes expressed apparently Eurocentric or hostile attitudes to Jews, parallel to the general Russian Judeophobia.[248] The following quotations from Gurland seem to prove this:

> Labour amongst Israel is not an easy task. There are many difficulties and anxieties to be passed. A field, that for many centuries had brought forth but thorns and thistles, requires ample time and continuous care to bring forth wheat instead of weeds. There are times when the Word of God seems to cause in the mind of inquiring Jews nothing but contradiction and antipathy, and sometimes one receives the impression that their opposition against Christ is the only tie that can bind them. The spirit of contradiction, gainsaying and aversion becomes hereditary and infectious like a malady and develops into a bulwark, which to remove is not an easy task, seeing that the Talmud and the whole Hebrew literature is fundamentally anti-Christian. . . ."
>
> The brighter my faith is within me the darker appears to me the night of Israel's unbelief and superstition. Present-day Judaism shows halfness, rigidity and crippling effect. Many promises without consummation, many hopes without supports. A lasting hatred against all nations based upon self-complacency and self-righteousness, the very cause of the fact that the history of mission work to Israel remains the history of a mighty religious war that creeps on very slowly.[249]

247. Brox, "Polarisering," 67–73, 69.

248. Klier, *Imperial Russia's*, 454–55.

249. Gurland, *IzW* (1911), 200. "Man erlebt viel schwere Stunden in der Arbeidt an Israel, ein Acker, der jahrhundertlang Dornen und Disteln trug, erzeugt nicht in kurzer Zeit eine Weizenernte! Es gibt Zeiten, wo Gottes Wort nur Wiederspruch und Umwillen zu verursachen scheint. Die Opposition gegen Christus dünkt mir oft das einzige Band zu sein, welches das zertreute Israel gegenwürtig noch zusammenhält. Dieser Wiederspruch und Wiederwille gegen das Christentum vererbt sich wie eine böse Krankheit von Geschlecht zu Geschlecht und wird zu einem inner Bollwerk, das nicht leicht zu beseitigen ist; beruht doch der Talmud und die ganze hebraische Literatur auf einer christenfeindlichen Tendenz. . . .

Je heller mir das Licht meines Glaubens scheint, um so dunkler erscheint mir die

This statement shows how Gurland maintains his argument about Talmud's destructive effect on the collective Jewish mentality in a way that could have resembled Eisenmenger.[250]

Gurland also describes strong affections for Germany and German values. In the correspondence from Gurland's years in Berlin and the following ministry in Kishinev, we get a glimpse of his feelings towards Germany. In a letter to Max Besser, Gurland declares himself a German, spiritually speaking.[251] Although he suffered much from his illness there, it is clear that his educational experience was very uplifting. Later, stationed in Bessarabia, he describes his longing for Germany and complains about being kept from the inspiring German environment. In this Gurland was representative of many Eastern European Jews, as there was a significant Jewish admiration of everything German in this period.[252] Nevertheless, the notes confirm the impression of Gurland as an assimilated Jew, or at least one who tried hard to walk that path.

This conclusion, however, would be rather one-sided considering the rest of the material. First of all, the statements about the Talmud's bad influence are congruous with Gurland's lifelong distaste for Talmud in general. Another element is his consistent identification with his Jewish background in several areas, like his use of Yiddish. In his interaction with Jews, it is not surprising that Gurland used his mother tongue as an advantage in his work. It is perhaps more significant that he seems to have continued using Yiddish in his own private writing. Some of his handwritten manuscripts, even well into the 1880s, are written in Yiddish.[253] The fact that he used his mother tongue even af-

---

Nacht des Unglaubens und Aberglaubens meines Volkes. Das gegenwärtige Judentum hat etwas Halbes, Starres, Verkrüppeltes. Lauter Verheissungen ohne Erfüllungen, Hoffnungen ohne jeglichen Halt in der Vernunft. Es ist ein ewiges Verneien und ein Hass gegen alle Völker, der auf Selbstgefälligkeit und Selbstgerechtigkeit gegrundet ist. Daher bleibt die Geschichte der Mission an Israel die Geschichte eines grossen religösen Kampfes, der nur langsam vorwarts kommen kann (*In Two Worlds*, English translation, 215–21).

250. Assuming that this was written after Gurland's return to the mission in the 1890s, which is indicated by Helene Gurland placing this text in the last chapters of *IzW*.

251. Gurland, *IzW* (1911), 130.

252. Klier, *Imperial Russia's*, 156.

253. It has not been possible so far to have these (two) manuscripts translated in length. However, Heike Arning made me in an email in February 2010 aware that the parts of the manuscript that is not Yiddish are texts in German Sütterlin, more pre-

ter becoming a prominent clergyman suggests that he did not try to wipe out traces of his Jewish background. In fact, the use of Yiddish was controversial within Eastern European Jewry, and for many Baltic Jews the use of Yiddish was regarded as uncultivated compared to the use of German and the preferred German assimilation in its wake.[254] Further, the Zionists embraced Hebrew while Yiddish increasingly became the language of the Jewish socialists (the *Bund*), along with Russian. As Gurland seems to have held on to Yiddish in this situation, it indicates some sort of social identification, and his use of the language cannot be related only to instrumental purposes like his mission activity. As several famous Jewish converts reflected some identification with the Jewish people, these observations on Gurland's behalf should not be overemphasized.[255] Nevertheless, this identification indicates some loyalty or positive consciousness about ethnic background, and these glimpses of his Jewish background were registered in different ways in his Christian surroundings.[256]

The Return to the Jewish Mission

What is probably a more important indication of Gurland's attitudes to the Jewish people is that in the 1890s he went back to "his first love," ministry towards the Jewish people. Soon after marrying Helene von Drachenfels, and having been Neander's successor in Mitau for two years, he applied to the Norwegian Israel Mission to become a full-time missionary in 1878.[257] The fact that in the end he moved his aristocratic family away from Kurland to Odessa is especially significant in this respect. Gurland probably could have gotten a job in Germany (after all, the Jewish mission societies in Germany had tried to make him come west), and the move to the Black Sea was probably not one the family found pleasant, if my interpretation of the son Rudolf Gurland's texts is

---

cisely passages from the Luther Bible of 1546, Jona 1-1-16 and Luke 15.1-10. Thanks to Nathaniel Finestone fort the assistance.

254. Hirschhausen, *Die Grenzen*, 152.

255. Zvi Gitelman claims that language has never been a defining characteristic for Jewish identity. However, he points out traditional Lithuanian Jews as a group that was particularly eager to avoid the use of Russian. Gitelman, "A Century," 11.

256. Fauerholdt, "National-Jüdiches Christentum," 23. Yiddish and the broken accent were associated with the traditional "Ost-Juden," which were regarded as scandalous ("a schande far di gojim"). Wolkoff, "Förnekande," 123–25.

257. Skarsaune, *Israel's venner*, 117.

correct. In the middle of the 1890s Gurland's health became dramatically worse, and although the climate at the Black Sea was a good reason for staying there, it certainly involved much work and less contact with Baltic Germans. It therefore seems reasonable to think that, for Gurland, the relative success in the Baltics did not have much personal significance, and even that he found the post of official minister in Mitau a dead end. Instead it looks like his involvement with the Jewish people had more weight. Not least, the fact that Gurland offered the Zion Union the option of reducing his annual salary from 6,000 to 2,000 rubles, as well as abandoning any right to a pension, is an indication of this in its own right.

Gurland's feeling of solidarity with the Jewish people seems to have been acknowledged in Jewish as well as Russian circles. The obituary in *Allgemeine Zeitung des Judentums* of June 30th, 1905, is written with the pogroms in Kishinev, and Gurland's efforts to help the victims, in mind.[258] For friends of the mission this attitude was not surprising. Readers of Gurland's reports already from the 1870s were well informed about his affection for the Jewish people. In one report he complains about the misery of Russian Jewry and how it burdens him personally.[259] The obituary in *Petersburger Zeitung* on June 8, 1905, states that he was forever loyal to the Jewish nation, and his grief for his people influenced his personality as well as drawing him back to mission work.[260] On several occasions Gurland made an effort to defend Jews from accusations, for example that Christian mission towards Jews is useless due to the Jews' stubbornness and inability to improve morally and culturally. In response, Gurland points to how Christianity itself has made it difficult for the Jews to understand how the Christian message could do them any good. The Jews are, therefore, neither worse nor better than other people are.[261]

Gurland not only felt that the accusations against his people were one-sided, but that they undermined the mission work as well:

---

258. Harling, "Zum Gedachtnis Pastor R. H. Gurlands," 86.

259. Gurland, *Bericht*, 15. In Odessa Gurland also met baptized Jews who tried to hide their Jewish bacground. Some of them he tried to persuade to be proud of their Jewish heritage. See Gurland, "Fra Russland," 150–52.

260. "Odessa," 3.

261. Gurland, *Bericht*, 12–13.

It is also true that in many Jewish converts there is little attractiveness but a good bit of difficulty for many gentile-Christian to understand them, and some Christian friends merely think that baptism should make of these Jewish men and women lovely children of light. In this wish we certainly side with our Christian friends but we are bound to ask them whether they are sure of themselves as to lacking nothing in Christlikeness! Baptism certainly is the bath of renascence but doesn't physical birth show us plainly that everybody, at the time of birth and long after, is and remains helpless, weak and liable to fall which everybody will consider as the proof of need of caring and nursing and teaching and assisting until physical and moral self-dependence may be attainable? ... At first some Jewish converts may, if this expression is admissible, look ugly, but what about Nathanael the Jew in whom even the Lord found no guile? Was Nathanael born a perfect Jew? And what about all those other Jewish Nathanaels who within your midst and before your eyes have fought the battles against Jewish and other prejudices and, having joined the church of God are now doing great credit to the church and bringing glory to the name of Jesus? Are they not the very prototype of the future people of Israel and the completion of the Kingdom of God.[262]

---

262. Gurland, *IzW* (1911), 201. The above text from the English manuscript differs somewhat from *IzW* 1911, which may be due to editorial changes from the first publication in 1907 (which may be the version the translator used), or to the translator's own efforts to turn the whole paragraph into several rhetorical questions: "Ja, es ist wahr, Proselyten sind vielfach nicht anziehend für den Christen, der sie nicht verstehen kann, und der erwartet, dass die Taufe sie in liebliche Kinder des Lichtes Wandeln sollte, ohne zu bedenken, dass auch ihm zu einem solchen noch manches mangeln mag. Gewiss ist der Taufe ein Bad der Wiedergeburt, aber wie der leibliche Mensch bei der Geburt hilflos, schwach und hinfällig ist und sorgfältiger, liebvoller Pflege bedarf, weil er erst im Werden und Wachsen begriffen ist, so ist's auch mit dem getauften Juden. ... Er sieht gewöhnlich noch recht hässlich aus, weil der neue Mensch noch nicht fertig ist. Aber es geht auch Nathanaelseelen, Israeliten ohne Falsch, die sich durch alle Jüdischen Vorurteile hindurchringen und die, in die Herberge der christlichen Kirche geflüchtet, derselbe zur Ehre gereichen. Sie gewähren einen Ausblick in die Zukunft Israels und Vollendung des Reiches Gottes.?"

In one of the last chapters of *IzW*, "Lestes Wirken unter Israel" ("The Last Work Unto Israel"), Gurland focuses on two of the major phenomena within Russian Jewry of the time: The rebirth of the Hebrew language and Zionist ideology. The date and context of the material is not given. Due to the time these phenomena became widespread in the Jewish communities in Russia, the reflections probably range from about 1890 to Gurland's death in 1905.

In other words, for Gurland, mission work toward the Jewish people was not only about saving souls, but was a confirmation of the Jews' human dignity and worth, and a spiritual defense against anti-Semitism. Although not mentioned explicitly, this sort of argument is probably aimed at the racist worldview of anti-Semitism, which regarded any efforts to help Jews take part in European civilization as futile. Banik points out how Zionism was seen as a tool for increasing some sort of national dignity for Jews, even among those who never considered emigration themselves. This was Herzl's expectation already in *Der Judenstat*, and this was the experience even for marginal Jewish communities in Norway and Sweden.[263] While Banik points out how Zionist activity became "a showcase for normality," proving that anti-Semitism and the European stereotypes of Jews were wrong, Anders Carlberg regards Zionism in the Scandinavian Diaspora as an act of solidarity with poor Jews in Eastern Europe.[264]

In addition to Zionism, the lies of anti-Semitism were also evident by looking at experiences from the mission fields, but regardless of this experience, the ideology contradicted the word of God itself.[265] In a letter, Gurland further explained why he avoided describing the faults of the Jewish people. Partly it was to defend mission activity as such, but it was also linked to a feeling of loyalty to the Jewish people. He claimed that in spite of their apostasy they were very dear to him, and he would not cause them any harm.[266]

Gurland's Attitude to Jewish Nationalism and Zionism

Gurland arrived in Odessa in 1896, the same year Herzl published *Der Judenstat*. The resultant enthusiasm and political activity among the Zionists naturally found interest among missionaries as well. Gurland probably knew the Zionist ideas already, as the movement had become a significant element in the Jewish community in the Baltic provinces. During the 1880s, Zionism won influence among the Jewish population in Kurland, and Hovevei Zion groups were established in several places, including Riga, Liepaja, Daugavpils and Krustpils. Already at the first conference of Hovevei Zion in Kattowitz, in 1884, there were

263. Banik, *Solidaritet og tilhørighet*, 55, 260.
264. Ibid., and Carlberg, "Sionismen," 146. See also Meyer, *Jewish Identity*, 69.
265. Gurland, *Erlebnisse*, 12.
266. Le Roi, *Rudolf Hermann Gurland*, 62.

delegates from the Latvian provinces. An important Zionist in Mitau was Rabbi Zvi Rabinovitch, who was the third delegate from Kurland at the Hovevei Zion Convention in Druskeniki in 1887.[267] The Jewish community in Bauska, close to Mitau, was a significant nest for Zionist ideology, with several famous preachers of Jewish national revival, like Rabbi Mordechai Eliasberg (1817–1889). The later chief rabbi of the Ashkenazi Jews in Palestine, Abraham Isaac Kook (1865–1935), resigned from his post as a rabbi in Bauska and moved to Palestine in 1904.[268]

When he settled in Odessa, Gurland would have had to deal with this movement on a daily basis, and he would have been expected to participate in the discussions about Zionism that were taking place both within the Jewish community and in mission circles. As the Jewish society in Odessa was one of the most important strongholds of the ideology, most of Gurland's material on Jewish nationalism probably was written during his years in the city, particularly after Herzl published *Der Judenstat*. In addition, one of his employers, the Mildmay Mission, was influenced by pre-millennialism. Within this theological scheme, Zionism in particular 'would attract much interest, as would Gurland's views on this movement. I therefore consider it most probable that the *IzW* material that deals with Jewish nationalism was written with the audience of the Mildmay Mission in mind.

For Gurland, Jewish nationalism was significant for two reasons: he saw the movement as part of prophetic fulfillment as well as another reason to reject anti-Semitic claims; like any other nation they wanted liberty and national independence. Whoever observed the movements that took place among the Jews in Eastern Europe "der kann nicht mer zweifeln, dass die gefängnissen Zions nach Erlösung seuszen und nach der herrlichen Freiheit der Kinder Gottes."[269]

Zionism was first of all a divine tool for the national redemption of Israel, spiritually as well as politically, and the key to understanding the movement theologically was found in the prophet Ezekiel:

> I look at the present movements of and within Israel only in the light of Ezekiel 37, and it seems to me that we have only just

267. Lipschitz, "Jewish Communities," 284.
268. Bobe, "Four Hundred Years," 11–15.
269. Gurland, *IzW* (1911), 201. ". . . cannot any longer doubt that the captives of Zion are sighing for salvation and for the redemption and the freedom of the children of God."

reached verse 7 where it is said: "... there was a noise, and behold a shaking, and the bones came together, bone to bone ... but there was no breath in them.[270]

For Gurland, the interpretation of Zionism as a fulfillment of the prophecy about the dead bones in Ezekiel 37 was something which "true Christians would acknowledge."[271] This is a strange statement, considering that Gurland had been seeking acculturation within pietistic orthodox Lutheranism. In these circles his interpretation of Ezekiel 37 would probably be associated with Anglo-Saxon philo-Semitism and "Restorationist" views, although there were German-speaking followers of this interpretation as well.[272] To label only this interpretation as "true Christian" is a rather exclusive statement not only against his own church tradition, but also against the mainstream interpretation of this chapter since Antiquity. Indirectly, Gurland here distances himself from traditional theological supersessionism. In addition, Zionism helps the Jewish people to rethink the concept of Jewish identity, which again could make them more open to the gospel.[273]

However, in spite of this and the new opportunities for the mission in the wake of Zionism, Gurland's evaluation of the new Jewish nationalism and consciousness for Jewish culture is not entirely positive. According to Le Roi, Gurland appreciated that the New Testament strengthened Jewish identity among some Zionists, but still this ide-

270. Ibid., 204. "Ich betrachte die gegenwärtigen Bewegungen in Israel nach dem Bilde von Hezekiel 37, und mich dünkt, wir sind erst beim 7.Verse angelangt, wo es heisst: "und siehe da rauschte es, und siehe es regte sich, und die Gebeine kamen wieder zusammen, ein jegliches zu seinem Gebeine, es war aber noch kein Odem in ihnen.""

271. Ibid., 46.

272. Considering Gurland's contact with Russian movements (like the Paschowites) inspired by Anglo-Saxon Christians, which often had a philo-Semitic profile, it is possible that Gurland's Zionist interpretation of Ezekiel 37 is a result of his contacts with such groups, but it could also be an example of Gurland reading the Old Testament in accordance with the Jewish tradition. According to Tromp, some Christian authors, like Justin Martyr and Irenaeus, began using Ezekiel 37 as an image of the eschatological resurrection beginning in the middle of the second century. This interpretation became the dominant understanding of the chapter in the church. Before this, the vision was held to be a promise about Israel's future restoration, which has been the mainstream interpretation in Jewish tradition and literature (Levey, *The Targum*, 103). However, according to Tromp, this view was also maintained by some Christian theologians in Antiquity, including Origen and Jerome. De Jonge and Tromp, *The Book of Ezekiel*, x and 61.

273. Gurland, *IzW* (1911), 46.

ology would only lead to political redemption and make them into a self-righteous people. Therefore, Zionism could very well end up as an attempt to restore Israel without Jesus.[274] Spiritually speaking, it was only God who could make the Jewish people alive again, and this could only be done through their conversion to Christ. Gurland therefore lamented the secular dimension of Herzl's work.[275] In spite of his theological perspective on the renewal of Hebrew and Zionism, Jewish nationalism was parallel to similar movements among most other nations.

Neither was he impressed by the new openness to Jesus found among many Zionists. When told that many Jewish nationalists appreciated Jesus and his teaching, Gurland held that many of them did not understand the nature of Christianity. In fact, the secular aspects of Zionism were its main handicap. For Gurland, these aspects of Zionism were not an isolated temptation in Jewish history, but could be added to numerous efforts at self-redemption. Each time these efforts ended in misery, and that was still a possible outcome of the Zionist movement.[276]

Christian Interpretation of Jewish Nationalism and Anti-Semitism

Although Zionism is an important variable in Jewish identity according to DellaPergola, to describe Gurland's affection and support for Zionism simply as an expression of Jewish identity would be superficial. The question is whether Gurland's Zionist sympathies were a product of mission ideology or his Jewish background. What was the reaction to Zionism and Jewish nationalism in the missions Gurland was related to, and what was Gurland's position in this regard?

Generally, German and Scandinavian friends of the mission to the Jews were ambivalent to Zionism, finding themselves both impressed by and reluctant about the movement. The reluctance was due to the secular attitude of the movement, which made it alien for people with a Christian worldview. On the other hand, many thought that this nationalism could be a turning point for the Jewish people's attitude to Jesus, an idea that sometimes was expressed in eschatological terms. Still, by the turn of the century *Saat auf Hoffnung* several times described

---

274. Le Roi, *Rudolf Hermann Gurland*, 42–47.
275. Gurland, *IzW* (1911), 202–3.
276. Gurland, *Erlebnisse*, 21.

and explained Zionism as a non-religious movement, sobering readers with eschatological expectations about the movement.[277] In his work on German mission activity towards the Jews, Christopher Clark claims the importance of Zionism lay in the question of whether mission strategy should seek absorption of the converts into the Gentile church or the founding of Jewish-Christian congregations. While pro-Zionists interpreted the development as a part of God's plan for Israel, people like Le Roi and Gustav Dalman held it to be the opposite. Zionism was a tool for salvation without God's redemption, a modern expression of how the Jews trusted in their own political and economic power.[278]

The evaluation of Zionism differed significantly among Jewish converts as well. One who openly disagreed with its sympathizers was Paulus Wolff, a missionary in Odessa for the Swedish Israel Mission between 1902 and 1911. Wolff was increasingly provoked by his Swedish leadership's positive attitude to Zionism. For him, Zionism was not an attempt for redemption, but a financial enterprise. Wolff therefore initiated a discussion about Zionism with Lindström, the mission's chairman in Stockholm. Most of this discussion was about the understanding of Gurland's key reference, Ezekiel 37. The debate between Wolff and his chairman centered on the exegesis of verses 1 and 14, and whether Israel could be restored *before* receiving the Spirit or if the Spirit could come before the new life and return to the land.[279] While Wolff said that conversion to Christ had to precede a restoration of Israel in its own land, Lindström understood the prophecy much like Gurland did, seeing the Zionist activity and the settlements as "a gathering of the bones" before the national conversion could take place. In fact, Gurland would express it more strongly. For him, true Christians would acknowledge Zionism as a fulfillment of this prophecy.[280]

Although Gurland did not doubt the eschatological significance of Zionism, he nevertheless found much of its importance in how it confirmed national Jewish dignity. Concerning anti-Jewish sentiments, Gurland was more cautious about his rhetoric when criticizing the Jewish community. Compared to friends of the missions like, e.g., Le

277. Dobbert, "Der Zionismus," 93.
278. Clark, *The Politics of Conversion*, 250–51.
279. In 1905, the Swedish mission had two of its five centers in Budapest and Odessa, Strack, *Yearbook* (1906), 110; and Edvardsson, *Kyrka och judendom*, 64.
280. Le Roi, *Rudolf Hermann Gurland*, 46.

Roi, he did not accuse Jews of being inhuman, nor did he claim that Jews suffered from a national lack of conscience.[281] In spite of his antipathy towards Talmud and its alleged crippling effect on the Jewish people, he appears not to have regarded Judaism as unable to create spirituality. While in the debate in Kishinev he expressed himself partly with traditional Christian terminology, he seems to have avoided the widespread anti-Semitic rhetoric of the time.[282]

Still, Gurland seems to have been ambivalent on Jewish nationalism. He did not relate the cause for the movement to anti-Semitism, but regarded it as proof that the Jewish people had the same national consciousness as the European nations.[283] Further, the Zionist movement showed that the Jews were aware of their need for redemption, and that they were eager to seek improvement of their conditions, disproving anti-Semitic claims and rhetoric that were also found in some mission circles. Still, Zionism was a national restoration without God. Just as the skeletons in the prophet's vision were without the Spirit of God, so this new reassembling of the Jewish people was without the presence of God so far.

Gurland's identification with Jewish nationalism was related to his strong feeling of solidarity with the Jewish people, which made him careful not to succumb to the widespread anti-Jewish rhetoric. However, as Gurland's ambivalent identification with Zionism and the new Jewish nationalism had parallels in mission circles as well as within the Jewish community, it is difficult to verify whether his views were influenced by his Jewish background or the Christian community. This is not surprising, though, considering Zionism's twofold origin, being a product of Jewish tradition as well as of the general modernization of Europe.

Lucky

LUCKY'S DIAGNOSIS OF THE JEWISH PEOPLE

When Lucky describes the contemporary situation of the Jewish people, he rarely comments on their poverty or the political situation of the Jews in Galicia or Eastern Europe.[284] When Lucky at times character-

---

281. Clark, *The Politics of Conversion*, 254–59.
282. Le Roi, *Rudolf Hermann Gurland*, 62.
283. Gurland, *IzW* (1911), 201.
284. Considering the political situation in Austria before WWI, and his own ex-

izes Eastern European Jewry in gloomy colors, it is usually related to its spiritual and cultural situation. In particular he laments the lack of dedication to prayer in the Jewish communities in Eastern Europe and the USA.[285] The widespread sympathy towards many contemporary ideologies among Jews, e.g., Marxism, is described as madness. If Marxism were to succeed, it would only lead to massive assimilation and the annihilation of the Jewish people.[286]

When he returned to Galicia and Stanislau in 1890, Lucky observed on his doorstep what he held to be the spiritual decline of the Jewish people: "In our days, the study houses will fall silent and all noise will cease in them. The youth—where are they? Those who are diligent for the Torah—who will find them?"[287] To change this development was one of Lucky's goals with his *Edut*. However, since the cultural decline was a product of the general modernization, the Jewish people could not recover without collectively accepting Jesus as Messiah.[288]

Jewish Nationalism and Palestinian Zionism

Lucky's feeling of solidarity with the Jewish people is particularly expressed in his sympathy for Jewish nationalism. His enthusiasm for Jewish nationalism and Zionist efforts appears to have started before he became a believer in Jesus, but increased around 1900. In 1909 *Sabbath Recorder* commented on how Lucky integrated Zionism as part of his work: "He is intensely alive to the Zionist movement and expects it soon will assume large proportions. Also believing it to be God's purpose that the Hebrew people shall recover the use of their own tongue, he publishes a paper called Eduth."[289]

Lucky's Jewish nationalism was never grounded on any racial theory; instead he claimed that one should love Israel because of John 3:16.[290]

---

periences from Bukovina that led to his emigration to the USA, one cannot expect that Lucky would be very explicit if he had critical views of the Austrian regime. Nevertheless, his silence about the social and economic misery of many of the Jews he was living amongst, is striking.

285. "What a Difference There Is Between . . . ," 10.
286. "Thoughts from the 'Edut,'" *Edut leIsrael* 1/2 (1888) 27.
287. "A Letter from Our Writer in Stanislawow," 7.
288. "Whatever Prayer or Supplication Is Made by Any Man (Chron. 6.29)," 13.
289. Philips, "Ch. Theophilus Lucky," 690–91.
290. "News in Israel," 45–50; 45.

In addition, for Lucky there could be no true national restoration of the Jewish people without a national embrace of Jesus.[291] In accordance with a traditional Christian interpretation of Jewish history, he claims that the rejection and murder of Jesus was a great sin that led to the destruction of the temple and the exile.[292] Lucky claims that when the nations have embraced the Word of God, this should also be done by the Jews, particularly since there had to be a national conversion to Jesus before the return to Palestine.[293]

In other words, the remedy for Israel was to be found in a combination of a national conversion to Jesus and the Zionist endeavors in Palestine, and the massive Jewish emigration to America was a national dead end. Lucky feared that the assimilation process that awaited them would destroy the people culturally. The strategy of assimilation had always been disastrous for the Jewish people.[294] According to Lucky the Zionists had understood this, but nevertheless it is only conversion to Christ that can give valid help.[295] Just as the Gentiles won peace and progress when they embraced Christ, this will also happen to Israel.[296] Already in its first issues, *The Peculiar People* supported Palestinian Zionism, and it praises the Jewish settlements in the Holy Land (sometimes the term "Palestine" is also used), particularly if Jesus-believing Jews appear to be included, like in the settlement of Artuf.[297] On the other hand, the journal criticizes the opposition to Zionism among the

---

291. Anonymous [N.S.Y.], "The Future of Our People, the People of Judah and Israel," 20; and "To Those Who Rise up Against Me," 24–25.

292. Anonymous [H.G.R.], "Israel's Salvation," 108–12. In fact, *Edut* even confirms the traditional understanding of Matthew 27:25, "His blood be upon us and our children," although indirectly by a contributor named J. M. Carman. See "Book review," *Edut leIsrael* 1/3 (1888) 59. Considering how the German pastors in Galicia described Lucky's aversion to the idea that the Jewish people had a moral responsibility for the death of Jesus, this is puzzling. Weidauer, "Erindringer," 175–78. As the comment in *Edut* is from 1888, it is possible that Lucky became more reluctant about this issue after he settled down in Galicia in 1890.

293. "The Dew of Heaven," 53–54; and "To the Dear Readers in the Camp of the Hebrews, the Edut Says," 67.

294. "The Salvation of Israel," 81.

295. Ibid., 84–85; and "A Great Need," 67.

296. "Answers to Rabbi M.G.," 115.

297. "News in Israel," 45–50; 50.

wealthiest classes: "The learned and the rich, unfortunately, do not sympathize with our aspiration: Palestine for the Jews."[298]

Lucky saw the national restoration of the Jewish people in relation to the settlement in Palestine in combination with a spiritual embrace of Christ. This is particularly evident in light of Lucky and Ernst Ferdinand Ströter's Christian Zionist group in Bukovina around 1903 and 1904.[299] It is possible that Lucky and Ströter met in New York, as Ströter in the 1880s cooperated with Arno Gaebelein's New York–based Hope of Israel.[300] This mission claimed the full right of Jewish converts to retain Jewish identity. Both Gaebelein and Ströter were dispensationalists who combined dispensationalism, philo-Semitism and traditional anti-Jewish accusations (e.g., that the Jews killed Jesus, were successful in business, etc.).[301]

Lucky believed that he lived in the time when his hopes about Israel would be fulfilled.[302] For any reader familiar with evangelical theology, this seems very similar to the premillennialism in Britain or the dispensationalism that was widespread in the USA by then. This intense messianic expectation was (and is) often combined with American patriotism, as people believed that the USA had a certain responsibility to assist the Jewish people prior to the advent of Jesus.[303] After the Civil War (1861–1865), dispensationalism gained enormous influence among American conservative evangelicals, and according to Ariel all

---

298. "Palestine," *The Peculiar People* 1 (1888–89) 69.

299. Johnson, "Vor missions," 92–99.

300. See also Ariel, *Evangelizing*, 23. also Meyer, "Protestant Missions," 93–115, 115.

301. Ariel, *Evangelizing*, 14 and 19. Before WWI, the interpretation of the eschatological texts convinced most dispensationalists that the demonic Gog in Ezekiel 38–39 had to be the Russian Empire. When Russia capitulated in autumn 1917, this among some other events seemed to be a fulfillment of the biblical prophecies. Weber, *On the Road to Armageddon*, 71–74.

302. Velthuysen, [title of article not given], 44.

303. Dispensationalism is the name of a certain version of Christian eschatology, established in the 1830s by the founder of the Plymouth Brethren, John Darby (1800–1882). According to this theology, history is divided into a number of periods, or "dispensations," for each of which God has a different plan for humanity. Dispensationalism holds that God's plans for the present as well as the future are found in the Bible, although the understanding of the details varies among different types of dispensationalists. Still, a main theme is the crucial role of the Jewish people in relation to the return of Christ. Dispensationalism attacks traditional Christian supersessionism, and generally holds that the prophecies to Israel in the Old Testament are not about the church but the Jews. Ariel, "In the shadow," 435–39; and McGrath, *Christian Theology*, 551–52.

of the several dozen Jewish missions that were created in the USA were marked by dispensationalism.[304]

However, Lucky's sympathy for Zionism is probably even more due to Zionist influence before his conversion. In his youth, particularly after 1867, many Galician Jewish intellectuals preferred assimilation to German society or culture. However, at the end of the century the situation had changed, as the majority now either preferred assimilation among the Poles or became Zionists.[305] Lucky probably belonged to the latter group, having been exposed to Zionist ideas during his studies in Breslau and Berlin a decade before Zionism became organized in Galicia during the 1880s. He probably met the most significant Zionist influence at Hildesheimer's seminary. Here the Zionist interest was religiously motivated, not driven by secular Zionism but by the vision of a Jewish return found in the Jewish tradition and liturgy.[306] In this case Lucky's Zionism was not a break with Judaism, but rather a result of the new activism of the Orthodox writers who created the ideology behind Hovevei Zion, particularly Hirsch Kalischer.[307] It is therefore reasonable to think that Lucky's Zionist agenda was based on religious Jewish Zionism in combination with Christian Zionism.

The Palestinian Arabs

It is reported that around 1909, Lucky expected the Turkish government to welcome Jewish immigration due to the anticipated economic growth, as well as expecting Jewish autonomy of some sort in the future.[308] For post-1948 readers this raises the question of how he regarded the Palestinian Arabs, but this topic is never discussed from Lucky's side.

---

304. Ariel, *Evangelizing*, 3.

305. Markovits and Sysyn, *Nationbuilding*, 94, 149.

306. Rürup, *Jüdische Geschicte*, 150.

307. Hirsch Kalischer (1795–1874) was among the early modern writers who argued for Jewish resettlement of Palestine. Already in 1862 Kalischer dealt in his writings with the religious and theological problems involved. He advocated the colonization of Palestine, the cultivation of land there, and the founding of an agricultural school and of a Jewish military guard. He held that the salvation promised by the prophets could come only gradually and by self-help on the part of the Jews. He caused the first colonization society to be established in Frankfurt-on-the-Main in 1861. Many Orthodox rabbis joined this movement, e.g., Israel Hildesheimer. http://www.jewishencyclopedia.com/view.jsp?artid=132&letter=Z&search=Messianic%20Judaism#328.

308. Philips, "Ch. Theophilus Lucky," 690–91.

Still, he must have been familiar with the question, as the issue was at times discussed among the different Zionist factions.[309] Lucky's silence on the issue could have been motivated by a wish more or less to ignore the problem, an attitude that may have been widespread in Zionist circles.[310] In fact, neither Pinsker nor Herzl discussed the security issue in their books. According to Saphira, an explanation of the sidestepping of the Arab problem is that before WWI the Arab neighbors were only one of several acute problems for the Jewish settlers, and at the time a much less relevant one.[311] In addition, the defensive ethos in the first decades of Jewish immigration from 1881 to the mid-1930s blurred the fact that there was a basic clash of interests in Palestine between the Jewish immigrants and the people already living there.[312] Still, while many of the first immigrants in the 1880s had no doubt that the land belonged to the Jews, whatever the demographic facts at the moment, others found the presence of the Arab Christians and Moslems traumatic. The first clash between Arabs and Jews was the riot in Petah Tikvah in March 1886, and as early as 1891 Ha'am expressed his worry about the settlers' attitude towards their Arab servants and workers.[313] Lucky's silence on this issue therefore resembles the attitude of many Zionists at the time.

However, as early as in 1890 *The Peculiar People* printed a text that clearly shows that the editors were aware of the situation and the potential conflict. The February issue includes Solomon Robitschek's criticism of a lecture by Mark Levy, where he argued for the Jewish return to Palestine "under a flag of Judah." Robitschek supports the restoration of Israel and the return of the Jews to Palestine, "but I do not believe, by any means, in a blood and iron theory or practice. The servants of Jesus do not fight, not even for their rights, much less for what is not their own. . . . There is nothing that stands in the way of Israel's restoration but their unbelief in Israel's God."[314] Unfortunately, this letter is not commented upon by the editor or any readers. Still, although this one event does not give us any information about Lucky's stand on the Jew-Arab issue, it at least tells us that the circle around Lucky was informed about the

309. Shapira, *Land and Power*, 56.
310. Ibid., 356.
311. Ibid., 45.
312. Ibid., 16.
313. Ibid., 56.
314. Anonymous, "Correspondence," 264.

debate, but was lying low on the Arab question. This is in contrast to the practice of other contemporary Jewish-Christian leaders, e.g., Samuel Schor. Schor, who participated on the second Zionist Congress in Basel in 1898, considered the return of the Jews to Palestine and the British conquest of the area confirmations of the scriptural promises. He would relate Zionism to these promises, and likewise he related the Arabs of Palestine to the descendants of Esau, who had no right to the land.[315]

Lucky and the Use of Hebrew

For Lucky, the choice of Hebrew for the Jewish journal was significant, and he was rather annoyed at tracts translated from German or English, which he characterized as "Goj feelings in crippled Jewishness."[316] The content as well as the language of *Edut* indicates that Lucky aimed his periodical at readers who were influenced by Jewish nationalism or Zionism. The choice of language, whether Hebrew, Yiddish or a European language, was an obvious identification marker for different groups within Jewish society. This identification was also expressed explicitly by Lucky. At the heart of the journal was a particular religious and nationalistic attitude, as expressed in its headline; *Edut* was a journal that testified to the Torah for Israel (Isaiah 8:20), and worked for all the national benefits of the Jewish people:

> I will testify to the Torah, which is our life and the length of our days, and will fight for our sacred books, whence all the house of Israel's glory derives. I will comment on all the events which take place in the camp of Israel, and will give instruction concerning the deeds we are called to perform, to enlighten the eyes of our precious people and their history and questions in life, and defend all the attributes of our nation against those who rise up against us. I will give them much honor and witnesses upon witnesses in order to enhance the glory of our holy language, Hebrew, God's tongue, the language of Moses and the prophets, envoys of the living God, and to adorn the wisdom of the house of Judah and its scribes.[317]

In other words, Lucky appears to have regarded a cultural and religious awakening among the Jewish people as just as important as the political

---

315. Migron, "Samuel Schor," 17–19.
316. Löwen, "Christian Theophilus Lucky," 15.
317. "Word to the Reader," 5.

and practical aspects of the Zionist movement. However, Lucky never appears to distance himself from the use of Yiddish, in contrast to many contemporary users of Hebrew.

By focusing on the Torah, Lucky wanted *Edut* to be a tool against the secularization and assimilation of Israel. The journal is very eager to stress that the Jewish people are one nation, like the Germans and the Poles, and comes back to this topic in several articles. Still, Israel is not a people like any other nation, but its existence is grounded by divine election. When the Jewish people throw away the Torah, the sign of its election, it is the result of a spiritual and cultural disease. Lucky therefore claims that *Edut leIsrael* is just like other conservative Jewish journals such as *Maggid, Meliz, Haz-Sephira,* and *Chabaseleth*. The difference between *Edut* and these is the journal's insight and viewpoints, including of course the belief that Jesus is the Messiah.[318]

Peace among Jews

The goal of *Edut* was to strengthen both Jewish and Gentile values in light of Jesus, and to work for peace among Jewish Christians and Jewish non-believers.[319] In other words, Lucky wanted acceptance for Jewish believers in Jesus within the Jewish people. Lucky is convinced that Jesus is the Messiah of Israel, and insists that all aspects of the past, present and future of the Jewish people must be seen from this perspective. Compared to more traditional mission journals, however, an evangelistic approach is not always obvious, although there usually is a clear testimony that the editor believes in Jesus. This leads *Edut* as well as *The Peculiar People* to frequently deal with the traditional accusation against Jewish Christians for being *meshummads*. The journal in return accuses the Jewish community for accepting any other belief than the Christian faith.[320] The Christian Jews do not only have the right to be Christians, but may be regarded as the *true* Jews. Lucky even describes Jesus-believing Jews as "not blind as their brethren and more earnest in their prayers."[321]

---

318. Ibid., 6.

319. Ibid., 5–7.

320. Zöckler, "Judentum und Christentum," (1892) 211. See also "As Others See Us," 90. The latter article is a response to accusations in the April and May issue of *The Jewish Voice*.

321. "What a Difference There Is Between...," 9.

Literally and practically, Lucky tried hard to live in the midst of his people, and he seems to have managed to gain some sort of acceptance in parts of the Jewish community. According to Courtiss I. Randolph, Lucky was in friendly contact with Solomon Schechter when he was visiting the USA, and in 1894 the Swiss pastor Laub was astonished by the reverence the local Jews showed Lucky when he followed him to Tysmenica.[322] It is a fact that there are few signs of Jewish hostility in most of the sources related to Lucky. While descriptions of Jewish opposition and harassment are central in the sources related to Isaac Lichtenstein as well as Gurland, they are almost absent in the stories about Lucky. It is puzzling that while Rabbi Lichtenstein met offensive attacks in liberal Budapest, Lucky seems to have avoided anything like that in spite of living in the traditionalist community in Eastern Galicia.[323]

Still, there is no doubt that the journal was not welcome in the Jewish community, making the editor describe the journal's situation as being lovesick.[324] Lucky's position and activity were heavily criticized by many Jews as well as Christians; at least this is the impression that is created by the journals. As one must take into account that many or most of the texts in *Edut* were produced by Lucky, it is natural to ask if Lucky had reasons to pretend there were Jewish opponents who wrote to the journal, or, on the other hand, to not report any personal harassment. Although the situation in Galicia was very different from the situation in the USA, the fact that *The Peculiar People* was criticized by Jewish circles in other journals, as well as in its own columns, tells us at least that the same could happen to *Edut*. On the other hand, *Edut* gives the impression that it was counted as significant enough in the Jewish community to generate responses to its editor, which could have been a motive for "creating" texts like that. Wiegand, however, explains Lucky's pseudonyms as representatives of a future Jewish-Christian church, and if that were the case, it would be strange to invent non-believers among the "congregation" to represent Jewish opposition. Still, although the

322. Randolph, "Christian Theophilus Lucky," 208, and Hruby, "Zur Problematik," 76–87. Solomon (Shneur Zalman) Schechter (1847–1915) was a Romanian Jewish scholar, educated at the rabbinic seminary in Vienna and at the Berlin University, famous for his discovery of the Cairo Genizah manuscripts. From 1901 he was president of Jewish Theological Seminary of America in New York. Schwarzfuchs, *A Consise*, 114.

323. Except for Pohlmann, who claims Lucky was assaulted and harassed in Romania in 1885–1886; Andersen, *Israelsmissionen*, 71–72.

324. "To Those Who Rise up Against Me," 24.

number of subscribers reportedly was low, the controversial profile of the Hebrew journal could, for some, be provoking enough to give such responses.

Regarding harassment or insults, it is possible Lucky never experienced such things, in spite of Pohlmann indicating the opposite.[325] But considering his antipathy against traditional mission methods, it could also have been left out because he wanted to avoid the traditional black-and-white image in mission periodicals describing the drama connected to new converts. Alternately, it could also be an expression of solidarity with his people, which made him avoid putting Jews in a bad light. According to Wiedauer, this was characteristic about Lucky. His love for his people made him blind to its bad sides and unfair in his judgment about the relationship between Gentile Christians and the Jews, claiming that the bad sides of the Jews were due to bad treatment by the Gentiles. As Lucky saw it, insofar as Israel had any responsibility for what happened to Jesus, the people's guilt was only tragic, and did not have any ethical character.[326]

However, Lucky does not seem to have been so one-sided as Weidauer thinks, as neither *The Peculiar People* nor *Edut* were free from accusations against the Jewish people. Instead, it is possible that it was Weidauer who had difficulties with his own prejudices: Weidauer admits some sympathy for the increasing anti-Semitic rhetoric, describing how this led to several tough confrontations between himself and Lucky.[327]

Lichtenstein

THE SPIRITUAL POVERTY OF THE MODERN JEWISH PEOPLE

In his arguments for the Jews to accept Jesus as Messiah, Lichtenstein often focuses on what he experienced as a depressing spiritual situation for his people. In many of his writings he gives a very grim diagnosis of the spiritual and national life of the Jewish people, describing how the different Jewish virtues are neglected. On this background, Lichtenstein

---

325. Andersen, *Israelsmissionen*, 70–75.
326. Weidauer, "Erindringer," 175–76.
327. According to Weidauer, even Herzl would say that Gentile Christians suffer under the Jews. On the other hand, Lucky focused on the blessing Jewish Christians had been for the church, and had a tendency to comment about people who had done something good, that they probably had some Jewish blood in them ("Erindringer," 175–78).

usually presents Jesus as the only doctor who can heal the nation. He admits that when speaking about social, economic and political conditions, the situation of the (Hungarian) Jews had never been better. Spiritually, however, Israel is not only in a period of decay, but is about to disintegrate.[328] In *Zwei Briefe*, Lichtenstein describes the situation for Israel as totally unbearable, claiming that only a radical treatment can save the nation.[329] The modern Jews try to the best of their ability to present themselves as non-Jewish, but nevertheless meet obstacles when applying for important jobs, etc. When Lichtenstein's son claims that he feels Jewish although he does not live like a Jew, the father replies in pathological terms: "This is just the cancer, the rotten worm-eaten character of our age, which in many other respects is brilliant. . . . Religion alone stagnates, is neglected, unconsidered."[330]

As Lichtenstein sees it, Israel is in a state of emergency.[331] The young generation of Jews believe they are enlightened compared to their limited and ignorant parents, but Lichtenstein says, the truth is that Israel has become tired of God. Israel's love for God has been like the relationship between a couple whose love for each other was strong in the first years of their marriage, but who later became tired of each other.[332] This is parallel to Israel's development from the establishing of the covenant at Sinai.[333] The result is that the rabbis are discouraged and exhausted, and in spite of all attempts by rabbinic conferences, they are not able to prevent this development or change anything for the better. People break the law continuously, and do not even tell their children about the Creator.[334] Israel has stopped taking the word of God seriously, and Jewish children grow up without fearing God. When Jewish parents celebrate a *Bar Mitzvah* with cigars and non-kosher food, they confuse their children and lead them astray.[335] For Lichtenstein this is extremely dangerous for the future of the Jewish people, as the children are the

---

328. Lichtenstein, *Two Letters; or What I really Wish*, 14.
329. Ibid., 15.
330. Ibid., 23.
331. Lichtenstein, *Die Liebe*, 1.
332. Ibid., 6–9.
333. Lichtenstein, *Die Liebe*, 12.
334. Ibid., 9.
335. Ibid., 26.

only way Israel can continue.[336] Consequently, the Neolog approach to this problem will not help, but only make the situation worse.

Peace between the Synagogue and Jewish Believers in Jesus

One of Lichtenstein's concerns in his writings is to defend Jewish believers in Jesus as part of the Jewish nation. Considering the history of the Jewish people, Lichtenstein admits that Israel's rejection of the Christian message is more than understandable. However, now the times have changed, and in the age of modernity and progress, it is now possible for any Jew to embrace Christ.[337] Considering the coherence between the New Testament and the Jewish tradition, there is no good reason for treating Jewish Christians as apostates.

In fact, it appears that Lichtenstein held the Neolog leadership to be the greatest threat to the Jewish people and its future. For centuries, Lichtenstein claims, Israel has followed false Messiahs, while Christian messengers often have called the Jewish people to repent before God. As a result, at the end of the 19th century, Israel has accepted everything from the modern world except Jesus. Historically, while it was difficult to find scriptural arguments for a great number of false messiahs—such as Asjer Lammlein, David Muri, Bar Kochba, and Sabbatai Zevi—Christ has been rejected. Therefore, the choice of martyrdom that often took place when the Jews were confronted by an aggressive church was odd for Lichtenstein.[338] Lichtenstein expresses ambivalence about the Jewish leadership that hailed the martyrs and praised Sabbatai Zevi, the deceiver and false Messiah of the seventeenth century, and at the same time rejected Jesus.[339] For Lichtenstein, the example of Sabbatai Zevi serves as a major contrast to Jesus in their respective claims about being Messiah. Particularly, he finds Sabbetai's attitude towards the law and Talmud as embarrassing compared to Jesus', and while Sabbetai titled several of his closest followers "kings," Christ made himself unpopular because he

---

336. Ibid., 30.

337. Lichtenstein, *Mein Zeugnis*, 14.

338. Lichtenstein, *Die Liebe*, 17.

339. After having claimed his messiahship, in 1666 Sabbatai sailed from Smyrna to Constantinople, aiming for Jerusalem, where he was expected by his masses of followers to restore Israel's political and spiritual power. He was arrested by the Ottoman regime, and some months later, he converted to Islam. Sharot, *Messianism*, 115.

criticized the scribes.[340] Since history shows that the Jewish leaders have erred in these things, they could not be carriers of the voice of God.

However, as the authority of Jewish giants like, e.g., Moses Mendelsohn had been restored after they were condemned by the Jewish leadership, Lichtenstein believes that the same restoration eventually will take place regarding Jesus. Not only will his position among the Jewish people change; at that time the walls between God and man, Jews and Christians, as well as between classes and races will fall.[341]

The tragic paradox in Jewish history is that the people of Israel, who honor their old teachers, ignore the one Jew who has changed the world like none other.[342] In addition, there is no one who has made the same sacrifice for the Jewish people as Christ and the (true) Christians.[343] It is therefore inconsistent that Jews who believe in Jesus should be excommunicated from the Jewish community, particularly since Reform Judaism, which has dramatically modernized the Jewish tradition and interpretation, is still regarded a part of this community.

This hostility towards Jewish believers in Jesus is even stranger when one considers how close parts of the Jewish worldview are to the New Testament, like the rejection of idols and the focus on faith. The New Testament and Christ represent the fulfillment not only of the Hebrew Bible, but also of the Jewish people itself.[344] Through Jesus salvation comes from the Jews, but not from assimilated Jews or modern Jews who do not even seek to make proselytes.[345] The strategy of keeping Jesus out of the Jewish nation means not only throwing away the "moral lifeline" and staying in the old spiritual ghetto, but is also a dangerous rejection of a divine call. Israel, which is God's chosen people on Earth, should again turn to God and the son of David, who demands that they should love God and neighbor.[346]

---

340. Lichtenstein, *Judenthum und Christenthum*, 9–10, 15.

341. Lichtenstein, *Two Letters, or What I really Wish*, 21, see *Zwei Briefe*, 18. Lichtenstein refers to Zachariah 12:10 and *Sukka* 52: "They will bitterly bemoan the Messiah, the son of Joseph, who was slain."

342. Ibid., 14.

343. Lichtenstein, *Die Liebe*, 32–33.

344. Lichtenstein, *Ein Geheimnis*, 35.

345. Lichtenstein, *A Jewish Mirror*, 16–18.

346. Lichtenstein, *Die Liebe*, 30.

ZIONISM/JEWISH NATIONALISM—In this situation Lichtenstein sees no help in contemporary attempts to reform Judaism, as these only make the people into transgressors of the law, and on some occasions he kicks back at the Neologs' modernization efforts. However, it is striking that in his writings he never discusses one of the major modern Jewish movements that took form around him, namely Zionism, or even modern Jewish nationalism in general. One reason for omitting this topic could be that in spite of Theodor Herzl being a Hungarian Jew, Zionism does not seem to have played a significant role in Hungarian Jewish society at the time. Zionism was actually fiercely attacked by the vast majority of the Hungarian Jews before WWI.[347] For most of the Hungarian Jews, the Zionists seemed to exchange security and relative success in Hungary with colonialism in the Middle East, risking either being suppressed by Muslim authorities or degrading Hungarian Jews into one of the other Hungarian minorities. However, in spite of these obstacles Zionism gradually won ground in Hungary as well, and in 1912 a Zionist conference was held in Budapest.[348]

Lichtenstein's silence on Jewish nationalism and Zionism may be explained by the specific debate on Hungarian Jewry in the last decades before 1914. Significant members of the Neolog community (and opponents of Lichtenstein) not only resisted Jewish nationalism, but also questioned the Semitic character of Hungarian Jews altogether. Rabbi Samuel Kohn, in his *A Zsidok Törtenete Magyarorszàgon* ("History of the Jews in Hungary"), promoted the theory that the Hungarian Jews originated not from ethnic Jewry, but rather traced their ancestry back to Khazar ancestors in the 10th century who had converted to Judaism before settling in Hungary. According to Bitton, this theory was embraced by the vast majority of Jewish assimilationists in Hungary, as it strengthened their belonging to Hungary. According to Kohn's Khazar theory, they were Hungarians of the Jewish religion, but he denied that there existed any Jewish nation.[349]

However, none of Lichtenstein's writings show any sign of support for this view of the origins of Hungarian Jewry. Instead he explicitly describes the Hungarian Jewish community and himself as the descen-

---

347. Kramer, *From Emancipation*, 27.
348. Bitton, "A Decade," 54.
349. Ibid., 25–27.

dants of Abraham, as well as Semites.³⁵⁰ Such remarks may have been a subtle way of mocking his opponents in the Neolog leadership.

Lichtenstein's reason for leaving out Zionism is probably related to Judaism. Lichtenstein claimed that a physical restoration of Israel would be preceded by a national spiritual revival. In several of his writings, Lichtenstein expresses hope that the Jewish people will be governed by Christ from Jerusalem.³⁵¹ The majority of Zionists were secular, and although they were hostile to the assimilationists, it is not very likely that Lichtenstein would support a movement that ignored most of the Jewish tradition altogether. For Lichtenstein, the primary cure for Israel was to turn to Christ, and secular Zionism would therefore be just as invalid as Reform Judaism. A movement like Zionism would not be included in Lichtenstein's eschatological framework. Israel should embrace Jesus as Messiah not only because it is a "moral lifeline," but primarily because it is only as followers of Jesus that the Jewish people can fulfill their destination among the nations. In spite of this fatal diagnosis of Israel, Lichtenstein believes that it is still God's chosen people and will play a crucial role in the salvation of the world.³⁵² In fact, it is only by serving Christ that Israel will complete its divine mission.³⁵³ The Zionist agenda would not fit into Lichtenstein's pattern. This would be consistent with the overall skepticism about secular Zionism from most (traditional and progressive) Jewish religious leaders before WWI.

As Lichtenstein's first publications in 1886 do not seem to reflect any explicit eschatology, it is possible that the expectations referred to in his later writings may be the result of Christian influence. However, Lichtenstein's eschatological chronology is exactly the opposite of that of his friend David Baron, who in his writings promotes a premillennial eschatology.³⁵⁴ According to Baron, the national conversion of the Jewish people to Christ follows *after* national restoration, while Lichtenstein seems to expect the events to follow the opposite order, in spite of the fact that premillennialists like Baron and Schönberger were his closest Christian friends. As far as I have seen, Lichtenstein was never influ-

---

350. Lichtenstein, *Die Liebe*, 28.

351. Lichtenstein, *Points of Contact*, 15; *An Appeal*, 21; *Judenthum und Christenthum*, 95; *Ein Geheimnis*, 38; *A Jewish Mirror*, 20–21.

352. Lichtenstein, *Points of Contact*, 3.

353. Lichtenstein, *Two Letters, or What I really Wish*, 18; see *Zwei Briefe*, 16.

354. Baron, *Det jødiske spørsmål*, 15–19; and idem, *The History of Israel*, 108, 181.

enced by Christians who claimed that the Jewish political restoration would take place after the national conversion to Christ. This indicates that Lichtenstein's eschatology was within the framework of traditional Judaism rather than a result of Protestant influences.[355]

Lichtenstein's Language

While leading Neologs, like Samuel Kohn, delivered sermons and writings in Magyar (Hungarian), Lichtenstein published his booklets in German. This was of course a practical approach, as German was the language of the modern Jews not only in Austria and Germany, but also in other parts of Central and Eastern Europe as well. The use of German is probably also related to Lichtenstein's Moravian background, where most Jews had German as their mother tongue. Still, it is also significant for understanding his position in the Jewish community, as it may indicate that he wanted to distance himself from the Magyarization of the Hungarian Jewish community. In the 1880s, many of the modern Hungarian Jews had gone through a language shift and used Magyar as their new mother tongue. They were probably able to read German as well, but it is evident that Lichtenstein did not want to be associated with the Magyarization of the Jewish community in Hungary.[356] The sources do not say to what extent he used Yiddish, which appears to have been associated with the Orthodox community (the obituary in *Judische Allgemeine Zeitung* is written in Yiddish). His use of Hebrew, which occurs in several of his writings, appears to have been limited to religious themes in the form of quotations from the Hebrew Bible as well as Talmud and other parts of the Jewish literature. There are no

---

355. For most Jews the expectations of Messiah and the restoration of Israel to its land were articles of faith until early modernity, before the disintegration of this theology in the wake of the reforms. In Jewish eschatology the messianic redemption included the return to the Land of Israel from exile, national independence and security; the borders of Judah and its cities would be extended and peace would rule among the nations as well as among individuals and nature. In addition, one looked forward to the knowledge of God spreading to all the nations, and other peoples would praise Israel for its spiritual superiority and ethical qualities. It was also common to expect a great increase in the population, healing of diseases and a lengthening of human life. The center of the millennium was the Land of Israel and particularly Jerusalem, but the expectations contained universalist as well as particularist elements. Sharot, *Messianism*, 45–49.

356. Lichtenstein found the Magyarization of the liturgy and prayers useless as a tool for strengthening Jewish spiritual life; Lichtenstein, *Die Liebe*, 13.

references in his pamphlets to the Hebrew movement, which probably is due to Lichtenstein's indifference to Zionism.

The Relationship to the Christian Tradition and Doctrines

Introduction

This chapter and chapter 4.5 relate to what Fredrik Barth called "boundary-crossing." Having investigated Gurland's, Lucky's and Lichtenstein's identification with Jewish tradition and the Jewish people, I will now discuss their identification with the Christian tradition and the Christian community. Did Gurland, Lucky and Lichtenstein consider that they had "crossed the Rubicon," as Lichtenstein put it?[357] Chapter 4.4 focuses on what it meant for Gurland, Lucky and Lichtenstein to relate to Christian tradition and church doctrine. Naturally, their attitude to baptism—perhaps the ultimate taboo—and church membership are central factors here. Just as interesting is how they related to Christian supersessionism (a key term in what has been called anti-Judaism) and contemporary discussions in the Christian communities about the Jewish people, Judaism and the Old Testament/Tanak. Often these topics will be seen in light of particular church traditions or denominational preferences. In chapter 4.5 I discuss how they related to some contemporary phenomena within the Christian community that were linked to the Jewish people: anti-Semitism and the emancipation and assimilation of Jews. To come to terms with these issues it is natural to discuss their relationships to some of the mission societies and/or churches, since these phenomena became subjects of heated debate within these circles.

Gurland

A Lutheran Pietist

Considering that Gurland was baptized in a Lutheran church and died as a Lutheran missionary and pastor, his identification with Lutheran doctrine is not very complicated. There is also no hint in the sources that he questioned parts of the church or the tradition with which he associated. Instead, he shows adherence to Luther and his work, in particular

---

357. Lichtenstein, *An Appeal*, 3–4.

his Bible translation.[358] However, the Lutheran tradition in Gurland's time had many different nuances, and generally Gurland seems to have identified with Lutheran pietism as it was expressed among German, Norwegian and American friends of the Christian mission to the Jews. He did not engage in doctrinal disputes, at least not directly, but his Christocentric worldview made him willing to cooperate with other Protestants as well, in particular the Paschowittes in Russia (his relations to this movement as well as to the Lutheran church in the Baltic will be discussed in the next chapter).[359] Still, as part of the German society, Gurland had to relate to an idea that was prevalent at his time, namely that Christianity had superseded Judaism. This was not a new idea, but found a new expression and new consequences in the tradition following Friedrich Schleiermacher.

Gurland and the Tradition after Schleiermacher

While Gurland's loyalty to Lutheran doctrine after his baptism in 1864 does not seem to have been questioned by anyone, his attacks on the religious system of Judaism were in accordance with a traditional Lutheran worldview. In spite of this, Gurland left little material in which he mentions Christian supersessionism explicitly, and his use of and attitude to the Old Testament appears to have contradicted contemporary theological tendencies to diminish the importance of the Hebrew Bible. This tendency was highlighted by the theologian Friedrich Schleiermacher (1768–1834, from 1810 professor in Berlin), one of the most influential theologians of the 19th century, who greatly impressed Gurland during his studies in Berlin.[360] To come to terms with Gurland's position in regard to the core concepts in the introduction, I will focus on his relationship to Schleiermacher as well as to contemporary Lutheran pietism.

Other than his explicit references to this in his letters to Max Besser, it is possible to detect Scheleiermacher's influence when it comes to Christianity's relations to other religions. In his lessons for confirmation candidates in Mitau, Gurland explicitly places paganism, Judaism and Christianity in relation to each other in a way that reminds one of the professor in Berlin: "Paganism is the oldest religion, from which Judaism

358. Gurland, *IzW* (1911), 124.
359. Ibid., 181, 207.
360. Ibid., 124.

comes, while Christianity is the flower of Judaism. . . . Judaism is the sunrise for the one who comes. Christ didn't come to abolish the law of God, but to fulfill it. Christianity is the only true and perfect religion."[361]

The quotation shows how Gurland sees an evolution in religion, from Paganism via Judaism to the perfect religion of Christianity. Gurland gives a relative approval of Judaism, but Judaism is not "the sun" itself, only "dawn," and clearly not as important as Christianity. This approach appears to fit neatly into the pattern of traditional supersessionism. The idea of Christianity as the most developed religion and worldview was common in Protestant Europe in the 19th century, and can be found in Schleiermacher. During this century, representatives of traditional Christianity who wanted scientific validation for mission activity would often regard Christianity as the highest level of universal religious development. For friends of Christian mission work this was a welcome approach, as it made Christian mission necessary for all.[362] Consequently Schleiermacher was much read and appreciated among traditional Christian believers for his lectures and writings defending religion and its legitimate function in the community. This must be understood in light of the rationalism of the Enlightenment, which had tried to marginalize religion and spirituality from the arena of science and reason.[363]

However, Gurland's outspoken sympathy for Schleiermacher does not correspond to Gurland's own theological views on central theological issues regarding mission to the Jews as well as traditional Christian doctrine. How can this paradox be understood? That Gurland was influenced by this thinking is not very surprising, considering Schleiermacher's position at theological institutions and among friends of the missions. Although Schleiermacher maintained the traditional supersessionist view that Christianity had supplanted Judaism, he nev-

---

361. Gurland, "Dritte Stunde, 17 Januar 1876": "Heidentum ist die älteste Religion; daran entstammte Judentum, dessen Blüte das Christentum ist. . . . Das Judentum ist die Morgenröhte des Kommenden. Christus kam nicht, Gottes Gesetz aufzulösen, sondern zu erfüllen. Das Christentum ist die einzig wahre, vollkommene Religion." The quotation is from the 3rd lesson in an unpublished, handwritten manuscript in German with over 50 lessons for Gurland's confirmation classes in Mitau in 1876. The manuscript is in the possession of Hans-Heinrich Gurland, who gave the author the opportunity to make a copy of some of the pages.

362. Berentsen, "Misjonstenkningen," 116.

363. Crouter, *Friedrich Schleiermacher*, 3, 74, 92, 293.

ertheless strongly opposed Jewish conversions to Christianity.[364] For Schleiermacher the passion of Christ has no place as redemption for sin, but is only a good example of how to endure suffering; the theological point of the passion narratives is the impression given by Jesus.[365] With a theological framework like this, there is no place for salvation history. Only the New Testament is normative, the Old Testament was incapable of expressing the Christian spirit and is only needed because of the historical link to the New Testament. Certainly, Christianity had nothing to look for in contemporary Judaism, which, he claimed, "is long since a dead religion."[366] Regarding most of these issues, Gurland's position was far from Schleiermacher's. When it came to practical Christian doctrines, Gurland seems to have been associated with the conservative camp. Particularly on the issue of Jewish mission and baptism of Jews, Gurland has a very different approach. That many Jews sought baptism for the sake of assimilation was well known. Gurland was critical of this, and according to Le Roi, Gurland wanted candidates for baptism to express an authentic religious conviction before baptism could take place. This was not due to Gurland's concerns about their Jewish identity, but rather because he feared some of them did not believe in the divinity of Jesus.[367]

Gurland's sympathy for the Old Testament also contradicts Schleiermacher's views, as Gurland was famous for his lectures and sermons about Old Testament topics. The question is whether Gurland's interest in the Hebrew Bible is reflected in his manuscripts.[368] In his lecture about the Old Testament ("Was enthält das Alte Testament?") Gurland rejects the notion that the Old Testament is a product of religious development.[369] Instead he claims it to be one coherent scripture with divine

---

364. Schleiermacher's views must be seen in the context of the ongoing debate about the emancipation of the Jews in Prussia around 1800, which he supported. In a series of five fabricated letters from 1799, Schleiermacher gives a number of reasons for not using baptism in this process. Some of them stem from his romanticist view that religions are organic entities, which makes transference between religions alien and even abhorrent for him. Beckmann, *Die fremde Wurzel*, 124–32; and Crouter, *Friedrich Schleiermacher*, 129.

365. Hägglund, *Teologins historia*, 332.

366. Crouter, *Friedrich Schleiermacher*, 126.

367. Le Roi, *Rudolf Hermann Gurland*, 18.

368. Gurland, *IzW* (1911), 142.

369. Gurland, "Was enthält das Alte Testament?"

salvation as its focus. This understanding of the Old Testament may be reflected in his lectures for his confirmation classes in Mitau, where each lesson is given a topic from Bible history or the Small Catechism of Martin Luther.[370] Approximately fifty percent of the content is related to narratives and other material from the Christian Old Testament. From the fifth lesson to the twentieth he dwells on the Creation and the Patriarchs, then finally comes to the Small Catechism, only to spend the next 10 lessons on the Ten Commandments.

However, Gurland's use of the Old Testament in these lectures is not necessarily due to his Jewish background, but may also be compatible with the methods of the German theologian and expert in ecclesial didactics Carl Adolf Gerhard von Zezschwitz (1825–1886). In his works he recommended a two-fold didactic method for the young members of the churches: first the biblical salvation history was presented, and then came the direct exposition of the Catechism, which was more focused on Christian doctrine. The purpose was to help the student to see himself/herself in light of salvation history; the overall perspective was more

---

370. Since the Reformation, confirmation in the Lutheran churches of Northern Europe had had a content that differed from the Roman Catholic version. While the Catholic Church regards it as a completion of baptism, as the confirmation candidate is given the Holy Spirit by the blessing by the bishop, the Lutheran churches held that the purpose of confirmation was the completion of the upbringing of baptized children. In other words, confirmation was held to be a pedagogic tool and not a sacrament. In most places confirmation classes in the Lutheran version were, and are, aimed at young people in the early or middle teens. The core curriculum of the classes was the Small Catechism of Martin Luther. Still, the didactic content and the structure of the teaching varied considerably both with regard to the historical period and geographical differences. Other than that, the content and organization of the teaching varied, depending on local and national tradition, church authorities and other circumstances, like the actual minister responsible for the confirmation. As the teaching material in confirmation classes was one of the key tools for reaching the ministers' parish members, didactic and theological consideration and updating were both needed and an arena for controversy. I have not found any work presenting the system of confirmation education in Kurland in this period. However, it is assumed that the system was not very different from the other Lutheran churches in Germany. In his survey on the worldwide use of Martin Luther's Small Catechism until the 1920s, J. M. Reu notes that in Latvia the German Lutherans used an edition prepared by Alexander von Oettingen. The year of publication of this version is not known, but in the 1920s it was out of print and was replaced by a number of others. It is probable that the German churches in Mitau used Oettingen's version. I then suppose that it was published when Gurland had his lectures in 1876. Reu, *Dr. Martin Luther's Small Catechism*, 299; Neander, *Die deutschen*, 10; and Jensen, "For 'døpte kristne,'" 21–34.

narrative than dogmatic.[371] It is therefore not unlikely that Gurland's lectures were influenced by Zezschwitz, considering the latter's dominating influence within Lutheran church pedagogics of the period. However, the lack of studies on this issue makes it difficult to say anything with certainty. A relevant question, though, is whether it would be expected that parish ministers spend almost 20 of 50 lessons on Genesis when teaching Baltic German teenagers.

On this background, Gurland's sympathy for Schleiermacher may be explained by Schleiermacher's skepticism towards rationalism, as his focus on affections and spiritual experience would find resonance in pietistic thinking. Arguing for religion as something that demands personal experience in contrast to the rationalistic approach, Schleiermacher naturally awoke interest among some pietists as well. The underlying theological implications of Schleiermacher's system were probably of little interest to Gurland. At least his affection for the Tanak was not interrupted by the nineteenth-century critical attitude to this scripture, but was connected to its traditional Christian interpretation, particularly pietistic Protestantism. Within this tradition, Gurland's general antipathy towards Talmud and parts of the Jewish tradition would fit neatly into traditional supersessionism combined with a strong identification with the Old Testament.

Lucky

Baptism

When Wiegand describes Lucky's baptism in Belgrade by unregistered Baptists, he explains that Lucky did not think the baptism had the same function for Jews as for Gentiles, as for the latter group the rite was a public refusal of idolatry. Later, to avoid the perception that he had left Judaism, he would not give clear answers to this question. This caused much tension between him and Jewish-Christian missionaries; they accused him of speaking with two tongues, and he would answer by calling them *meshummads*.[372]

---

371. Koziol, *Katechumenat heute*, 39, 62. This scheme may also be found in other Lutheran material on the Catechism, e.g., in the Norwegian schoolbooks after 1891 which were inspired by Zezschwitz. See Saxe, *Katekismeundervisningen*, 17.

372. Wiegand, "Chajim Jedidjah Lucky," 46.

As suggested in the biography chapter, Lucky's understanding of baptism seems to have been influenced by a Baptist and spiritualistic theology. This appears to be confirmed by Gisle Johnson's description of one of Lucky's followers in Budapest in the 1920s. The oldest member of Johnson's group of Jewish believers in Budapest was a baptized Jew named Karl Achs, who was affiliated with the Scottish mission. He had been a friend of Lucky's, and for years he took part in the discussions between Johnson and some of the members of Johnson's group about baptism. According to Achs, Christian baptism was nothing other than a version of "Jewish baptism."[373]

Sabbath Observance

However, when Lucky associated himself with the SDB, the reason was not so much the church's doctrine on baptism as its Sabbath observance. Lucky's ideas about the relationship between Jewish tradition and the New Testament went far beyond what would be acceptable not only in most Jewish communities, but in most Christian communities as well. Seventh Day Baptists are some of the few Christians who claim observance of the Shabbat (Saturday):

> You know my love to the Seventh-day Baptist Denomination. And why do I love them? Because they—as a denomination—walk in the ways of God. They "keep the commandments of God, and have the testimony of Jesus Christ." The church at large has thrown aside the obedience to God's commandment. I love God's Word and his commandments, therefore my heart was made glad when I learned to know there is a group of non-Jewish Christians who are obedient to God, doing what he command[s].[374]

Lucky shared the conviction that observance of the Sabbath is not only relevant for Jews and Jewish Christians, but for all Christians: The observance of Sunday is generally characterized as a practice which is "desecrating the Sabbath of God."[375] It should be noted, however, that I have found such strong statements from Lucky only in sources from the SDB. Although Lucky's membership in this church was well known among his contemporaries, the doctrine of Sabbath observance for all

---

373. Terray, *Et liv i grenseland*, 118–21, 170. It is not clear what Achs, or Johnson, meant by this expression, but it might refer to the Jewish ritual bath.

374. Anonymous, "The Work of Brother Ch. Th. Lucky," 267.

375. Ibid., 268.

Christians does not seems to have been pursued very much by Lucky in other circles. Lucky does not seem to have had any problem participating in Sunday services or other non-Jewish Christian traditions, e.g., Christmas celebrations.[376] However, as *Edut* explicitly laments Sunday observance, there is no reason to believe that Lucky only was pretending to hold this doctrine to put himself in a positive light from a Seventh Day Baptist perspective.[377] In any case, considering that Lucky's main goal was to work for a modern Jewish Christianity, it cannot be expected that Lucky would highlight his view on this issue when the outcome probably would have marginalized him and his position even more.

The Interdenominational Seventh Day Baptist

Despite associating himself with Protestant Christianity and his membership in the SDB, Lucky usually tried to place himself outside denominational struggles.[378] This appears to have been accepted by at least some members of the SDB leadership, considering that *The Peculiar People*, mostly run by pastor Daland, appears to have followed much the same practice concerning church relations. According to Daland, *The Peculiar People* was characterized as not being the organ of any mission society. Although it was not undenominational, it wanted to be *interdenominational*.[379] This also seems to be a correct way to describe Lucky, who already before he went to New York had contact with Baptists as well as Lutherans. Lucky was famous for fighting for his theological views, not to follow up the traditional quarrels between the churches, but to counter the churches' views on Judaism and the Jewish people.

However, issues like anti-Judaism and supersessionism are seldom discussed explicitly in Lucky's writings or in *The Peculiar People*, in spite of his aversion to all of these ideas. While mainstream mission periodicals felt it necessary to discuss anti-Semitism, Lucky appears to have gone

---

376. Petra Volf describes how Lucky participated with much enthusiasm in the Christmas celebrations with her family, not only singing Danish Christmas carols but also taking the initiative to visit a seriously ill member of the evangelical congregation on Christmas Eve. Lucky led the little procession through the town, carrying a little Christmas tree (!) (Volf, "Reminiscences about Lucky," 97–99).

377. "The Sabbath Day," 1–15. According to Dr. Main there was some suspicion and reluctance in the SDB leadership concerning Lucky. Randolph, "Christian Theophilus Lucky," 207–8.

378. Ibid.

379. *The Peculiar People* 2 (1889) 194.

beyond this issue. Lucky's ideas about the continuity between Jewish tradition and the New Testament, his support of Jewish nationalism and his struggle for a Torah-observant Jewish Christianity fundamentally challenged supersessionism as well as any theological anti-Judaism in its own right. Nevertheless, there is no doubt that Lucky was conscious that he by his faith in Jesus had crossed a boundary in the eyes of the Jewish community. The way he seems to have obscured the date of his baptism, is in itself an indication of this.

Lichtenstein

BAPTISM

The core of the tension around Lichtenstein in the Christian community lay in his status as being unbaptized. Like Lucky, Lichtenstein had a very ambivalent relationship to the churches and mission societies, just as the Jewish missions appear to have been almost as ambivalent towards him. He was probably well aware that cultivating friendship with missionaries the way he did, would be a serious transgression of the traditional border of the Jewish community, but these flaws would have been more devastating if he were baptized in public. As he never accepted an official baptism, the consequence was much frustration in his relationships with most Christian contacts, even with his best friends David Baron and C. A. Schönberger.

The frustration is most clearly expressed by Le Roi in his work on the Jewish mission in the 19th century, where Lichtenstein's position is regarded as highly problematic from a Christian perspective.[380] Le Roi supports the Jewish-Christian missionary A. Venetianer, who already in 1886 wrote a public letter to Lichtenstein in which he criticized Lichtenstein's national consciousness, thinking it prevented him from taking the final step to Christianity.[381] Apparently Venetianer and Le Roi associate Lichtenstein with the contemporary progressive Jewish circles in Vienna and Budapest who stressed the continuance between Judaism and Christianity. In Le Roi's opinion, both orally and in writing

---

380. Le Roi, *Geschichte*, 2:277.

381. A. Venetianer was baptized by the missionary C. A. Schönberger in 1873 in Prague. From 1879 he worked for the Scottish Free Church in Hungary and later in Triest, where he wrote a book about the history of the evangelical Christians in the area in 1887. Ibid.

Lichtenstein claims that Judaism and Christianity are so close that no conversion is necessary.[382] Consequently he doubts that Lichtenstein is an authentic believer in Christ, and although Lichtenstein writes enthusiastically about Christ he has not become his own savior. The issue of Lichtenstein's rejection of baptism shows this; his interest in Christ is only an interest in history of religion. In spite of this pessimistic evaluation of Lichtenstein, for Le Roi Lichtenstein is still a sign of the new era in the Jewish people's relation to Jesus.[383] However, Lichtenstein supported Jews who wanted to be baptized, as long as they were authentic believers in Jesus. Philippus Gordon quotes a correspondence between Lichtenstein and a Jewish wife from Czernowitz, who after having read Lichtenstein's writings wanted to be baptized. In her letter she asked for advice about which church she should make contact. Lichtensteins's answer was that this was up to her, as long as she turned to a church that clearly had its foundations on the New Testament.[384]

Gjessing is the only source that refers to Lichtenstein's self-baptizing. Gjessing's obituary is not very substantial on this point, mentioning only that he baptized himself on a "particular Friday in a Sabbath mikve."[385] I believe one must consider the possibility that Gjessing constructed this information in an effort to satisfy his Norwegian and German readers. First, there are no other sources that confirm his version. Second, for the conservative Lutherans in the Norwegian mission society Lichtenstein's refusal of baptism was not only a breach with church tradition but a refusal of the sacrament, and thereby salvation. The story in Gjessing's obituary could therefore serve as some sort of comfort for Lichtenstein's Norwegian sympathizers. As Lucky and *The Peculiar People* several times pointed out, many mission periodicals in the Jewish missions were not alien to "freshening up" the news from the mission work with overly optimistic reports.[386] Third, as Gjessing's narrative wrongly dates the Tisza Eszlar affair to 1876, this may indicate that he was not very well informed.

---

382. Le Roi, *Geschichte*, 1:290. Generally Le Roi's opinion is that the British mission societies suffer under a philo-Semitic tendency of glorifying the Jews; Le Roi, *Geschichte*, 2:279.

383. Le Roi, *Geschichte*, 2:277, 279.

384. Gordon, *På Missionresor*, 85.

385. Gjessing, "Rabbi Isak (Ignaz) Lichtenstein," 175.

386. "Editorial Notes," *The Peculiar People* 1 (1888–89), 112.

Nevertheless, personally I doubt that Gjessing made up this story. Gjessing had lived in Budapest between 1893 and 1897 and knew Lichtenstein personally, and the Norwegian periodical *Missions-Blad for Israel* claims Gjessing was one of Lichtenstein's best friends during those years.[387] Gjessing was not regarded as a very practical or successful missionary, but his reports were factual and detailed to an extent that even could be regarded as a problem for the Norwegian mission periodical.[388] For that reason, it is not very surprising that he would know details others did not know or care much about.

In addition I doubt that Gjessing's story would be very comforting for his readers. Such an auto-baptism would usually not be accepted as an authentic baptism by most Lutherans at the time, be they friends of the Jewish mission or not. Instead, the narrative about Lichtenstein's individualistic approach to the sacrament could have been seen as rather unfortunate and even offensive, and would not necessarily make critical readers more sympathetic to Lichtenstein. When Gjessing gives us this information, he also refers to how Yechiel Herschensohn-Lichtenstein at the *Institutum Judaicum* in Leipzig did the same thing in the 1850s, together with some friends. What Gjessing does not say, however, is that Herschensohn-Lichtenstein later accepted an official baptism, something which would be well-known to many of his readers. In addition, it may be that the obituary in *Jüdische Allgemeine Zeitung* refers to this event when it states that Lichtenstein was never *formally* baptized.[389]

Still, if Gjessing's information is correct, the question remains: why did Lichtenstein not reveal the event to Baron and others, or why did they not pass on this information? Lichtenstein's motives for giving personal information to Gjessing, like the anecdotes from his childhood or his auto-baptism, we do not know. However, for Lichtenstein, an overall goal was to avoid being legally regarded as a *meshummad*, and discretion would therefore be necessary. If Baron had the same information, it is possible that he quite simply maintained the same discretion in his obituary, only mentioning the obscure reference to the baptism in the *Algemeine Jüdische Zeitung*.[390] Considering the emotional turmoil in Lichtenstein's family in the days before his death, it

387. Anonymous, "Rabbi Lichtenstein og hans Omvendelse," 72.
388. Aasen, *Ragnvald Gjessing*, 21–28.
389. Baron, "Rabbi Ignatz Lichtenstein," 265.
390. Ibid.

is possible that he feared the consequences for the family and perhaps for Lichtenstein's grave if he wrote about it explicitly. In addition, it is possible that the question of baptism was a minor matter for Baron, as long as Lichtenstein appeared to have grasped the spiritual message of Christianity. Due to his association with the Mildmay Mission and its leader John Wilkinson, it is possible that Baron shared Wilkinson's opinion about Rabinowitz's eagerness concerning baptism, which Wilkinson characterized as "sacramentalism."[391] In that case, Baron would be more concerned about Lichtenstein's general aversion to being identified with apostates than the isolated question of baptism.

If one accepts Gjessing's report as authentic, it tells us that at some point Lichtenstein decided to accept baptism, but totally within the framework of Judaism—as he saw it.

Another relevant question is why Isaac Lichtenstein did not follow Joseph Rabinowitz in Kishinev when the latter arranged a public baptism with representatives from different Protestant churches present, and which was not registered in any church register. The Mildmay Mission gave active support to Rabinowitz, and probably Baron (who worked for Mildmay Mission in the 1880s) or others suggested this solution for Lichtenstein. Rabinowitz met Rabbi Lichtenstein on at least two occasions in Budapest, and here the circumstances of Rabinowitz's baptism in 1884 almost certainly were presented as an option for Lichtenstein as well. The only outcome of these meetings was that Lichtenstein's reluctance in relation to the issue frustrated Rabinowitz. Lichtenstein did not want to follow Rabinowitz's pattern, but we do not know exactly why. Whatever Rabinowitz's motives for the non-denominational profile of his baptism, the extraordinary arrangement did not reduce the distance between himself and most other Russian Jews. From their point of view, he was still regarded as an apostate. For Lichtenstein, who wanted to remain within the Jewish community, this solution would probably be of no use. Instead this arrangement of the baptism led Rabinowitz into an open conflict with Rudolf Faltin, who probably expected to baptize Rabinowitz. Another explanation for Lichtenstein's refusal to follow Rabinowitz could be that Lichtenstein thought that Rabinowitz in one way or another was cheating, trying to escape a problem with a hybrid solution, regardless of the judicial aspects.[392]

391. Kjær-Hansen, *Joseph Rabinowitz*, 108–9.
392. Ibid., 174–75.

The Sins of Israel

In *Zwei Briefe*, Lichtenstein's son Emmanuel points out that his father treats Christianity with too much one-sided sympathy to be taken seriously in the Jewish population. Although I do not think this accusation is unfounded, it would be wrong to say that Lichtenstein turned a blind eye to the dark side of the church's traditional relationship to the Jewish people. In several writings he dwells on the horror of this part of Jewish history, but claims that the aggression was not executed by true Christians. While anti-Semites think they document the truth of their Christianity by hating Jews, genuine believers in Christ are rather led by compassion to Israel.[393] For Lichtenstein the problem is how even pious Christians become anti-Semites, alienating Jews even more from Christianity.[394] Referring to Christ's warnings against false prophets, Christians need to express love to the Jewish people. True Christians do not condemn others, but are stricter with themselves than with others.[395] Neither does true Christianity know any barriers between races, but will rather combat anti-Semitism. Anti-Semitism, by its very nature, is against not only Jews but also Christianity itself, not least because Jesus himself was a Jew.[396]

Still, several of Lichtenstein's writings carry harsh criticism against the Jews. By referring to James 3:1–13 and Talmud *Erachin* 16, as well as Romans 2:17–23, Lichtenstein states that Israel, like all people, sins "with every step."[397] The Jewish nation has people in its midst who are Jews only in name, and who even sin against their own countrymen. Just like everyone else, the Jew therefore must seek repentance.[398] Several times Lichtenstein explicitly relates the suffering of the Jewish people to the people's rejection of Christ. Although this theme is touched upon at other times as well, e.g., in his address in Leipzig in 1895, this theme is particularly central in the little pamphlet *Das Blut Christi, ein Nachklang*

---

393. Lichtenstein, *Die Liebe*, 33.
394. Referring to Matthew 18:7 and 23:37–39; Lichtenstein, *The Points of Contact*, 14.
395. Lichtenstein, *Die Liebe*, 19.
396. Ibid., 22.
397. Lichtenstein, *Ein Geheimnis*, 9–10.
398. Lichtenstein, *An Appeal*, 5.

aus dem Midrasch Echa, which is an attempt to show how the suffering of the Jewish people is due to their rejection of Jesus.[399]

The pamphlet builds on *Midrash Echa*, the midrash on the Book of Lamentations, a commentary or exposition of the sin of Israel before the destruction of Jerusalem, particularly the murder of the priest Zechariah (2 Chronicles 24:20–22 in combination with Ezekiel 21:28). The story is combined and introduced with the following lines from the liturgy for the 9th of Av, the memorial for the destruction of the temple:

> O day of sorrow, how woefully it affects me!—The day when my transgression reached its height, and my bold hand was imbrued in the blood of the prophet; truly this innocent blood will not rest until it is avenged, and the judgement has been marked and wonderful. Mourning and lamentation resound throughout the realm of Judah.[400]

After this introduction, Lichtenstein follows up with a short paraphrase of the midrash, with the last sentence from the liturgy above repeated several times between the paragraphs.[401]

---

399. Lichtenstein, *Points of Contact*, 11; and "Das Blut Christi," 229–32.

400. Lichtenstein, *The Points of Contact*, 11. At this point Lichtenstein also refers to the murder of Zechariah, which is what the midrash starts with.

401. The midrash contains two versions of this text; Lichtenstein seems to have used the slightly extended version:

R. Yudan asked R. Aha, "Where did the Israelites kill Zechariah? Was it in the courtyard of women or in the courtyard of the Israelites?"

He said to him, "It was neither in the in the women's courtyard nor in the Israelites' courtyard, but in the priests' courtyard.

"But they did not dispose of his blood like the blood of a hind or a ram: 'He shall pour out the blood thereof and cover it with dust' (Lev. 17:13).

"But here: 'For the blood she shed is still in her, she set it upon a bare rock; she did not pour it out on the ground to cover it with dust' (Ez. 24:7).

"'She set her blood upon the bare rock, so that it was not covered, so that it may stir up my fury to take vengeance' (Ez. 24:8)."

Seven transgressions did the Israelites commit on that day: They murdered a priest, prophet, judge, they spilled innocent blood, they blasphemed the divine name, they imparted uncleanness to the courtyard, and it was, furthermore, a Day of Atonement that coincided with the Sabbath.

When Nebuzaradan came in, the blood began to drip. He said to them, "What sort of blood is this dripping blood?"

They said to him, "It is the blood of oxen, rams, and sheep that we offered on the altar."

He forthwith sent and brought oxen, rams, and sheep and slaughtered them in his presence, but the blood continued to drip.

Lichtenstein's point is that just as the Jewish nation suffered due to its sins towards the prophets, for the last 19 centuries the Jews have been facing the punishment for the murder of Jesus. To underline this he quotes Matthew 27:25 and the story of the woman who was healed by touching the clothes of Jesus in Mark 5:25–34. Lichtenstein also refers to this last event in *Zwei Briefe*, and the point is the same: Israel is in the same situation as this woman, and like her, the nation can only be healed by Jesus.[402]

That the sufferings of the Jewish people are due to their rejection of Christ is an established tradition in Christian literature and teaching before the Holocaust, and it is reasonable to think that *Das Blut Christi* is a clear example of how Lichtenstein adopted this Christian tradition after his conversion. This interpretation of Jewish history was commonly accepted in the Jewish mission circles as well, although it usually was combined with philo-Semitism. Helene Gurland also reflects this traditional attitude when describing the horror of the Kishinev pogrom in

---

He said to them, "If you tell the truth, well and good, but if not, I shall comb your flesh with iron combs."

They said to him, "What shall we tell you? He was a prophet who rebuked us. We conspired against him and killed him. And lo, years have passed, but his blood has not stopped seething."

He said to them, "I shall appease it."

He brought before him the great Sanhedrin and the lesser Sanhedrin and killed them, until their blood mingled with that of Zechariah: "Oaths are imposed and broken, they kill and rob, there is nothing but adultery and licence, one deed of blood after another" (Hos. 4:2).

Still the blood seethed. He brought boys and girls and killed them by the blood, but it did not stop seething.

He brought youngsters from the school house and killed them over it, but it did not stop seething.

Forthwith he took eighty thousand priests and killed them on his account, until the blood lapped the grave of Zechariah. But the blood did not stop seething.

He said, "Zechariah, Zechariah, all the best of them have I destroyed. Do you want me to exterminate them all?"

When he said this, the blood forthwith came to rest.

Then he considered repenting, saying, "Now if one soul matters so, as to that man who has killed all these souls, how much the more so!"

He fled and sent a parting gift and converted. (Petihta Twenty-Three)

Text according to Neusner, *Israel After Calamity*, 21–22.

402. Lichtenstein, *Zwei Briefe*, 28.

1903, and when Lucky rejected the idea that Israel was morally responsible for the death of Jesus, this frustrated even his closest sympathizers.[403]

There is no doubt that when referring to Matthew 27:25 as a key to understanding the midrash and the history of the Jewish people, Lichtenstein seems to confirm this traditional Christian position. However, both the midrash and the text from Matthew are used to build up an appeal for the readers to embrace Christ, and in itself Lichtenstein's pamphlet does not give any legitimacy to Christians harassing the Jews. As Lichtenstein points out, this aggression is the main reason why the Jewish people shun Christianity.[404] The pains of Israel are due to the rejection of Messiah, but the Jews have not seen this because it was Christians who killed and persecuted them. The Christians, for their part, should see the hand of God in Israel's rejection of Christ, since this brought the gospel and the Jewish Bible to the rest of the world.[405] In fact, the situation now is that Israel has won a victory of historical dimensions, as true Christians pray for Israel.[406]

Still, relating Lichtenstein's use of *Midrash Echa* solely to Christian or New Testament influence would be superficial. Lichtenstein's interpretation of the midrash as a key to interpreting Jewish history, seems to be consistent with traditional Jewish exegesis, and may even be related to the widespread Jewish self-accusations in the Jewish literary tradition from the Middle Ages. The midrash points out idolatry and social injustice among Israel as the reasons for the destruction by the Babylonians in 587 BC, and later the Roman destruction in AD 70.[407] Lichtenstein's general statement about the reason for Israel's suffering seems therefore primarily to be based on a rabbinic text. The only novelty in Lichtenstein's use of the midrash (not insignificant from a rabbinic point of view), is the way he relates it to the death of Jesus. The crucial factor in Lichtenstein's perspective is that he challenges the established identification of who is to blame for the Jewish people's trauma and suffering: It is the Jewish people itself, and not primarily the non-Jewish or Christian neighboring peoples.[408]

---

403. Weidauer, "Erindringer," 175–78.
404. Lichtenstein, *Points of Contact*, 12.
405. Ibid., 25.
406. Ibid., 5.
407. Neusner, *Israel After Calamity*, 14, 46.
408. Alexander, "Toward a Theory of Cultural Trauma," 15.

Given the associations between traditional Christian accusations against the Jewish people as "Christ-killers" and the rather bizarre imagery in Lichtenstein's pamphlet, it is unfortunate that we do not know much about how *Das Blut Christi* was used or read after its publication. In a short notice about the mission work in Lithuania in the early 1920s, *Missions-Blad for Israel* describes which of Lichtenstein's writings were sold by the Swiss mission society *Verein des Freunde Israels in Basel*'s shop in Vilnius, and mentions these three titles: *Zwei Briefe, Ein Judenspiegel*, and *Ein Geheimnis aus dem Talmud*. However, we cannot be sure that this list was complete. The two first titles were also translated into English by David Baron's Hebrew Christian Testimony.[409] Probably the selection of pamphlets to be translated, as well as which were to be sold at mission stations, reflects which publications were regarded as most useful for evangelistic purposes. In that case, *Das Blut Christi* at least does not seem to have been the most popular work.

In summary, Lichtenstein seems to have preferred to baptize himself more or less in secret, instead of undergoing a traditional baptism that would have cut him off from the Hungarian Jewish community. The paradox is that Lichtenstein, who insisted so strongly on being Jewish and would not cross the boundary represented by baptism, nevertheless found it natural to relate the tragic parts of Jewish history to the death of Jesus, a view strikingly parallel to traditional Christian anti-Judaistic rhetoric.

---

409. Lichtenstein, *Points of Contact*, 2.

The Relation to the Christian Community

Assimilation, Anti-Semitism, and Mission Strategies before WWI

For the majority of Jews in Eastern Europe, baptism and identification with Christianity remained a taboo in the Jewish community. In addition, Gurland, Lucky and Lichtenstein experienced some degree of alienation in the Christian community due to their Jewish background. Often this experience of being "neither fish nor fowl" was related to historical situations and ideological influence outside their control. They were bound to respond to the new nationalist ideas in Europe and modern anti-Semitism, and they became involved in the missions at a time when the traditional assimilation of converts was challenged and the question of national churches was raised. The controversy over mission strategies highlighted the situation for many Jewish converts—at least those who still wanted to identify themselves as Jewish in some way or another. Consequently, I will discuss Gurland's, Lucky's and Lichtenstein's attitudes to these questions, as well as their personal relations to the mission societies and their workers.

The increased number of baptisms and the following assimilation of Jews into European communities were caused by processes in Jewish as well as Christian society. It is usually assumed that for most of the 200,000 Jews baptized according to records from the 19th century, the major motives were to overcome the legal and political restrictions on the Jewish population as well as leaving the traditional Jewish way of life. In Russia, Prussia and Hungary, the conversions appear to be the result not of state involvement or systematic policy, but rather of new social mobility, particularly related to intermarriage.[410] A political consequence of the Napoleonic wars was the governments' new efforts to strengthen and modernize the European states. It was therefore no coincidence that the establishment of *Die Berliner Gesellschaft zur Beförderung des Christentums unter den Juden* in 1822 was supported by the Prussian king, as the conversion of the Jews was regarded as a reasonable approach in this process.[411] However, already before the middle of the century the governments had become much more ambivalent to mission activities towards the Jews. In Germany, the Berlin Society

---

410. Schainker, "Imperial Hybrids," 315.
411. Clark, *The Politics of Conversion*, 125–26.

and other missions increasingly found themselves politically marginalized. In Russia, the Russian Orthodox Church had much doubt about the motives of the converts, while the tsarist regime was sensitive to the anti-Jewish sentiments in the population and became increasingly less liable to believe that the traditional goal of assimilating Jews was realistic or desirable.[412]

In spite of the long history of Judaeophobia in European history, the nationalist and ethnic element of the Jew-hatred from the middle of the 19th century was something new. Traditionally, the hostility and accusations of ritual murder and sacrileges of the sacrament were grounded in the religious rivalry between Christianity and Judaism. Stereotypes about the greedy and dishonest Jew were related to Jewish over-representation in the trades, and the establishment of the Rothschild financial empire in the early 1800s fueled the idea of Jewish political influence, in spite of the fact that most Jews in Eastern Europe were impoverished. In the 1850s and 1860s, the idea of the Jew as an alien and a capitalist was increasingly combined with the new Social-Darwinist ideas of races.[413] Now Jews were labeled Semites, which disconnected the Jewish question from religion, making it a question of biology instead. From the end of the 1870s anti-Semitism became a popular movement in Germany and in Eastern Europe, headed by the German court chaplain Adolf Stoecker and the professor of history Heinrich von Treitsckhe. Although anti-Semitism in itself was not enough to build a political platform, the economic and social upheaval in the last decades before WWI made anti-Semitic rhetoric useful for political mobilization of the masses.[414] This rhetoric associated the Jews with liberal ideas and regarded the relatively high representation of Jews in the German public as damaging for the European nations.

The missions' attitude towards emancipation and anti-Semitism was just as complex and ambivalent as it was to the Zionist movement.[415] Central mission leaders, like Le Roi, Herman Strack, Richard Bieling and particularly Franz Delitzsch, rejected a number of anti-Semitic works from the 1870s onwards, conveying strong criticism against anti-

---

412. Schainker, "Imperial Hybrids," 115–17.
413. Stokke, "Auswanderer," 26–29.
414. Ibid., 31.
415. Clark, *The Politics of Conversion*, 281. Clark here is referring to Ernst Bloch.

Semites such as Eugen Düring and Adolf Stöcker.[416] Nevertheless, many of them were using much of the widespread anti-Semitic rhetoric.[417] Le Roi used much the same list of allegedly anti-Christian citations from the Talmud as the average anti-Semitic literature.[418] Like many others, Le Roi experienced the modernization of German society as a crisis, and although he acknowledged that the Jews had a merely incidental relation to this process, he claimed that they were particularly able to adapt to and exploit the new opportunities due to the characteristic alleged egoism of the Jew. The Jews were instrumental in the introduction of modern ideas and the new secular individualism, which consequently would undermine the culture as well as the Christian values of Germany.[419] The mission periodicals lamented the pogroms, but nevertheless explained much of the anti-Semitic attitudes as understandable reactions to the damage caused by the Jews.[420] The physical ghetto was the result of the spiritual ghetto of Talmud, which made a barrier between the Jews and any Christian influence. According to Clark, many missionaries thought that Judaism was unable to create a spirituality that went beyond outer observance, and that the withdrawal of Talmud from Jewish life in modern times would only leave an empty space for materialism and religious indifference.[421] Talmud had also not been able to help the Jewish people to seek improvement for their own conditions by manual labor. Not unexpectedly, similar accusations were found among contemporary anti-Semites.

The attacks on anti-Semitism from the mission leaders were meant not only to defend the Jews, but also to defend the mission activity. Anti-Semitism's answer to the Jewish Question was a threat to the Jewish missions and undermined their own answers to the same issues.[422] Le Roi distanced himself explicitly from racial anti-Semitism, but nevertheless

---

416. The struggles over anti-Semitism caused much strife in the German mission societies. In 1882, Delitzsch described to the Norwegians how the question of the Russian pogroms destroyed *Zentralverein*'s general assembly that year; Skarsaune, *Israels venner*, 164.

417. E.g., not helping idolaters or not giving back a heathen's lost property; Clark, *The Politics of Conversion*, 259, 273.

418. Ibid., 254–59.

419. Ibid., 264–69.

420. Ibid., 276.

421. Ibid., 255–59.

422. Ibid., 252.

held that the gospel had become a rearguard in the struggle against the Judaization of German society. Although he held that there was a certain unchanging ethnic character to the Jews, he could not accept that race made Jews unable to experience spiritual transformation, and he could certainly not accept the outspoken attacks on Christian doctrine. In addition, while he described the contemporary influence of the Jews on German culture rather gloomily, he was optimistic about what would happen after the expected mass conversions to Christianity. Just as they now were in the frontlines of undermining Christianity, they would then become the foremost servants for Christian mission to the world.[423]

One of the mission leaders who became particularly involved in the debate about anti-Semitism was Franz Delitzsch, who held that modern anti-Semitism was nothing less than a dangerous poison.[424] In 1871, the Austrian professor August Rohling published his book *Der Talmudjude*, which had great influence on the increasing anti-Semitism in Central Europe. Several times Delitzsch attacked Rohling in writing for lies and wrong methods. Like others, he could prove that Rohling had copied and paraphrased large portions of the anti-Semitic book *Entdecktes Judenthum*, by J. A. Eisenmenger, from 1700. In 1881, he published the book *Rohlings Talmudjude beleuchtet*, which stirred a heated discussion between himself and Rohling. For Delitzsch, anti-Semitism was just as anti-Christian as it was anti-Jewish, infecting German communities with hate.

Generally, Protestant and Catholic missions combined the spreading of the gospel with the spreading of the national culture of the missionaries, and consequently most converts to Christianity were expected to cross over the boundary to European culture as well as accepting Christian teaching. This was the background for the discussions about mission strategy in the last decades before WWI, a debate that took place in periodicals as well as at mission conferences. European missionaries were very much of a piece with European and English civilization, and their missionary identification was heavily influenced by the contemporary Eurocentric worldview and the awareness that they were embodying European superiority.[425] The missionary assumption was that assimilation to the norms of Protestant Europe was the best one

---

423. Ibid., 278.
424. Wagner, *Franz Delitzsch*, 411.
425. Bonk, *The Theory*, vi.

could give the converts; their intention was to prove that new Christians in Africa and Asia could be as good Europeans as anyone else.[426] This did not mean that all missionaries were nationalists, but simply that they thought their culture was a fruit of Christianity, or that their home nation was the best tool for spreading the gospel.

During the 19th century there were an increasing number of missionaries who believed that the new Christians in Africa and Asia should keep close bonds with their national society, to reduce the alienation between the converts and their ethnic and cultural backgrounds. Parallel to this new emphasis on the value of national cultures on the mission field, many Jewish missions also became concerned about contextualization of the Christian message, which led several to promote congregations of Jewish believers.[427] As a consequence, the Jewish missions became involved in passionate discussions about mission strategy and potential Jewish-Christian congregations. In this climate Gurland, Lucky, Lichtenstein and other Jewish converts would find themselves in the crossfire between sympathizers of European assimilation, Christian universalism and Jewish nationalism.

Gurland

The Baltic German Community and Underground Russian Evangelicals

One of the reasons the Baltic Lutheran synods established mission work towards the Jews in the 1860s was that the conversion of Jews to Christianity would be an alternative to the political emancipation being signaled by the Russian regime.[428] Ideologically, the tsar's initiative was associated with political and economic liberalism, and part of a general reform of the agrarian and feudal character of Russian society. Fearing that increased Jewish influence would undermine the Christian (and perhaps Baltic German) way of life in the wake of emancipation, some

---

426. Walls, *The Missionary Movement*, 105.

427. The work of Leon Rosenberg (Gurland's assistant and successor) in Odessa was an attempt of the Mildmay Mission to continue Rabinowitz's pioneer work in the 1880s and 1890s. Glaser, "A Survey," 109.

428. The primary argument was Christian love. Müller, "Ueber Judenmission," 89–116.

pastors, like the Baltic German pastor Müller, wanted the Jews to be assimilated instead, religiously as well as culturally.

To what extent did Gurland sympathize with these views? As far as we know, Gurland always ties his motives for his work to Christian love for the Jews, and there are no sources where he mentions any political motives for the mission work. Considering his life story, though, he would fit neatly into the general paradigm that Jewish converts were to be Germanized and cut any bonds to the Jewish people. Not only had he been living and studying in Berlin, he also made sure that his daughter had a German upbringing. His later marriage with Helene von Drachenfels, as well as his prominent position in Mitau, seems to confirm the pattern.

However, we also know that his educational background and his reluctance to join the resistance against Russification led to some frustration with him among the Baltic German clergy. At the beginning of the 1890s, the relationship between Gurland and some of the leadership of the Lutheran church in Kurland had become rather cold. While Helene Gurland in 1907 explains this development by referring to different personalities, misunderstandings and Gurland's reluctance towards the Baltic German resistance to Russification, his son Rudolf as well as the obituary in *St. Petersburger* refer to the different educational backgrounds of the former rabbi/seminarian and the university theologians in Kurland.[429] Fauerholdt, however, seems to think the frustrations were due to the fact that Gurland's cultural integration into Baltic society was incomplete. For some of the clergy and church authorities Gurland was neither fish nor fowl, as he never was regarded as truly assimilated into Baltic German society.[430] However, that Gurland's Jewish background became a problem for him in Kurland does not mean that he was a victim of anti-Semitism, which does not seem to have been widespread in the Baltic provinces at the time.[431] Still, Gurland was aware of the existence of this movement, as his positive remarks on Jewish nationalism and the Zionist movement function as arguments against anti-Semitic claims about the Jewish character.[432]

429. Bitter and Gurland, *Unsichtbare kirche*, 23.
430. Fauerholdt, "National-Jüdiches Christentum," 23.
431. Laserson, "The Jews and the Latvian Parliament," 98; Šteinmanis and Anders, *History of Latvian Jews*, 33.
432. See above 4.3.2.3 [x-ref].

While Gurland's relationship to the leading strata in the Baltic German churches seems to have become somewhat awkward and ambivalent, he developed friendships with significant members and leaders of the Paschowittes, the movement of Russian Protestant revivalists between the 1870s and WWI. Gurland's contact with revivalist Protestantism was not new; after all, Faltin as well as Delitzsch were associated with this tradition in a neo-Orthodox Lutheran context. In addition, Gurland's friend and penpal from the time he studied in Berlin, Max Besser, was working with Professor Friedrich August Tholuck in Halle, who exercised much influence on Protestant pietism and revivalist circles. The Paschowittes, however, were spirituality associated with the English Free Church, and were regarded with suspicion by the Russian regime. Helene Gurland claims that Gurland not only felt sympathy with Paschkow, but also met him and corresponded with him when he was in exile. According to *IzW*, for Gurland personal love for the Savior was so crucial that differences in liturgy and "minor matters" (probably theological differences) did not disturb him.[433] The same reference mentions that Gurland cooperated with persecuted Stundists (possibly also Baptists, who were close to the Stundists) in and around Odessa, just like Paschkow.[434] Both Russian Stundists and Baptists made efforts to reach Jews and had Christian Jews in their ranks, also in the Odessa area (like Julius Feinstein, who was a member of the Baptist church in Odessa). Rabinowitz also had some correspondence with Pasckhow in the 1880s, and in 1913 the Stundists for some time used Rabinowitz's hall in Kishinev for their own meetings.[435]

In April 1884, the Russian authorities took action to suppress the evangelical movements. The leaders were exiled, and Paschkow died in Rome in 1902. Notably, these actions were supported by the Baltic

---

433. Gurland, *IzW* (1911), 181, 207.

434. Originally a movement focusing on Bible-reading and a Christian lifestyle within the Russian Orthodox Church in southern Russia and Ukraine in the 1860s and '70s, in the last decades before 1905 the Stundists became an underground movement due to increased persecution by the church and political authorities. The Paschowites had several members in central positions who often tried to help some of the Stundists. It is possible that the visits by princess Lieven and others in Odessa were not only to the Gurland family, but also to keep in touch with local Stundists. Hebly, *Protestants in Russia*, 49–61; and Diedrich, *Siedler Sekterier*, 149.

435. Kjær-Hansen, *Joseph Rabinowitz*, 216.

German leadership, which feared Baptist influence.[436] According to Diedrich, some of the reasons for this move were political, as some feared that the democratic organization of the movement would strengthen the opposition to the Baltic German hegemony, just like the traditional Moravian movement had done.[437] However, Gurland was not alone in his support for these groups in the Baltics. As the evangelical movement now took the character of an underground movement until the Toleration Act of 1905, Gurland's friend Princess Lieven became a central figure for the groups of revivalists.[438]

In short, there is no doubt that Gurland identified significantly with the German and Baltic German culture and way of life after his conversion, and seems to have encouraged his children to socialize within this context without any bonds to his own Jewish background. This affiliation to German culture nevertheless had its limits, as he never associated with the Baltic German patriots or was fully accepted by everyone in the fellowship of pastors. In addition, he openly supported evangelical groups that were regarded with suspicion by Russian as well as Baltic German authorities, which cannot have reduced the tensions in his ambivalent relationship with the Baltic German community.

Gurland's Relation to the Mission Societies

As described above, Gurland had few difficulties in cooperating with revivalists of different denominational flavors. Nevertheless he claimed affection for mission societies with a certain Lutheran profile, and he does not seem to have found their traditional mission strategies problematic. In his job application to the Scandinavian-American *Sionsforeningen for Israel* (Zion Union for Israel) in 1891, Gurland describes his own preferences regarding different mission societies: "(I) would prefer to stand in your honourable Zion Union instead of a service with a Jewish mission in England or Germany, wherefrom I already have got requests."[439] Given that he cooperated closely with the Bible work of the Mildmay Mission in Russia for 18 years (from 1887 to his death in 1905), this statement is puzzling. Gurland does not say what he finds wrong with the British or German societies, but praises the impression he has gotten about the

---

436. Meyer, *Zinzendorf*, 95.
437. Diedrich, *Siedler Sekterier*, 98.
438. Hebly, *Protestants in Russia*, 64.
439. Waldeland, *Jøderne og Jødemisjonen*, 97.

spiritual character of the American society. In other words, Gurland did not challenge the mission strategy or methods of these societies, but was considering their theological profile. This may refer to the Lutheran pietism that characterized many of the Scandinavian congregations in the American Midwest. His statements could be an attempt to make himself more interesting to the society, although it is difficult to see the motives for this. As far as I can see, with his background and established network within the German and British missions, Gurland would probably not have any problems getting a job with most of them. After all, he had already rejected job offers from Lutheran mission societies in Germany several times.

However, as Gurland suggests that the Scandinavian-Americans can reduce his salary drastically, he appears eager to be employed. In addition to a preference for a Lutheran society, this move may also be related to his (or his family's) wish to stay in Kurland. As none of the established missions had any work in either Kurland or Riga, this suggestion may have served as an attempt to make them believe that this was the right moment to establish such a work.[440]

It seems that Gurland himself was not only comfortable doing the mission work Lucky so despised, but he even longed for it. His positive perspectives on Jewish nationalism did not lead him to challenge the methods of the mission, but he seems to have distanced himself from the idea that mission work was a way to rescue the Christian community from Jewish influence. For him, mission work was about leading Jews to Christ and the Christian church, not a political tool to maintain German hegemony in the Baltic provinces.

Lucky

THE MISSION SOCIETIES AND JEWISH SURVIVAL

What many observers found characteristic about Lucky was his opposition to Jewish mission societies. This conflict was not because he opposed Jews believing in Jesus, but because he thought traditional mission activity was only able to created *meshummads*; in other words, it became a national threat to the Jewish people as well as a social tragedy

---

440. In Glaser's survey of the Jewish mission societies in the twentieth century, the Baltic provinces of Russia do not seem to have had a high priority in these circles compared to Poland and the southern parts of the empire.

for the Jewish individual.[441] Lucky's criticism was directed at anything that undermined Jewish continuity and survival. This, of course, made him absolutely hostile against anti-Semitism. Lucky did not only react against Adolf Stöcker and the anti-Semitic newspaper *Reichsbote* (Berlin), he also protested fiercely when local German papers in Galicia showed anti-Semitic sentiments.[442] In fact, Lucky seems to have thought that the goals of anti-Semitism and traditional Christian mission work were two sides of the same coin. According to Wiegand, Lucky had come to the conclusion that mission work toward the Jews was just another version of anti-Semitism in the early 1870s, before he became a believer in Jesus. This was the result of a meeting he had with Joh. de Le Roi, who worked as a missionary for the Berlin society in Breslau at the time.[443] Although I have not found this parallel stated explicitly by Lucky, there is no doubt that he regarded traditional mission work as a threat to Jewish survival and continuity.

When a Jew was baptized he would officially become part of a church, but would usually not be welcomed in his new community—and in addition he would be rejected by his own people.[444] Nevertheless, Lucky was convinced that Jews had to accept Christ as Messiah. In short, the Jews needed Christ but not the mission. Jews living in the midst of Christian communities in Europe and America could read the Bible and participate in the local Christian community on their own initiative. The best thing the churches could do was to cultivate a good spiritual life in their own congregations, which could reveal the gospel to the Jews among them.[445] According to Daland, this was not to be understood as a debunking of Christian mission work in general, but of sending paid missionaries to work among Jews where there were Christians all around them, i.e. "in enlightened Christian lands." Sending missionaries to places like Southeastern Europe was something else, as these were "compact

---

441. Dalman, "Falsche Wege," 163. Lucky was particularly targeting British missions, possibly because of their dominance among missions to the Jews before WWII.

442. Weidauer, "Erindringer," 177.

443. Wiegand, "Chajim Jedidjah Lucky," 42.

444. After observing what happened with most baptized Jews in Galicia, Weidauer shared Lucky's view, stating that when a person was ripped out of the Jewish nation it would be wrong to name this activity "Jewish mission" (Weidauer, "Erindringer," 179–80).

445. Wiegand, "Chajim Jedidjah Lucky," 56.

centers of talmudic Judaism, into which neither a true Christianity nor the light and spirit of recent times has penetrated."[446]

Consequently, Lucky considered it an absolute trespass for him to be employed by any mission, and even avoided working as a teacher at non-Jewish institutions.[447] While traditional Jews regarded a public *baptism* as the ultimate break with the Jewish people (see Isaac Lichtenstein), for Lucky this taboo was associated with the *missions*. Still, his position was seen as a paradox by most representatives of the Jewish missions. While the director of the Barbican Mission, Rev. Christlieb T. Lipshytz, regarded Lucky as a faithful coworker, he nevertheless claimed that he knew no one who had fought against the methods of the mission societies as much as Lucky.[448] The question is how Lucky, who even found his attachment to the Berlin Society in the early 1890s unbearable, could put up with a situation where he worked as a traditional missionary for Pohlmann in Romania in the period 1885–1886, and for more than a decade was willing to help missionaries in Galicia, people who became his close friends.[449]

There is reason to think that Lucky would distinguish between formal and informal relations to a mission society. Due to the nature of Pohlmann's work in New York, Lucky's mission work in Romania was probably based on the personal relationship and mutual trust between Pohlmann and Lucky, and not organized formally under a mission board or a similar official entity. Indeed, it is difficult to see how Pohlmann's church was able to pay a missionary at all. After all, Pohlmann's congregation appears to have been a fellowship of poor immigrants with very limited resources, not even able to pay their pastor regularly.[450] This way of organizing his work would be consistent with Lucky's strategies in relation to the SDB as well as to the Berlin Society. According to Dr. Main,

---

446. *The Peculiar People* 2 (1889) 194. In fact, *Edut* even defends Christian mission, and parallels it to the way non-Jews could become proselytes in the Old Testament; see "Book review," *Edut leIsrael* 1/8 (1888) 159.

447. According to Zöckler, Lucky rejected many offers of positions as a teacher or professor in order not to be associated with opportunists (Zöckler, "Christian Theophilus Lucky," 7).

448. Velthuysen, "Christian Theophilus Lucky," 196.

449. Kjær-Hansen, "On Lucky's Whereabouts," 18.

450. It is possible that one of the reasons for Lucky to return to New York was the end of money for his work. Another would probably be to take up the plans for the periodicals with his friends in SDB.

a Seventh Day Baptist who supported Lucky, Lucky preferred financial support in the form of sporadic donations, not a regular salary. Likewise, he wanted to give informal reports instead of regular reports to a mission board. Naturally, the mission societies found this way of organizing mission work difficult to accept. In fact, Lucky's preferences appear to have made the mission boards suspicious about his motives.[451]

At any rate, Lucky never avoided contact with missionaries or mission societies as such, as long as he could be regarded as a partner. What was crucial for Lucky was whether the connection to missions or churches would undermine Jewish independence and Jewish continuity, or let Jewish Christians remain Jewish. This is probably one of the reasons why Lucky did not see any conflict between being a friend to missionaries and guiding them in their work, and still being an enemy of the mission societies. As long as he felt that the personal relationships were characterized by mutual respect, he was happy with the situation, even when dealing with missionaries who did not share his views, like Gisle Johnson. Another reason was probably that these friendships gave him an opportunity to try to influence the thinking in the mission societies. These efforts, however, led to frictions that eventually led to direct or indirect accusations of heresy against him (see below).

Mission Strategy: Protecting the Jews against the Missions, or Protecting the Missions against Lucky?

What Lucky was looking for was to create acceptance for the Jewish-Christian movement he expected in the near future. This approach not only created much frustration with Lucky among the missions, but also

---

451. Randolph, "Christian Theophilus Lucky," 207–8. The conflicts between Lucky and the missions concerning how to organize the financial support for his work appear to have been part of the general difficulties when Jewish Christians initiated mission work to Jews in North America in the decades around 1900. These individuals usually organized their work in accordance with business customs in Eastern Europe, only to find themselves dependent on financial support from societies or churches with completely different expectations for handling money, stemming from European and American middle-class culture. Actually, antagonists of the Jewish missions demanded that the missions keep standards that were usually not common among freshly arrived Jewish immigrants. According to Ariel, many Jewish enterprises and associations in America as well as in Eastern Europe were run on a casual basis as far as bookkeeping was concerned. Jewish organizations therefore followed much the same pattern. For cultural reasons it was not easy to adapt to American middle-class standards when it came to organizing and administering an enterprise. See Ariel, *Evangelizing*, 72.

caused much strife between the mission societies and the individual missionaries themselves.

This struggle first manifested itself in the debate between Müller and Wiegand vs. Dalman, Strack and Löwen in the early 1890s.[452] According to Wiegand, the speeches by Faltin and Rabinowitz at the mission conference in Leipzig in 1895 initially were meant to follow up parts of that debate.[453] In 1904, P. L. Anacker accused Lucky's companion, Professor E. F. Ströter, of confusing Israel's future with the contemporary mission to the Jews.[454] In the last years before WWI, the Danish Mission was particularly troubled by conflicts surrounding Lucky, and in the period 1905-1906 its board had to deal with a conflict between their new missionaries in Prmyzel, Stephan and Petra Volf, and the society's other workers. Volf supported Lucky's views on Jewish mission, which among Danish friends of the Jewish mission was seen as an attack on the society's work, in particular the work of the Jewish Christian Philemon Petri in Copenhagen.[455]

Between 1910 and 1911, the controversy around Lucky seems to have reached its peak, culminating at the Eight International Jewish Mission Conference in Stockholm, June 7-9, 1911.[456] Here the key word appears to have been "Ebionitism." According to Weidauer, Lucky used this expression himself as a description of his way of life and poverty.[457] However, at the Stockholm conference it was the theological connotations of the term that were in focus: Did the strategy proposed by Lucky (and Waldemann) imply a Judaizing of Christianity? The controversy was related to Lucky's Declaration of Law-observing Hebrew Christians,

452. Kjær-Hansen, "Lucky and the Leipzig Program," 23-26.

453. Wiegand, "Chajim Jedidjah Lucky," 59.

454. Ströter, *Die Judenfrage und ihre göttliche Lösung* and Anacker, "Zu Prof. Ströter's Judenfrage," 33-39. Generally, the relationship between Ströter and Lucky invites further studies.

455. In 1914 Volf's successor, Emil Clausen, who apparently did not share Volf's sympathy for Lucky, complained in several letters to the mission board that Lucky acted like a "spy and poacher of our young Nathanaels," and confirms Schönberger's statement that Lucky works like a mole in the mission fields ("Lucky treibt Maulwurfsarbeit"). Whether Lucky knew of this label on himself is not clear, but it is interesting that his friend Wiegand affirms its use. See Kjær-Hansen, "Mrs. Petra Volf's Reminiscences," 28-31; and Wiegand, "Chajim Jedidjah Lucky," 48.

456. Kjær-Hansen, "Lucky and Waldmann's" 39-45; Kjær-Hansen, "Controversy about Lucky," 46-64.

457. Weidauer, "Erindringer," 167.

as well as the two papers on the issue presented by the Jewish convert and mission leader C. T. Lipshytz and pastor T. Lindhagen, chairman of the mission society in Sweden.

Lipshytz rejects the declaration, claiming that "it is possible to love Christ and also love the (Jewish) nation."[458] Referring to Rabinowitz, he states that to accept the declaration would be to lead Jewish converts away from authentic Christianity:

> For us, the missionaries, to cultivate Rabbinism is to neglect the duty of winning the Jews from the traditions of men, and of bringing them into definite association with the great Teacher as followers, disciples, brethren. Joseph Rabinowitz discovered this. The Jews suspected him while he spoke of "Christ our brother." When, however, he was baptized, everyone knew what he meant, and he was rightly regarded as a Christian out-and-out.[459]

For Lindhagen, the main reason for *supporting* the declaration was his fear that the assimilation of Jewish Christians would destroy the Jewish people.[460] The Christian church should follow the General Assembly of the Episcopal Church of the USA in 1907, and let the Jewish Christians follow their Christian liberty and let their children be circumcised.[461]

Kjær-Hansen suggests that the delegates at the conference suspected that the reason for the declaration was to hide Lucky's true agenda, namely to make Torah observance an obligation for Jewish believers, in spite of the declaration's insistence of the opposite.[462] In other words, the rejection of the declaration was due to the circumstances and not the content of the document itself. Otherwise, this decision in Stockholm would have been a complete debunking of the views virtually all of the societies present had supported since the early 1890s. Kjær-Hansen points out that since the days of Rabinowitz, whose work and person

---

458. Lipshytz, "Ebionitism," 71–77, 73–74.

459. Ibid, 77.

460. Lindhagen, "Is there Ebionitism," 78.

461. Ibid., 83.

462. Kjær-Hansen describes the reception of the declaration as "cold." For Wiegand, who had brought the declaration with him to the conference, this would probably be an understatement. Wiegand accuses the leaders of the conference of not letting the audience respond to the addresses by Lindhagen and Lipshytz. Wiegand had been given only five minutes to present and explain the proclamation, but there was not given room for any further discussion (Wiegand, "Die 8. Internationale Konferenz," 113).

were a significant reference in the declaration, the idea of Jewish-Christian congregations with voluntary Jewish law observance was generally accepted in these circles. The problem in Stockholm was that the majority did not trust Lucky.

Kjær-Hansen's theory appears to be confirmed by David Baron's attacks on Lucky's program in the *Scattered Nation*.[463] In this article, Baron quite directly accuses Lucky and his partner Philip Cohen for making observance of Jewish festivals, circumcision, a modified synagogue liturgy, and everything connected to Zionism into a biblical obligation for Jewish believers.[464] Baron has some sympathy for Lucky and Cohen as long as the agenda is understood as a reaction against traditional mission methods, whose main objective may appear to be to absorb and denationalize the Jews. However, the program for Torah observance described in the proclamation is unbiblical as well as a waste of time, as neither Lucky nor his Jewish followers had succeeded in reducing the opposition to Christ in the Jewish communities. In addition, it would lead many believers into a religion of merit. Despite repeated assurances from Lucky and his supporters that there is no thought of merit attached to this movement, Baron thinks there are nevertheless many Jews who will not understand this distinction between merit and pure national observance.[465]

Due to the absence of open debate in Stockholm, it is of course difficult to know whether Baron's opinion—that Lucky's position was a gateway for backsliding into Judaism—was representative for the participants at the mission conference. Lindhagen at least seems to have been aware of the suspicion about Lucky's agenda, as he refers to a statement from Lucky at a Jewish-Christian conference in Stanislau, in August 1903, to explain Lucky's intentions:

> I do not demand from my fellow-believers the complete and strict observance of all Jewish customs at any price. Here is my brother who says "We live in exile and are not our own masters, and though I would like to keep the entire ceremonial law, and all the more because I am a disciple of Jesus, I cannot do it. I am

---

463. Baron, *Messianic Judaism*, 418–32.

464. Baron is referring to the first issue of *The Messianic Jew*, published in 1910.

465. According to Baron, Lucky admitted to him that he preferred the maximum program, only adding the name of Jesus now and then into the traditional Jewish liturgy. See Baron, *Messianic Judaism*, 5, 15.

a soldier and must eat barrack fare. I must rest on Sunday for the sake of my daily bread." Well, he is my brother nevertheless. I do not judge his conscience, nor is he to let me be a conscience to him in the matter of meats, or of the Sabbath, all of which are only a shadow of that which we have the substance in Christ. On the other hand, another says "Because I believe in Christ therefore I give up the Sabbath." Well, he is not less acceptable to God on that account, and I do not despise him for it or condemn him. But I am sorry for him, and it hurts me to the depth of my heart because he too is a child of Israel and should help us to build up the walls of Jerusalem.[466]

In other words, the mission leaders did not need to fear Lucky as a threat to Christian liberty, as Lindhagen saw it. It is possible that the handling of the declaration, as well as Baron's article, are best understood in light of the general climate that was prevailing in Protestant missions around 1911. The conference in Stockholm was held the summer after the great world mission conference in Edinburgh, where the creation of national churches for new non-European Christians was one of the topics. It is probably no coincidence that the declaration refers to significant church leaders who at this conference argued for this cause.[467] In other words, the declaration not only tried to identify with the work of Rabinowitz, but placed itself in the mainstream ideology from Edinburgh. In this light the rejection of the declaration becomes even more remarkable.

However, concerning the nationalizing of churches, the history of Protestant missions also shows that there was a large gap between mission theory and practice. For the participants in Stockholm, the problem

---

466. Lindhagen, "Is there Ebionitism," 80.

467. Kjær-Hansen, "Lucky and Waldmann's 'Declaration,'" 43. As only 19 of the 1,215 official delegates at the Edinburgh conference were from the non-Western world (only one of them was from Africa, and about 1,000 were from Britain and Northern America), it might be surprising that the declaration refers to this conference as an argument for a Jewish national church. Nevertheless, the conference was consistent in its enthusiasm for indigenous mission workers and cultural diversity in the expression of the Christian faith. This positive approach to non-Western cultures was often associated with a theology held by several of the delegates that Christianity was a sort of fulfillment of other religions, in particular elite Hinduism, which was regarded as superseded by Christianity. Further, the conference encouraged the political powers to have the welfare of the native populations in the colonies as their primary concern. This enthusiasm, however, was based on contemporary theories of race, which also made mission leaders reluctant to work at establishing national and independent churches as such for decades later. Stanley, *The World Missionary*, 12, 207, 307.

was that a practical concretization of the ideology came alarmingly close. If the majority of the delegates shared the Eurocentrism common to the Protestant mission, the program in the declaration would put the missions in a delicate situation, forcing them either to reject not only the work of Rabinowitz but the signals from Edinburgh as well, or to accept a strategy they found unnatural.[468] Add the questions about heresy, and it is possible the leadership quite simply found it best to silence the matter altogether.

In short, Lucky's position in the Christian community, and in particular among the mission societies, seems to have been extremely ambivalent. His views on Jewish national continuity and nationalism made him despise traditional mission methods toward Jews as a sort of anti-Semitism, or at least as a destructive force that made Jewish Christians into non-Jews. From the early 1880s he nevertheless nurtured friendships and partnerships with missionaries and church leaders in the USA and Europe in an effort to evangelize Jews, but he tried to avoid any connection to mission societies or institutions that could threaten his feeling of independence. While he was able to inspire many in these societies to rethink and discuss their practices, he also stirred a lot of controversies between and within the mission societies. Finally, five years before his death, his efforts ended in the anti-climax in Stockholm, where his ideas were more or less neglected by the majority of the mission leaders and representatives.

Lichtenstein

The Jewish Guest

Although he identified with the New Testament and central Christian doctrines, Lichtenstein would not identify with the Christian community in the sense of joining a church. Nevertheless, he shared fellowship with several missionaries, particularly David Baron and C. A. Schönberger. That this caused confusion and frustration is quite understandable from the missions' point of view, as Lichtenstein's position was very atypical of most Jewish believers in Jesus. In the last decades before WWI a great number of Hungarian Jews were baptized; according to Glaser in 1898–1903 more than 2,000 baptisms were recorded.[469] This

---

468. Ibid., 307.

469. Of the 2,000, more than 1,400 became members of the Roman Catholic Church, the majority church in Austria and Hungary. Glaser, "A Survey," 119.

was, of course, mostly due to the ordinary assimilation process among Hungarian Jews, often related to intermarriage, but it nevertheless made Lichtenstein's situation very special.[470] Of the converts that converted for religious reasons, many of the most famous came from Hungary. The Presbyterian missionaries from Scotland dominated the efforts to evangelize the Hungarian Jews from 1839 to WWII, and their work had resulted in some important Jewish Christians like Alfred Edersheim, Alexander Tomoroy, G. R. Lederer, Bishop Joseph Scherschewski, and Israel and Adolf Saphir.[471] Generally, for decades the Scots tried to integrate the converts into the Reformed church, but Lichtenstein never seems to have considered this option for himself.[472]

The explanation was that Lichtenstein did not feel any connection to any established church, as he felt "they lacked the Jewish spirit," as Gjessing puts it.[473] In other words, Lichtenstein's desire to remain within the Jewish community in Hungary was not a formality but a matter of belonging and identification. Lichtenstein did not only reject the contemporary assimilation process that was taking place among Jews in Hungary and the rest of Central Europe, he wanted the Jewish community to be strengthened in its Jewish identity. Consequently, in the Christian community Lichtenstein to some extent seems to have wanted to be a guest, not a member.

In the Christian community the views on Lichtenstein differed quite a lot. In spite of the sympathy Lichtenstein won among some British missionaries, other prominent mission leaders would not even describe him as a true Christian. This seems to have been the case particularly among the German societies, and missionaries like Venetianer and Le Roi publically announced their skepticism about Lichtenstein. Although Lichtenstein in his three first booklets hails Jesus as the Jewish Messiah, as late as at the end of the 1890s Le Roi seems unwilling to accept him as an authentic Christian.[474] Not least, he was criticized by Rabinowitz, who could not accept Lichtenstein's views about being baptized. The topic of Lichtenstein's baptism was also in the annual report of the Free Church of Scotland in 1889, in a letter from Rabinowitz in which he

470. Ibid., 115.
471. Kool, *God Moves in a Mysterious Way*, 108.
472. Kovács, *The History*, 373.
473. Herman, "Den ungarske rabbiner Lichtenstein," 75–76.
474. Le Roi, *Geschichte*, 2:277.

criticized Lichtenstein for not being baptized like he was.[475] This letter was written before Lichtenstein's two meetings with Rabinowitz, which took place in Budapest in October 1891.[476]

However, his contacts and network of Christian leaders and missionaries was significant, and must have been known in the Budapest Jewish community. At the least, it was seen by the obituary in the *Jüdische Algemeine Zeitung* as an example of his transgression of boundaries. Generally, Lichtenstein seems to have had a much better relationship with the British missionaries than with the Germans. In a letter to Baron he comments on how he has experienced the spiritual atmosphere differently in Britain than in Hungary, but he does not elaborate further. It is tempting to think this feeling is connected to Lichtenstein's experience of Christianity as the civil religion in Hungary and Eastern Europe compared to the free-church networks in Britain.

One of the first missionaries who came in touch with Lichtenstein already in the mid-1880s was Moody, who encouraged him to publish the three first pamphlets in 1885/1886.[477] While Frank, the missionary in Hamburg, was important later, in the period after Lichtenstein's resignation until he moved to Budapest, the relationships with Baron and Schönberger seem to have been of most significance for him. From 1890 he was financially supported by Frank, and from 1892/1893 by the committee set up by Baron and Wilkinson in London. This committee was probably parallel to a similar committee for supporting Rabinowitz, which was established in 1887.[478] As in Rabinowitz's case, the committee supporting Lichtenstein had an unofficial character and was initiated as an ad-hoc enterprise, and the sponsors as well as the clients were without any formal responsibility for each other except for the things they had agreed on.

This way of organizing financial support was, for Rabinowitz as well as for Lichtenstein, an attempt to avoid being associated too strongly to the missions, giving them an opportunity to claim that they were independent. The same arrangement, in which the Jewish believer and Christian

---

475. Kjær-Hansen, *Joseph Rabinowitz*, 175.

476. Ibid., 174–75.

477. Andrew Moody, missionary for the United Free Church of Scotland and leader of its mission work in Hungary. Glaser, "A Survey," 119–21.

478. Dalman, "Theorie und Praxis," 118.

sponsors established a partnership instead of a mission society taking the individual on as an employed missionary, was also tried out by Lucky.[479]

In his obituary, Lichtenstein's friend David Baron also has some reservations about Lichtenstein's position. According to him, Lichtenstein's first writings show many defects in relation to Christian doctrine, and he claims that Lichtenstein never fully understood the parable about the new and old wine. However, Baron thought one could observe an increased understanding of Christian doctrine over the years.[480] When, after several years, Lichtenstein still did not want to join the group of prominent Jewish Christians, one can ask why the financial support did not decline. It is tempting to suggest that it must have been the close relationships between Baron, Schönberger and himself that kept the support from the committee going from 1893 to 1908.

True Christians are Philo-Semites

In contrast to Lucky, who joined the SDB but nevertheless attacked the mission work towards Jews, Lichtenstein never became a member of any church but never seems to have attacked the work of the missions. For the most part he seems to have regarded them, particularly the committee in London, as a resource for his own activities and people who were interested in the well-being of his people.[481] In spite of the increasing anti-Semitism and the Tisza Eszlar affair in 1882–1883, Lichtenstein does not dwell on anti-Semitism in his writings, except to claim that the Jews' true friends in combating anti-Semitism will be found among friends of the Christian mission. Several times he encourages his Jewish readers to admire the piety and attitude of true Christians, including the missionaries. Philo-Semites like Delitzsch, Lichtenstein claims, do not wish to turn the Jews away from their people, but rather to bring them to "Christ, as to Him in whom Jehova dwells, and who has appeared to

---

479. To establish such partnerships was an extraordinary way of organizing the work for the Jewish missions, but nevertheless this arrangement appears to have been met with understanding in Britain as well as Germany. The companionship between Löwen and Lucky from 1889 to 1892 was built on the same principles, and this was possibly the case also when he worked as a missionary for Pohlmann in Austria in 1885–1886. However, as Löwen points out, Lucky was troubled by what he found to be a sense of losing independence and perhaps also integrity with this solution. See Dalman, "Theorie und Praxis," 119.

480. Baron, "Rabbi Ignatz Lichtenstein," 256.

481. Lichtenstein, *The Points of Contact*, 9.

redeem his people; as to Him also in whom Faith, Hope, and Love, those three heavenly powers, which are the arteries of true Judaism, course together in their original source and heat."[482]

Still, associating himself officially with a mission society seems to have been a transgression of boundaries from which he would refrain. His contact with the missionaries seems to have been motivated by his personal need for support from and fellowship with other believers in Jesus, but also by the idea that when the Jewish people are in danger, the nation's best friends are found among the Christian missionaries.

The Relationship to Jewish-Christian Groups and Individuals

Introduction

In the following, I will discuss Gurland's, Lucky's and Lichtenstein's relationships or identification with other Jewish believers in Jesus who in different ways insisted that they were Jews. The relationships between these people were complex and characterized by a mixture of friendship, cooperation, enmity or no contact at all; sometimes the factor that could unite or split people was the question of Jewish identity and Christian faith, and at other times other issues were more relevant. Still, the fact that this more-or-less loose community or phenomenon existed makes it natural to relate Gurland, Lucky and Lichtenstein to each other as well as to other Jewish Christians in order to understand their ideas about being Jewish and believing in Jesus. These people were something Gurland, Lucky and Lichtenstein could identify with or reject, and I find it interesting to see what they said and did in this regard in light of Jewish identification and crossing of boundaries.

This means that I will focus on some Jewish Christians they related to—or were rejected by. Some of these were famous, at least within the circles of the mission societies, particularly Joseph Rabinowitz, David Baron and Yechiel Herschensohn-Lichtenstein.[483] I also discuss the

---

482. Lichtenstein, *An Appeal*, 17–19.

483. Yechiel Zevi (Hirschensohn/Herschensohn) Lichtenstein (1831–1912) had a Hasidic background in Jassay in Romania, and baptized himself in 1855. He married Rabinowitz's sister in Kishinev in 1878. For Hirschensohn-Lichtenstein Jewish Christianity would not make either Judaism or the Jewish people disappear into Christianity, but would rather revitalize Christianity. When Delitzsch and the *Zentralverein* established the *Institutum Judaicum* in Leipzig in 1885, Herschensohn-

relations between Gurland, Lucky and Isaac Lichtenstein themselves when natural. In cases where the sources say that Gurland, Lucky and Lichtenstein were in contact with an established fellowship of Jewish believers in Jesus (e.g., the Hebrew Christian Alliance), I include their attitude to such fellowships in the discussion. Finally, I pay attention to Gurland's, Lucky's and Isaac Lichtenstein's position in the debates about Torah observance for Jewish believers in Jesus and Jewish-Christian congregations, discussions that in a particular way focused on the relation to Jewish tradition, the Jewish community, Christian tradition and the Christian community at the same time.

Jewish Christians and Jewish-Christian Fellowships before WWI

Regarding the attitude and relation to Jewish-Christian (in an English-speaking context: Hebrew-Christian) fellowships as an identification marker, it must be emphasized that such groups were extremely marginal phenomena at the time, and the concept of Jewish-Christian *congregations* was more like a controversial vision than a reality in the century before WWI. Most Jewish Christians tried to live their lives in the Christian community within an established traditional church after they were baptized. Nevertheless, the idea of such fellowships was known. Particularly in the Anglo-Saxon context there were several attempts to build groups of Jewish Christians during the 19th century, although they apparently were all short-lived.[484] In his overview of the contemporary Messianic movement, Rich Robinson refers to at least ten unions or "brotherhoods" of Jewish Christians between 1823 and 1887, most of them in the USA.[485] Robinson claims that this phenomenon was, on the one hand, due to the cold shoulder Jewish believers could meet in the American churches, and on the other hand an assertion of Jewish identity among Jewish immigrants in the USA. According to Menachem Benhayim, Hebrew Christianity and Jewish nationalism were nurtured in the same environment. In a period of assimilation and disintegration of Jewish identity in the Western countries, combined with increasing

---

Lichtenstein became one of the lecturers, a post he kept until his death. Zipperstein, "Heresy," 212; Quiñónez, "An Introductionary," 79.

484. According to Schainker, in many places in Russia the converts maintained separate communities. However, this statement is not elaborated, and should be studied further. Schainker, "Imperial Hybrids," 25 n. 13.

485. Robinson and Rothstein, *The Messianic*, 40–47.

anti-Semitism, there was a strengthened recognition of the need for Jewish expression, both for religious and secular Jews. The same tendency took hold among Jewish Christians. Many accepted being part of the non-Jewish culture, but nevertheless many maintained a strong sense of having a Jewish background. In this period there emerged a minority of Jewish Christians who sought to maintain their place within the Jewish community, and saw the establishing of Jewish-Christian congregations and Torah observance as the key tool for this.[486]

The first fellowship of Jewish believers that was able to maintain some sort of continuity was the Hebrew Christian Alliance of Great Britain and later the Hebrew Christian Prayer Union. The alliance was established in 1866 by Dr. Carl Schwartz (d. 1870), and its members were Jewish Christians in the Church of England as well as in the British free churches. In 1882, the Hebrew Christian Prayer Union was formed to strengthen the spiritual fellowship between Jewish believers in different countries. At the end of the 1880s, the union had 536 members, including both Gurland and Lucky as well as Rabinowitz. Members of the society, who lived all over Europe as well as in America, promised to pray for the evangelization of the Jews on Saturdays, and in Britain they tried to arrange at least one meeting annually, on Yom Kippur.[487] In 1901, the Prayer Union merged with the Hebrew Christian Alliance. Generally these societies, both before and after 1901, focused on the ethnic identity of the members more than on discussions about Torah observance.

In the USA, however, the issue of Jewish law observance for Hebrew Christians was to become a matter of more significance. In 1901, Dr. E. S. Niles convened the "Hebrew Christian Conference" with 25 members in New England, where he advocated the voluntary observance of some rabbinic Jewish customs. Partly as a response to this initiative, in July 1903 in Mountain Lake, Maryland, a conference of Jewish believers opposing Niles established a committee led by the Jewish missionary Luis Meyer. The participants in the conference represented a variety of views on Torah observance, and the question of the observance of Jewish customs was raised at the meeting by the Jewish Episcopalian minister Mark Levy, who held that one should keep the commandments of the

---

486. Benhayim, "The Emergence," 49.
487. Le Roi, *Geschichte*, 2:350.

Pentateuch.[488] However, the vast majority of the participants rejected this proposal. This was partly due to theological reasons, and partly due to fear of resentment from their different denominations. Levy's view was instead supported by the Methodist missionaries in New York, Gaebelein and Ströter, as well as the Episcopal Church, which was later to issue a statement about Jewish Christians' right to Torah observance.[489]

On the European continent, the situation was even more difficult. The attempts to create Jewish-Christian fellowships (not to mention those who aimed to become congregations) were not only few, but also extremely dependent on the leaders.[490] When leaders like Joseph Rabinowitz, Lucky, and L. W. Horowitz died or left, the fellowships in Kishinev, Stanislau/Lemberg, and Braila disintegrated. In addition, the efforts were characterized by different theological and strategic profiles. While Lucky and his followers found the creation of Jewish-Christian fellowships and continued Torah observance as being two sides of the same coin, Rabinowitz would stress his Jewish ethnic background but be more light-handed when it came to Torah observance.

Gurland

THE LEIPZIG STRATEGY

At the mission conference in 1895 in Leipzig, issues like Jewish-Christian congregations and Torah observance for Jewish believers were discussed with much intensity. Here both Gurland and Lichtenstein participated,

---

488. The different views on Torah observance and assimilation later led to the establishing of two national bodies of Hebrew Christians in the USA: the HCAA (today MJAA) in 1915, and the IHCA (today IMJA) in 1925. However, these bodies never included more than a minority of all Jewish believers in the USA. In other words, most of them joined established churches. Robinson and Rothstein, *The Messianic Movement*, 47. In 1903 Mark Levy also founded the Society for the Advancement of the Gospel of the Circumcision in Virginia, Richmond; Strack, *Yearbook* (1906), 118.

489. Ariel, *Evangelizing*, 48.

490. Already in 1740 the leader of the Moravians, Count Zinzendorf, agitated for Jewish-Christian fellowships within the church. However, the aspirations for a Jewish-Christian church in the nineteenth century were also connected to developments in Palestine. Particular attention, and disappointment, was given to the Jewish-Christian Anglican bishop of Jerusalem between 1846 and 1849. Some years later Israel Bick (or Pick) also did not succeed in his efforts for Jewish Christianity in Palestine; Dalman, "Theorie un Praxis," 118.

as well as Lucky's closest German friends, Wiegand and Zöckler.[491] In spite of detailed minutes from the heated discussion at the conference, the outcome was not very substantial if one is looking for what Gurland and Lichtenstein thought about the issue, except that both of them seem to have been rather skeptical and cautious of Wiegand's lecture.[492] Wiegand argued that baptized Jews should be encouraged to stay within the Jewish society they belonged to, instead of being assimilated into their Gentile surroundings. The main argument for this strategy was that the traditional loss of Jewish identity also made the converts lose their opportunities to witness about their faith to their fellow Jews.

Almost all the Jewish-Christian participants, including Gurland, opposed Wiegand's view in a statement they made together. Except for this, Gurland is not reported to have said a word during the debate itself. This behavior resembles his silence regarding these issues in *IzW* as well as in the rest of the source material. Still, considering his views on Zionism and Israel's expected salvation, Gurland seems to expect the Jewish people's continued existence after its future national conversion to Christ. The question is what strategy he found most compatible with these ideas, particularly in relation to the contemporary strategic debate in the German, British and American missions.

Between 1888 and 1890, the *Zentralverein* and the Leipzig institute worked out a new strategy for Jewish mission: Instead of sending out missionaries to work directly with Jews, one should build up congregations for Germans in Eastern Europe that would be attractive for Jews. Those Jews who wanted to convert should be encouraged to stay in their Jewish environment and thereby maintain their Jewish identity as much as possible. Although this strategy was in accordance with Delitzsch's ideals, it became particularly associated with the new leadership of William Faber in the early 1890s, as well as with Lucky's ideas.[493] This strategy led to much criticism from within the *Zentralverein* as well as from other societies. Dalman withdraw from the society for some time, while Le Roi held the strategy to be a German version of what he called

---

491. The questions had been discussed since the late 1880s, in the wake of the Jewish-Christian fellowship in Kishinev established by Joseph Rabinowitz.

492. See the minutes by Dalman in *Die Allgemeine Konferenz für Judenmission*, 3, 16–22. Dalman was not regarded as a neutral agent on these issues, as he had opposed parts of Lucky's agenda since the early 1890s.

493. Skarsaune, *Israels venner*, 185.

the British "obsession" with philo-Semitism.⁴⁹⁴ Although Le Roi and Dalman did not deny the possibility of a Jewish-Christian church in the future, their opinion was that contemporary mission work should focus on the individual.

Although Gurland never explicitly revealed what he thought about this debate, the fact that he took a position as a traditional missionary in Riga and Odessa at least shows that he did not reject traditional mission work. Although this choice was partly due to other factors such as his declining health and the conflict in Mitau, Gurland obviously did not believe that the new Leipzig strategy was the only solution for Jewish mission.

Jesus-Believing Jews

It is a puzzling fact that Gurland refrains from taking sides in the most controversial debate among the Jewish mission societies in the last 20 years of his life. The only text I have found in which he possibly addresses this controversy is the following brief note from his reflections on the movements among the Jews in the last decades before his death:

> Many well-educated and judicious Jews, who speak of Jesus and his teaching with great respect, see in the contrast between Christianity and Judaism only a struggle of civilization that will

---

494. Le Roi, *Geschichte*, 1:175, 290 and 2:386. While Le Roi and SDB held Lucky to be the source behind this new strategy, Skarsaune points out how the leaders of the *Zentralverein* had begun the reorientation already before Lucky returned to Europe. However, at that point *Edut leIsrael* and *The Peculiar People* had been published, and read, for months. In Leipzig, the leadership of the *Zentralverein* was enthusiastic about *Edut* and *The Peculiar People*, although the society would suffer internal conflicts due to this profile later. Dalman, "Missionsrundschau," 59. If Lucky was not the force behind this strategy from the start, he nevertheless was soon identified with it, as the *Zentralverein* found significant support from Lucky, practically as well as ideologically. Still, Le Roi does not debunk the idea completely. He also refers to some attempts to establish Jewish-Christian fellowships in the USA, like Jacob Freshman's founding of a Jewish-Christian congregation in New York in 1882; also Andersen, *Israelsmissionen i New York*, 40–57. Other examples are the Jewish-Christian fellowships in 1867 and 1868 in New York and Chicago, which employed J. Lotka as their missionary. This phenomenon is, according to Le Roi, due to what he describes as the peculiar social situation in America. Le Roi, *Geschichte*, 2:388; and Skarsaune, *Israels venner*, 185.

When describing Schönberger, the only fault Le Roi finds is the philo-Semitism that characterized him, and his engagement in the opposition to the growing anti-Semitism: "The strangest glorification is so strong in the British society, that only a few of its workers can get away untouched by it" (Le Roi, *Geschichte*, 2:279).

end with the victory of truth, but what does it help if a man admits that he sees in Jesus the greatest prophet, moral teacher and martyr?! If Jesus was not the son of the living God then he was a blasphemer who deserved death. Only one thing or the other is possible![495]

As the context deals with Jewish nationalism, I tend to believe that Gurland here refers to the interest in Jesus one could find among the early Zionists. Still, it is also possible that he refers to the groups "New Israel" and "the Spiritual Biblical Brotherhood," led by Jacob Priluker and Jacob Gordin in southern Russia in the 1880s.

Sometimes the sources explicitly reveal that Gurland was familiar with the existence of Russian Jewish believers in Jesus, baptized or not, who stuck to the Jewish tradition. On one of his journeys he had an encounter with an old rabbi who had lost his whole family; the last daughter had also become a Christian at the hospital in Riga. Living more or less like an eremite, he confessed his faith in Jesus and observed Jewish customs like the talith when he prayed.[496] However, already in the 1870s he also describes a disappointing experience with a group of Christianity-inspired Jews in Vilnius. The group's leader was a certain rabbi named Eliah Moische, with whom Gurland had been corresponding for some time before he was invited to come down and discuss the relationship between Christianity and Judaism with them, as well as their plans to emigrate to America and establish a Jewish-Christian community.[497] The meeting turned into a dispute about millennialism and

495. Gurland, *IzW* (1911), 202. "Viele gebildete und urteilsfähige Juden, die mit Ehrfurcht von Jesus und seiner Lehre sprechen, sehen in dem Gegensatz zwischen Christentum und Judentum nur einen Kulturkampf, der mit dem Siege der Wahrheit enden muss. Aber was hilft es, dass zugeben wird, Jesus sei der grösste Prophet, Sittenlehrer und Märtyrer gewesen, war er nicht der Sohn Gottes, so ist er ein Gotteslästerer gewesen und hatte den Tod verdient. Hier gibt es kein entweder-oder." The last sentence in the English manuscript (p. 218), is not a correct translation of the German "Hier gibt es kein entweder-oder"; these versions actually contradict each other. However, as the English version seems more consistent with the rest of the cited paragraph, I believe that the sentence from *IzW* 1911 is the result of a spelling mistake in the German ("ein" and "kein").

496. Gurland, *Erlebnisse*, 10.

497. Although not stated explicitly, this group appears to have been some sort of farming project. Such agricultural colonies for Jewish immigrants in the USA were initiated as part of the attempt by established American Jews to distribute the newcomers over the country. As the initiative was taken by American Reform Jews, it is possible that the Russian group in Gurland's narrative considered the colony "Jewish-Christian"

whether it was wise to immigrate to America or not. Based on references like Isaiah 2:4 and Zachariah 3:8, Moische proclaimed that the future messianic kingdom and the millennium would begin from this community. Further he claimed he had Christian friends in England who were willing to support the project. According to Gurland, the main motivation seemed to be the wish to emigrate, and all his warnings against the project were in vain.[498] Gurland summarized his own view on the issue like this: "The in itself correct and comforting hope of Israel's conversion and future glorious kingdom must, however, by honest Jews who want to be saved, be regarded as a minor matter."[499] When he finally challenges the participants on the need for baptism and repentance, he is rejected as "ein wahrer Goi" ("a true Gentile"). At the end of his report he relates this circle to another group of Jewish emigrants from Romania who soon thereafter left for Nebraska.

In spite of his pessimism about the group's project, I find it interesting that Gurland seems to have been theoretically open to the idea of some sort of Jewish-Christian congregational structure already in the 1870s. At least he was willing to discuss the matter with them. Why, then, did he not involve himself in the debate in the 1880s and 1890s on Jewish-Christian congregations and observance of Jewish customs? Gurland never used his many opportunities to criticize or comment on the idea of Jewish-Christian congregations, and I believe that in these circumstances some consideration of Gurland's network is relevant to explaining this silence. Gurland probably chose to be quiet due to his relationships with Rudolf Faltin and Joseph Rabinowitz. In a brief commentary *IzW* reveals that Gurland had become friends with Rabinowitz.[500] The fact that Gurland's spiritual father had been having a fight with Rabinowitz for years, since 1887, just around the corner in Odessa, is not mentioned, and we can only guess why.[501] One explanation can be that Faltin was still alive in 1907 when *IzW* was published, and Gurland's

---

for this reason. Rom, *The American Jewish Attitude*, 105.

498. Gurland, *Bericht*, 20–26.

499. Ibid., 22. "Die an und für sich gewiss berechtigte und trostreiche Hoffnung auf Israels Bekehrung und zukünftige Reichsherrlichkeit muss doch dem einzelnen ernstgesinnten Juden, der selig werden will, als Nebensache erscheinen."

500. Gurland, *IzW* (1911), 197.

501. Kjær-Hansen, *Joseph Rabinowitz*, 132.

widow would probably not want to irritate the elderly Faltin if she had material about Gurland that he would have found embarrassing.

However, there were probably also more practical reasons for this friendship. In Odessa Gurland was employed by the Mildmay Mission, which was also Rabinowitz's most significant sponsor, and the year after Rabinowitz's death Gurland was appointed superintendent for all the Mildmay Mission's workers in the Russian Empire. Although Rabinowitz was independent, his economic and spiritual connections with Wilkinson and the Mildmay Mission would probably make it interesting for both Gurland and Rabinowitz to keep in touch. Openly supporting either Faltin or Rabinowitz could therefore not only destroy some of Gurland's personal relationships, but also put a strain on his relations to the Mildmay Mission as well as some of the German mission circles. Kjær-Hansen claims that Faltin caused problems for Rabinowitz in relation to the Russian authorities. At the same time, several of the mission societies and central figures of the missions, like Delitzsch and Dalman, continued to support both him and Faltin.[502]

Considering Gurland's Christocentric and ecumenical profile, it is quite possible that Rabinowitz and Gurland had sympathy for each other in spite of Gurland's work as a traditional missionary. From Gurland's perspective, relating to Rabinowitz would not be much different from relating to other evangelistic Protestant movements in Russia, like the Stundists and Paschowittes.

A practical consequence of the friendship between Gurland and Rabinowitz was that Jews from Kishinev who wanted to be baptized after Rabinowitz's death in 1899, came to Gurland in Odessa.[503] We do not know the number of these, but can assume that they are included in the statistics of his work, although Gurland never says so. In addition to this, he clearly has a positive attitude to the growing Jewish nationalism in Russia. In fact, Gurland appears to have been more sympathetic towards Zionism than Rabinowitz. When Rabinowitz publically announced his newfound sympathy for Jesus in the early 1880s, it was a result of his disappointment with Hovevei Zion and the settlement movement when visiting Palestine in 1882. In some ways Rabinowitz seems to have rejected the Zionist approach as a way of redemption for the Jewish people, at least before Herzl's *Der Judenstat*, and instead re-

---

502. Ibid., 115, 139.
503. Gurland, *IzW* (1911), 197.

placed it with a Christianity for Jews. The spiritual redemption of Israel had to come first, and eventually God would let the people return to their land.[504] Although ambivalent to the movement, Gurland did not share this pessimism about Zionism, but instead integrated the movement into his Christian worldview and eschatology.

In addition to his friendship with Rabinowitz, Gurland developed a warm relationship with the Ukrainian Jewish couple Julius and Esther Feinstein. Julius and Esther had become believers in Jesus several years before Julius was employed by the Mildmay Mission and became Gurland's assistant in Odessa. As Esther and Julius had tried to make *aliyah* in the 1880s, this tells us that they probably were influenced by Hovevei Zion long before they met Gurland. In his report to the Mildmay Mission, Julius Feinstein is particularly concerned about how well Gurland has been treating him. If there were differences of opinion between Feinstein and Gurland on Jewish nationalism and Jewish identity, this does not seem to have been a hindrance for their friendship, and it is certainly possible that this relationship included some mutual understanding on these things. After all, they were both witnesses to Rabinowitz's work in Kishinev and southern Russia, and these questions must have been touched upon between them.

In spite of his silence on matters like Jewish-Christian fellowships and the ongoing debate within the mission societies, Gurland seems to have been rather cold towards Lucky's agenda and the Leipzig strategy, preferring a role as a missionary working for a mission society. On the other hand, he was willing and able to establish friendly relations and even cooperate with persons and groups that tried to work out ways to remain Jewish while believing in Jesus. This suggests that he was open to the idea that Jewish Christians could maintain their Jewish identity, at least more than had traditionally been the case until then.

Lucky

Lucky's Relation to Other Jewish Christians

Lucky's relationships with other Jewish Christians seem to have been ambivalent. His key principle was that Jewish converts do not have to become renegades or be assimilated. From this perspective he would regard some converts as renegades, and Lucky could have a critical and

---

504. Skarsaune, *Israels venner*, 168.

bitter attitude towards proselytes/converts who had left the Jewish people.[505] In particular, he found the marriages some of them had made with non-Jewish women repulsive. On the other hand, others were described as heroes.[506] In particular, Lucky presents two individuals as pioneers and models for Jewish Christians: Israel Pick (Bick) and Yechiel Herschensohn-Lichtenstein.[507]

Israel Pick was born in Senftenberg in Bohemia, and was baptized on January 1, 1854, by the minister and missionary Daniel Edwards in Breslau. He had a difficult childhood and turned to pantheism. He later became involved in a synagogue in Bucharest, where he began arguing for a Jewish-Christian union, without finding support from any camp. In 1853, he left the congregation and spent time in Amsterdam and Berlin until he was baptized in Breslau. Shortly after his conversion, he published several pamphlets and books on Jewish-Christian issues: *Ein Wort an mein Volk: Israel hat eine Idee zu tragen, die letzte Lüge der sterbenden Synagoge* (Breslau 1854), *Der Stern aus Jakob* (autobiography, Barmen 1856), *Die sterbende Jüdin im Gitschiner Spital, Kol Nidre Nacht, Ist kein Arzt da?* and *Israel und dessen Propheten*. Pick argued enthusiastically for the restoration of Israel, and migrated to Palestine in the 1850s. Here he became the leader of a small group of followers who called themselves "Amenites." In 1859 he disappeared, and was presumed dead. The several references to Pick's efforts in *Edut* are not very detailed, but it is clear that Lucky somehow wanted to establish his journal in the tradition of Pick.[508]

Edut is more substantial in its enthusiastic references to Herschensohn-Lichtenstein. The question is how this enthusiasm fits with Löwen's narrative about a conflict between Lucky and Herschensohn-Lichtenstein on Lucky's return to Europe in the summer of 1889.[509] The alleged bitterness is difficult to trace in sources other

---

505. Zöckler, "Judentum und Christentum," (1892) 214.

506. Ibid., 104.

507. "Word to the Reader," 5–6.

508. Le Roi, *Geschichte*, 2:279, 318–19. Was Löwen's and *Edut*'s address in Lemberg only a curious coincidence? According to the headlines the address was "J. Pick, Copernicusstrasse 4, Lemberg." Considering Lucky's playing with words and names, it is possible this was a part of his attempt to be associated with Pick. On the other hand, several of Israel Pick's family became associated with the missions in Galicia and Romania. See Anonymous, "News," 280; and Le Roi, *Geschichte*, 2:279–80.

509. Löwen, "Christian Theophilus Lucky," 17. According to Löwen, Lucky was

than Löwen, and particularly in the Hebrew journal the references to Herschensohn-Lichtenstein generally are positive. In *HaEdut*'s review of Yechiel Lichtenstein's commentary on the New Testament (published by Dalman in Leipzig in 1897), there are no signs of any hard feelings between Lucky and Lichtenstein. In fact, the Jewish spirit of Jesus-believing Jews, and in particularly that of Herschensohn-Lichtenstein, is claimed to far surpass what is found in contemporary Jewish communities.[510] For spiritually longing Jews, Lichtenstein's commentary is regarded as the ultimate advisor. Lucky seems to be particularly grateful for the way Lichtenstein combats anti-Judaistic interpretations of the New Testament:

> He desires to prepare an arsenal of weapons for every Jew who is a disciple of Yeshua, so that he can stand firm if he is attacked by the opponents of Yeshua who base their claims on the books of the NT . . . He has taken burnt dust from the Talmud and midrashim and other sources and turned it into bullets and put them in his revolver and put the barrel into the hands of Jewish disciples of Yeshua so they can walk confidently in their paths and not be afraid of those who rise up against them to accuse them.[511]

Still, some sort of tension is revealed. Lucky blames Lichtenstein's advisors and publisher (in particular Gustaf Dalman) for forcing Lichtenstein to make the commentary too short. He seems to regard Lichtenstein as some sort of prisoner under Dalman: "When will the day come when writers will do their work according to the guidance of their spirit and not in accordance with those who stand outside the camp?"[512] In other words, Lucky laments Herschensohn-Lichtenstein's situation of being employed by the institute in Leipzig. This, however, does not necessarily confirm Löwen's story about personal strife between Lucky and Herschensohn-Lichtenstein. The revealing of such private controversy is perhaps not to be expected in a journal, but as *Edut* was not very irenic when discussing similar issues, this explanation does not seem sufficient.

---

particularly upset about the fact that Herschensohn-Lichtenstein had married a non-Jewish woman.

510. "What a Difference There Is Between . . . ," 10.
511. "Book review: Lichtenstein's commentary on the New Testament," 11–15; 14.
512. Ibid.

In other words, the relationship between Herschensohn-Lichtenstein and Lucky appears somewhat obscure.

Regarding Lucky's connections with other leading Jewish Christians, his relationship with Rabinowitz is the most striking due to its rapid shift in attitude. After his meetings with Faber and Delitzsch in Leipzig in July 1889, Lucky stayed with Joseph Rabinowitz in Kishinev for two months. In a letter from Lucky, quoted by Daland (dated September 3, in Kishinev), he explains his stay with Rabinowitz: 1. He wants to establish congregations using the one in Kishinev as a model; 2. He wants to convince Rabinowitz to abolish the observance of Sunday, as the congregation observes both the Sabbath and Sunday.[513]

However, in the decades following the meeting between Lucky and Rabinowitz in Kishinev, we do not hear much about Rabinowitz. While *The Peculiar People* in 1889 is happy to publish Rabinowitz's articles of faith in Hebrew and English, the magazine for the next decade is almost silent about the work in Kishinev.[514] However, in a book review in 1893, Daland reveals his own lack of sympathy with Rabinowitz:

> All he tells us about Rabinowitz is rather mythical than historic. Rabinowitz is not leader of a great Jewish Christian community; he has not even a small Jewish Christian church; he has never had a real following, in the sense that Pastor Kruger and other Gentile Christians understand it. Rabinowitz and his household are baptized Christians, and are registered in Russia as Christians of the Reformed Church, and that is all. For national Jewish Christianity there is no perceptible gain. The idea of remaining Jews has died out even in the family of Rabinowitz himself.[515]

In fact, Daland's verdict on Rabbi Lichtenstein is no better: "The 'movement' of Rabbi Lichtenstein, of Tapio Szele, amounts next to nothing. Rabbi Lichtenstein appears to be about to have as little influence as Rabinowitz."[516] The reason for this lack of further contact may lie with Rabinowitz or Lucky himself, or most likely a combination of both. Rabinowitz never did follow Lucky's advice about abolishing Sunday observance.

---

513. Daland, "Brother Lucky's Travels," 625.

514. See Rabinowitz's creed for the "Sons of the New Covenant"/ "New Testament Israelites" in Anonymous, "A Jewish Christian Confession of Faith," 232–39.

515. *The Peculiar People* 6 (1893) 165.

516. Ibid., 166.

Paradoxically, while Lucky was able to establish cordial fellowship with non-Jewish missionaries and ministers, he seems to have failed to do the same with Jewish believers. He was able to create a great personal network among the mission societies in Europe and in the USA, which were both inspired and/or provoked by him, but he never did the same among the most prominent Jewish believers who shared many of his views from the start.[517] We do not even know if he ever met Rabbi Lichtenstein, and the relationship between himself and Yechiel Lichtenstein appears to have become ambivalent. Neither do we know if Lucky ever met Paul Levertoff or Mark Levy, and we hear nothing about them in *The Peculiar People, Edut* or other sources related to Lucky.[518]

Another question is why, during his years in New York, Lucky did not associate with some of the congregations or fellowships there which consisted of Jewish Christians, namely Jacob Freshman's Hebrew Christian congregation or the Jewish Christian Leopold Cohen's mission work. Instead he publically denounces the work by Jacob Freshman. Although within a Methodist tradition, the congregation was non-denominational and related to the Apostolic Creed in its statement of faith. In addition to arranging services on Sundays, there were prayer

---

517. The same can probably be said about Rabinowitz, who in addition to rejecting the authenticity of Isaac Lichtenstein's conversion, appears not to have had much contact with Herschensohn-Lichtenstein after his own conversion, in spite of their being brothers-in-law.

518. In his article about Philip Cohen and Lucky in *The Scattered Nation* in 1911, Baron refers to at least one discussion between him and Lucky. This may have taken place during his travels in Eastern Europe (if not by correspondence). On these journeys he was accompanied by Levertoff, who worked with Baron between 1901 and 1909, and it is quite possible Lucky and Levertoff met on some of these occasions. We know however, that that they disagreed on some issues, and the relationship was at times strained: According to Strack, Levertoff was present at the mission conference in Stockholm which turned down the declaration by Waldmann and Lucky, which may indicate Levertoff's attitude to Lucky. Brian Reed sent me in August 2013 a copy of a letter from Lucky to Levertoff, where Lucky asks Levertoff for forgiveness and reconciliation, while at the same time challenges him to explain his feelings for the mission work he is doing., "Letter Luiky Williams to Levertov," in email from Brian Reed August 8. 2013. Concerning Rabbi Isaac Lichtenstein, in referring to the 1887 annual report of the Hebrew Christian Prayer Union in London, Lucky is more concerned about an address in a letter from Rabbi Lichtenstein in Hungary than the union's contact with Queen Victoria. Lucky calls him R. Y. Lichtenstein and claims that he is rabbi of the Yeshurun congregation in Hungary. Due to the name of the town and the abbreviation, it is not clear whether he refers to Isaac Lichtenstein or Herschensohn-Lichtenstein. See "The Fifth Annual Report of the Hebrew Christian Prayer Union, London 1887," 77.

meetings and sermons aimed at a Jewish audience on Fridays and Saturdays as well.[519] In contrast to larger missions, Leopold Cohen held that Jewish Christians like himself were the best missionaries. In addition, he claimed the right of converted Jews to hold on to certain Jewish identification markers, like the Sabbath. According to himself he practiced Jewish customs in his own family, and did not want converts to assimilate too much.[520]

In spite of his ambivalence towards these efforts to create Jewish-Christian congregations, Lucky was a member of the Prayer Union in London, which he held as a sign of the new era replacing the 1,500-year period of assimilation of Jewish Christians. *Edut* even compares this union with the work of Ezra and Nehemiah, and refers to the meetings of the union in New York and to its leaders without any critical remarks.[521]

Instead of associating with fellowships organized by Jewish Christians in the New York area, Lucky preferred Seventh Day Baptists. This was perhaps due to the lack of adherence to Jewish tradition in Cohn's and Freshman's societies, combined with the fact that this church gave him the opportunity to form a work in his own image, centering around the journals. In addition, Lucky may have made the same impression on Jewish Christians that he did on Moses Löwen in Stanislau: Lucky's emphasis on Jewish law observance made them back off, even if they wanted a strong Jewish identity themselves.

According to Löwen, Lucky's personality had had this effect upon sympathizers and friends long before he became a believer. When he organized groups of young Jews who wanted to learn political theory and philosophy in Galicia and Bukowina, after a while most of them became tired of Lucky's intense regime. That the Jesus-believing Lucky apparently had more sympathizers among non-Jewish than Jewish Christians, was a fact that also struck his friends. According to Wiegand, this was

---

519. Freshman was son of a Jewish convert and Methodist pastor in Canada. In 1881 he was sent by the Methodist Church in Canada to New York to establish a congregation for Jewish Christians. From its start in 1882 to 1885 the little congregation had different addresses, until it was able to raise its own building at N. 17 St., Mark's Place, on October 11. Freshman's only salary came from the congregation and gifts, and I have not been able to find out what later happened to this work. See "Letters," 22; and Andersen, *Israelsmissionen*, 40–57.

520. Ariel, *Evangelizing*, 33.

521. "News in Israel," 49; and "'That They Might Gain Insight into the Words of the Torah' (Neh. 8.13)," 87.

due to the fact that most Jewish Christians were too assimilated into traditional thinking and non-Jewish culture. They had invested too much in the Christian community and were too integrated into traditional Christian thinking to see Lucky's point of view. Instead, Wiegand claims, one should consider how the *new* Jewish Christians would think.[522]

Lucky's Ideal of Jewish-Christian Congregations

Lucky's views on modern Jewish Christianity could perhaps be labeled Jewish-Christian utopianism, partly due to the lack of support for his agenda and partly due to lack of results from his own work. Compared to the evangelistic profile of Isaac Lichtenstein's writings, Lucky's Hebrew- and English-language publications are more concerned with accusing the methods of the Jewish missions, as well as defending and explaining his own position. The apologetic approach was probably due to his goal of creating a space for Jewish Christians within Judaism.

Lucky did not accept that Jewish believers in Jesus should be treated as aliens by the Jewish community. In fact, he regarded the rejection of Jewish believers in Jesus as part of the internal Jewish divisions.[523] Nevertheless, being accepted within the Jewish people was in the end only Lucky's first goal. According to Wiegand, Lucky's aspiration was not really to get Jewish Christians into the *church*; his ideal of the future was rather that the *synagogue* would be filled with believers in Christ. From this, Kjær-Hansen suggests that Lucky was not quite honest about his agenda, and that the participants at the Stockholm conference suspected this. However, Lucky's goal was known to careful readers of *Edut* quite early. Already in the early 1890s, Zöckler describes these aspirations with much sympathy in his article in *Saat auf Hoffnung*.[524] According to Wiegand, when these Jewish believers were numerous enough they could raise their own scribes and authorities, insisting that the traditional Jewish leaders should not be the only spiritual leaders within the Jewish community.[525] As Zöckler understood Lucky's efforts to establish small fellowships of followers in Galicia (and probably in New York as well), they were made in order to realize this hope. Lucky therefore

---

522. Wiegand, "Chajim Jedidjah Lucky," 59–60.

523. "To the Dear Readers in the Camp of the Hebrews, the Edut Says," 102.

524. Zöckler, "Judentum und Christentum," (1893) 53.

525. Wiegand, "Chajim Jedidjah Lucky," 60. Wiegand explicitly mentions the Hasidic leaders.

claimed that this community needed to be ethnically homogenous and protected from influences that could threaten the embryonic group that would develop into the greater national Jewish community of believers in Jesus.[526] Eventually, when Israel recognized Jesus in the future, Jewish tradition and Jewish spiritual life would not only be renewed and transformed, but Israel would take the leading role in spreading the gospel, being a congregation of divine witnesses (*edut*).[527]

Torah Observance for Jewish Christians

A key word in the Stockholm mission conference in 1911 was "Ebionitism," referring to a group of Jews in the early church that was condemned because of its theology, in which the divinity of Jesus was rejected.[528] In the lectures in Stockholm no one questioned Lucky's Christology; instead the focus was solely on the practical and soteriological aspects of Lucky's program vs. Christian liberty. The headlines of the lectures therefore may seem misplaced, but Lucky actually seems to have described himself as an "Ebionite," in the sense that he was a poor Jew (which Weidauer claims is the literary meaning of the term).[529]

From Lucky's literary activity alone, it is difficult to get a systematic overview of what Torah observance for Jewish believers in Jesus would mean in real life.[530] In the years before WWI, however, he explained publically what he wanted in practical terms. Around 1910, in cooperation with Philip Cohen and Dr. Waldmann from Lemberg, he formulated two alternative programs for Torah observance for Jewish Christians. For Jewish individuals who wanted to live as jewishly as possible, they recommended "the maximum program." For those who, for various reasons, could not live up to this goal, they recommended "the minimum program," which basically was to observe the minimum of what is necessary for the continuity of Jewish tradition: circumcision,

---

526. Zöckler, "Judentum und Christentum," (1893) 51.
527. Ibid., 53–54.
528. McGrath, *Christian Theology*, 330; Skarsaune, "The Ebionites," 419–62.
529. Weidauer, "Erindringer" (1923), 167. For details on the term, see Skarsaune, "The Ebionites," 424–27.

530. The main exception seems to be Zöckler's statement in the early 1890s, that when it came to out-dated laws, Lucky wanted to follow the orthodox interpretation and practices. Zöckler, "Judentum und Christentum," (1892) 252.

the Sabbath and the festivals.[531] The maximum program included kosher observance (the dietary laws) as well. According to Baron, Lucky once told him he preferred the maximum program himself, which was about observing Jewish customs in all things, only "adding the Name of Jesus now and then." According to Baron's experience with Lucky and Cohen, the programs expected the observant individual to support Jewish nationalism and Zionism.[532]

In spite of his efforts to establish homogenous fellowships of Jewish believers in Jesus for decades, Lucky did not manage to get support from many Jewish Christians, who stepped back due to his intensity and bitterness towards the way of life most traditional Jewish Christians had chosen. His main idea, that Jewish believers in Jesus should voluntarily observe Jewish customs, nevertheless seems to have found interest among some Jews as well as Christian missionaries, although Lucky was not able to build a lasting fellowship.

Lichtenstein

LICHTENSTEIN AND OTHER JEWISH CHRISTIANS

According to Baron, Lichtenstein would have liked to establish a Hebrew Christian congregation if he were younger, a desire he is supposed to have repeated several times.[533] Nevertheless, these aspirations are never expressed in his publications, and neither can one find any explicit references to the embryonic Jewish-Christian movement—or other contemporary Jewish Christians for that matter. It is unlikely that his silence on the topic was because Lichtenstein was simply indifferent or uninformed about the question. Lichtenstein seems to have been generally well informed about the world around him, particularly as he praises the contemporary progress of humanity as well as lamenting the spiritual situation of the Jewish people.

Not least, Lichtenstein was invited to participate in the discussion, for instance at the mission conference in Leipzig in 1895. In the minutes, Dalman notes briefly that Rabbi Lichtenstein was cautious about Wiegand's proposals regarding Torah observance: "Also Rabbi

---

531. Lindhagen, "Is there Ebionitism," 78.

532. Baron, *Messianic Judaism*, 4–5, 15.

533. Baron, "Rabbi Ignatz Lichtenstein," 260. See also Herman, "Den ungarske rabbiner Lichtenstein," 78.

Lichtenstein would only hear about a keeping of the law in a spirit of humbleness, devotion and love."[534] Dalman obviously understood this remark as critical to Wiegand. However, as neither Wiegand nor Lucky would have disagreed with Lichtenstein's utterance, it is difficult to grasp the relationship between Lichtenstein's and Lucky's points of view from this short sentence. Lichtenstein could just as well have tried to modify or supplement Wiegand's claims. At least, it is probably an oversimplification to place Lichtenstein among Wiegand's (and thereby Lucky's) opponents based on this statement.

Lichtenstein's sermons in Tápiószele became inspired by the New Testament about the same time that Joseph Rabinowitz began his work in Kishinev. Consequently, in the following 25 years Lichtenstein could observe the development of the nascent Jewish-Christian movement and the debate about it. Indeed, many in the Jewish missions considered him a part of it. On this background, Lichtenstein's scarce contact with other Jewish believers in Jesus, except for Baron and Schönberger, is striking.

However, we know Lichtenstein discussed his faith in Jesus with Rabinowitz. In 1891, they met on two occasions in Andrew Moody's home in Budapest, and although Moody states that they had a very interesting conversation, the outcome was limited, if anything. Already in 1889 Rabinowitz had announced his disapproval of Lichtenstein's understanding of Christianity in a letter to Moody, in which he asked Moody to greet Lichtenstein with the words from John 12:23–24 and Romans 6:4 (the last text referring to baptism).[535] It seems that Rabinowitz and Lichtenstein differed particularly on the question of baptism. In spite of his sympathy for Rabinowitz and his work, Wilkinson accused Rabinowitz of holding "sacramentarian" views, indicating that he had much faith in the spiritual effect of Holy Communion as well as baptism. If Wilkinson's impression were correct, it would partly explain Rabinowitz's critical attitude to Isaac Lichtenstein's refusal of baptism. In addition to the issue of baptism, before his conversion Rabinowitz had already expressed a critical attitude towards Talmud.[536] According to Kjær-Hansen this was not a new stance conditioned by his new faith, but

---

534. Dalman, *Die allgemeine Konferenz für Judenmission*, 19.

535. Kjær-Hansen, *Joseph Rabinowitz*, 175. While the text in John deals with how Jesus parallels his own fate to the death of a seed bringing forth new life, Romans 6:1–11 is about baptism.

536. Ibid., 108–9.

was an old concept which he held on to, quite similar to Gurland. In spite of this skepticism towards Jewish tradition, Rabinowitz used parts of the Talmud and midrashic literature, as well as Kabbalah, when expounding for instance Christology. Rabinowitz insisted that his Christian faith had not made him a former Jew, and he maintained that every Jewish believer was free to observe Jewish traditions or not. Theoretically, he did not distance himself from anyone who maintained Jewish customs, but in practice, he disagreed strongly with Lichtenstein.[537]

Lichtenstein, however, does not seem to have been very eager to come in touch with Rabinowitz, or other Jewish believers in Jesus for that matter. Except for his encounters with Rabinowitz on the occasions arranged by Moody, it seems that Lichtenstein relied on Baron and Schönberger in his relations to other Jewish Christians, e.g., when he met Paul Levertoff in Budapest in 1905. On that occasion, Levertoff was following Baron on his journey to the Balkans.[538] In addition, Lichtenstein, at least in his writings, was also silent about his views on Jewish-Christian congregations. One explanation for this could be that all of the famous Jewish supporters of a Jewish-Christian church were associated with the mission societies, even Lucky. In the Jewish community most of them were regarded as apostates. If Lichtenstein had associated himself in public with these, he would have been in the same category himself—something he at any cost wanted to avoid.

However, this explanation is not obvious. Although Lichtenstein did not refer to any specific Jewish Christians in his publications, at the same time he was not afraid of describing Gentile missionaries in a very flattering manner in his evangelistic writings. According to the reference in Baron's obituary to the notice of Lichtenstein's death in the Jewish newspaper, Lichtenstein's friendly acquaintance with representatives from the missions and their financial support were commonly known among the Jews. The question is whether his silence about Jewish Christianity could be related to his silence about contemporary Jewish

---

537. Ibid., 233.

538. Paul Philip (Feivel) Levertoff (1874–1954) was from Belarus, and became Herschensohn-Lichtenstein's successor at the Leipzig Institute. Like Lichtenstein, he had a Hasidic background, and much of his scholarship was related to studies of Hasidism. Before he began in Leipzig, he worked for several Jewish missions between 1896 and 1911, including the Hebrew Christian Testimony in 1901–1910. While working in this society, he traveled much with David Baron, and published a number of works on Judaism and Christianity. Quiñónez, "Paul Phillip Levertoff," 24–25.

nationalism. When discussing Lichtenstein's attitude to Zionism, I mentioned that he may have been influenced by the general skepticism of the movement in the Hungarian Jewish community, or that he neglected the topic for the sake of his readers. As the idea of a contemporary Jewish Christianity could be regarded as a fruit of Jewish nationalism, the phenomena could therefore have been treated the same way. Lichtenstein's goal was for the Jewish people to embrace the form of Christianity expressed in the New Testament, not to create a Jewish-Christian community. As he saw it, it was not a limited group of Jewish believers who should lead the nations in the work of the gospel, but the Jewish nation as a whole. Israel, as a people, should not exclude itself from the nations, but lead them to Christ. Lichtenstein's primary focus in his writings was therefore the evangelistic approach, not the establishment of groups of Jewish believers in Jesus.

The Paradox of Torah Observance for Jewish Believers in Jesus

In his letter to his father in 1887, Emmanuel Lichtenstein expresses confusion about his father's actions and intentions, and rather exasperatedly asks him, "What do you really wish?"[539] This question becomes particularly relevant when it comes to Lichtenstein's attitude to Jewish Christians' relationship to Torah observance. The topic is never discussed systematically in his pamphlets, but is left as a paradox. At times he fiercely attacks contemporary Jewry and Reform Judaism for its lack of law observance, and he regrets that Jewish Christians are assimilated into the European cultures and are lost to the Jewish nation. Still, at the same time his writings encourage Jews who find themselves unable to live according the law, to convert to Christianity as a "moral life-line" (but never in the sense of becoming official members of a church). While ordinary rabbis, as he puts it, will try to prevent any Jew from being baptized, even individuals who cannot take care of themselves, Lichtenstein points out with pride that he does exactly the opposite.[540] At the same time, he underlines the similarities between Christianity

---

539. Lichtenstein, *Two Letters, or What I really Wish*, 12.
540 Herman, "Den ungarske rabbiner Lichtenstein," 73–74.

and Judaism to such an extent that Le Roi accuses him of undermining the need for conversion.[541]

The lack of a theoretical explanation in his publications is not due to a lack of interest in the topic.[542] Lichtenstein is aware that Jewish Christians usually turn non-Jewish, or at least their children do. However, this is not only the fault of the Jewish Christians or the churches. This practice is due to the Jewish people itself as well, as the stigmatization of Jewish believers in Jesus causes alienation between the believer and the Jewish community: "So long as the sons of Israel who confess Jesus are thus treated, there will continue to be alienation between Jews and Jewish-Christians."[543]

Lichtenstein's answer to the dilemma of Jewish continuity vs. faith in Jesus can probably be found in his own life: The position of limbo. I do not believe this was only an expression of confusion, but rather illustrative of what he held to be the situation for any Jew who has embraced Christ and awaits God's promise of the future salvation of the Jewish nation. Lichtenstein knew that Jewish Christians as individuals usually assimilated with Gentile Christians and were lost from the nation in the first generation. Nevertheless, the people would remain, based on the divine pledge:

> It is usually the endeavour of Jewish Christians in the very first generation to be rid of every Jewish impress, to amalgamate with the Christians, and be lost among others. The individual is lost, but the people remain. Israel, as the elect people, the everlasting witness to the peoples, cannot, and ought not, to disappear in the tumult of the nations. For this we have a sure word, a divine pledge, "For I am the Lord, I change not; therefore ye sons of Jacob are not consumed" (Mal 3:6).[544]

By turning to Jesus, Israel will not cease to be a nation nor be absorbed into its Christian surroundings, but will become the head of the nations, which is its calling from God.[545] The continuity of the Jewish people is solely dependent on God, and is not based on observance of Jewish customs as such. However, Lichtenstein regards the decrease of

541. Le Roi, *Geschichte*, 2:277, 279.
542. Lichtenstein, *Die Liebe*, 19.
543. Lichtenstein, *A Jewish Mirror*, 7.
544. Lichtenstein, *Two Letters, or What I really Wish*, 25.
545. Lichtenstein, *Die Liebe*, 20. See Zech 8:23; Isa 2:2–5.

Torah observance as a symptom of a fundamental spiritual crisis in the Jewish community. The attempts of religious reform are not only in vain in dealing with this crisis, they are themselves a part of the problem. Embracing Jesus as Messiah is therefore not the next-best solution for Jews who cannot deal with Torah observance; it is to enter into the core of the destiny and goal of the Jewish people. In other words, believing in Jesus is a way not only to come to terms with the divine demands of law observance, but to live an authentic Jewish life. Lichtenstein therefore wants Israel to wake up from its spiritual apathy and take the leadership in promoting the gospel, like Moses, who placed "himself in the gate of the camp, and shouted with clear, ringing voice: 'Come to me all who are on the Lord's side!'"[546]

In other words, Lichtenstein's thoughts about the observance of Jewish customs may be consistent, in spite of the lack of systematic discussion of the topic. He wanted the Jewish people to embrace Jesus and thereby be renewed in its Jewishness, and possibly felt that discussions about Jewish-Christian fellowships and Torah observance were missing the point. This would also partly explain his silence about other famous Jewish Christians.

---

546. Lichtenstein, *Two Letters, or What I really Wish*, 26.

5

Conclusion

Three Jewish-Christian Identities

When comparing Gurland's, Lucky's and Lichtenstein's identification as Jews, a major characteristic is the difference between Gurland and the other two in their attitudes to and affection for Jewish tradition.

Gurland

Concerning both Jewish tradition and his relationship to Christian doctrines, Gurland appears to have crossed the boundaries of traditional Jewish identity. To him, Talmud contains man-made speculations that have led the Jewish people astray from God to spiritual darkness and depravity. The true way to God for the Jewish people is in Christ, the Messiah, as he is revealed in the New Testament and prophesied in the Hebrew Bible. In addition to this doctrinal reorientation, the break with the Jewish religious community in many ways was solidified by Gurland's marriage with Baroness Helene von Drachenfels; this is most clearly seen in the fact that his children from this marriage did not have any contact with the Jewish people.

On the other hand, Gurland maintained some bonds to his Jewish family and parts of the Jewish community, and continued to identify with the Jewish people. On some occasions he also was willing to keep some Jewish customs. This pattern brings into question the stereotypical image of an apostate who had turned his back on his Jewish origin. It seems more relevant to describe Gurland as having a dual identity, at some points identifying strongly with a Christian worldview while also continuing to identify with Jewish identification markers such as, e.g., Zionism and Yiddish. Gurland's identification with the Jewish people was related more to the Hebrew Bible, the Jewish cultural heritage and the contemporary Jewish political situation and aspirations than to elements like the Talmud.

Gurland makes an absolute distinction between Talmud and the Hebrew Bible. The former is, to a large extent, a corrupt product of men, and its influence keeps the Jewish people in bondage. The continuity of the Jewish people is not discussed as a topic, in spite of his identification with his people even after his conversion. What is clear is that for Gurland, a Jewish national identification based on Talmud would have a negative effect for the Jewish people. Gurland regarded the increased Jewish nationalism and the renaissance of the Hebrew language as a Jewish national awakening as well as a process of liberation from Talmud. However, as the alternative to traditional Judaism for the majority seemed to be modern paganism and unbelief, the outcome of this process would not necessarily be positive. If the national awakening of the Jewish people could lead to any real progress, it had to be based on the spirituality of the Hebrew Bible as well as the New Testament. Christian mission work therefore seems to have been the natural solution not only to save individuals, but to rescue the Jewish people as authentically Jewish, spiritually speaking. Although Gurland did not reject the idea of a future national Jewish conversion to Christ, he regarded contemporary individual conversions as a far more significant matter.

In spite of a successful church career and identification with traditional Lutheran doctrine and German culture, as well as his marriage to a Baltic German baroness, Gurland seems to have been partly marginalized within the Baltic German public and leadership. The reluctance or dismay about his person was apparently related to his cultural and educational background, combined with his lack of support for the resistance against Russification in the last decades before 1905. Gurland's life story therefore seems representative for Fredrik Barth's notion of how individuals who crossed ethnic boundaries in poly-ethnic communities were free to participate in the new society, but often suffered under the majority language and culture.[1] Although his relationship to the Baltic

---

1. Barth, "Introduction," 32.

German community was ambivalent, Gurland identified himself with German and Russian Protestant revivalist movements. Some of these groups were to some extent alien and even critical to Baltic German church leadership and theology. Some of Gurland's most significant personal relationships in the Baltic and St. Petersburg were built on a shared sympathy to these movements. In this context, the locus for Gurland's identity or loyalty was his theological preferences, not Baltic German culture or society as such. Comparing Gurland's sympathy for German culture and Eurocentric attitudes with his positive views on Jewish nationalism, the assumption that Gurland adapted a dual identity seems to be verified.

Gurland never established or publicly encouraged the establishing of Jewish-Christian churches, and he was clearly against law observance for Jewish believers. Instead he placed himself in the more or less traditional role of a missionary to the Jews both before and after his ministry in Kurland. However, in spite of his close relations to German mission circles, he never openly criticized or discussed Rabinowitz's work or ideas about Jewish-Christian congregations. In fact, in contrast to Lucky (and partly Lichtenstein), Gurland seems to have had friendly relationships with Rabinowitz and other Jewish Christians.

Lucky and Lichtenstein

For Lucky and Lichtenstein, the traditional dichotomy between Christianity and Judaism was anachronistic and false. Instead they underlined the spiritual bonds between Judaism and Christianity, even more than contemporary missionaries with a positive and nuanced attitude to the Jewish tradition. Still, they also claimed there was a difference of crucial importance between Judaism and Christianity: Israel's attitude to Jesus as its Messiah. This was a question of authentic Judaism and Jewish spiritual life. When Israel eventually would turn to Jesus as Messiah, this would revitalize the spiritual life of the Jewish nation, as *Jewish*.

While Gurland debunked the oral tradition more or less completely, Lucky and Lichtenstein insisted that their faith in Jesus was compatible with the Jewish faith and heritage. Still, in reality not even Lichtenstein and Lucky regarded the New Testament and Talmud as equals with regard to spiritual authority. Although Lichtenstein belonged to the Neolog community in Hungary, he disliked the contemporary reforms of Jewish practices and observance, and in particular he feared the consequences for Jewish continuity and Jewish spiritual life. The only legitimate reasons he found for religious reforms were in the New Testament, or more precisely in the teaching of Jesus. Even Lucky, when it came to dealing with, e.g., kosher observance, would give the New Testament primacy in relation to Jewish tradition.[2] In spite of this respect for the primacy of the New Testament, they continued to hold the Jewish tradition in high esteem, as it was generally regarded as part of the divine revelation as far as it converged with the New Testament.

The main difference between Lichtenstein and Lucky seems to be their different attitudes to Zionism, intermarriage and Torah observance. While Lucky regarded Zionist efforts to be important for the establishment of a modern Jewish Christianity, Lichtenstein does not even mention Jewish nationalism. Lucky held observance of Jewish customs to be highly important for Jewish believers in Jesus. It was therefore essential that Jewish believers in Jesus voluntarily maintain Jewish customs and traditional piety as much as possible, a practice he claimed was confirmed by the New Testament. To be able to do this, intermarriage had to be avoided, considering how Jewish identity was related to Jewish family life. Around 1910 he argued for two levels of such Torah observance, the maximum and minimum programs.

Parallel to his silence on Zionism, Lichtenstein was not very concerned with the practical aspects of how Jewish customs were to be observed. Instead he cared about the motivation for such observance.[3] For him, faith in Jesus would strengthen adherence to Jewish tradition by itself; in the New Testament the Jewish people would find a new and reinforced motivation for being Jewish.

Both Lucky and Lichtenstein seem to have regarded a realization of the millennium and Christ's divine kingdom on earth, centered in Jerusalem, as a natural consequence of the future national conversion to Christ. Lucky and Lichtenstein claimed that a national embrace of Jesus by the Jewish people would lead to a spiritual revival of Jewish piety. This revival of authentic Jewish values could only be caused by a national embrace of Jesus. Both were worried about the spiritual decline of the Jewish people and the contemporary disintegration of the

---

2. the regulations in Acts, compared to the traditions of Hillel and Shammai. "The Watch of HaEduth," *HaEdut* 5/2 (1898) 34.

3. Dalman, *Die allgemeine Konferenz für Judenmission*, 19.

Jewish way of life. Lichtenstein was particularly worried about this, and felt that Reform Judaism only made things worse. For both Lucky and Lichtenstein, New Testament Christianity functioned as the fulfillment of Judaism and the Jewish tradition, but for Lichtenstein it was also a cure for Israel's national spiritual and religious crisis. This is probably the reason Lichtenstein did not discuss how Jewish believers in Jesus should maintain their Jewish identity. To embrace pure New Testament doctrines would not only make Israel the leader in the evangelization of the world, but also renew the Jewish way of life.

While both of them saw the rejection of Jesus by the national Jewish leadership in the Gospels as tragic, they differed on whether this was the reason for Israel's calamities. While Lucky denied that Israel had any responsibility for its sufferings, Lichtenstein regarded Israel's sins as a major explanation for the tragedies in Jewish history. For him a Jewish national embrace of Jesus would not only help Jewish individuals, but change the Jewish destiny altogether. For both Lucky and Lichtenstein, Israel's bondage was related to the Gentiles, due to either the traditional oppression of the Jews or the modern assimilation process. For Lichtenstein a national conversion to Jesus (but not to the Christian churches), would solve this threat, as Israel would then attain its rightful position among the nations as a *Jewish* people. For Lucky this national conversion would be the perfection of Judaism, as long as the Jewish Christians were allowed to maintain Jewish traditions.

Other than Lucky's attempts to establish a Jewish-Christian settlement in Palestine, neither he nor Lichtenstein made any effort to establish Jewish-Christian congregations, but welcomed a Christianization of the Jewish people without cultural and theological influence from traditional church bodies. However, both of them cultivated friendship and partnership with Protestant missionaries and mission societies. From Lichtenstein's point of view, this was not very problematic, but Lucky found such cooperation challenging and threatening for the development of an authentic Christian Jewish community. For him it was crucial to be regarded as an independent agent who could not be accused of being in the service of non-Jewish mission societies, something that most mission societies found difficult to understand.

On the other hand, Lichtenstein had more difficulties concerning baptism than did Lucky. While Lichtenstein was more relaxed with his non-Jewish partners, he was nevertheless not willing to undergo an official baptism that would cut him off from the Jewish community in Hungary. Although I have found no sources in which Lucky or Lichtenstein discussed the theology of baptism explicitly, it seems that both of them had a spiritualistic or symbolic view, more than a sacramental understanding, of baptism. Certainly they regarded baptism in the New Testament as a private matter which did not have to be officially registered. While there is some uncertainty as to whether Lichtenstein underwent an immersion ceremony that he counted as baptism for himself, there is little doubt that Lucky was baptized in public, perhaps even more than once.

Lucky's and Lichtenstein's struggles with their relationship to the Christian community must be seen in light of the general debate concerning Jewish continuity in their day. According to Jonathan Sacks, until the 20th century, the Jewish strategy for continued existence was based on segregation from the non-Jewish community.[4] As I see it, Lucky, and to some extent also Lichtenstein, followed this strategy when they played out their faith in Jesus in a Jewish context, where they found it necessary to distinguish themselves from the Christian community. They did not seek segregation for its own sake, but their strategies were seen as steps on the road to intensify and renew Jewish spiritual life in light of the New Testament.

However, this strategy alone did not do much for Jewish survival, and certainly not for Lucky and Lichtenstein. As Sacks points out, for the Jewish communities the traditional segregationist strategy did not succeed in maintaining Jewish continuity in itself, but because they prioritized the Jewish identification of their children by establishing schools and living Jewish communities.[5] Lucky and Lichtenstein were not able to establish communities or institutions that could shape what they believed was Jewish-Christian identity. In fact, Gurland was the only one of the three who involved himself in Jewish education or the education of Jewish children. However, these schools were associated to Christian ideas or the *Haskalah* movement, and were efforts to detach Jewish children from Talmud and the synagogue. For Lucky and Lichtenstein this would not have been an option.

Gurland's, Lucky's and Lichtenstein's attitudes to Jewish tradition seem to have been shaped greatly by their experiences with Judaism

4. Sacks, *Will We Have Jewish Grandchildren?*, 85.
5. Ibid.

before their conversion. In general, their new Christian/New Testament interpretation and worldview seems to have had a minor effect on their identification with Jewish tradition as well as with the Jewish people. This may explain the diversity of views among them with regard to their Jewish identification. From the perspectives of religious studies and studies of Christian missions, the fact that Jewish believers in Jesus before WWI found different solutions regarding their Jewish identity is not surprising. In fact, this study seems to confirm Rebecca Norris's statement about religious converts and their relationship to their background:

> Having found a tradition that satisfies specific needs, the concepts and practises of the adopted religion are filtered through the convert's language and associations. This affects not only the meanings of ideas and symbols but also the attitude of the convert toward ritual requirements. Some converts take on their adopted religion with rigorous adherence; others perform selectively, accepting only what corresponds to pre-existing attitudes.[6]

Further Perspectives

A striking characteristic of the three individuals in this study is the paradoxical similarity in the outcome of their activity. In different ways, the reactions of the Jewish and Christian communities to Gurland, Lucky and Lichtenstein show how the very idea of being a Jew who believes in Jesus apparently made the concepts "Jewish" and "Christian" meaningless for many. Their insistence on being Jewish and Christian at the same time disregarded the established boundaries between Judaism and Christianity. Kurt Hruby claims that Lucky's experience shows that the idea of a modern Jewish Christianity is anachronistic, and that Lucky was overlooking the historical experience of the Jewish people as well as the developments in Judaism and Christianity over almost two millennia.[7] Lucky's contemporary opponents, e.g., Gisle Johnson and David Baron, would describe his ideas as an illusion or an expression of heresy, while Rabbi Lichtenstein's public identification with the New Testament did not only lead the Jewish leadership in Hungary to demand his resigna-

---

6. Norris, "Converting to What," 179.

7. Hruby, "Zur Problematik," 86. Hruby comments that sympathizers of a modern Jewish Christianity fail to see that it is one thing to feel solidarity with the Jewish people, another for the Jewish society to accept baptized Jews.

tion, but even made some of them ask him to be baptized. Lichtenstein's refusal to undergo a public baptism did not make him socially acceptable in the Jewish community in Hungary (except in Tápiószele), although he did maintain his judicial right to be buried in the Jewish cemetery. He was also not accepted within the Christian camp, where many found his position theologically and socially abnormal. Already in his first publications, Lichtenstein is hostile to and estranged from the cultural and religious development and the Magyarization of Hungarian Jewry. Later, in spite of addressing his writings to the contemporary German-speaking middle and upper classes of East Central Europe, he did not find enough support to allow his ideas to manifest themselves in form of a community (if he ever wanted such a community).

Lucky's and Lichtenstein's praise of Jewish tradition, as well as their different attitudes to modern Jewish movements, does not appear to have had any impact on their position in the Jewish community. In any case they were marginalized. Both had contact with small groups of Jewish individuals, but many practical efforts to reach the Jewish community, be they written publications or Zionist efforts, were made with help from Protestant mission societies, networks or individuals.

On the other hand, Gurland's break with Judaism and association with Baltic-German society and Christian missions did in the end not make his position more socially successful. When Baltic German society found itself culturally and socially threatened by Russification in the last decades before 1914, Gurland's position as a stranger grew stronger. Gurland, who at first appears to have been one of several Jewish converts who found a career and prominent position after baptism, was to some extent marginalized because of his unwillingness or inability to be totally assimilated into his new community. This does not mean that he found more public acceptance in the Jewish community.

In other words, it appears that whatever they did, as long as they in one way or another claimed in public to have faith in Jesus and still maintained some sort of Jewish identity, they found themselves in a fragile and potentially marginalized position within both communities of faith. Robert L. Wolkoff's statement about the Jewish experience in general also fits them: They "were damned if they did and damned if they didn't."[8]

---

8. Wolkoff, "Förnekande," 121.

Gurland's, Lucky's and Lichtenstein's ambivalent position in the Jewish and Christian/non-Jewish communities seems to have its parallel in what Hannah Arendt called the "conscious pariah." These were emancipated Jews who had chosen the role of the "conscious pariah," who transcended national boundaries but did not hide his origin (in contrast to the "parvenu," who tried to succeed in the non-Jewish community without being able to escape his Jewish roots). The pariah was alienated not only from the European community, but from the Jewish community as well. These individuals (like Disraeli, Heine and Kafka) constituted a hidden tradition, hidden because there were no links between them other than the conditions that evoked their reaction.[9] Not being fully included in either community, they nevertheless used both communities as platforms from which to gain an insight into the other, and insisted on the right to think independently from established ideologies and political categories. In particular, this is parallel to Lucky and Lichtenstein, who insisted on thinking independently from established theology and religious categories as well. They could subject the experience of the Jews to the criticism of the Christian tradition, just as they could use their perspectives as Jews to analyze and criticize the Christian community and tradition.

Spiritually speaking, Gurland, Lucky and Lichtenstein did not regard themselves as those who had crossed a border or were living on the outskirts of the Jewish people; instead, they found their position to be in the center of Jewish spiritual life and faith. In fact, for all three of them, the hope for Israel's spiritual survival was to be found in Jesus. They thereby not only wanted to believe in Jesus as Messiah while still identifying with the Jewish people and/or Judaism, but also fundamentally challenged the traditional concept of what and who is Jewish. The extraordinary thing about Lucky and Lichtenstein (and also Gurland) was that they changed a major traditional boundary marker, faith in Jesus, from a taboo into a fundamental element in Jewish identity. In that sense, being Jewish was still a matter of religion for them, and secular identification markers like Zionism were not the constitutive element in their Jewish identity.[10]

---

9. Arendt, *The Origins*, 56–68; 65 n. 26.

10. Gurland, Lucky and Lichtenstein would seem to agree with the idea that Jewish identity is a religious concept; see Sacks, *One People?*, xii.

It may be natural to see this dissertation as a post-structuralist attempt to bring to light a long-time marginalized social group, and it is not a coincidence that contemporary representatives of Reconstructionist and Reform Judaism treat contemporary Messianic Judaism in this way. In books written by such people, Messianic Jews are not only an example of oppressed and marginalized Jews, but a significant attack on the very idea of what is "normal." In his analysis of the Marranos and their identity challenges in and outside the Iberian Peninsula, Yirmiyahu Yovel makes this explicit. He claims that the Marranos represent the modern perspective on modernity.[11] Finding themselves in a vacuum between Spanish Catholic and Jewish identity, the New Christians were not only the first Europeans to separate religion (Judaism) from ethnicity (the Jewish people). They also discovered (or invented) the notion of human subjectivity, one of the cornerstones of modern culture. Here the individual anchored his or her knowledge, ethics and rights. For Yovel, the Marranos also describe the basic and genuine non-integral character of human existence, anticipating the modern experience. To him, the Spanish and Portuguese Inquisitions represent all integral forces, which not only may lead to common self-deception, but are potentially harmful as well. Yovel's perspective of identity as a kaleidoscopic phenomenon rejects the existence of any Archimedean point for human identity.

I believe that placing Gurland, Lucky and Lichtenstein within this dichotomy between essentialism and constructivism is not very accurate for their situation. Understanding Gurland's, Lucky's and Lichtenstein's claims as a question about the right to exist within the Jewish framework—like, e.g., Reform Judaism—is missing something of what was felt to be at stake in the controversy around them in Jewish and Christian communities. Lucky, Gurland and Lichtenstein did not question the idea of an essential Jewish identity, but by insisting on a Jewish identity while professing faith in Jesus, they fundamentally challenged what should be considered the core and the boundaries of Judaism or the Jewish people as such. The challenge of their faith in Jesus was not only about giving them *Lebensraum* in the Jewish community, but was probably felt in the Jewish camp as implying a question about the legitimacy of traditional (rabbinic) Judaism and the Jewish way of life. Instead of questioning the existence of an essential Jewish identity, Gurland, Lucky and Lichtenstein found their faith in Jesus to be the authentic Archimedean

---

11. Yovel, *The Other Within*, xii, 365.

point for evaluating Jewish (and human) existence. As described in the introduction, modern Israeli Jews tend to identify more with Jews from Antiquity than with Eastern European Jews from the 19th century.[12] Likewise, Gurland, Lucky and Lichtenstein found a key to Jewish identity in a scripture from Antiquity: the New Testament.

Nevertheless, Lucky's and Lichtenstein's affiliations to the Jewish tradition, their insistence on living in the midst of the Jewish community or their Torah observance did not change their social position as apostates in the Jewish community. None of them were able to establish carrier groups that were able to communicate their ideas on Jewish identity and faith in Jesus successfully within the Jewish community. The traditional concepts of Christian and Jewish identities appear to have been regarded as of an essential nature, and were not a topic for discussion, at least not on the terms dictated by contemporary sympathizers with a Jewish-Christian church. Due to this, Lucky's and Lichtenstein's arguments seem to have been neglected rather than challenged in their own right within Jewish communities. A discussion about Jewish identity for Jewish believers in Jesus, where Lucky's (and to some extent Lichtenstein's) views were discussed, only appeared in the forums of the Jewish missions. Here the discussion was mainly concerned with the soteriological aspects vs. the legitimacy of a national church for Jewish Christians, and hence the question was whether a manifest Jewish identity of this kind was in accordance with the Bible and Christian (Protestant) doctrine. Still, even in this context Lucky (or at least his non-Jewish followers) and Lichtenstein did not feel they were taken seriously. This was particularly evident at the mission conference in Stockholm in 1911, where Lucky's proposals were more or less laid aside in silence.

In short, then, the proper conditions for a public discourse about a modern Jewish Christianity do not seem to have been present in the decades before WWI. The consequence was an increased social marginalization of Lucky and Lichtenstein in Jewish as well as most Christian circles, a destiny that to some extent was shared even by an acculturated Jewish Christian like Gurland.[13]

---

12. Paine, "Israel," 126.
13. Fauerholdt, "National-Jüdiches Christentum," 23.

Appendix

The False Doctrines of Talmud

Introduction

A major point in my analysis of Gurland, particularly when I discuss the debate in Kishinev in 1864, is that his attitude to the Jewish tradition is related to his background as a *maskil*. I have therefore added the whole narrative as an appendix. The following text is copied from the English manuscript of *In zwei Welten*, pages 90–105. For German versions, see Hennings, "Aus dem Tagebuch," pages 82–103, for the 1864 narrative; and *IzW* 1911, pages 79–92, for a more edited version.[1] The Norwegian version from 1912, *I tvende verdener*, tends to follow Hennings' text from 1864. I have not tried to give a full explanation of the text-critical history of the narrative.

---

1. See the manuscript *In Two Worlds*, English translation of *IzW* (manuscript found in the possessions of Hans-Heinrich Gurland, Hildesheim; date and translator unknown). Generally, *IzW* 1911 (and the English version) tightened the original 1864 text used by Hennings, but also included Gurland's Talmud references in full, making it easier for the reader to follow the arguments. While the 1864 text places "Ich" in front of Gurland's part of the dialogue, other participants in the debate are likewise identified as "NN," etc. In *IzW* this is omitted and edited, probably for the sake of fluency for the reader. Generally, the 1864 text is longer, as it includes some additional examples from Jewish tradition and references to Gurland's discussions with his father and grandfather in his childhood. Hennings, "Aus dem Tagebuch," 87.

Text: "False doctrines of the Talmud"

On March 8th my fellow-lodgers who also had leanings toward the Christian religion and often came to my room in order to hear more about it, rushed into my room at 6 o'clock in the evening and shouted: "We have been betrayed! We are lost!" "Everything has been found out! The whole town is up against us! We are to be stoned to death!"

I told them to be calm but they shouted: "Jakob (Eng.: James) and Moses have already been locked up by the synagogue-superintendent, and have been demanded to tell this evening, why they went with us in the pastor's church. Everybody says you are at the bottom of it, and they intend to call you before the congregation this evening."

One of them continued: "See what they gave me for a reminder," and with these words he pointed to his bruised face and arms, "this is what my uncle and my other relatives did to me, and it would have been worse still, had I not succeeded to escape."

I was reminded of Zechariah 13.6: "And one of them will say unto him: What are these wounds in thine hands? Then he shall answer: Those with which I was wounded in the house of my friends."

I had not very long to wait for their summons to appear before the congregation. I went first to the Pastor who strengthened me by divine instructions and by prayer, and after I had entrusted myself into the hands of the Lord, I went in good cheer. It was very bad weather. Rain was pouring down and I shivered on account of the cold temperature, but within myself there was a fire aflame. Pain, gladness, woefulness and great excitement filled my heart.

Before I entered the congregation-hall I lifted up, once more, a silent prayer: "O Lord, be mighty in me weak one."[sic.] I could hear loud voices shouting in the hall and, quickly entering, I called to them: "Peace be with you, brethren!"

Everybody became quiet and I became aware of those two men who, for their faith's sake, had been brought before congregation, and I asked all who were present: "What wrong have these brethren done?," when H. R replied: "These fools have only you to thank for the suffering; they allowed you to take them to the church!"

"But that is not true," interjected some of my previous followers. "These men are liars, it is not possible!"

I asked: "Why do you not believe these innocent ones?" and I was answered: "Because of that rule that stands for us once and for ever: No true Jew can become a Christian!"

"This very sentence should be reversed," I replied, "as it should run: Every true Jew has to become a Christian."

Some other men now cried out: "O God, O God! now we see that it isn't only a rumour!"

Others, again, exclaimed: "What is it that makes you say such nonsense?"

I answered: "The Word of God! The Old Testament as well as the New Testament!"

"What did you say! The New Testament is God's Word?!" somebody interjected.

"Yes it is," I replied, "and the Old Testament is quite unintelligible for anyone who does not know the New Testament, for the latter rests upon the Old Testament and is its fulfilment."

"O woe unto us, woe unto us who have been ear-witnesses to such blasphemy!" cried many of the people present, "O cherem, cherem (Damnation, damnation). He has blasphemed God!"

Others again, shouted: "Patience, brethren, patience! Let us at first try to bring him and his followers back to our creed and away from their error."

"Pardon me, brethren," I interjected, "and suffer me to explain my views closer, or tell me wherein I am erring."

"Is there any explanation necessary at all? In stead of our one-God of Israel you are proclaiming the heathen-god."

I answered: "I act like a true Jew when acknowledging our Triune-God, for already our forefathers Abraham, Isaac and Jacob have served this triune God!"

"That is not true! A triune God, that is not true!" they shouted.

"Beloved brethren," I continued, "our people, the people of Israel already for two thousand years Israel resisted the truth. We are the people that sit in darkness, believing we have the light. What help are to us our law and our work? All our praying, imploring and fasting does not avail, neither our weeping, as long as we reject and despise the Messiah whom Moses and all the prophets have foretold?! Woe unto us, if we believe those talmudists and wait for their Messiah! They contradict each other and lead us astray."

"Away with him, away with him, we will not any longer hear him," so some shouted, whereas others called out: "Let him tell us what he has to say against the Talmud!"

I replied to them: "Brethren! I herewith declare publically that the Talmud has brought me to despair! Covetous of self-honour and self-glory, and in a fantastic manner the Talmudists have darkened, through false interpretations, all such places in the Old Testament which are beaming forth clear light. Please listen to me patiently and test my words as to truth, and you will see I am telling you the truth!"

"As far as my memory can go back, even in my early days of boyhood, I was continually tortured by doubt, and I was anxious to hear and know: when was the world created? When will its end be? Is there a world beyond? Why has God created me? What is the purpose of my life on earth? Will my life be ended when I die? All such questions filled my mind since my boyhood-days. I went several times and with great zeal through all the holy scriptures and read nearly all commentaries, I had learned some mekhiltot of the Talmud Babli with all supporting explanations, but all these did not disperse my doubt and many places in Holy writ remained a riddle to me. The more I tried to get rid of my doubts by studying Talmud and Midrash the keener they became. Yea, I must confess that, when at age 22 I became a rabbi, and that notwithstanding my knowledge of Talmud Babli and Jerushalemi as well as Midrash and Sohar, I was not able to find a satisfactory answer to the smallest question of my boyhood-days.

I took then to studying the latest Jewish books, hoping to find the truth through those famous writers, but in vain! Instead of honey I tasted poison. Plenty of questions and doubts everywhere, but no satisfactory answers! For all these writers simply condemn whatsoever is unintelligible to them.

What regret did I personally feel whenever adherents of mine came and bewailed the plight of their hearts, or whenever I was asked for my opinion concerning the Talmud! When I saw that many brethren together with the Talmud rejected also the Old Testament, I always considered it my duty to publicly declare that the Old Testament must not be put on the same level with the Talmud and to explain the difference between them, and to urge them to stick to the Old Testament which to me is a most holy book. You know how uproariously these my interventions were treated at Wilkomir.

The False Doctrines of Talmud 349

I must, however, also mention that, though in my public addresses I endeavoured to explain [the?] Holy Writ, I felt and saw that I could not much convince my opponents, simply because all the Messianic prophesies and citations were also to me but great mysteries. Not until I had started reading the New Testament did I receive understanding of these prophesies."

Here I was interrupted by shouts from all sides: "We do not wish to hear anything about the New Testament!"

"My dear brethren," I continued, "I do not say that there are no rays of light at all in the Talmud; everybody reading the Talmud attentively cannot but notice much longing for truth, but truth itself is nowhere to be found in the Talmud.

The writers of the Talmud attach immoderate value to their own prudence and are so proud of their own sagacity, that the prophet Isaiah's words found in chapter 29 verse 14 befits [sic.] them: 'The wisdom of their wise men shall perish, and the understanding of their prudent men shall be hidden.' Isn't it true that all the Talmudists declare their teachings as equal with God's own word, nay even as higher than the latter? You will find in Berachoth page 4, column 2: 'Everybody who transgresses on the Scriptures incurs for penalty the offering of an expiatory offering (chatos); anybody who transgresses on the teachings of the sages incurs for penalty of death.' And in Chagiga page 10, column one, we read: 'When passing from studying Halacha (the traditions) to studying Old Testament, no man will find peace.'

With how much self-esteem they looked upon themselves becomes evident to everybody reading how one Talmudist ascribes to the other the most fabulous and numerous deeds of wonder. They declare that, on their word the river-waters banked up for them to pass through; at their command the clouds in the sky obeyed and discharged water; at a beckoning with their hand the windows of heaven closed; they had power over death; they argued with God and came off victorious, as told by Baba Mezia in vainglorious and disrespectful words; they praised themselves as standards for lowliness, truth and virtue. You can judge for yourselves now, whether it is true or not true that, along with some beams of light the Talmud does not contain very much untruthfulness, deceit, and nonsense."

Some now called out: "Stop these blasphemies! It does not behove to us to criticise the traditions of the rabbis. Maimonedes the great sage taught that all our knowledge points to the fact that we know nothing; therefore we must rest content with blindly following the ancient fathers!"

I replied: "I can find no place in the Scripture obliging you to consider the teachings of the ancient fathers as God's word, and therefore there is no justification for blind following, especially since we can see for ourselves how these wise men contradicted one another! In addition we can see that these wise contradict each other. For instance: Beth Hillel says:—Mutthar,—it is allowed, and Beth Shamai says:—asur,—it is forbidden, very frequently concerning the same matter, and yet we are expected to consider both contradictionary statements as utterances of the living God.

Our reason is liable to lead us astray so that we need a source from which to draw unalloyed truth; we need a stone with which we can test the genuineness, the purity of gold. Such source is the word of God concerning which David says: 'With Thee oh God is the living fountain, and in Thy light we see The Light.' Therefore, dear friends, let us return to that pure fountain; let us return to Moses and the Prophets! We have turned away from daylight and are walking in darkness; we have rejected that great King for whom our forefathers had longed, and we have handed him over to the Gentiles, who now have the Light and are rejoicing! Oh brethren, I adjure you: search ye the Scripture so that the dead bones may become alive again!"

"You seem to have much too great opinion of your own person," said the superintendent of the synagogue, Mr. Z, "If you think that you have found the light and all our rabbis should have led us astray. If, in reality, there is anything dark in our Scriptures, we can obtain light from later rabbis."

I replied: "I would not agree to that, for amongst all the commentaries there is not one that solves those many contradictions or that could throw any satisfactory light on them. In a great many places we are given commentaries of greatest profligacy and indecency, especially in the writings of Rabbi Salomon ben Isaak, the famous rabbi, whose commentaries are esteemed most holy equal to holy scripture, and they are often subject for sermons. I do not care for citing here some of such places but I will, at least, mention some other places in order to prove what sort of nonsense the so-called acumen of those Talmudists has discovered by subtle arguments.

You will find in Genesis 12.14 the words . . . 'When Abraham was come into Egypt . . . ,' whereas a talmudical commentator says that this should read: . . . 'When they (Abraham and Sara) went to Egypt' . . . , and the commentator states that Abraham had hidden Sara in a case, so that the Egyptians could not see her until they demanded that the case should be opened in order that the rate of custom-duties might be ascertained! Furthermore: Our father Abraham was the greatest amongst all the giants; he was as big as 74 persons in height and size. Eliezer king of Basa, and often also called Og, was another giant whom Abraham, however, used to place him on his hand when he wanted to talk to him, and that one day he lost one of his teeth which Abraham got hold of and made a bedstead of it in which he slept.

In Gittin 69 we are told concerning Assmodai, the chief of devils, that he deceived, swallowed and spued again out at the end of the world that famous king Solomon, and that there, notwithstanding all his wisdom, this king for some time king Salomo was condemned to live as a beggar. Some talmudists add, that Salomo never reigned anymore and that in his poverty and misery he wrote the book Kohelet (=Preachers), and that in the meantime Assmodai in Salomo's figure and counterfeit sat on David's throne and reigned as king over Israel and over Salomo's wives and concubines. Of Assmodai, furthermore, it is reported, that, together with all the holy angels, he studied in the heavenly college and had the same voting power as the angels.

Baba Mezia (page 80) says: 'Once upon a time all the angels and the whole heavenly college disputed against God, and when none of the parties would way, they appealed to Rabbi Chanina who, at the time, still lived on earth, asking him to be arbiter for them. Chanina who wanted to please God decided that God was in the right.'

Also in those stories well known to you and concerning Aba and Levi in Berachot page 18 those rabbis ascribed to themselves divine power as never told of any other any human being. It is impossible for me to submit to such obvious nonsense and contradictions but, at the same time I do not wish to cause the impression in you that I expect of you to consider my words as infallible."

Here again I was interrupted by some men who had already for some time been very restless and said: "How, then, dare you to criticise our ancient fathers?!"

"You would, indeed, be justified in accusing me of impudence, if only judging from my own understanding I would have uttered disapproving and distrustful remarks about our ancient fathers, for I am but human and, therefore, liable to make mistakes! But I possess a better test stone than my power of reasoning, namely the genuine and true word of God as revealed from God to Moses and His holy prophets, and it is a holy duty for every son of Abraham to discern what God said from words uttered by human beings. As nothing but man's word, however, all that has to be considered which is not in agreement with God's own word, and God's Judgment is hanging over our poor people who permit that they are led astray."

"It is just your teaching that is perditious and misleading," several men called out, "to us there is nothing holier than the Talmud!"

"Is, then, all that holy to you," I replied, "which Rabbi Bechai (page 4) drivels? He says that God committed a sin in not creating the moon as big as the sun, seeing that in Genesis 1, 16 it is said: 'God created two great lights.' And that God has wronged the moon and, therefore, commanded to Israel to offer up a redeeming sin-offering. In our present generation we are content with one prayer which we pray at the appearance of every new moon, because we are now without a holy temple. Could that be Holy Scripture that declares God himself, Him the Holy one of Israel, a sinner?! Shame, shame on all such men who call God a sinner and the cause of all sins as another blasphemy says in the Talmud (Berachoth, page 32): 'God is the cause to all sin,' and who imagine that they can prove this from Jeremiah 14.6, Mika 4.6 and Ezekiel 36.26–27."

At this point all the Jews present cried out: "You impudent fellow, you dare to blaspheme our holy faith! But you are not the first and only one; Israel had more of such perverters but Israel also outlived them, such as Erter, Ginsburg, Lebensohn and others more! Israel will be faithful to his faith, but the perverters will go to their perdition!"

"My dear friends," I answered, "I am in no wise making fun of you or mocking you! This matter is much too serious to me! My heart bleeds because my brethren go astray. Do not consider me one of those critics who not only reject the Talmud but also contest all foundation of Scripture and are solely in favour of materialism and rationalism. You are my witnesses who I have walked hitherto and you know, that also I used to despise Christianity in my ignorance but now God in his mercy has removed from my eyes the cover of Moses and I have found His

Messiah, my personal Saviour Jesus Christ through God's own word. All those places in the Old Testament concerning Messiah are now clear to me! I urge you to implore God that He may also open your eyes and also you may find in His word the clear truth as it is in Christ Jesus! I hope you will not misunderstand me and that you will realise that I am only aiming at the truth and the salvation of Israel."

Some of my hearers were, evidently, deep in thoughts and looked very earnest; others whispered to each other and finally someone said: "We have, indeed, very much cause to bewail that we are without king, without prophet and without Sanhedrin (judges) or you would have received such an answer as a seducer and a blasphemer like you should receive. If you think you have conquered us, as nobody is refuting you, you are very much mistaken! Our dreamy thoughts about Messiah, namely that he has already come, can in no wise be considered as a fact! We stick to the Talmud with full conviction and, therefore, we tell you that Messiah is still to come and he will bring to nought all blasphemers like you! Therefore we command you to stop your proclamations. They were such as incur the penalty decreed by that sentence by our old rabbis: 'Every learned man who rebels against our words has to be strangled.' Our Chachamim (wise men) have proved from Deuteronomy 17.11 that every man who doubts their interpretation is guilty of death, for it is said: 'If the Chacham tells you that your right hand is you left hand and vice versa, on pain of death you are bound to believe it and obey.'"

Another man called out: "How is it possible for you to go three times every day through that prayer saying: 'Oh that all gainsayers would be robbed of all hope, and that all the wicked would perish quickly and, with them, all those who purposely do evil should be rooted out. Humble Thou them speedily in our days . . . etc etc.!' Can such a man as you say this prayer, seeing that you are one of those seducers and traitors in Israel?!"

I replied: "Alas, alas! With David I lament that amongst my own kin I am a stranger! I long to bring them peace but they are out for war! And with Isaiah I say to you: 'Woe unto those who call evil good and good evil, that put darkness for light and light for darkness, that put bitter for sweet and sweet for bitter!' And with Jeremiah I call out: 'How do we say, We are wise and the Law of the Lord is with us? Lo, certainly in vain made he it; the pen of the scribes is in vain. The wise men are ashamed they are dismayed and taken; Lo, they have rejected the word of the Lord;

and what wisdom is in them?' (Jer. 8.7–9). Oh my brethren, these words, are they not a true picture of our Chachamim (wise men)? Not only have they pronounced the death sentence upon men who dare to question their teaching, but even God's Holy Word have they put under restraint, for they demand everybody to keep away from the Mikra (Bible). No wonder that we have nearly forgotten the Hebrew language, for we withhold from our children the treasure of Holy Writ and, instead, we give them talmudical trifles! No wonder that on becoming independent our boys wrestle themselves free from that power of fanaticism and that they scoff at Talmud and Midrash and sink into despair and vice! What is a child to think when reading on page 7 of Berachot: God prays daily twice! In support of which impropriety the child is made believe that the proof for such monstrosity is to be found in the 7th verse of the 56th chapter of the prophet Isaiah's book saying: 'I will make the joyful in my house of prayer, and that the house of prayer was at Salem.' What is a boy to think when reading in Ber. Rab, page 56 that God every day, when he saying his prayers, puts on his Tephilin (the phylacteries) in which, so they say, the words of Isaiah 62.3 are inscribed! In Menachot, column 2, page 35 the rabbis say: 'God, when speaking to Moses (according to Exodus 33.23): And when I shall take away my hand thou shalt see my back but not my face, showed to Moses his phylacteries!' And what about Chagiga, page 5 where it is said that God every day weeps when He thinks of Jerusalem's destruction! On page 7 in Berachot it is said: 'God once demanded of Rabbi Ismael, the high priest, that he should say a blessing on God's head, and that, when that rabbi complied, God was so pleased that he nodded with his head as if saying: amen!'"

At this moment some of my hearers began to shout wildly, but I urged them to let me finish; and after a long uproar they agreed and I continued:

"Dear brethren! Why don't you examine yourselves the teachings of the Chachamim as to whether they agree with the Holy Writ?! Take for instance, the 5th commandment! In Pesachim, page 49 column 2, Rabbi Eleasar says: 'It is permitted to tear open the nostril of an Anamharetz (unlearned person) even on the day of Atonement when it falls on a Saturday. And to this his disciples is reported to have answered: Rabbi, perhaps you better say, it is permitted to slaughter the man, and the rabbis is said to have answered: This would make it necessary to say a special blessing, and this should be avoided!' Now, tell me please, how can this be consistent with the commandment love thy neighbour?! And regarding anyone who is not a learned man the Talmud has only words of mockery and disdain and says moreover: 'An Amhaaretz (unlearned person) may be torn like a fish,' and for those rabbis the word Amhaaretz means those who though having studied The Old Testament did not study Gemara (Talmud)!

Rabbis have declared, that no exception can be made with regard to the inhibition to marry such an unlearned man's daughter who would be no better than an animal, and that nobody should stay overnight in the house of the unlearned in order to avoid to be suspected of murder! And still another sample from the Talmud: 'The unlearned is forbidden to eat meat, for this privilege is reserved exclusively for those who learn the Law!' There [are] thousands of similar teachings in the Talmud, and from my boyhood-days I remember that during such lessons I did not know whether to I should laugh or weep! Surely who has some conscience left within him must take exception from such coarseness. From such teaching nothing but conceit and impiety can arise! No wonder that Jesus the Son of Man once cried out: 'Woe unto those haughty and self-righteous Pharisees!' No wonder that to such men Jesus who is the very Truth and Love and Mercy and Meekness is but an eyesore! If you are honest to yourselves you can but admit that everyone of you has similar if not the same thoughts on the Talmud but nobody is courageous enough to speak out, although you know it is true what I said!"

These words roused the people and made them bitter against me. Only very few sighed: "Yes, it is so indeed," whereas a few others said: "Wherewith will you replace our loss, if we drop the Talmud which, after all, contains also some truth and good points?! How shall our souls find rest, if we despise the Talmud which opens up some precious prospects to us, such prospects as the Old Testament withholds from us. Heavenly prospects of refreshing times they are, whereas the Law and the Prophets do nothing but announce temporal punishment?! No, No! It is far better for us to stick to the Talmud!"

I interrupted them and said: "My dear brethren! If you are really anxious about your souls' salvation, I say to you: Search the Scriptures which God gave us, search them with an holy earnest and you will, certainly, find Him the true Messiah who alone can save you! None of us (are) just, no not one! You know Isaiah's words (64.6): 'And all your righteousness are as filthy rags,' and the same prophet says also (43.24):

'Only the Lord is our righteousness and strength!' If we believe in Jehova Zidkenu (The Lord our Righteousness) who has borne our curse on the Cross then His righteousness will be accounted unto us. There is no other way of salvation!"

They replied: "Supposing it is as you say; who will guarantee that your Jesus is the real Messiah?"

This gave me an opportunity to repeat and explain to them many other Messianic sayings in the Old Testament, and when, by means of false interpretations, they tried to pervert the Scripture I read to them the 53rd chapter of Isaiah, at which prophecy they were so perplexed that they were silent. After that I read to them prophesies that clearly speak of Jesus, but one of the men jumped up and shouted at the top of his voice: "Your Bible is falsified! What you have read is not in the Tanach" (Old Testament). Some other men were joining him in shouting: "His Tanach is false!," so that great disorder set in, but I answered them calmly: "You are quite at liberty to inspect my Bible and compare it with yours. You will find no difference whatsoever!" Some of them, indeed, inspected my Bible, and when they ascertained that it did not differ from theirs, their anger and bitterness grew still worse. Some shouted: "Jesus Christ destroyed the Holy Law of God!" I replied: "That is not true! Jesus has not destroyed the Law, he fulfilled it and He is the End of the Law!" They retorted: "How is that possible?!" I answered: "Gladly will I endeavour to tell you in as few words as possible, if you care to listen: Through Adam's fall Sin came into the World; and since we all have sinned (this also the Talmud teaches!), Death has come to every man. Transgression of the Law is followed, as a matter of course, by the sinner's punishment, but God who loves the world does not want that the sinner die, and therefore He sent, so many years ago, His prophets who were to call us to repentance so that we should know our sinful state and, if longing for redemption, should confess our guilt. Each prophet points to redemption through the Messiah; and when the appointed time had come, the son of God came down to this earth and took upon Himself the form of man. He is the end of the Law and the only one who fulfilled it. As an unspotted Lamb He offered Himself a ransom for our sins, and Christ's merit God accounts unto all who come to Him through faith in Jesus Christ. The propitiational sacrifice of the Old Testament was the prototype of the atonement which Jesus brought about on Golgotha for mankind. Hence everyone who in his heart believes that Jesus of

Nazareth is his personal Messiah, obtains forgiveness of sins and eternal salvation, and now every poor soul may walk his life's path rejoicingly in the knowledge that his Redeemer lives! And how much happier still can such a man or woman die, knowing that Jesus died and rose from the dead and, sitting at the right hand of God the Father, draws all men to Him into eternal glory! Seek Jesus, my dear brethren, and His light! He is the only one who can help you!"

Gurland had hardly finished, when all those who during his speech had given signs of impatience and rage rose from their seats and, with curses and wild gesticulations, rushed at him shouting: "What do we still wait for? Why did we allow this ungodly fellow to go on with such blasphemy?! Away with him and with all who belong to him! Away with that enemy of Israel!" The uproar increased more and more, and but for timely help Gurland would have been attacked. Two of Gurland's personal friends helped him quick to the door and urged him that he should not show himself in the street more than unavoidably necessary. "We shall make endeavours to call on you," they said, "for we want to hear more about Christianity!" On the next day Gurland was informed that he had been anathematised by the synagogue-authorities, and that copies of this announcement were published in the synagogue and affixed to every street-corner.

Bibliography

Primary Sources

Sources on Gurland

Gurland, Helene. *In Two Worlds*. English translation of *In zwei Welten*. (Manuscript found in the possession of Hans-Heinrich Gurland, Hildesheim. Date and translator unknown.)

———. *In zwei Welten: Rudolf Hermann Gurland: Ein Lebensbild*. Vierte Auflage; Dresden: von T. Ludwig Ungelenk, 1911.

———. *I tvende verdener: et livsbillede*. Translated from German into Norwegian by Wilhelm Pettersen, Chicago: Zions røst, 1912.

Gurland, Rudolf Hermann. *Bericht über die Arbeit an Israel seitens der evang.luth. Kirche in den baltischen Provinzen Russlands im Jahre 1874*. Mitau, 1875.

———. *Erlebnisse eines Judenmissionars*. St. Johannis Drückerei, Dinglingen (Baden). (Date of publication unknown.)

———. "Fra Russland. (Af Missionær Gurland i "Lutheraneren")." *Missions-Blad for Israel* 78 (1904) 148–52.

———. Lectures from his confirmation classes in Mitau/Jelgava in 1876.

———. "Was enthält das Alte Testament?" (Unpublished lecture, date unknown).

Gurland, Rudolf Hermann, and G. Seesemann. "Fra de russiske Østersjøprovinser." *Missions-Blad for Israel* 48 (1874) 58–64, 72–80.

Sources on Lucky

Anonymous (presumed to be written by Lucky, Christian Theophilus). "Answers to Rabbi M.G." *Edut leIsrael* 1/6 (1888) 112–15.

———. "Book Review." *Edut leIsrael* 1/3 (1888) 54–62.

———. "Book Review." *Edut leIsrael* 1/8 (1888) 156–59.

———. "Book Review: Lichtenstein's Commentary on the New Testament." *HaEdut* 4/4 (1897) 11–15.

———. "The Fifth Annual Report of the Hebrew Christian Prayer Union, London 1887." *Edut leIsrael* (in the translation called *HaEdut*) 2/4 (1890) 77–79. In the footnotes the pagination follows the English translation by Hilary Le Cornu.

———. H. G. R., "Israel's Salvation." *Edut leIsrael* 1/6 (1888) 108–12. This article is continued from issue 4–5, 79–85, where no author is named.

———. H. G. R. "Israel's Salvation." *Edut leIsrael* 1/7 (1888) 123–26.

———. "The History of the Life of Franz Delitzsch" *Edut leIsrael* 1/4–5 (1888) 95–97.

———. J. D. N. "Testimony in Jacob." *Edut leIsrael* 1/8 (1888) 152, 155.

———. K. I. M. "The Story of Passover." *Edut leIsrael* 1/7 (1888) 126–40.

———. "A Letter From Our Writer in Stanislawow." *Edut leIsrael* 2/1 (Sivan 1890 [The volume is not given, but is assumed to be the second]) 6–8. In the footnotes the pagination of the article before the semicolon follows the reference to the Hebrew text by Hilary Le Cornu, while the page(s) that follow indicate the location in the Hebrew text calculated by me.

———. "Letters From England." *Edut leIsrael* 1/4-5 (1888) 72–74

———. "Letters From England." *Edut leIsrael* 1/6 (1888) 103–6.

———. "Letters From Galicia." *Edut leIsrael* 1/4-5 (1888) 67–72.

———. "Letters From Romania." *Edut leIsrael* 1/8 (1888) 146–52.

———. "Memorial Stone in the Book." *Edut leIsrael* 1/4-5 (1888) 85.

———. "News in Israel." *Edut leIsrael* 1/3 (1888) 45–50.

———. N. S. Y. "The Future of Our People, the People of Judah and Israel." *Edut leIsrael* 1/2 (1888) 29–32.

———. "The Sabbath Day." *HaEdut* 5/3 (1898) 1–15.

———. "The Salvation of Israel." *Edut leIsrael* 1/4-5 (1888) 79–85.

———. "Shavuot—by a Faithful Celebrant." *Edut leIsrael* 2/1 (Sivan 1890) 9–13.

———. "'That They Might Gain Insight into the Words of the Torah' (Neh. 8.13)." *Edut leIsrael* 1/4-5 (1888) 85–89.

———. "This is the Task Set Before 'The Witness.'" *Edut leIsrael* 1/1 (1888) 6–7; 6. Pagination according to the Hebrew text.

———. "Thoughts From the 'Edut.'" *Edut leIsrael* 1/2 (1888) 25–29.

———. "Thoughts From HaEdut." *Edut leIsrael* 2 (the volume is not given but from the year I assume it is the second, issue 1, Sivan 1890) 5.

———. "To Those Who Rise up Against Me." *Edut leIsrael* 1/2 (1888) 24–25.

———. "To the Dear Readers in the Camp of the Hebrews, the Edut Says." *Edut leIsrael* 1/4-5 (1888) 65–67

———. "To the Dear Readers in the Camp of the Hebrews, the Edut says." *Edut leIsrael* 1/6 (1888) 101–3.

———. "The Watch of HaEdut." *HaEdut* 4/2 (1897) 1–3.

———. "The Watch of HaEdut." *HaEdut* 4/4 (1897) 1–10.

———. "The Watch of HaEdut." *HaEdut* 5/2 (1898) 25–34.

———. "What a Difference There Is Between . . . " *Edut leIsrael* 1/1 (1888) 9–11.

———. "Whatever Prayer or Supplication Is Made by Any Man (Chron. 6.29)." *Edut leIsrael* 1/1 (1888) 11–15.

———. "Word to the Reader." *Edut leIsrael* 1/1 (1888) 1–8. In the Hebrew text the pagination is 1–6 (according to email from Hilary Le Cornu to the author, September 7, 2012).

Lucky, Christian Theophilus. "Judenchristliche Gedanken und Hoffnungen." *Saat auf Hoffnung* 37 (1900) 7–35. (The article consists of anonymous letters to August Wiegand, but according to Weidauer, the author is Lucky. See Weidauer, "Erindringer," 172.)

———. "Passah-Ereignisse. Von Eliakim." *Nathanael* 4/6 (1888) 165–86.

———. "Letter Luiky Williams to Levertov." Email from Brian Reed August 8, 2013.

The Messianic Jew: Organ of the Jewish Messianic Movement 1/1 (1910) (May 14, 2011). Online: http://vineofdavid.org/remnant_repository/theophilus_lucky/.

Sources on Lichtenstein

Ewell, Monika. "A Secret from the Talmud, by Rabbi J. [sic] Lichtenstein (Budapest, Trommelgasse 52)." Unpublished English translation from German of *Ein Geheimnis aus dem Talmud*, 2004.

Lichtenstein, Isaac/Ignaz. *Eine Bitte an die geehrten Leser*. Vienna: L. Schönberger, date of publication not given. In my references, I use the English version: *An Appeal to the Jewish People, by the Late Rabbi I. Lichtenstein, Budapest*. London: the Hebrew Christian Testimony to Israel, translated by Mrs. Baron, year of publication unknown.

———. "Das Blut Christi, ein Nachklang aus dem Midrasch Echa." *Saat auf Hoffnung* 30 (1893) 29–32.

———. *Ein Geheimniss aus dem Talmud*. Vienna: L. Schönberger, 1900.

———. *Ein Judenspiegel*. Vienna: L. Schönberger, 1896. I refer to *A Jewish Mirror or the Scriptures reflecting Christ*. London: the Hebrew Christian Testimony to Israel, third edition, year of publication unknown. Translation by Mrs. Baron.

———. *Judenthum und Christenthum*. Hamburg: A. Scheibenhuber, 1891 or 1892.

———. *Die Liebe und die Bekehrung: Ein sehr ernstes Wort zu sehr ernster Zeit*. Budapest: Hornyánszky, 1886.

———. "Ein Neujahrsgruß für die Neugebornen im Herrn zum Heilsjahre 1902." *Saat auf Hoffnung* 39 (1902) 5–8.

———. *The Points of Contact between Evangelical and Jewish Doctrine. An Address by Rabbi I. Lichtenstein (delivered at Leipsic)*. Translated from the German by Mrs. Baron (London: Mr. Fegan's Homes, 1908). This is the English translation of "Welche Anknüpfungspunkte findet die evangelische Verkündigung bei den Juden?" In *Die allgemeine Konferenz für Judenmission in Leipzig, abgehalten vom 6. bis 8. Juni 1895*, edited by Gustaf Dalman, 40–55. Leipzig, 1896. (Schriften des Institutum Judaicum in Leipzig, No. 44–46).

———. "Svar på spørsmål i Israel." ("Answers on Questions in Israel"). Translated from German into Norwegian by Ragnvald Gjessing, in *Missions-Blad for Israel* 67 (1893) 53–58.

———. *Der Talmud auf der Anklagebank durch einen begeisterten Verehrer des Judenthums*. Budapest: Hornyánszky, 1886.

———. "Ein Weihnachts- und Neujahrsgruß für die auserwählten Kinder des Lichtes." *Saat auf Hoffnung* 37 (1900) 35–40.

———. "Ein Weihnachts- und Neujahrsgruß an alle Neugeborenen im Herrn." *Saat auf Hoffnung* 36 (1899) 5–9.

———. *Mein Zeugnis*. Budapest: Hornyánszky, 1886.

———. "Zwei Briefe' oder 'was ich eigentlich will.'" *Saat auf Hoffnung* 30 (1893) 9–36. I refer to the English translation, I. Lichtenstein, *Two Letters; or What I really Wish* (London: Hebrew Christian Testimony to Israel, translated by Mrs. Baron, year of publication unknown).

Secondary Literature

Aasen, Asbjørn. *Ragnvald Gjessing 1859–1927: Pionermisjonæren i norsk Israelsmisjon—en studie i hans liv og tjeneste*. Oslo: Spesialavhandling ved Det teologiske Menighetsfakultetet, 1992.

Ahituv, Shmuel, ed. *Historical Atlas of the Jewish People*. London: Continuum, 2003.

Alexander, Jeffrey C. "Toward a Theory of Cultural Trauma." In *Cultural Trauma and Collective Identity*, edited by Jeffrey C. Alexander et al., 1–30. Berkeley: University of California Press, 2004.

Alexander, Sidney. *Marc Chagall: A Biography*. London: Cassel, 1978.

Amir, Moshe. "Dvinsk." In *The Jews in Latvia*, edited by M. Bobe et al., 262–68. Tel Aviv: Association of Latvian and Estonian Jews in Israel, 1971.

Anacker, P. L. "Meine Reise nach Galizien." *Saat auf Hoffnung* 36 (1899) 78–91.

———. "Zu Prof. Ströter's Judenfrage." *Saat auf Hoffnung* 41 (1904) 33–39.

Andersen, R. *Israelsmissionen i New York: Historisk fremstillet*. København: Chr. Christensen, "Bethesda," 1887.

Anonymous. "1910 census." Subchapter in the article "History of the Jews in Hungary" (October 2, 2009). No pages. http://en.wikipedia.org/wiki/History_of_the_Jews_in_Hungary#20th_century:_success.2C_persecution.2C_and_destruction.

Anonymous. "Alfred (village), New York." June 25, 2008. No pages. http://en.wikipedia.org/wiki/Alfred_(village),_New_York.

Anonymous. "As Others See Us." *The Peculiar People* 2/2 (1889) 90–91.

Anonymous. "At Least be Corteous." *The Peculiar People* 6 (1893) 94–96. The pagination of the article in my copy is incomplete.

Anonymous. *Belarus and Lithuania: Census & Family Lists from Various Districts, 1795–1900* (February 8, 2009). page 1237, registration: 90, source: LVIA/515/25/112, Glue: Stakliskes18May185890. Online: http://search.ancestry.com.

Anonymous. "Book Review." *The Peculiar People* 3 (1891) 156–160. The pagination of the article in my copy is incomplete.

Anonymous. "Brother Lucky's Work." *Sabbath Recorder* 46/26 (1890) 409.

Anonymous. "Christian Theophilus Lucky." *Seventh Day Baptist Yearbook*. Seventh Day Baptist General Conference 1917: 22–23.

Anonymous. "Correspondence." *The Peculiar People* 2 (1890) 264.

Anonymous. "Deaths." *Sabbath Recorder* 82/5 (1917) 159–60.

Anonymous. "Editorial Notes." *The Peculiar People* 1 (1888–89) 71.

Anonymous. "Editorial Notes." *The Peculiar People* 1 (1888–89) 110–12.

Anonymous. "Fra saafeltet." *Missions-Blad for Israel* 97 (1923) 150–56.

Anonymous. "A Great Need." *The Peculiar People* 2 (1889) 67–69.

Anonymous. "Herzl's Interview with Von Plehve." Subchapter in the article "Zionism." December 7, 2008. No pages. http://www.jewishencyclopedia.com/view.jsp?artid=132&letter=Z&search=Messianic%20Judaism#328.

Anonymous. "Horowitz, Arye Leib Ben Eleazar Ha-Levi." In *Encyclopedia Judaica Jerusalem*, edited by Cecil Roth and Geoffrey Wigoder,: 8:986. Jerusalem: MacMillian, 1973.

Anonymous. "Israelitiche Allianz zu Wien." http://www.jewishencyclopedia.com/view.jsp?artid=332&letter=I.

Anonymous. "An Israelite indeed." *The Peculiar People* 5/1 (1892) 273.

Anonymous. "Jechiel Zevi Lichtenstein." *Missions-Blad for Israel* 86 (1912) 122–27.

Anonymous. "A Jewish Christian Confession of Faith." *The Peculiar People* 2 (1889) 232–39.

Anonymous. "Jewish Identity." In *The Oxford Dictionary of the Jewish Religion*, edited by R. J. Zwi Werblowsky and Geoffrey Wigoder, 370. Oxford: Oxford University Press, 1997.

Anonymous. "Messianic Testimony." February 23, 2012. No pages. http://www.messianictestimony.com/aboutus.html.

Anonymous. "Mikulov." Paragraph in the chapter "Trips in the Czech Republic." April 2, 2008. No pages. http://www.dartmore.cz/content/JewishStudies/trips.html.

Anonymous. "Mikulov (Nikolsburg), Czech Republic." April 2, 2012. No pages. http://www.shtetlinks.jewishgen.org/Nikolsburg/homeniko.htm.

Bibliography

Anonymous. "Missionen i Stanislau." *Missions-Blad for Israel* 82 (1908) 159–60.
Anonymous. "News." *The Peculiar People* 2 (1889) 280.
Anonymous. "Odessa." In *Enclycopedia Judaica*, CD-Rom edition. Jerusalem: Judaica Multimedia, 1997.
Anonymous. "Odessa." March 10, 2010. No pages. http://www.jewishvirtual library.org/jsource/judaica/ejud_0002_0015_0_15016.html.
Anonymous. "Odessa: (Rudolf Gurland)." *Petersburger Zeitung* 179 (26th of May [8th of June] 1905) 3.
Anonymous. "Palestine." *The Peculiar People* 1 (1888–89) 68–69.
Anonymous. "Purjesz (Hungary)." February 4, 2010. No pages. http://www.porges.net/FamilyTreesBiographies/Porjes.html.
Anonymous. "Rabbi Lichtenstein og hans Omvendelse." *Missions-Blad for Israel* 71 (1897) 65–73.
Anonymous, "Sefirot." In *The Oxford Dictionary of the Jewish Religion*, edited by R. J. Zwi Werblowsky and Geoffrey Wigoder, 618–619. Oxford: Oxford University Press, 1997.
Anonymous. "Southern Moravian Region, Mikulov Chateau." April 2, 2008. No pages. http://www.czechatlas.com/southern-moravian-region/mikulov-chateau/.
Anonymous. "Stanislav." In *Encyclopedia Judaica Jerusalem*, edited by Cecil Roth and Geoffrey Wigoder, 15:338. Jerusalem: Keter, 1973.
Anonymous. "Stirner, Max." In *Store norske leksikon*, edited by Petter Henriksen, 13:655. 4th ed. Oslo: Aschehoug og Gyldendal, 2006.
Anonymous. "Tapio-Tzele." In *The Encyclopedia of Jewish Life Before and During the Holocaust*, edited by Shmuel Spector and Geoffrey Wigoder, 3:1287–88. Jerusalem: Yad Vashem, 2001.
Anonymous. "Tápiószele." *Zsidó Lexicon*. Edited by Peter Ujvàri. Translated by Ildiko Szayer. Budapest 1929. Wesbite of Electronic Library of Hungary, The Hungarian Jewish Lexicon (Magyar Zsidó Lexicon). No Pages. http://mek.niif.hu/04000/04093/html/telepules.htm.
Anonymous. "A Translated Extract from the Hebrew Monthly 'Eduth l'Israel' (Witness Unto Israel)." *The Peculiar People* 1 (1888–1889) 30–53.
Anonymous. "Tysmenitsa." In *Encyclopedia Judaica Jerusalem*, edited by Cecil Roth and Geoffrey Wigoder, 15: 1492. Jerusalem: Keter, 1973.
Anonymous. "The Work of Brother Ch. Th. Lucky." *Sabbath Recorder* 70/9 (1911) 267–68.
Anonymous "What's In a Name?" *The Peculiar People* 1 (1888–89) 110.
Anonymous. "Zwei neue jüdische Zeitschriften." *Saat auf Hoffnung* 34 (1897) 163–68.
Arendt, Hannah. *The Origins of Totalitarianism*. New York: Harcourt, Brace & World, 1966.
Ariel, Yaakov. *Evangelizing the Chosen People: Missions to the Jews in America, 1880–2000*. Chapel Hill: University of North Carolina Press, 2000.
———. "In the Shadow of the Millennium: American Fundamentalists and the Jewish people." In *Christianity and Judaism,* edited by Diana Wood, 435–50. Studies in Church History. Cambridge: Blackwell, 1992.
Baehr, Peter. *Hannah Arendt, Totalitarianism, and the Social Sciences*. Stanford: Stanford University Press, 2010.
Balodis, Agnis. *Lettlands och det Lettiska Folkets Historia*. Stockholm: Lettiska Nationella Fonden, 1990.

Banik, Vibeke Kieding. *Solidaritet og Tilhørighet: Norske Jøders Forhold til Israel 1945–1975*. Acta humaniora 392. Oslo: Universitetet i Oslo, 2009.

Baron, David. *The History of Israel*. London: Marshall Morgan and Scott, 1925.

———. *Det Jødiske Spørsmål og Dets Løsning: Israels Nutid og Fremtid*. Christiania (Oslo) L. M. Berntzen, year not given. (Norwegian translation from the English original *The Jewish Problem—Its Solution or, Israel's Present and Future*. London: Morgan & Scott, 1894.)

———. *Messianic Judaism; or Judaizing Christianity*. London: Morgan and Scott, n.d. Reprint of Baron, David. "Messianic Judaism; or Judaizing Christianity." *The Scattered Nation* 68 (October 1911).

———. "Rabbi Ignatz Lichtenstein. In Memoriam." *The Scattered Nation, Hebrew Christian Testimony to Israel* 57 (January 1909) 251–266.

Barth, Fredrik. "Introduction." In *Ethnic Groups and Boundaries: The Social Organization of Culture Difference*, edited by Fredrik Barth, 9–38. Oslo: Universitetsforlaget, 1969.

Bascomb, Neal. *Rødt mytteri: Elleve skjebnedøgn på slagskipet "Potemkin."* Oslo: Schibsted, 2008.

Baumann, Arnulf H. "The History of the Archives of the Zentralverein." *Mishkan* 49 (2006) 25–30.

Beckmann, Klaus. *Die fremde Wurzel: Altes Testament und Judentum in der evangelischen Theologie des 19. Jahrhunderts*. Göttingen: Vandenhoeck & Ruprecht, 2002.

Benhayim, Menachem. "The Emergence of Messianic Jews." In *Jewish Identity and Faith in Jesus*, edited by Kai Kjær-Hansen, 49–58. Jerusalem: Caspari Center, 1996.

Berend, Ivan T. *History Derailed: Central and Eastern Europe in the Long Nineteenth Century*. Berkeley: University of California Press, 2003.

Berentsen, Jan-Martin. "Misjonstenkningen 1500–1900." In *Missiologi i Dag*, edited by Jan-Martin Berentsen et al., 110–32. 2nd ed. Oslo: Universitetsforlaget 2004.

Berg, Miriam. "Keren Ahvah Meshihit: Reproducing Material from the 19th century." *Mishkan* 49 (2006) 39–41.

Bilmanis, Alfred. *A History of Latvia*. Princeton: Princeton University Press, 1951.

Bitton, Livia Elvira. "A Decade of Zionism in Hungary, the Formative Years, the Post-World War 1 Period: 1918–1928." PhD diss., New York University, 1968.

Bitter, Stephan, and Hans-Heinrich Gurland. *Unsichtbare Kirche. Rudolf Gurlands Erleben des Bolschewismus und des Nationalsozialismus*. Rheinbach: CMZ, 2000.

———. "Gurland, (Chaim) Rudolf Hermann." *Biographisch-Bibliographischen Kirchenlexikon* 26 (2006) cols. 551–72. Online: http://www.bautz.de/bbkl/g/gurland_r_h.shtml.

Blegen, J. H. *Zionsforeningens Historie: Et Tilbakeblikk ved Femogtyveårsjubileet*. Minneapolis: The Zion Society for Israel, 1903.

Blom, Jens Gunvald. "Reiseerindringer." *Missions-Blad for Israel* 66 (1892) 120–24, 148–53, 173–75.

Blystad, Stig-Øyvind O. "Muslimske Jesus-disipler." *Ropet fra Øst* 40/3 (2010) 6–7.

Bobe, M. "Four Hundred Years of the Jews in Latvia (A Historical Survey)." In *The Jews in Latvia*, edited by M. Bobe et al., 21–77. Tel Aviv: Association of Latvian and Estonian Jews in Israel, 1971.

———. "Riga." In *The Jews in Latvia*, edited by M. Bobe et al., 243–61. Tel Aviv: Association of Latvian and Estonian Jews in Israel, 1971.

Bogojavlenska, Svetlana. *Die jüdische Gesellschaft in Kurland und Riga 1795–1915*. Paderborn: Ferdinand Schöningh, 2012.
Bonk, Jonathan. J. *The Theory and Practice of Missionary Identification 1860–1920*. Lewiston, NY: Edwin Mellen, 1989.
Boyarin, Daniel. *Border Lines: The Partition of Judaeo-Christianity*. Philadelphia: University of Pennsylvania Press, 2004.
"A Brief Notice of a Brief Life." *The Peculiar People* 2 (1889) 61–63.
Brox, Ottar. "Polarisering i norsk islamismedebatt." *Nytt Norsk Tidsskrift* 8 (2009) 67–73.
Burgmester, Karl. "Franz Delitzsch und der Zentralverein." In *Zeugnis für Zion: Festschrift zur 100-Jahrfeier des Evang.-Luth. Zentralverein für Mission unter Israel*, edited by Reinhard Dobert, 13–29. Erlangen: Verlag-Druckerei Karl W. Goldhammer, 1971.
Butenschøn, Nils A. *Midt-Østen: Imperiefall, statsutvikling, kriger*. 2nd ed. Oslo: Universitetsforlaget, 2009.
Carlberg, Anders J. "Sionismen som uttryck för judisk identitet." In *Judisk identitet*, edited by Jackie Jakubowski, 141–52. Stockholm: Natur och kultur, 1993.
Carlebach, Elisheva. *Divided Souls: Converts from Judaism in Germany, 1500–1750*. New Haven: Yale University Press, 2001.
Chandler, Paul-Gordon. *Pilgrims of Christ on the Muslim Road: Exploring a New Path between Two Faiths*. Chicago: Cowley, 2007.
Chazan, Robert. *Jewish Suffering: The Interplay of Medieval Christian and Jewish Perspectives. Lectures on Medieval Judaism at Trinity University*. Kalamazoo: Western Michigan University, Medieval Institute Publications, 1998.
Chulos, Chris J. *Converging Worlds: Religion and Community in Peasant Russia, 1861–1917*. DeKalb: Northern Illinois University Press, 2003.
Clark, Christopher M. *The Politics of Conversion: Missionary Protestantism and the Jews in Prussia, 1728–1941*. Oxford: Clarendon, 2000.
Clark, Elizabeth A. *History, Theory, Text: Historians and the Linguistic Turn*. London: Harvard University Press, 2004.
Clay, Eugene J. "Orthodox Missionaries and 'Orthodox Heretics' in Russia, 1886–1917." In *Of Religion and Empire: Missions, Conversion, and Tolerance in Tsarist Russia*, edited by Robert P. Gerachi and Michael Khodarkovsky, 38–69. Ithaca: Cornell University Press, 2001.
Coad, F. Roy. *A History of the Brethren Movement: Its Origins, Its Worldwide Development and Its Significance for the Present Day*. Exeter: Paternoster, 1968.
Cohen, Jeremy. "The Mentality of the Medieval Apostate." In *Jewish Apostasy in the Modern World*, edited by Todd Endelmann, 20–47. New York: Holmes & Meier, 1987.
Cohn-Sherbok, Dan. *Messianic Judaism*. London: Continuum, 2000.
Crawford, Howard Toy. "Neander, Johan August Wilhelm." May 29, 2009. No pages. http://www.jewishencyclopedia.com/view.jsp?artid=147&letter=N.
Crouter, Richard. *Friedrich Schleiermacher: Between Enlightenment and Romanticism*. Cambridge: Cambridge University Press, 2005.
Daland, William C. "Brother Lucky's Travels." *Sabbath Recorder* 45 (1889) 652.
Dalman, G. *Die allgemeine Konferenz für Judenmission in Leipzig vom 6. bis 8. Juni 1895*. Schriften des Institutum Judaicum. Leipzig: Akademischen Buchhandlung, 1896.
———. "Falsche Wege." *Nathanael* 7 (1891) 161–181. [The article is anonymous, but according to Rengstorf the author was Dalman, see Karl Heinrich Rengstorf. "85 Jahre Instiutum Judaicum Delizschianum." In *Zeugnis für Zion: Festschrift*

zur 100-jahrfeier des Evang.-Luth. Zentralverein für Mission unter Israel, edited by Reinhard Dobert, 30–68; 44, note 96. Erlangen: Verlag-Druckerei Karl W. Goldhammer, 1971.]

———. "Mein Verhaltnis zur Leipziger Judenmission." *Nathanael* 8 (1892) 93–94.

———. "Missionsrundschau." *Saat auf Hoffnung* 26 (1889) 59.

———. "Theorie und Praxis der Judenmission im allgemeinen." *Nathanael* 7 (1891) 97–128.

Danby, Herbert. *The Mishnah: Translated from the Hebrew with Introduction and Brief Explanatory Notes*. Peabody, MA: Hendrickson, 2011.

Davis, Lawrence B. *Immigrants, Baptists, and the Protestant Mind in America*. Urbana: University of Illinois Press, 1973.

Dawidowicz, Lucy S. *The Golden Tradition: Jewish Life and Thought in Eastern Europe*. New York: Schocken, 1967.

DellaPergola, Sergio. "Jewish Identity/Assimilation/Continuity: Approaches to a Changing Reality." Jewish People Policy Planning Institute: Avraham Harman Institute of Contemporary Jewry, the Hebrew University of Jerusalem, January 3, 2014. http://research.policyarchive.org/17720.pdf.

———. *World Jewry Beyond 2000: The Demographic Prospects*. Oxford: Oxford Centre for Jewish Studies, 1999.

Delitzsch, Franz. "Ein südrussiches Vorspiel der Zukunft." *Saat auf Hoffnung* 21 (1884) 106–10.

Dieckhoff, Alain. *The Invention of a Nation: Zionist Thought and the Making of Modern Israel*. New York: Columbia University Press, 2003.

Diedrich, Hans-Christian. *Siedler Sekterier und Stundisten*. Leipzig: Evangelische Verlagsanstalt, 1985.

Dribin, Leo. "Kurzeme's and Zemgale's Jews." March 11, 2009. No pages. http:/www.lu.lv/studiju-centri/jsc/pilsetas/zemgale/kurzeme_zemgale.html.

Dubin, Lois C. "The Social and Cultural Context: Eighteenth-Century Enlightenment." In *History of Jewish Philosophy*, edited by Daniel H. Frank and Oliver Leaman, 636–59. Routledge History of World Philosophies 2. New York: Routledge, 1997.

Duzmans, Karl. *Lettland för och nu*. Stockholm: Ernst Wessmans, 1926.

Eberhardt, Piotr. *Ethnic Groups and Population Changes in Twentieth-Century Central-Eastern Europe: History, Data, and Analysis*. New York: M. E. Sharpe, 2003.

Eder, Klaus, et al. *Collective Identities in Action: A Sociological Approach to Ethnicity*. Burlington, UK: Ashgate, 2002.

Edvardsson, Lars. *Kyrka och judendom: Svensk judemission med särskild hänsyn till Svenska Israelsmissionens verksamhet 1875–1975*. Lund: Liber Läromedel/Gleerup, 1976.

Eichorn, David. *Evangelizing the American Jew*. New York: Jonathan David, 1978.

Ellenson, David. "The Orthodox Rabbinate and Apostasy in Nineteenth-Century Germany and Hungary." In *Jewish Apostasy in the Modern World*, edited by Todd Endelmann, 165–88. New York: Holmes & Meier, 1987.

Endelmann, Todd. "The Social and Political Context of Conversion in Germany and England, 1870–1914." In *Jewish Apostasy in the Modern World*, edited by Todd Endelmann, 83–107. New York: Holmes & Meier, 1987.

Eyerman, Ron. "Slavery and the Formation of African American Identity." In *Cultural Trauma and Collective Identity*, edited by Jeffrey C. Alexander et al., 60–111. Berkeley: University of California Press, 2004.

Fauerholdt. P. "National-Jüdiches Christentum." *Saat auf Hoffnung* 48 (1912) 13–24.
"The Feast of Tabernacles." *The Peculiar People* (1888–89) 66–67.
Feher, Shoshanah. *Passing over Easter: Constructing the Boundaries of Messianic Judaism.* Walnut Creek, CA: AltaMira 1998.
Feiner, Shmuel. *Haskalah and History: The Emergence of a Modern Jewish Historical Consciousness.* Portland, OR: Littman Library of Jewish Civilization, 2002.
Freehof, Solomon B. "Introduction." In *The Reform Movement in Judaism*, by David Philipsson, i-xvi. New York: Ktav, 1967.
Friese, Heidrun. "Introduction." In *Identities, Time, Difference, and Boundaries*, edited by Heidrun Friese, 1–13. New York: Berghhahn, 2002.
Gelber, N. M. "The Wiznitzer Tzadikim Dynasty." October 16, 2009. No pages. http://www.jewishgen.org/yizkor/Bukowinabook/buk1_089.html.
Gershenson, Olga. "Ambivalence and Identity in Russian Jewish Cinema." In *Jewishness: Expression, Identity, and Representation*, edited by Simon J. Bronner, 175–94. Jewish Cultural Studies 1. Oxford: Littman Library of Jewish Civilization, 2008.
Giesen, Bernhard. "The Trauma of Perpetrators: The Holocaust as the Traumatic Reference of German National Identity." In *Cultural Trauma and Collective Identity*, edited by Jeffrey C. Alexander et al., 112–54. Berkeley: University of California Press, 2004.
Gintere, Sandra. "August Bielenstein als Theologe." In *Internazionale wissenschaftliche Konferenz. Sammelband der Konferenz*, 140–48. Riga: Domus Rigensis, 2007.
Gitelman, Zvi. "A Century of Jewish Politics in Eastern Europe." In *The Emergence of Modern Jewish Politics: Bundism and Zionism in Eastern Europe*, edited by Zvi Gitelman, 3–19. Pittsburg: University of Pittsburg Press, 2003.
Gjessing, Ragnvald. "Rabbi Isak (Ignaz) Lichtenstein." *Missions-Blad for Israel* 82 (1908) 171–76.
———. "Rabbi Isaak (Ignatz) Lichtenstein." *Saat auf Hoffnung* 46 (1909) 3–10.
Glaser, Mitchell Leslie. "A Survey of Mission to the Jews in Continental Europe 1900–1950." PhD diss., Fuller Theological Seminary, 1998.
Godin, Abraham. "Jewish Traditional and Religious Life in the Latvian Communities." In *The Jews in Latvia*, edited by M. Bobe et al., 217–21. Tel Aviv: Association of Latvian and Estonian Jews in Israel, 1971.
Gordon, Benjamin. *Between Two Worlds.* New York: Bookman, 1951.
Gordon, Philippus. *På Missionresor Bland Judar i Östeuropa, Egypten och Det Heliga Landet.* Stockholm: Israelsmissionens Andelsförenings, 1926.
Gottesman, Itzik Nakhmen. *Defining the Yiddish Nation: The Jewish Folklorists of Poland.* Detroit: Wayne State University Press, 2003.
Griffin, Robert J., ed. *The Faces of Anonymity: Anonymous and Pseudonymous Publication from the Sixteenth to the Twentieth Century.* New York: Palgrave MacMillian, 2003.
Groth, Bente. *Jødedommen.* Oslo: Pax, 2000.
Gurock, Jeffrey S. "Jewish Communal Divisiveness in Response to Christian Influences on the Lower East Side, 1900–1910." In *Jewish Apostasy in the Modern World*, edited by Todd Endelman, 255–71. New York: Holmes & Meier, 1987.
Guttry, Aleksander von. *Galizien: Land und Leute.* Munchen: Georg Müller, 1916.
Hägglund, Bengt. *Teologins historia: En dogmhistorisk oversikt.* Lund: Gleerups, 1981.
Handler, Andrew. *Blood Libel at Tiszaeszlar.* East European Monographs. New York: Boulder, 1980.

Handy, Robert T. *A History of Union Theological Seminary in New York*. New York: Columbia University Press, 1987.
Harket, Håkon. *Historien om en moderne idé*. Oslo: Universitetsforlaget, 2001.
Harling, Otto von. "Katholische Missionsbestrebungen unter den Juden." *Saat auf Hoffnung* 51 (1914) 71–74.
———. *Pionerarbeide i Galati*. Oslo: Den Norske Israelsmisjon, 1948.
———. "Zum Gedachtnis Pastor R. H. Gurlands." *Saat auf Hoffnung* 42 (1905) 85–87.
Harris-Shapiro, Carol. *Messianic Judaism: A Rabbi's Journey through Religious Change in America*. Boston: Beacon, 1999.
Haumann, Heiko. *A History of East European Jews*. Budapest: Central European University Press, 2002.
Hebly, J. H. *Protestants in Russia*. Grand Rapids: Eerdmans, 1976.
Helmreich, William B. *The World of the Yeshiva: An Intimate Portrait of Orthodox Jewry*. New Haven: Yale University Press, 1982.
Hennings, Ralph: "'Aus dem Tagebuch eines bekehrten russischen Rabbiners.' Ein adversus-judaeos-Text aus der evangelischen-lutherischen Kirche in Russland." In *Beiträge zur ostdeutschen Kirchengeschichte, Folge 6. Der Pietismus und seine Nachwirkungen im östlichen Europa*, edited by Peter Maser et al., 74–105. Münster: Des Vereins für ostdeutsche Kirchengeschichte, 2004.
Henry, John. *The Scientific Revolution and the Origins of Modern Science*. 3rd ed. New York: Palgrave Macmillan, 2008.
Herman, "Den ungarske rabbiner Lichtenstein." *Missionsblad for Israel* 68 (1894) 53–59; 72–78. [Translation of an article by Professor Herman in *Freund Israels* (the Swiss mission society *Verein des Freunde Israels* in Basel), Herman's first name, and the date and name of his original article is not given.]
Herzl, Theodor. *Jødestaten: Forsøk på en moderne løsning av jødespørsmålet*. Oslo: L. S. P., 2005. [A Norwegian translation of *Der Judenstaat: Versuch einer modernen Lösung der Judenfrage* from 1896.]
Hilker-Siebenhaar, Carolin. *Wegweiser durch das jüdaische Berlin*. Berlin: Nicolaische Verlagsbuchhandlung Beuermann, 1987.
Hindmarsh, Bruce D. *The Evangelical Conversion Narrative: Spiritual Autobiography in Early Modern England*. Oxford: Oxford University Press, 2005.
Hirschfeld, Ekkehard. «Ernst Ferdinand Ströter; Eine Einführung in sein Leben und Denken», 1. June 10, 2014. http://ub-ed.ub.uni-greifswald.de/opus/volltexte/2013/1543/pdf/diss_Hirschfeld_Ekkehard.pdf. Hirschhausen, Ulrike von. *Die Grenzen der Gemeinsamkeit: Deutsche, Letten, Russen und Juden in Riga 1860–1914*. Kritische Studien zur Geschichtswissenschaft. Band 172. Göttingen: Vandenhoech & Ruprecht 2006.
Hödl, Klaus. *Als Bettler in die Leopoldstadt: Galizische Juden auf dem Weg nach Wien*. Vienna: Bölau, 1994.
Hoffman, Joel M. *In the Beginning: A Short History of the Hebrew Language*. New York: New York University Press, 2004.
Holthaus, Stephan. "Weitblick des Glaubens. Friedrich Wilhelm Baedeker—der Evangelist Russlands." April 2, 2009. No pages. www.bruederbewegung.de/pdf/holthausbaedeker.pdf.
Hruby, Kurt. "Zur Problematik des jüdischen Menschen in der christlichen Gemeinde: Chaim Jedidjah Pollak (Christian Theophilus Lucky)." In *Der Verein der Freunde Israels 150 Jahre*, edited by Kurt Hruby, 76–87. Basel: Schweizerische Evangelische Judenmission, Stiftung für Kirche und Judentum, 1980.

Bibliography 369

Hunsberger, Bruce. "Swimming Against the Current: Exceptional Cases of Apostates and Converts." In *Joining and Leaving Religion: Research Perspectives*, edited by Leslie J. Francis and Yaacov J. Katz, 233–48. Leominster, UK: Gracewing, 2000.

Hvalvik, Reidar. "A New Sect within Judaism." In *Jewish Identity and Faith in Jesus*, edited by Kai Kjær-Hansen, 19–26. Jerusalem: Caspari Center, 1996.

Illmann, Karl-Johan, and Tapani Harviainen. *Judisk historia*. Åbo: Åbo akademi, 1997.

Jacobs, Jack. *Jewish Politics in Eastern Europe: The Bund at 100*. New York: Palgrave, 2001.

Jacobs, Joseph. "Moses Margoliuth." September 30, 2008. No pages. http://www.jewishencyclopedia.com/articles/10409-margoliuth-moses.

Jensen, Oddvar Johan. "For 'døpte kristne' eller 'udøpte hedninger'? Til debatten om Pontoppidans katekisme forklaring på 1800-tallet." *Tidskrift for Teologi og kirke* 61 (1990) 21–34.

Jocz, Jakob. *The Jewish People and Jesus Christ: The Relationship between Church and Synagogue*. 3rd ed. Grand Rapids: Baker, 1979.

Johnson, Gisle. "Fra vor missions fortid, vor berøring med Lucky." *Missions-Blad for Israel* 97/19 and 97/21 (1923) 225–27 and 248–51.

Jonge, Henk Jan de/Tromp, Johannes. *The Book of Ezekiel and Its Influence*. Aldershot: Ashgate, 2007.

Kahn-Paycha, Danièle. *Popular Jewish Literature and Its Role in the Making of an Identity*. Jewish Studies 21. Lewiston, NY: Edwin Mellen, 2000.

Karabelnik, Gabriela. "Competing Trends in Messianic Judaism: The Debate over Evangelicalism." Senior thesis, Yale University, 2002.

Katz, Jacob. "The Identity of Post-Emancipatory Hungarian Jewry." In *A Social and Economic History of Central European Jewry*, edited by Yehuda Don Karady and Victor Karady, 13–32. London: Transaction, 1990.

Kirby, David. *The Baltic World, 1772–1993: Europe's Northern Periphery in the Age of Change*. New York: Longman, 1995.

Kjær-Hansen, Kai, "Controversy about Lucky." *Miskhan* 60 (2009) 46–64.

———. "Isaac Lichtenstein—a Jesus-believing Hungarian Rabbi." May 25, 2012. lcje.net/papers/2007/intl/Hansen5.doc.

———. *Joseph Rabinowitz and the Messianic Movement: The Herzl of Jewish Christianity*. Edinburgh: Handsel, 1995.

———. "Lucky and the Leipzig Program." *Miskhan* 60 (2009) 22–27.

———. "Lucky and Waldmann's 'Declaration of Law-observing Hebrew Christians.'" *Miskhan* 60 (2009) 39–45.

———. "Lucky—Controversial and Challenging." *Miskhan* 60 (2009) 3.

———. "Mark Kinzer and Joseph Rabinowitz." *Mishkan* 48 (2006) 4–7.

———. "Mrs. Petra Volf's 'Reminiscences about Lucky (1917).'" *Miskhan* 60 (2009) 28–38.

———. "Neither Fish nor Fowl?" In *Jewish Identity and Faith in Jesus*, edited by Kai Kjær-Hansen, 9–18. Jerusalem: Caspari Center, 1996.

———. "On Lucky's Whereabouts in 1885–1886." *Miskhan* 60 (2009) 17–21.

———. "Occupation of the Field." *Mishkan* 52 (2007) 4–5.

Klier, John Doyle. *Imperial Russia's Jewish Question, 1855–1881*. Cambridge: Cambridge University Press, 1995.

———. "State Policies and the Conversion of Jews in Imperial Russia." In *Of Religion and Empire: Missions, Conversion, and Tolerance in Tsarist Russia*, edited by Robert

P. Geraci and Michael Khodarkovsky, 92–114. Ithaca: Cornell University Press, 2001.
Kohn, Jerome. "Preface." In *The Jewish Writings. Hannah Arendt*, edited by Jerome Kohn and Ron H. Feldman, ix–xxxii. New York: Schocken, 2007.
Kool, Anne-Marie. *God Moves in a Mysterious Way: The Hungarian Protestant Foreign Missions Movement 1756–1951*. Zoetermeer: Boekencentrum, 1993.
Kornblatt, Judith Deutsch. *Doubly Chosen: Jewish Identity, the Soviet Intelligensia, and the Russian Orthodox Church*. Madison: University of Wisconsin Press, 2004.
Kovács, Ábrahám. *The History of the Free Church of Scotland's Mission to the Jews in Budapest and Its Impact on the Reformed Church of Hungary, 1841–1914*. Frankfurt am Main: Peter Lang, 2006.
Koziol, Klaus. *Katechumenat heute: Der Katechumenat bei C. A. G von Zezschewitz und in der Gegenwart*. Theologische arbeiten 27. Berlin: Evangelische Verlagsanstalt Berlin, 1968.
Kramer, T. D. *From Emancipation to Catastrophe: The Rise and Holocaust of Hungarian Jewry*. Lanham, MD: University Press of America, 2000.
Kühl, Jørgen. *Tyskere i Øst*. Århus: Aarhus Universitetsforlag, 1997.
Landmann, Isaac. "Gutman, David von," and "Gutman, Wilhelm von." In *Universal Jewish Encyclopedia* 5. March 28, 2010. No pages. http://www.publishersrow.com/Preview/PreviewPage.asp?shid=0&clpg=1&per=100&pid=1&bid=2870&fid=31&pg=147&o=1258016591748. [The source given for both articles is Wiedmann: *Festschrift anlässlich des vierzigjärighen Geschäftsjubiläum des Hauses Gutman*, in *Jewish Chronicle*, May 24, 1895.]
Laserson, M. "The Jews and the Latvian Parliament." In *The Jews in Latvia*, edited by M. Bobe et al., 94–186. Tel Aviv: Association of Latvian and Estonian Jews in Israel, 1971.
Le Roi, Joh. F. A. de. "Daniel Landsmann." *Der Messiasbote: Ein Nachrichtenblatt der Berliner Judenmission* 1 (1909) 52–56.
———. *Geschichte der Evangelischen Judenmission seit Entstehung des neueren Judentums*. 3 vols. 2nd ed. Schriften des Institutum Judaicum in Berlin 9. Leipzig: J. C. Hinrichs'sche Buchhandlung, 1899.
———. "John Wilkinson." *Nathanael: Zeitschrift für der evangelischen Kirche an Israel* 24/1 (1909) 50–58.
———. *Judentaufen im 19. Jahrhundert: Ein statistischer Versuch*. Schriften des Institutum Judaicum in Berlin 27. Leipzig, 1899.
———. *Rudolf Hermann Gurland: sonderabruck aus Nathanael*. Leipzig: Zeitschrift für der evangelischen Kirche an Israel, 1906.
Levin, Dov. "Jelgava." In *Pinkas Hakehillot Latvia v'Estonia*. Jerusalem: Yad Vashem, 1988. http://www.jewishgen.org/yizkor/pinkas_latvia/lat_00149.html.
———. *The Litvaks: A Short History of the Jews in Lithuania*. Jerusalem: Yad Vashem, 2000.
Levey, Samson H. *The Targum of Ezekiel: Translated, with a Critical Introduction, Apparatus, and Notes*. Edinburgh: T. & T. Clark, 1987.
Lillevik, Raymond. "Lucky—møteplager eller veileder?" *Misjonsblad for Israel* 127/6 (2006) 22–24.
———. "Rudolf Hermann Gurland, Israelsmisjonens første rabbiner; bør han helst glemmes?" *Misjonsblad for Israel* 178/3 (2005) 22–23.

Lindhagen, Theodor. "Is there Ebionitism in the Jewish Mission?" In *Yearbook of the Evangelical Missions among the Jews 1. The Committee of the International Jewish Mission Conference. Minutes from the 8th International Conference for the Jewish Missions in Stockholm 7–9th of June, 1911*, edited by Herm. L. Strack, 78–84. Leipzig: J. C. Hinrichs'sche Buchhandlung, 1913.

Lipshytz, Christlieb T. "'Ebionitism' in the Jewish Mission? The Relation of Christianity to the National Consciousness of the Jews." In *Yearbook of the Evangelical Missions among the Jews 1. The Committee of the International Jewish Mission Conference. Minutes from the 8th International Conference for the Jewish Missions in Stockholm 7–9th of June, 1911*, edited by Herm. L. Strack, 71–77. Leipzig: J. C. Hinrichs'sche Buchhandlung, 1913.

Lipschitz, Shaul. "Jewish Communities in Kurland." In *The Jews in Latvia*, edited by M. Bobe et al., 276–84 Tel Aviv: Association of Latvian and Estonian Jews in Israel, 1971.

Longum, Leif. *Drømmen om det frie menneske: Norsk kulturradikalisme og mellomkrigstidens radikale trekløver Hoel—Krog—Øverland*. Oslo: Universitetsforlaget 1986.

Löwen, Moses Gotthold. "Christian Theophilus Lucky. Versuch eines Lebensbildes." *Nathanael. Zeitschrift für die Arbeit der evangelichen Kirche an Israel* 33 (1917) 1–25.

———. "Zur Abwehr wieder eine neue Verunglimpfung der Judenmission." *Nathanael. Zeitschrift für die Arbeit der evangelichen Kirche an Israel* 9 (1893) 33–50.

Magocsi, Paul Robert. *Galicia: A Historical Survey and Bibliographic Guide*. Toronto: University of Toronto Press. 1983.

———. *Historical Atlas of Central Europe*. 2nd rev. and expanded ed. Seattle: University of Washington Press, 2002.

Mahler, Raphael. "The Economic Background of Jewish Emigration from Galicia to the United States." *YIVO Annual of Jewish Social Science* 6 (1952) 255–67.

———. *Hasidism and the Jewish Enlightenment: Their Confrontation in Galicia and Poland in the First Half of the Nineteenth Century*. New York: The Jewish Publication Society of America, 1985.

Malino, Frances, and David Sorkin. *From East and West: Jews in a Changing Europe, 1750–1870*. Oxford: Blackwell, 1991.

Männchen, Julia. *Das Herz zieht nach Jerusalem: Gustaf Dalman zum 150. Geburtstag*. Greifswald: Der Theologischen Fakultät der Ernts-Moritz-Arndt-Universität Greifswald, 2005.

Markovits, Andrei S., and Frank E. Sysyn. *Nationbuilding and the Politics of Nationalism: Essays on Austrian Galicia*. Cambridge, MA: Harvard University Press for the Harvard Ukrainian Research Institute. 1989.

Marton, Zsolt. "Zsidók útja a világ Messiásához." Master's thesis. Budapest: Baptista Teológiai Akadémia Hittudománi Kar, 2012.

McCagg, Wiliam O., Jr. *A History of the Habsburg Jews, 1670–1918*. Bloomington: Indiana University Press, 1992.

———. "Jewish Conversion in Hungary in Modern Times." In *Jewish Apostasy in the Modern World*, edited by Todd Endelmann, 142–64. New York: Holmes & Meier, 1987.

McCaul, Alexander. *The Old Paths, or the Talmud Tested by Scripture being a Comparison of the Principles and Doctrines of Modern Judaism with the Religion of Moses and the Prophets*. 2nd ed. London: London Society's House, 1880.

McGrath, Alister. *Christian Theology: An Introduction*. 2nd ed. Oxford: Blackwell, 1997.
Melchior, Bent. "Jødedommens historiske fundament: Loven." In *Jødene og jødedommen: Fra det gamle testamente til Midt-Østen konflikten*, edited by Egil A. Wyller and Terje Gudbrandson, 32–49. Oslo: Universitetsforlaget, 1977.
Mendes-Flohr, Paul, and Jehuda Reinharz, eds. *The Jew in the Modern World: A Documentary History*. 2nd ed. Oxford: Oxford University Press, 1995.
Meyer, Dietrich. *Zinzendorf und die Herrnhuter Brüdergemeinde, 1700–2000*. Göttingen: Vandenhoeck & Ruprecht, 2000.
Meyer, Louis. "Protestant Missions to Jews: A Sketch." In *Yearbook of the Evangelical Missions to the Jews*, edited by Hermann L. Strack, 93–115. Leipzig: J. C. Hinrichs'sche Buchhandlung, 1906.
Meyer, Michael A. *Jewish Identity in the Modern World*. Seattle: University of Washington Press, 1990.
———. *Response to Modernity: A History of the Reform Movement in Judaism*. Oxford: Oxford University Press, 1988.
Meyersohn, Th. "Das Unterrichtswesen der Juden in Wilna." *Saat auf Hoffnung* 26 (1889) 196–202.
Michaeli, Z. "Jewish Cultural Autonomy and the Jewish School Systems." In *The Jews in Latvia*, edited by M. Bobe et al., 186–88. Tel Aviv: Association of Latvian and Estonian Jews in Israel, 1971.
Migron, Yoelit. "Samuel Schor, the Man and His Time." *Mishkan* 37 (2002) 5–20.
Moody, Andrew. "Budapest. Report of Rev. Andrew Moody." *Free Church of Scotland, Report of the Committee of the Conversion of the Jews* (1892) 4–6.
———. "Budapest. Report of Rev. Andrew Moody, B.A." *Free Church of Scotland, Report of the Committee of the Conversion of the Jews* (1894) 7–8.
———. "Report of the Rev. Andrew Moody." *Free Church of Scotland, Report of the Committee of the Conversion of the Jews* (1887) 9–12.
———. "Report of Rev. Andrew Moody." *Free Church of Scotland, Report of the Committee of the Conversion of the Jews* (1891) 6–7.
Mullan, John. *Anonymity: A Secret History of English Literature*. Princeton: Princeton University Press, 2008.
Müller, Johannes. "Bericht über die zwanzigjärige bisherige Thatigkeit des Zentralvereins." *Saat auf Hoffnung* 27 (1890) 156–68.
———. "Die Evangelisation Israels im Lichte des Reiches Gottes." *Saat auf Hoffnung* 28 (1891) 7–12.
———. "Entgegnung auf die 'Biblischen Gedanken über Judenmission.'" *Saat auf Hoffnung* 28 (1891) 65–77.
Müller, W. "Ein offenes Wort an den Herrn Rabbiner S. Pucher zu Mitau von einem kurlandischen Synodalen." *Baltische Monatsschrift* 16 (1867) 374–85.
———. "Ueber Judenmission: Vortrag, gehalten auf der Kurl. Privinzial-Synode 1865 von W. Müller, Pastor zu Sauken." *Mitheilungen und Nachrichten für die evangelische kirche in Russland* 22. (1866) 89–116.
———. "Zur Characteristik des modernen Judenthums." *Baltische Monatsschrift* 13 (1866) 483–99.
Neander, Wilhelm. *Die deutschen ev.-luth. Gemeinden Lettlands im Jahre der Umsiedlung 1939*. Hamburg: Harry v. Hofmann, 1966.
Nerel, Gershon. "Eusebius' *Ecclesiastical History* and the Yeshua Movement." *Miskhan* 39 (2003) 65–86.

———. "The 'Flagship' of Hebrew New Testaments: A Recent Revision by Israeli Messianic Jews." *Mishkan* 41 (2004) 49–56.

———. "Nostra Aetate: Between Hebrew Catholics and Messianic Jews." *Mishkan* 46 (2006) 47–58.

Neusner, Jacob. "Mishnah and Messiah." In *Judaisms and Their Messiahs at the Turn of the Christian Era*, edited by J. Neusner et al., 278–81. Cambridge: Cambridge University Press, 1987.

———. *Jews and Christians: The Myth of a Common Tradition*. Valley Forge, PA: Trinity, 1991.

———. *Israel After Calamity: The Book of Lamentations*. Valley Forge, PA: Trinity, 1995.

Norris, Rebecca Sachs. "Converting to What?" In *The Anthropology of Religious Conversion*, edited by A. Buckser and S. Glazier, 171–82. Oxford: Rowman & Littlefield, 2003.

Omer-Sherman, Ranen. *Diaspora and Zionism in Jewish American Literature: Lazarus, Syrkin, Reznikoff, Roth*. Hanover: University Press of New England, 2002.

Paget, James Carleton. "The Definition of the Terms Jewish Christian and Jewish Christianity in the History of Research." In *Jewish Believers in Jesus: The Early Centuries*, edited by Oskar Skarsaune and Reidar Hvalvik, 22–52. Peabody, MA: Hendrickson, 2007.

Paine, Robert. "Israel: Jewish Identity and Competition over 'Tradition.'" In *History and Ethnicity*, edited by in Elizabeth Tonkin et al., 126–36. New York: Routledge, 1989.

The Peculiar People 2 (1889) 1–4. The article has no title.

The Peculiar People 2 (1889) 193–95. The title of the article is lacking, and the pagination in my copy is incomplete.

The Peculiar People 6 (1893) 161–67. My copy lacks the title of the article, which is a book review, and the pagination is therefore incomplete.

The Peculiar People 9/1 (1896) 1.

The Peculiar People 9 (1897) 237–240; 239. The title of the article is lacking, and the pagination in my copy is incomplete.

Penslar, Derek J. *Israel in History: The Jewish State in Comparative Perspective*. New York: Routledge, 2007.

Phillip, Wolfgang. "Spätbarock und frühe Aufklärung das Zeitalter des Philosemitismus." In *Kirche und Synagoge: Handbuch zur Geschichte von Christen und Juden*, edited by K. H. Rengstorf and S. von Kortzfleisch, 2:23–86. Stuttgart: Ernste Klett, 1970.

Philips, William B. "Ch. Theophilus Lucky." *Sabbath Recorder* 67/22 (1909) 690–91.

Polkinghorne, Donald E. "Narrative Psychology and Historical Consciousness: Relationships and Perspectives." In *Narration, Identity and Historical Consciousness*, edited by Jürgen Straub, 9–18. Oxford: Berghahn, 2005.

Prusin, Alexander Victor. *Nationalizing a Borderland: War, Ethnicity, and Anti-Jewish Violence in East Galacia, 1914–1920*. Tuscaloosa: University of Alabama Press, 2005.

Pruter, Karl. *Jewish Christians in the United States: A Bibliography*. New York: Garland, 1987.

Pucher, Solomon. *Offener Brief an den Herrn Pastor Gurland von Salomon Pucher, Rabbiner der Jüdischen Gemeinde in Mitau*. Riga: Leopold Mende, 1875.

———. "Offenes Sendschreiben an die Kurländischen Herren Synodalen von S. Pucher, Rabbiner zu Mitau." *Baltische Monatsschrift* 16 (1867) 217–41.

Quiñónez, Jorge. "The Doyen of 19th Century British Jewish Missions." *Mishkan* 43 (2005) 75–82.

———. "An Introductionary Bio-Bibliography to Jechiel Zebi Herschensohn-Lichtenstein." *Kesher* 15 (2002) 78–89.

———. "Paul Phillip Levertoff: Pioneering Hebrew-Christian Scholar and Leader." *Mishkan* 37 (2002) 21–34.

Rambo, Lewis R. *Understanding Religious Conversion*. New Haven: Yale University Press, 1993.

Randolph, Courtiss I. "Christian Theophilus Lucky." *Sabbath Recorder* 83/7 (1917) 206–8.

Ranki, Vera. *The Politics of Inclusion and Exclusion: Jews and Nationalism in Hungary*. St. Leonards, Aus.: Allen and Unwin, 1999.

Raun, Toivo. *Estonia and the Estonians*. 2nd ed. Stanford: Hoover Institution, 1991.

Ravitzky, Aviezer. *Messianism, Zionism, and Jewish Religious Radicalism*. Chicago: University of Chicago Press, 1993.

Reinen, I. Ch. "Missions: Correspondence." *Sabbath Recorder* 48/33 (1902) 518.

Rengstorf, Karl Heinrich. "85 Jahre Instiutum Judaicum Delizschianum." In *Zeugnis für Zion: Festschrift zur 100-jahrfeier des Evang.-Luth. Zentralverein für Mission unter Israel*, edited by Reinhard Dobert, 30–68. Erlangen: Verlag-Druckerei Karl W. Goldhammer, 1971.

Reu, Johan Michael. *Dr. Martin Luther's Small Catechism: A History of Its Origin, Its Distribution, and Its Use*. Chicago: Wartburg, 1929.

Robinson, Richard A., and Naomi Rose Rothstein. *The Messianic Movement: A Field Guide*. San Francisco: Purple Pomegranate Productions, Jews for Jesus, 2005.

Roden, Frederick S. "Introduction. Jewish/Christian/Queer: Crossroads and Identities." In *Jewish/Christian/Queer: Crossroads and Identities*, edited by Frederick Roden, 1–18. Burlington, UK: Ashgate, 2009.

Roemer, Nils. *Jewish Scholarship and Culture in Nineteenth-Century Germany: Between History and Faith*. Madison: University of Wisconsin Press, 2005.

Rom, Kirsti. "The American Jewish Attitude towards Eastern European Jewish Immigrants, 1881–1908, as Reflected in 'The American Israelite.'" Master thesis, University of Bergen, 2003.

Rosen, Ilana. "Hasidism versus Zionism as Remembered by Carpatho-Russian Jews between the Two World Wars." In *Jewishness: Expression, Identity, and Representation*, edited by Simon J. Bronner, 213–38. Jewish Cultural Studies 1. Oxford: Littman Library of Jewish Civilization, 2008.

Roshwald, Aviel. *Ethnic Nationalism and the Fall of Empires: Central Europe, Russia and the Middle East, 1914–1923*. London: Routledge, 2001.

Roth, Cecil. "Kayserling, Meyer." In *Encyclopaedia Judaica Jerusalem*, edited by Cecil Roth and Geoffrey Wigoder, 12:42. Jerusalem: Keter, 1971.

Rudnick, Ursula. *Studium zum christlich-jüdischen Gespräch seit 1945: Auf dem langen Weg zum Haus des Nachbarn. Positionen der evangelischen Kirche im christlich-jüdichen Gespräch seit 1945 und ihre Verortung in der Theologie*. Hannover: Hora, 2004.

Rürup, Reinhard. *Jüdische Geschicte in Berlin: Essays und Studien*. Berlin: Edition Hentrich 1995.

Rüsen, Jörn. *History, Narration, Interpretation, Orientation*. Oxford: Berghahn, 2005.

Sacks, Jonathan. *One People? Tradition, Modernity, and Jewish Unity*. London: Littman Library of Jewish Civilization, 1993.

———. *Will We Have Jewish Grandchildren? Jewish Continuity and How to Achieve It*. London: Valentine Mitchell, 1994.

Sadan, Tsvi. "Jesus of Nazareth in Zionist Thougth: 1881–1945." *Mishkan* 49 (2006) 59–64.
Saphiro, Marc B. *Between the Yeshiva World and Modern Orthodoxy: The Life and Works of Rabbi Jehiel Jacob Weinberg, 1884–1966*. Portland: Littman Library of Jewish Civilization, 1999.
Saxe, Oluf. *Katekismeundervisningen: En ledetråd til opbyggelig undervisning i skole og hjem*. Christiania: J. W. Cappelen, 1889.
Schaeffer, E. "Bilder des Rückblicks aus hundert Jahren Missionsgeschichte." In *Leben und des Herrn Werk verkündigen: Die Jahrhundertfeier der Gesellschaft zur Beförderung des Christentums unter den Juden am 4. und 5. Februar 1922*, edited by E. Schaeffer, 34–53. Berlin: Bertelsmann Gütersloh, 1922.
Schainker, Ellie R. "Imperial Hybrids: Russian-Jewish Converts in the Nineteenth Century." PhD diss., University of Pennsylvania, 2010.
Scheiber, Alexander. "Kohn, Samuel." In *Encyclopaedia Judaica Jerusalem*, edited by Cecil Roth and Geoffrey Wigoder, 12:264. Jersusalem: Keter, 1971.
Schreckenberg, Heinz. *Die Christlichen Adversus-Judaeos-Texte und ihr literarisches und historisches Umfeld (13.–20. Jh.)*. Europeische Hochschulenschriften. Frankfurt am Main: Peter Lang, 1994.
Schwarzfuchs, Simon. *A Concise History of the Rabbinate*. Oxford: Blackwell, 1993.
Sconfield, Hugh. *The History of Hebrew Christianity from the First to the Twentieth Century*. London: Duckworth, 1936.
Sevener, Harold A. *A Rabbi's Vision: A Century of Proclaiming Messiah: A History of Chosen People Ministries, Inc. Centennial Edition, 1894–1994*. Charlotte: Chosen People Ministries, 1994.
Seventh Day Baptists in Europe and America: A Series of Historical Papers Written in Commemoration of the One-hundredth Anniversary of the Organization of the Seventh Day Baptist General Conference, Celebrated at Ashaway, Rhode Island, in 1902 (New Jersey: the American Sabbath Tract Society, Plainfield, 1910), 348–49, 380–81, 384–91, 438, 1338–39, 1346–47, 1382–83.
Shapira, Anita. *Land and Power: The Zionist Resort to Force, 1881–1948*. Stanford: Stanford University Press, 1999.
Sharot, Stephen. *Messianism, Mysticism, and Magic: A Sociological Analysis of Jewish Religious Movements*. Chapel Hill: University of North Carolina Press, 1982.
Shazar, Zalman. "The Idea of Redemption in Hassidic Thought." In *In the Time of Harvest: Essays in Honor of Abba Hillel Silver on the Occasion of his 70th Birthday*, edited by Daniel Jeremy Silver, 401–20. New York: MacMillan, 1963.
Siegel, John Howard. *Depression and Level of Self and Object Representation in Minority Group Religious Converts: Jews and the "Jews for Jesus."* San Diego: California School of Professional Psychology, 1992.
Silver, Abba Hillel. *A History of Messianic Speculation in Israel: From the First through the Seventeenth Centuries*. Glouchester: Peter Smith, 1978.
Singer, Steven. *Jewish Religious Thought in Early Victorian London*. Cambridge: Cambridge University Press, 1985.
Sípos, Ete Álmos. *'Bittet den Herrn der Ernte.' Guyla Forgács (1879–1941). Pioner der Ungarischen reformierten Inneren Mission*. Zoetermeer: Boekencentrum, 2007.
Skarsaune, Oskar. "The Ebionites." In *Jewish Believers in Jesus: The Early Centuries*, edited by Oskar Skarsaune and Reidar Hvalvik, 419–62. Peabody, MA: Hendrickson, 2007.
———. *Israels venner—Norsk arbeid for Israelsmisjonen 1844–1930*. Oslo: Luther, 1994.

———. "'En Lærd af Guds Naade.' Carl Paul Caspari 1814–1892: En biografi." Unpublished manuscript.
Skrypek, Stanislaw. *The Problem of Eastern Galicia*. London: The Polish Association for the South Eastern Provinces, 1948.
Slouschz, Nahum. *The Renascence of Hebrew Literature*. Philadelphia: The Jewish Publication Society of America, 1909.
Solomon, Simon. *In the Thicket*. Philadelphia: The Jewish Publication Society, 1963.
Spekke, Arnolds. *History of Latvia: An Outline*. Stockholm: M. Goppers, 1951.
Stanislawski, Michael. "Jewish Apostasy in Russia: A Tentative Typology." In *Jewish Apostasy in the Modern World*, edited by Todd Endelmann, 189–205. New York: Holmes & Meier, 1987.
———. *A Murder in Lemberg: Politics, Religion, and Violence in Modern Jewish History*. Princeton: Princeton University Press, 2007.
Stanley, Brian. *The World Missionary Conference: Edinburgh 1910*. Cambridge: Eerdmans, 2009.
Šteinmanis, Josifs, and Edward Anders. *History of Latvian Jews*. East European Monographs. New York: Columbia University Press, 2002.
Stern, David H. "Court Cases and the Struggle for Aliyah." In *Jewish Identity and Faith in Jesus*, edited by Kai Kjær-Hansen, 87–96. Jerusalem: Caspari Center, 1996.
Stokke, Karin Margrete. "Auswanderer, Einwanderer, Durchwanderer, Rückwanderer: Die Allgemeine Zeitung des Judentums og østjødisk migrasjon 1881–1903." Master's thesis, University of Oslo, 2003.
Ströter, Ernst Ferdinad. *Die Judenfrage und ihre göttlicher Lösung nach Römer Kapitel 11*. Kassel: Ernst Röttger, 1903.
Strozier, Robert M. *Foucault, Subjectivity, and Identity: Historical Constructions of Subject and Self*. Detroit: Wayne State University Press, 2002.
Talmage, F. E., ed. *Disputation and Dialogue: Readings in the Jewish-Christian Encounter*. New York: Ktav, 1975.
Telchin, Stan. *Some Messianic Jews Say, Messianic Judaism is Not Christianity: A Loving Call to Unity*. Grand Rapids: Chosen, 2004.
Terray, Laszló G. *Et liv i grenseland: Gisle Johnson 1870–1946: Et liv for Israel i Romania og Ungarn*. Oslo: Lunde, 2003.
Thompson, Alfred E. *A Century of Jewish Missions*. Chicago: Fleming H. Revell, 1902.
Torm, Axel. *50 Aars arbejde for Israel: Tilbageblik over Den danske Israelsmissions historie*. København: O. Lohse, 1935.
Unbegaun, B. O. *Russian Surnames*. Oxford: Clarendon, 1972.
Velthuysen, Gerhard. "Christian Theophilus Lucky." 82/7 (1917) 196–98.
———. [name of article not given.] *Sabbath Recorder* 82/2 (1917) 44.
Vital, David. *A People Apart: A Political History of the Jews in Europe, 1789–1939*. Oxford: Oxford University Press, 1999.
Volf, Petra. "Mindeblade om Pastor Johannes Volf (27.02.1873–21.10.1911." *Hjemliv og trosliv: Mindeblade fra Indre Missions Vaartid* 13 (1945) 92–118.
Wagner, Peter. "Identity and Selfhood as a Problematique." In *Identities, Time, Difference, and Boundaries*, edited by Heidrun Friese, 32–55. Oxford: Berghhahn, 2002.
Wagner, Siegfried. *Franz Delitzsch, Leben und Werk*. München: Chr. Kaiser, 1978.
Waldeland, O. *Jøderne og Jødemissionen: En historisk fremstilling om Jødernes religiøse og borgerlige Stilling samt Jødemissionen*. Minneapolis: Den forenede kirkes trykkeri, 1896.

Walls, Andrew F. *The Missionary Movement in Christian History: Studies in the Transmission of Faith.* Edinburgh: Orbis, 1996.

Walton, Stephen J. *Skaff deg eit liv! Om biografi.* Oslo: Det Norske Samlaget, 2008.

Wandycz, Piotr S. *The Price of Freedom: A History of East Central Europe from the Middle Ages to the Present.* 2nd ed. New York: Routledge, 1992.

Weber, Timothy P. *On the Road to Armageddon: How Evangelicals Became Israel's Best Friends.* Grand Rapids: Baker Academic, 2004.

Weidauer, Max. "Erindringer om Lucky." *Missions-Blad for Israel* 97 (1923) 140–43, 166–68, 171–80. [Norwegian translation of the original German article: Max Weidauer, "Erinnerungen an Ch.Th. Lucky." *Saat auf Hoffnung* 60 (1923) 166–68, 171–80, 209–14.]

Wiegand, August. "Die 8. Internationale Konferenz für Judenmission in Stockholm 1911." *Saat auf Hoffnung* 48 (1911) 106–23.

———. "Chajim Jedidjah Lucky, ein gesetztreuer Judenchrist." *Nathanael, Zeitschrift für die Arbeit der evangelischen Kirche an Israel* 33 (1917) 41–63.

———. "Eine kritische Stimme über die Judenmission." *Nathanael, Zeitschrift für die Arbeit der evangelischen Kirche an Israel* 9 (1893) 150–56.

———. "Inmitten Israels, Beobachtungen und Gedankern eines jungen Theologen." *Saat auf Hoffnung* 28 (1891) 138–50.

———. "Judenchristliche Gedanken und Hoffnungen." *Saat auf Hoffnung* 37 (1900) 59–152.

Wilkinson, Samuel Hinds. "Colporteur Julius Feinstein." *Trusting and Toiling* (April 1899) n.p.

———. *The Life of John Wilkinson, the Jewish Misionary.* London: Morgan & Scott, 1908.

———. *In the Land of the North: The Evangelization of the Jews in Russia.* London: Marshall Brothers, 1905.

Wittram, Reinhard. *Baltische Geschichte: Die Ostseelande Livland, Estland, Kurland 1180–1918.* München: R. Oldenburg, 1954.

Wolkoff, Robert L. "Förnekande och självhat som identitet." In *Judisk identitet*, edited by Jackie Jakubowski, 119–32. Stockholm: Natur och kultur, 1993.

Yovel, Yirmiyahu. *The Other Within: The Marranos: Split Identity and Emerging Modernity.* Princeton: Princeton University Press, 2009.

Zake, Ieva. *Nineteenth-Century Nationalism and Twentieth-Century Anti-Democratic Ideals: The Case of Latvia, 1840s to 1980s.* Lewiston, NY: Edwin Mellen, 2008.

Zalkin, Mordechai. "Scientific Literature and Cultural Transformation in Nineteenth-Century East European Society." *Alef* 5 (2005) 249–71.

Zaretsky, Tuvya, ed. *Jewish Evangelism: A Call to the Church.* Lausanne Occasional Paper 60. Forum for World Evangelization hosted by the Lausanne Committee for World Evangelization in Pattaya, Thailand, September 29 to October 5, 2004.

Ziethe, W. *Funzig Jahre der Judenmission: Eine Denkschrift zur funfzigjärigen Jubelfeier der Berliner Geshellschaft der Förderung des Christentums unter den Juden.* Berlin: Der Berliner Geshellschaft der Förderung des Christentums unter den Juden, 1872.

Zipperstein, Steven J. "Heresy, Apostasy, and the Transformation of Joseph Rabinovich." In *Jewish Apostasy in the Modern World*, edited by Todd Endelmann, 206–31. New York: Holmes & Meier, 1987.

———. *Imagining Russian Jewry: Memory, History, Identity.* Seattle: University of Washington Press, 1999.

Zöckler, Lillie. *Gott Hört Gebet: Das Leben Theodor Zöcklers.* Stuttgart: Quell-Verlag Stuttgart, 1951.
Zöckler, Theodor. "Aus Galizien." *Saat auf Hoffnung* 51 (1914) 131–42.
———. "Christian Theophilus Lucky." *Saat auf Hoffnung* 60 (1917) 2–8.
———. "Die Missionsarbeit in Galizien." *Saat auf Hoffnung* 33 (1896) 216–20.
———. "Judentum und Christentum in ihrem Verhältnis beleuctet von Jüdischen Christen. Die hebraische Zeitschrift Eduth le-Israel." *Saat auf Hoffnung* 29 (1892) 205–15, 249–65, and *Saat auf Hoffnung* 30 (1893) 44–54.

Index of Subjects and Names

d'Abling, Baroness H. 168
Abraham (in the Old Testament/ Tanak) 54, 55, 164, 218, 226, 229, 234, 271, 347, 351
Achs, Karl 279
Acts (in the New Testament) 54, 196, 206, 210-11, 254, 336
Adler 67, 72, 74
Adversus judaeos 176-77
Alfred (Centre) 117, 120-21, 139
Aliases 104
Aliyah 86, 245-46, 319
Ambrose 202
Am'haaretz 179, 180, 219-20, 335
Amiel 136
Amos (in the Old Testament/ Tanak) 223
Anti-Semitism 4-5, 23, 25-26, 32, 37, 79, 93, 98, 134, 152-53, 168, 219, 238-42, 247, 252, 255, 257, 273, 280, 285, 290-93, 295, 299, 306, 309, 312, 315
Anti-Judaism 177-78, 205, 239, 273, 280-81
Apostate/ Meshummad 2, 56, 60, 64, 91, 102, 173, 182, 188, 192, 210, 222, 264, 268, 278, 283-84, 298, 329, 343
Anarchism 96, 104
Arabs 22, 261-263
Assimilation 4-5, 8, 23, 25, 31-32, 35, 37, 57, 82, 84, 95-96, 121, 150-51, 177, 182-83, 189-90, 201, 214, 230, 239-40, 245, 249, 258-59, 261, 264, 270-71, 273, 276, 290, 293-94, 296, 303, 307, 311, 313, 324, 337
Augustine 202
Ausgleich 35, 92
Austria/ Austrian 7, 30-32, 34-35, 49, 92-93, 95, 112, 126, 139, 143, 150-51, 156-158, 235, 239, 240, 244, 257-58, 272, 293, 306, 309
Axenfeld, Carl 65, 191

Baal Shem 202
Baptism 4, 25-26, 44, 53, 56-57, 60, 62-63, 72, 90-91, 98, 101, 103, 106-8, 112-13, 115-16, 118, 132-133, 136, 143, 161, 166-67, 170, 189, 217, 239-40, 251, 273-74, 276-79, 281-84, 289-90, 300, 306-7, 317, 328, 337-38, 340
Baron, David 130, 135, 142, 146, 151-73, 189, 228, 230, 236, 242, 271-72, 281-83, 289, 304-10, 323, 327, 329, 339
Bauer, Simon 136-37
Bausk 67, 72, 253
Belarus 30, 35, 45, 47, 52, 64, 109, 184, 329
Belgrade 103, 106, 108, 378
Berlin (the city) 11, 38, 57-58, 63-64, 77, 81, 94, 97-107, 121-22, 125-29, 135, 138, 140, 200, 248, 261, 265, 274, 295-96, 299, 320
Berliner Heidenmissionshause 57
Die Berliner Gesellschaft zur Beförderung des Christentums unter den Juden (the Berlin Society) 38, 57, 125-29, 194, 290, 299-300
Bessarabia 8, 31-32, 53, 63-64, 105, 156, 248
Besser. Max 57-58, 248, 274, 296
Blasphemy 71, 176, 347, 352, 357
Boethuseans 207
Bogatirowa, Gisa 45, 50, 52, 64
De Boodschapper 130, 139
Boundaries 5, 14-16, 164, 238, 246, 308, 310, 333-34, 339-42
Braila 135-37, 313

Breslau 94, 97–98, 261, 299, 320
Briggs, C. A. 111
Brüll 158–59
Budapest 32, 40, 90, 137, 142–65, 168, 170–73, 217, 230, 232, 256, 265, 270, 279–84, 308, 328–29
Bukowina 104–5, 108, 134, 324
Bulgaria 126
Bund 18, 32, 243, 249
Burial 22, 88, 172, 175

Caspari, Carl Paul 39, 56, 175, 188
Cemetery 137, 140–41, 144, 151, 172–73, 217, 230, 340
Ceremonial law 175, 198, 204, 212, 236, 304
cherem 175, 189, 347
Chernowitc/ Czernowitz 38, 104, 117, 282
Christology 6, 119, 164, 199, 227–30, 326, 329
Christmas 201, 280
Church
  Anglican 37–38, 106, 166, 179, 313
  Baptist 85–86, 89, 94, 103, 106–7, 113–14, 116, 139, 143, 155, 172, 278–80, 296–97
  Congregationalist 111
  Episcopal 116, 303, 312–13
  Free (included Scottish) 37, 40, 155, 165–66, 168
  Lutheran 9, 39–40, 55, 57–61, 65–66, 69, 71–73, 77, 80, 90, 105, 107, 109–16, 13–132, 140, 146–47, 155, 175, 178, 189–90, 195, 198, 254, 273–74, 277–83, 294–98, 334
  Methodist 313, 323–24, 110, 112, 114, 116, 135
  Presbyterian 110–11, 116, 162, 307
  Reformed 129, 139, 145, 147, 155, 307, 322
  Roman (and Greek) Catholic 5–6, 59, 63, 69, 94, 114, 124, 131, 147, 156–57, 205, 277, 293, 306, 342
  Russian Orthodox 5, 18, 53, 59–65, 69, 84–85, 124, 176, 178, 186, 291, 296

Seventh-Day Baptist 40, 89–90, 94, 107, 109, 112–13, 117–18, 120, 124, 126, 139, 195, 214, 279–80, 301, 324
Circumcision 84, 210, 212, 223, 231, 304, 313, 326
Cohen, Leopold 175, 188–89, 323–24
Cohen, Philip 118, 129–30, 304, 326–27
Conscious pariah 341
Constantinople 86, 126, 268
Conversion narrative 12, 44, 49, 54–56, 64, 90–91, 101, 103
Conversions 3, 5, 37, 55, 59–62, 64, 72, 84, 143, 149–50, 175, 188, 239–40, 276, 290, 293, 334
Convert 4–5, 12, 15–17, 37, 39, 44–45, 47, 49, 52, 54–62, 64, 67, 70, 72–74, 78–79, 85, 87, 93–94, 103–4, 106, 112, 114–16, 121, 127, 141, 147, 149–50, 157, 160, 167, 175–79, 183–86, 188, 191–92, 196, 201, 212, 214, 221, 249, 251, 256, 260, 266, 268, 270, 287, 290–95, 303, 307, 311, 314, 319–320, 324, 330, 339–40
Cottrell, Ira Lee 113
Covenant 126, 194, 204–6, 216, 222, 227, 234, 267, 322

Daland, William C. 89, 109, 113, 117, 120, 280, 299, 322
Dalman, Gustaf 123–24, 128, 132, 164, 168, 199, 213, 256, 302, 314–15, 318, 321, 327–28
Den Danske Israelsmission (The Danish Society) 40, 126, 130–32, 302
Delitzsch, Franz 39, 58, 75, 85, 101, 105–9, 113, 116, 120, 123, 153, 188, 291–93, 296, 309–10, 314, 318, 322
Deuteronomy (in the Old Testament/ Tanak) 156, 228, 235, 353
Dichotomy/ dichotomization 14, 335, 342
Dispensationalism 26, 135, 260–61
Dubnow, Simon 243

Index of Subjects and Names

Dworkowitz 80

Ebionitism 138, 302, 326
Edersheim, Alfred 307
Edinburgh 130, 305–6
Edwards, Daniel 320
Edut leIsrael 11, 38, 98, 109, 117–29
Eisenmenger, Johann Andreas 178–79, 248, 293
Einspruch, Henry 137
Emancipation 4, 66, 68, 147, 149, 151, 239–40, 246, 273, 276, 291, 294
Erachin (in Talmud) 285
Eschatology/ eschatological 245, 255–56, 260, 271–72, 319
Essenes 220
Essentialism 20, 342
Der Evangelisch-Lutherische Zentralverein für Mission unter Israel 123–25, 127, 292, 310, 314–15
Ezekiel (in the Old Testament) 136, 227, 253–54, 256, 260, 286, 352
Ezra (in the Old Testament) 193

Faber, Wilhelm 120, 123, 125, 314, 322
Faltin, Ernst Karl Rudolf 53–58, 62, 67, 85, 124, 178–81, 284, 296, 302, 317–18
Feinsilber, Robert 171–72
Feinstein, Julius(Yiddle) and Esther 86, 296, 319
Festival 108, 212–13, 216, 223, 229, 231, 304, 327
Frank, Arnold 161–63, 167
Freshman, Jacob 315, 323–24
Friedlander, Zevi Hermann 107, 116–18, 120, 122
Gaebelein, Arno 114, 135, 260, 313
Galicia 31–32, 35, 40, 90, 92–96, 103–6, 108, 112, 117, 119–41, 147, 157, 171, 181–86, 202, 208–9, 213, 257–61, 265, 299–330, 320, 324–25
Geiger, Abraham 98–99, 200
Gemara 144, 180, 355
German culture 19, 51. 57–58, 67, 93, 246, 293, 297, 334–35

Gjessing, Ragnvald 11, 142–45, 151–67, 170, 217, 230, 232, 236, 282–84, 307
Gordin, Jacob 84, 316
Gospel of Luke 227, 235, 249
Gospel of Mattew 53, 101, 154, 156, 199, 209–12, 214, 220, 224, 232, 259, 285, 287–88
Gospel of Mark 156, 208, 225, 227, 232, 287
Gospel of John 101, 156, 229, 258, 328
Goy 52, 121, 189, 249, 263
Gurland, Raphael (Feidel or Faytel) 45–46
Gurland, Helene 11, 43–44, 46, 49–50, 72–78, 81, 189, 191, 248, 287, 295–96, 333
Gurland, Ida 45, 78, 101
Gurland, Marie 45, 50, 56–57, 64, 77
Gurland, Rudolf 79–81, 189, 249, 295
Gurland, Sophie 52–53, 57, 64, 69, 77, 190

Ha'am, Ahad 82, 243–44, 262
Hasidism/Hasidic 5, 32, 35, 47, 50, 52, 83, 86, 95–96, 100, 105, 117, 202, 208–9, 222, 245–46, 310, 325, 329
Haskalah/maskilim 5, 32, 47–52, 68, 82–83, 96, 181–88, 209, 240–41, 338, 345
Halacha/ halakic 21, 23, 83, 182, 209, 211, 349
Harling, Otto von 130, 135
Hebrew (the language) 2, 11, 22, 32, 39, 45–51, 63, 80, 82, 93–94, 97, 101, 104–6, 111, 117–19, 123, 128, 133, 140, 157, 165, 173, 178, 183–86, 195, 238, 241, 249, 251, 263, 272, 322, 325, 334, 354
Hebrew Christian Alliance of Great Britain 26, 106, 311–12
Hebrew Christian Prayer Union 212, 323–24
The Hebrew Christian Testimony 39, 170, 172, 289, 329
Heder 47, 70–74, 94, 144
Hertzl, Theodor 16, 242, 270
Hess, Moses 242

Hibbat Zion/ Hovevei Zion 82, 242–45, 246, 253, 261, 318–19
Hillel 101, 211, 336, 350
Die Hochschule für die Wissenschaft des Judentums 97–102, 209
Horowitz, L. W. 135–37, 313
Hungarian/Magyar 35–36, 145–53, 157, 161, 167, 223, 232, 236, 267, 270, 272, 306–7

Identification 5, 14–15, 19–25, 55, 61, 91, 93, 121, 158, 175, 176, 190, 195, 213, 225, 238–41, 246, 249–50, 257, 273, 278, 307
Idolatry 211, 235, 278, 288
Institutum Judaicum Delitzschianum 105, 123, 131, 222, 283, 310
intermarriage 84, 121, 214, 217, 290, 307, 336
Isaiah (in the Old Testament/ Tanak) 54–55, 187, 207, 216, 223–29, 263, 317, 349, 353–56
Israelitischer Landessekretariat (See also Judaism: Reform) 148
Israelitische Landskanzlei / Neolog (See also Judaism: Traditional/ Orthodox) 148–52, 158–60, 172, 217, 223, 230–31, 236–37, 268, 270–72, 335

James' Letter (in the New Testament) 285, 346
Jeremiah (in the Old Testament/ Tanak) 156, 194, 205, 228, 352–53
Jerusalem 156, 210–11, 227, 241, 245, 268, 271–72, 286, 305, 313, 336, 354
Johnson, Gisle 11, 89–90, 107, 131, 134, 136–37, 170, 279
Judaism
    Traditional/ Orthodox 3, 5, 17, 32, 47, 49–52, 56, 83, 95, 97–100, 102, 119, 122, 145, 148, 151, 172, 181–86, 188, 192, 201–3, 213, 223, 226, 230, 236, 238–39, 241–46, 249, 261, 265, 271–72, 200, 304, 325, 334

Reform (see also Israelitische Landskanzlei / Neolog) 5, 17, 32, 47, 51–53, 66, 71, 78, 96–102, 119, 269, 330, 337
Judaeophobia 30, 37, 291

Kabbalah 46, 48–51, 184, 208–9, 329
Kalischer, Hirsch 246, 261
(Neo-)Karaites 92, 187, 201, 221–22

Kayserling, Meyer 158–61
Kishinev 218, 220, 243, 248, 250, 257, 284, 287, 296, 310, 313–14, 318–19, 322,, 328, 345
Kohn, Samuel 158–161, 270, 272
Kosher (kashrut)/ Dietary laws 22, 78, 84, 133, 151, 175, 189, 191, 210–11, 230–31, 236, 267, 327, 336
Kovno 47, 51
Kurland 35, 43, 46, 64–81, 87–88, 139, 175, 189, 249, 252–53, 277, 295, 298, 335

Landow, Joseph 117–18, 120, 122
Landsmann, Daniel 107, 109–10, 113
Latvians 66, 68–69, 79
Lemberg (L'vov/L'viv) 40, 49, 64, 92, 120, 122, 126–27, 140–41, 145, 213, 313, 320, 326
Letter to the Galatians 132, 206, 224
Letter to the Hebrews 206
Letter to the Romans 136, 167, 215, 224, 232, 235–36, 285, 328
Levinsohn, Isaac Baer/ Ber 50, 179, 182
Levertoff, Paul 171, 208, 222, 323, 329
Levy, Mark 262, 312–13, 323
Lewy, Israel 102–2, 108
Lichtenstein, Abraham Jakab 144–45
Lichtenstein, Emmanuel (son) 161, 170, 219, 285, 330
Lichtenstein, Emmanuel (grandson) 146, 170–71
Lichtenstein, Fáni 145–46
Lichtenstein (or Herschensohn), Yechiel 7, 26, 83, 105, 107, 125–26, 199, 208, 213, 222, 283, 310, 320–23, 329

Index of Subjects and Names

Lieven, Countess 76–77, 81, 296–97
Lillienthal, Max 50
Lindhagen, Theodor 40, 135, 138, 303–5, 327
Lipshytz, Christlieb T. 300, 303
Liturgy 105, 148, 220, 261, 272, 286, 296, 304
London Society for Promoting Christianity amongst the Jews 4, 38, 57, 59, 67, 125, 179
Löwen, Moses 11, 90, 93, 96–113, 120–30, 135, 137–39, 194–95, 203, 213, 263, 302–9, 320–21, 324
Luther, Martin 110, 277

Maimonides, Moses 48, 110, 229
Margoliuth, Moses 106, 109
Marrano 45, 158–159, 342
Marx, Karl/ Marxism 96, 119, 258
Maximum program 304, 326–27, 336
McCaul, Alexander 186, 218–20
The Messianic Jew 129–30, 304
Messiah 48, 101–2, 108, 137, 147, 154–56, 168, 172, 176–77, 181, 188, 193, 195–200, 207–14, 217, 221, 223–26, 229–30, 245, 258, 264, 268–72, 288, 299, 307, 332–35, 341, 347, 351, 355–57
Meyer, Luis 114, 312
Micha (in the Old Testament/ Tanak) 223
Mikve 162, 166, 262
Mildmay Mission to the Jews 4, 38, 253, 284, 294, 318–19
Minimum program 304, 326–27, 336
Mishnah 144, 215, 245
Mitau 8, 65–67, 70–81, 88
Moische, Eliah 316–17
Moody, Andrew 155–60, 165–67, 308, 328–29
Moravia 144, 147, 272
Moravians (The Moravian movement) 66–67, 297, 313
Moses (in the Old Testament/ Tanak) 51, 102, 156, 187, 193, 198–99, 203–4, 207, 209, 213, 215, 228–29, 263, 332
Muller, Johannes 120, 123–28, 302

Müller, W. 66–67, 72, 240, 295
Mysticism 95, 101, 104–5, 208–9

Nationalism 334–36
Neander, Eduard 66, 74
The New Testament 80, 86, 101–5, 119, 153–54, 156, 169, 176, 193–96, 199–200, 203–6, 209–11, 214, 220–24, 229, 231–34, 237, 254, 268, 269, 276, 279, 281–82, 288, 321–22, 328, 330, 333–39, 343, 347, 349
New York 11, 89, 93, 106, 109–14, 117, 120–22, 135, 213, 260, 265, 280, 300, 315, 323–25
Nikolsburg (Mikulov) 143–44
Niles, E. S. 312
Nordau, Max 241
Den Norske Israelsmisjon (The Norwegian Israel Mission) 7, 40–41, 76, 80, 90, 127, 131, 135–36, 142–42, 149

Odessa 38, 40, 53, 63, 75, 80–89, 189, 191, 240, 242, 249, 252–53, 256, 294, 296, 315, 317–19
Old Testament (The Hebrew Bible/ Tanak) 71, 111, 133, 136, 179–80, 187–88, 191, 194–95, 201, 219, 224, 226, 229, 254, 260, 273–78, 300, 347
Oral tradition 48, 176–77, 179, 181, 184, 187, 201–2, 209–10, 219, 223, 335
Ordo salutis 44, 55–56

Pale of Settlement 32, 35, 59, 61, 65
Palestine/ Eretz Israel 38, 82, 86, 99, 126, 135–40, 143, 213, 224, 241–46, 253, 259–63, 313, 318, 320, 337
Pantheism 96, 320
Paschkow, Wassilij Alexandrowitsch/ Paschowittes 76–77, 296
Pastor primaries 66, 74, 76
Paul (the apostle) 53, 56,112, 116, 119, 133, 167, 197.198, 203, 210, 224
Paulinum 133

Pesach/ Passover 22, 108, 153
Pesachim (in Talmud) 179–80, 220, 354
Peter (the apostle) 119, 210
Pharisees 194–95, 199, 206–212, 214–15, 220, 355
Pick, Israel 313, 320
Pietist 5, 12, 39, 55, 66–67, 178, 180, 254, 273, 278
Pinsker, Leo 82, 242, 262
Philo-Semite/ philo-Semitic 45, 141, 254, 260, 282, 287, 309, 315
Pogroms 32, 82, 84, 87–88, 93, 140, 168, 183, 240, 242, 250, 292
Pohlmann, H. 107, 110, 112–13, 265–66, 300, 309
Poland/ Poles 30, 32, 35, 57, 89, 92, 139, 147, 298
Pollak, Aaron and Esther 93
Poverty 32, 61, 93–95, 119, 133, 257, 266, 302, 351
Pork 209, 231
Powell, S. S. 120
pre-millennialism 253
Pressburg (Bratislava) 97–98, 151
Priluker, Jacob 83–84, 316
Proverbs (in the Old Testament/ Tanak) 224
Psalms (in the Old Testament/ Tanak) 194, 228
Pseudonyms 91, 122–23, 203, 265
Pucher, Shlomo 70–75, 175

Rabbi Akiba 202
Rabbi Meir 202
Rabbi Pinchas 202
Rabbi Simlai 196, 223
Rabbiner Seminar für das Orthodoxe Judentum 97, 200, 261
Roi, Joh. de le 7, 11, 44, 75–76, 98, 107, 116, 256–257, 281–282
Rabinowitz, Joseph 284, 294, 296, 302–8, 310, 312–14, 317–19, 323, 328–29, 335
Rappoport 202
Rationalism 181, 188, 223, 275, 278, 352
Renegades 319

Repentance 196, 203, 285, 317, 356
Reuter 121
Reval (Tallinn) 77, 274
Revelation, divine 48, 99–100, 102, 111, 186–87, 200, 202, 214, 224, 336
Revelation (in the New Testament) 220
Riga 65, 68–69, 73, 75–76, 80–82, 252, 298, 315–16
Rohling, August 240, 293
Rosenberg, Leon 38, 87, 294
Rothschild, Baron 242, 291
Rotterdam 139, 168
Russia 1, 5, 18, 30–35, 39, 46–47, 51, 53–54, 56–66, 71–72, 74–76, 81–83, 86–87, 133, 135, 139, 177–79, 181–82, 185, 188, 191, 240, 243, 260, 274, 290, 294–97, 311, 316
Russbaum 104–5, 112
Russification 35, 68–69, 139, 177, 295, 334, 340
Ruth (in the Old Testament/ Tanak) 216

Sabbath 82, 113, 116–17, 126, 141, 151, 167, 171, 192, 196, 199, 212, 214–16, 230–232, 236, 279–80, 305, 322, 327
The Sabbath Tract Society 40
Sabbetai Zvi 268
Sadducees 207
Salary 80, 86, 110, 115, 126, 250, 298, 301, 324
Salkinson 39
Saunders, Earl 113
Schechter, Solomon 265
Schleiermacher, Friedrich 274–78
Schor, Samuel 263
Schönberger, Charles Andrew 39–40, 156, 162–64, 170–72, 271, 281, 302
Schwartz, Carl 312
Seesemann, Gustav 65, 67
Shammai 211, 336
Shavuot/ Pentecost 216, 231
Shoa (the Holocaust) 4, 7, 24
shtetl 61, 92
Sionsforeningen 40, 80, 297

Smolenskin, Peretz 242
Socialism/ Socialist 18, 30, 32, 37, 96, 105, 192, 214, 240, 243, 249
Social Darwinism 31, 37, 240
Somerville, Andrew 167
Soteriology 6, 314, 326, 343
Spener, Philip Jakob 178
Stirner, Max 96, 104
Supersessionism 25-26, 109, 178, 254, 260, 273, 275, 278, 280-81
Stanislau (Ivanov Frankovsk) 92, 122, 126-35, 140, 217, 258, 304
Status Quo 148
Stockholm 135, 138, 146, 256, 302-6, 323, 325-26, 343
Stöcker (Stoecker), Adolf 291-92, 299
Ströter, Ernst. F. 135-36, 260, 302, 313
Strychance 112
Stundists 85, 296, 318
Suffering 187, 200, 226, 245, 276, 285-87, 337
Svenska Isralesmissionen(The Swedish Society) 40,
Szarvason 146

Talith 119, 316
Talmud 174-237
Talmud-bokur 144
Tápiószele 144-46, 151-52, 156, 158-63, 168, 170, 230-32
Tholuck, Friedrich August 58, 296
Tisza Eszlar 152-53, 282, 309
Torah observance 26, 95, 97, 130, 138, 152, 193-94, 201, 209, 211-13, 230, 303-4, 311-13, 326-27, 330, 332, 336, 343
Trinity 6, 208, 221-22, 227, 229
Tysmienica/ Tysmienitsa 92, 95

Ukrainian/ Ruthenian 93, 95, 104, 127, 319
Union Theological Seminary 89, 109

Velthuysen, Gerard 139
Venetianer, A. 281, 307
Vienna 32, 40, 92, 109, 146, 156, 235, 242, 265, 281
Violence 64, 88, 92
Vilnius 45-47, 50-51, 65, 70, 72, 78, 190, 289, 316
Volf, Johannes and Petra 130-32, 140, 280, 302
Volozhin 47, 49, 184, 246

Wagenseil, Johann Christoph 178
Warsawiak, Hermann 115
Weidauer. Max 11, 89-91, 101, 107, 131, 134-35, 140, 299
Wiegand, August 11, 90, 95, 124-26, 128, 131-32, 138, 140, 302-3, 314, 324-25
Wilkinson, John 38-39, 163, 284, 308, 318, 328
Wilkomir (Ukmerge) 50-51, 74, 183-84,
Withford, W. C. 120
Wolff, Paulus 256
Wygoda 106

Yiddish 149, 171, 183-84, 241, 248
Yom Kippur 22, 200, 312

Zechariah (in the Old Testament/ Tanak) 228, 286-87, 346
Zezschwitz, Carl Adolf Gerhard von 277-78
Zionism/Zionist 10, 18-19, 21-23, 32, 82, 93, 96, 99, 136-37, 183, 186, 217, 239, 241-46, 249, 251-64, 270-73, 291, 295, 304, 314, 316, 318-19, 327, 330, 334, 336, 340-41
Zöckler, Lili (born Bredenkamp) 132
Zöckler, Theodor 11, 91, 128, 131-35, 140, 194-213, 264, 300, 314, 325

www.ingramcontent.com/pod-product-compliance
Lightning Source LLC
Chambersburg PA
CBHW071231290426
44108CB00013B/1365